Salad for the Social.

Avery Sc

Salad for the Social:

By the Author of

"Salad for the Solitary."

"Some coarse, cold salad is before thee set;
Fall on."—— BEN JONSON.

NEW YORK:
DE WITT & DAVENPORT, 160 & 162 NASSAU STREET.
LONDON:—RICHARD BENTLEY.
1856.

W. H. Tinson, Stereotyper. George Russell, Printer. G. W. Alexander, Bin

For

All whose Intellectual Tastes prefer Wholesome Diet to

Literary Confectionery,

This Salad

Has been Especially Prepared,

By

"An Epicure."

"A DINNER of fragments is often said to be the best dinner; so there are few minds but might furnish some instruction and entertainment of their scraps, their odds and ends of thoughts. They who cannot weave a uniform web, may at least produce a piece of patchwork."

GUESSES AT TRUTH.

"To the man of robust and healthy intellect, who gathers the harvest of literature into his barn, thrashes the straw, winnows the grain, grinds it in his own mill, bakes it in his own oven, and then eats the true bread of knowledge, we bid a cordial welcome."

SOUTHEY'S DOCTOR.

Introductory.

"I WOULD go fifty miles on foot, to kiss the hand of that man whose generous heart will give up the reins of his imagination into his author's hands—be pleased, he knows not why, and cares not wherefore." STERNE.

SOUTHEY remarks that there are some persons who are willing to be pleased, and thankful for being pleased, without thinking it necessary that they should be able to *parse* their pleasure, like a lesson, or give a rule or reason why they are pleased. It is the aim and design of the following pages to put the reader in this precise condition; believing, with Sydney Smith, "that all mankind are happier for having been happy; so that if you make them happy now, you make them happy twenty years hence by the memory of it." Old books by great authors are not in everybody's reach; and though it is better to know them thoroughly than to know them here and there, yet it is a good work to give a little to those who have neither time nor means to get more. When in any fragrant, scarce old tome the bookworm discovers a sentence or an illustration that does his own heart good, he should hasten to give it currency. Most readers—readers *con amore*, have some snug little corner in the storehouse of memory, in which they treasure up choice passages of their favorite authors. It requires more than a mental process to reduce such a heterogenous collection to something like order. The present volume, with its antecedent, originated in some such an attempt. These desultory chapters are the fruitage of many pleasant, recreative hours spent in the highways and by-ways of literature. Whenever a tempting thought-blossom decoyed us by its alluring beauty, the prize was captured to enrich and grace our collection. Such gleanings may by some be deemed trifles, but

"Though high philosophy despise such things,
They often give to weightier truths their wings;
Convey a moral, or correct bad taste,
Though aptly called light learning, still not waste.
A spark of nature's fire will not despise,
A word sometimes makes brighter, lovelier eyes;
A flash of wit disarms old care of wrath,
A happy line throws beauty in our path;
Though sages say light learning wisdom stifles,
There *is* delight in stringing useful trifles."

If trifles are facts, they cease to be trivial; and in these stirring times, when our allotted leisure is becoming infinitessimally small, the terse and epigrammatic are to be preferred to the discursive and the diffuse, in our reading. Somewhat after the manner of old Burton, these chapters are fertile of quotations—being compounded mainly of the thoughts of others—a species of literary amalgam. This will scarcely be considered an objection, since it gives the essence of many minds instead of one. A quaint writer asserts that "every book is itself a quotation." As with the jeweller, if in some instances the setting may be rudely done, yet the gem still retains its original value; and we are free to confess, as did Goldsmith of his "Vicar," (and with vastly more reason), that "there are a hundred faults in this thing; yet a book may be amusing with numerous errors, or it may be dull without a single absurdity." It would be great temerity to appropriate to our humble essay the witty analysis of the witty author already cited, and affirm—that "it has profundity without obscurity, perspicuity without prolixity, ornament without glare, terseness without barrenness, penetration without subtlety, comprehensiveness without digression, and a great number of other things without a great number of other things."

The present work might not inaptly be styled *an odd* volume, were it not intended to be *even* with its predecessor, of which, indeed, it forms the counterpart. It is odd in its plan and arrangement, consists of odd sayings and selections, from many odd and out-of-the-way authors. It is, moreover, fitted for odd readers, and odd half-hours, and, oddly enough, is the handiwork of a very odd specimen of an author. Oddities are not, however, without their use; they sometimes dispel *ennui*, the headache, and even the heartache.

Our design has been to minister to intellectual entertainment with instruction, mingling

Sayings fetched from sages old,
Laws which Holy Writ unfold,
Worthy to be graved in gold;
Lighter fancies not excluding,
Blameless wit, with nothing rude in,
Sometimes mildly interluding.

For we hold, with Rabelais, that the funds of wit and merriment are not yet exhausted—that the wings of fancy are not yet clipped, and that our ancestors have not said and sung all our good things.

"What more refreshing than a Salad, when your appetite seems to have deserted you, or even after a generous dinner—the nice, fresh, crisp salad—full of life and health, seems to invigorate the palate and dispose the masticatory powers to a much longer duration."*

* Soyer.

"Salads," according to a modern French authority,* "refresh without exciting, and make people younger." The Salad we offer *ought* to have this effect; and we hope everybody will bring to it—what everybody wishes for, and as soon as possessed, loses—a good appetite. Salads are not generally suited for weak digestions, or sickly folk; yet we have it certified on professional authority that this salad *is* adapted for the especial cure and comfort of any who may have such malady as that complained of by the author of *Elia*, who thus piteously portrays his sufferings to Bernard Barton: "Do you know what it is to succumb under an insurmountable *day-mare*—an indisposition to do anything, or to be anything—a total deadness and distaste—a suspension of vitality—an indifference to locality, a numb, soporific good-for-nothingness—an ossification all over, an oyster-like indifference to passing events—a mind stupor—a brawny defiance to the needles of a thrashing-in conscience—with a total irresolution to submit to water-gruel processes?"

After sundry erasures, blottings, corrections, insertions, enlargings and diminishings, with interlineations, we have at length completed the work, which, whatever may be alleged against it, shall be innocent of all heresy of necromancy, geomancy, alchymy, exorcism, phantasmagoria, witch-craft, metoposcopy, sorcery, or thaumaturgie.

As this is a Salad for the Social, it is to be hoped that it will prove savory to the palate of a goodly number of good-natured guests; since even frugal fare is rendered relishable by the presence of smiling faces and happy hearts, while the most costly viands often lose their zest where these are not. Foremost among the pleasures of the table are, what an elegant novelist has termed "those felicitous moods in which our animal spirits search, and carry up, as it were, to the surface, our intellectual gifts and acquisitions." The invitation to this repast is,

* Brillat Savarin.

therefore, respectfully tendered all genial spirits who will bear company with the humble host; and being unknown to the great world, "I will tell you, sirs, by way of private, and under seal, I am a gentleman, and live here obscure, and to myself."*

F. S.

* Ben Jonson.

The Ingredients.

BOOK-CRAFT.

—— "Mightiest of the mighty means,
On which the arm of Progress leans—
Man's noblest mission to advance,
His woes assuage, his weal enhance,
His rights enforce, his wrongs redress—
Mightiest of the mighty is the *Press!*"—BOWRING.

"Books are spectacles with which to read nature. They teach us to understand and feel what we see, to decipher and syllable the hieroglyphics of the senses."—DRYDEN.

BOOKS are an essential element of our social economy. The best minds of every age are trained by

"Those dead but sceptred sovereigns, who still rule
Our spirits from their urns."

From books they receive most of their culture; and by them are disciplined in youth, stimulated in manhood, and solaced in age. "When I am reading a book," said Swift, "whether wise or silly, it seems to me to be alive or talking to me." Such is the feeling of every student who appreciates the author he reads.

"There are those who desire a book as a living companion of the mind; and to such, a good work is society to his loneliness—a balm to his troubles—a friend to the friendless—wealth to the poor, and, moreover, can keep the mind in action, though the body dies. It was Plato who went to play when he was elected to the consulship, but the evening before he died, he read. Mind lives by mind as it has been developed and preserved; and man, by this medium, has shown himself in action like an angel, in words like a god. Take this from him and he is nothing."*

"In books we have friends for every mood—comforters for every sorrow; a glorious company of immortals, scattering their sweet influences on the worn and beaten paths of our daily life. Shapes 'that haunt thought's wilderness' are around us, in toil, and suffering, and joy: mitigating labor, soothing care, giving a keener relish to delight; touching the heroic string in our nature with a noble sentiment; kindling our hearts, lifting our imaginations, and hovering alike over the couch of health and the sick pillow, to bless and cheer, and animate and console."

Book-making, once a science, acquired by long laborious toil, has, by the appliances of modern machinery, become a mercantile pursuit of almost unlimited extent. In olden times, the *stylus* and parchment were the mechanical essentials of a book, and years were often devoted to its production; now, by the magic of metal type and the steam-press, volumes are multiplied almost by the hour. Formerly, a book, both as to its mind and mechanism, was the sole work of the monk or scribe; now, there is a division of labor—the author writes it, the steam-press prints it, and the publisher is its purveyor to the public.

* Henry Giles.

By this expedient, the universal diffusion of knowledge has been promoted, and each department of the labor been rendered more perfect. But for this, the light of learning would not have been reflected from the luminous page, while the Cimmerean gloom of the "dark ages" would have still cast deep shadows over the nations.

> "The PEN and the PRESS, bless'd alliance! combined
> To soften the heart and enlighten the mind;
> For *that* to the treasures of knowledge gave birth,
> And *this* sent them forth to the ends of the earth;
> Their battles for truth were triumphant, indeed,
> And the rod of the tyrant was snapped like a reed.
> They were made to exalt us, to teach us, to bless,
> Those invincible brothers—the PEN and the PRESS."*

A book has been curiously defined, "brain preserved in ink;" and when there is plenty of the fruit, it is a conserve to tempt the most capricious palate. In ancient times, books were written on the bark of trees; hence the Latin word *liber*, from which we derive our English term "library." "Book" is from the Saxon, "*boc*," a beech-tree.

A tablet made from the main body of a tree was called *codex* or *caudex*. Scipio Maffeï distinguishes square and round books by the terms *codex* and *liber*, respectively. It is doubtful whether barks or stones were first written on; although the Decalogue, the first writing of which we have any authentic account, was on the latter. The leaves of plants were long used for writing on—chiefly those of the palm, papyrus,† tiles, &c. Leather, and goat-skins were used by the Egyptians. Plates of

* J. C. Prince.

† The invention of parchment is ascribed to Eumenes, who reigned more than two thousand years ago. He was the founder of an extensive library, into which the new manufacture was largely introduced. Parchment volumes were commonly rolled on a round stick, with a ball at each end, and the composition began at the centre. These were called volumes, and the outsides were inscribed just as we now letter books,

copper and lead were also used in the East. According to Josephus, the children of Seth wrote their inventions in Astronomy, &c., on stone pillars. Hesiod's works were first written on tables of lead—Solon's laws on wooden planks. The wood was sometimes covered with wax, so that the writing could be easily effaced. Pliny thinks that writing on lead succeeded that on barks.

The term "volume" is from *volvo*, to roll, the earlier manuscripts being in the form of a scroll or roll.

The Chinese manufacture paper of linen, the fibres of the young bamboo—of the mulberry; the envelope of the silkworm—of a native tree called *chu* or *ko-chu*—but especially of cotton. They were in possession of the art long before it was known in Europe; and, as Mecca was a sort of depot for the fabrics of China, it is by some very reasonably supposed, that the paper was brought from that country. Whatever might have been its origin, the art was undoubtedly employed and improved by the Arabs, who, in their career of conquest, carried it into Spain, about the beginning of the tenth century. Other accounts ascribe the invention of cotton paper to Greece; indeed, not only its origin, but the various improvements in its manufacture, and the different substitutions of new materials have long been the subject of controversy.

Cotton paper was called *charta bombycina:* it was very white and strong, but not equal to that in which linen is a constituent.

With regard to linen paper, authorities differ widely. By some accounts, its manufacture was not introduced into Europe until the latter part of the fourteenth century, a mill having

The Greek MSS., in Herculaneum, consist of papyrus, rolled, charred, and matted together by the fire, and are about nine inches long, and one, two, or three inches in diameter, each being a volume or separate treatise.

Cotton and silk paper were in use at an early period, but linen rags were not used till A. D. 1200. This invention has been placed earlier by some good authorities, but it would appear that they have confounded the cotton with the linen paper. The first paper-mill was erected in England, towards the end of the sixteenth century.

been, in 1390, established at Nuremberg. In 1366, however, the Republic of Venice granted a patent to the town of Treviso, for the exclusive manufacture of linen paper; and it is also stated, that the Arabs, when in Spain, on account of the scarcity of cotton, and the abundance of flax and hemp, substituted the latter material in its preparation. Their first manufactories were at Xativa, now San Felipe.

Forty years ago, three men, by handwork, could scarcely manufacture 4,000 small sheets of paper a day, while now they can produce 60,000 in the same time. It has been calculated, that if the paper produced yearly by six machines could be put together, the sheet would encircle the world.

Nowhere is paper so much used as in the United States. In France, with 35,000,000 of inhabitants, only 70,000 tons are produced yearly, of which one-seventh is for exportation. In England, with 28,000,000 of inhabitants, 66,000 tons are produced; while in this country the amount is nearly as great as in France and England together.

A large proportion of this consumption of paper is directed to the 2,000 newspapers which are incessantly springing up in all sections of this country—some to flourish, but more born but to die, and make room for the succession.

When first the art of Printing was discovered, only one side of a page was impressed: the printers had not yet found out the expedient of impressing the other. When the editions were intended to be curious, they omitted to print the first letter of a chapter, for which they left a blank space, that it might be painted or illuminated, at the option of the purchaser. Several ancient volumes of these early times have been found, where these letters are wanting, as they neglected to have them painted. It was the glory of the learned, when the art was first established, to be correctors of the press, to the eminent printers. Physicians, lawyers, and bishops, as well as authors, occupied this department. The printers then added frequently to their names those of the correctors of the press; and editions were valued according to the abilities of the corrector.

About the close of the fourteenth century, the world was blessed with the invention of this art. Three German cities—Haarlem, Mentz, and Strasburg—claim, each one, the honor of having been the place of the original discovery, but the evidence rather inclines to favor the claim of Mentz; for, at this city, either by John Guttenberg or Peter Schoeffer, in the year 1440, were invented movable types; with which movable types, the first book printed was the Bible, and that in the year 1450, though some authorities declare that the Latin Bible, or Vulgate, was first printed on the Continent, in 1462. Lawrence I. Coster, of Haarlem, discovered the art of impressing characters on paper, by means of wooden blocks, in the year 1430; and we may here remark that the ground of doubt between Guttenberg and Schoeffer seems to be an opinion pretty well authenticated, that the types of the former were of wood—those of the latter of metal; and that while the invention of the one happened in the year 1440, that of the other was consummated at some time during the following ten years.

John Faust, or Fust, was only concerned as a patron of Schoeffer, but as such he was sincere and energetic. Some writers declare that Fust went to Paris, carrying with him for sale a number of printed Bibles. That the similarity of all these books caused the French to distrust him as a conjuror. That at first they threatened to indict him, and thus extorted the secret. And they add that from this affair, the popular story of Dr. Faustus took its rise. This, however, is false. Haywood tells us (see "Goethe's Faust"), that "Johann" (or John) "Faust" (or Faustus—that is, the conjuror) "was born at Kunklingen, within the territory of Würtemberg, of parents '*low of stock*' (as Marlow expresses it), some time towards the fifteenth century. He must not be confounded with Faust (or Fust), the printer, who flourished more than half a century before."

To the German triumvirate belongs the honor of having been the first to employ movable types, matrices, and punches in printing.

Trithemius, a contemporary, ascribes the invention of movable types jointly to Gutenberg and Faust, and an ancient chronicle at Cologne notes that, after ten years' preparation, the art of printing began to be practised in the year 1450. The former authority further states that the parties expended in the printing of the first twelve sheets of the Bible, 4,000 florins. The Bible in question is the Latin Vulgate, commonly known by the name of the Mazarin Bible, from a copy of it having been discovered, in the middle of the last century, in the *Bibliothèque Mazarine.**

It is worthy of note that the advent of the "divine art" was sanctified by religion. It was fitting that it "should thus first be devoted to the Sacred Oracles, since no book had been so

* In Timperley's amusing volume on "Printers and Printing," it is stated that John Muller (surnamed Regiomontanus) who died at Rome, in the year 1476, was for some time suspected of being the inventor of printing.

frequently transcribed in earlier times, and none, we may add, has been so often reprinted in later. The majority of all the books ever published owe much of their essence and genius to its inspirations. The muse of Milton, Cowper, and a host of others in sacred song, have found in the Bible their Pierian spring; and even the world's poet, Shakspeare, is no exception to the fact. Its lessons are the essence of religion, "the seminal truth of theology, the first principles of morals, and the guiding axioms of political economy." It has moulded the finest minds that have ever blessed humanity; it has sustained the heart alike of prince and peasant, under suffering and sorrow, shed a halo of glory around the grave, and lit up a pathway to a brighter world.

Gutenberg was the inventor of the art, and Faust, a goldsmith, furnished the necessary funds. Had it been a single page, or even an entire sheet, which was then produced, there might have been less occasion to have noticed it; but there was something in the whole character of the affair, which, if not unprecedented, rendered it singular in the usual current of human events. This Bible was in two folio volumes, which have been justly praised for the strength and beauty of the paper, the exactness of the register, and the lustre of the ink. The work contained twelve hundred and eighty-two pages, and, being the first ever printed, of course involved a long period of time, and an immense amount of mental, manual, and mechanical labor, and yet for a long time after it had been finished and offered for sale, not a human being, save the artists themselves, knew how it had been accomplished. Of the printed Bible, twenty-six copies are said to be in existence; some of them are printed on vellum. Of the known remaining copies, ten are in England, there being a copy in the libraries of Oxford, Edinburgh, and London, and seven in the collections of different noblemen. The vellum copy has been sold as high as $2,500. Thus, as if to mark the noblest purpose to which the art could ever be applied, the first book printed with cut metal types was the Bible, in 1444-1460.

Faust displaced Gutenberg from the partnership in 1455, and subsequently carried on the business with Schœffer; one of their first works was a Psalter, which appeared in 1457. Faust is supposed to have died of the plague in 1466. After his death, Schœffer had the meanness to arrogate to his family the entire invention of the art of printing—and succeeded so far as to obtain from the Emperor Maximilian some lucrative privileges authenticating his pretensions. By this act of the Emperor, Gutenberg was robbed of his deserved reputation—his discoveries being attributed to his rival, and he regarded as a pretender. He was dead, however, before Schœffer dared advance his claim. Upon quitting his partners, he had established a printing press at Mentz, under the patronage of Dr. Conrad Humbracht, who advanced the necessary funds. In 1460, he printed the great Latin dictionary, *Catholicon Johannis de Balbus.* In 1465, he was attached to the Count Adolphus, of Nassau; and is supposed to have died in 1468.

The Dutch have disputed with the Germans the honor of the invention of printing, claiming it in behalf of Laurence Coster, a citizen of Haarlem. Their claim will not, however, bear investigation, and vanishes beneath the scrutiny to which it has been subjected by rigid inquiries.

After these pioneer printers had dissolved partnership, in a few years the business began to expand itself to such an extent that, in 1530, there were upwards of 200 printing-presses in Europe.

Gutenberg at first took impressions from his types by fastening them upon a table—coloring them with writing-ink—spreading the paper over them, and pressing it with a rubber of horn.

Faust invented printing-ink, and Gutenberg constructed a rude printing-press. Iron presses were earliest employed by Lord Stanhope.

2

Between the years 1467 and 1475, printing-offices were opened at Cologne, Augsburg, Nuremberg, and Lubec. Monks, called "Brothers of common life," founded printing establishments at Brussels and Louvain, in Belgium. In the year 1467, a press was transported to Rome; some years afterwards, to Venice, Milan, and Naples. The printing art came to Paris in 1469. It met with obstacles on the part of copyists, who feared to lose their means of subsistence; but the king, Louis XI., protected the printers.

The art was conveyed from Haarlem to England in 1468, and by Bourchier, Archbishop of Canterbury. This prelate sent to Haarlem, Turner, master of the robes, and a merchant named William Caxton, to learn the art. Caxton prevailed with Corseilles to come over to Oxford, and there set up a press. But before he left the continent, he translated from the French, and in the year 1471 published at Cologne, *the first book ever printed in the English language*, entitled, *The Recuyell of the Historyes of Troye.* "An imperfect copy of this work," says Duppa, in his notes to Johnson's Journal of a Tour to Wales, "was put up to sale in 1812, when there was a competition amongst men eminent for learning, rank and fortune; and, according to their estimation of its value, it was sold for the sum of £1,060 10s." In the year 1474 (having in the meantime returned to England), he published *the first book ever printed in England.* It was entitled, "The Game and Playe of the Chesse: Translated out of the Frenche, and emprynted by me William Caxton. Fynysshid the last day of Marche, the yer of our Lord God a thousand four hondred, lxxiiij."

Caxton, who died at the age of 81, in 1491, and who, in addition to having had the honor of introducing into England the "divine art"—fitly styled "ars artium omnium conservatrix"—was an eminent instance of the successful cultivation of letters, combined with mechanical pursuits. Amidst the onerous charge of an extensive printing-office in one of the chapelries of Westminster Abbey, containing twenty-four presses, with about a hundred workmen, this indefatigable man actually gave to the world no fewer than five thousand closely printed folio pages from his own pen, consisting chiefly of translations from the French, or the stock of his own vernacular literature. Several of his works have subsequently passed through successive editions, and about sixty of his books still exist. His just estimate of Chaucer, which he first printed, evinces his uncommon critical acumen. On more accounts than one, therefore, may Caxton be fitly styled the father of the English press. The well-known names of Pynson, who died 1529, Wynkin de Worde, in 1534, and Wyer, in 1542, although justly celebrated for the improvements they effected in the typographic art, the former having first constructed and introduced into use the Roman letters, claim a passing mention.

Printing hitherto had been for the most part in Latin; but the Italians in 1480 began to print with Greek and Hebrew types, and they were the first to use these.

In the sixteenth century, according to Dr. Gregory, there appeared various editions of books in Syriac, Arabic, Persian, Armenian, Coptic or Egyptian, characters.

Anthony Koburger, of Nuremburgh, was a person eminent for his learning as well as for his elegance in printing. He was styled the *prince of printers*, and was likewise a very extensive bookseller. Besides a spacious warehouse at Lyons, he had agents in every important city in Christendom, and kept sixteen open shops, with a vast number of warehouses. He printed thirteen editions of the Bible in folio, which are esteemed as extremely beautiful specimens of the art; but his *chef-d'œuvre* was the *German* Bible, printed in 1483, folio, the most splendid of all the ancient German Bibles, being embellished with many curious wood-cuts.

About the year 1547, we find honorable mention made of the name of Robert Copland, formerly engaged in Caxton's office; he was a stationer, printer, author, and translator. The "Rose Garland," in Fleet-street, was his well-known residence. Anthony Scoloker was another, who translated several works which he printed, one of which, affording no unequivocal proof, however, of his prophetic skill, was intituled, "A Juste Reckenynge, or Accompte of the Whole Number of the Yeares, from the Beginnynge of the Worlde unto the present Yeare of 1547; a Certayne and Sure Declaracion that the Worlde is at an Ende." Robert Stephens, the renowned Parisian printer and scholar, was his contemporary; his erudition as a critic and etymologist, is sufficiently evinced by his great work, "Dictionarium seu Latinæ Linguæ Thesaurus." De Thou, the historian, passed the following merited eulogium upon this distinguished scholar:—"Not only France, but the whole Christian world, owes more to him than to the greatest warrior that ever extended the possessions of his country; and greater glory has redounded to Francis I. by the industry alone of Robert Stephens, than from all the illustrious, warlike, and pacific undertakings in which he was engaged. His son and successor was also of great classical attainments, and wrote many learned works." We next come, in the order of date, to the name of John Day, the equally prolific printer and parent—having introduced into the world two hundred and forty-five books, and twenty-seven children! He lived in the neighborhood of Holborn Conduit."

Richard Grafton, of London, was distinguished alike for his erudition, as well as being an eminent printer. He was a linguist, and also the friend of Cranmer and Lord Cromwell. Grafton lived in the house of the Grey Friars, since known as Christ's Hospital.

His first work was the English Bible, printed abroad in 1535, which he presented to Archbishop Cranmer and Lord Cromwell.

Thoresby mentions the New Testament printed at Paris by Bishop Bonner's means. In November, 1539, the king, by his letters patent, "directed to all and singular printers and booksellers within this his realm," &c., appointed the Lord Cromwell, keeper of his privy seal, to take special care and charge "that no manner of person or persons within his realm shall enterprise, attempt, or set in print any Bible in the English tongue, of any manner of volume, during the space of five years next ensuing the date thereof, but only all such as shall be deputed, assigned, and admitted by the said Lord Cromwell." Accordingly, it appears, by the Bibles printed this very year, his lordship assigned others besides Grafton and Whitchurch, as John Biddel, Thomas Berthelet, etc., to print Bibles in the English tongue.

The first of these, printed this year, was a Bible in large folio, with the following title: "The Byble in Englyshe, that is to say, the Content of all the Holie Scripture bothe of the Olde and Newe Testament, truely translated after the Veryte of the Hebrue and Greke Textes, by the dylygent Studye of dyuerse excellent learned men, expert in the forsayde tonges.

"Prynted by Richard Grafton and Edward Whitchurch,

"*Cum priuilegio ad imprimendum solum.* 1539."

Grafton was in so much favor, that we find, in Rymer's *Fœdera*, a patent dated January 28, 1543, as follows :—

"*Pro divino servicio, de libris imprimendis.*"

In 1545, he printed King Henry VIII.'s Primer, both in Latin and English, with red and black ink, for which he had a patent, that is inserted at the end, expressed in much the same words as the preceding one of 1543.

In the first year of Edward VI., Grafton was favored with a special patent, granted to him for the sole printing of all the Statute Books. This is the first patent that is taken notice of by that diligent and accurate antiquarian, Sir William Dugdale.

An eminent printer was Christopher Plantin, of Antwerp, who lived in the latter part of the sixteenth century. "I am well aware," says his biographer, "that many illustrious men have flourished as printers, such as the Aldi of Italy, the Frobens from Germany, and the Stephenses from France; but these were all eclipsed in the single name of Plantin: if these," he continues, "were the stars of their own hemispheres he was the *Sun*, not of Antwerp merely, nor Belgium, but the world!" His offices at Antwerp, Germany, and France seem to have been established upon the most magnificent scale, and, like one of his great predecessors, Stephens, he indulged himself in the luxury of *silver types*. At one time, he is reported to have paid to his proof-readers and compositors no less than one hundred golden crowns *per diem*, no equivocal evidence of the extent of his operations. He also retained, not only in his friendship, but in his employ, a host of the literary men of his day, among the number the renowned De Thou. His *chef-d'œuvre*—which has been styled the eighth wonder of the world—was his *Biblia Polyglotta*, in eight folio volumes, copies of which, not being now rare, produce no extraordinary sums at auction.

Then we have the no less illustrious names of Francis Raphelengius, the celebrated scholar, and printer to the University of Leyden; and Louis Elzevir, of the same place (temp. 1595—1616), the founder of the most learned family of printers that ever adorned the republic of letters. Elzevir, is said to have been the first who observed the distinction between the use of the consonant *v*, and the vowel *u* (which had been recommended by Ramus and other writers long before, but never regarded), as also the vowel *i* from the consonant *j*. Aldus Manutius, with whom terminated a family of printers scarcely less distinguished in the literary history of their times, extending to upwards of a century, was grandson to the celebrated Aldus.

His extraordinary precocity was displayed by the successful publication of a production from his own pen in his eleventh year; and his great work, *De Veterum Notarum Explanatione*, has not only immortalized his name, but has been long since acknowledged as a standard for reference by the learned. In the reign of the second Charles, we find the name of John Ogilby, geographical printer to the Court, and noted as having written some books, including a pompous account of the coronation of that monarch, which he was appointed to write, in 1661. He also published a magnificent Bible, with illustrations, for which he was remunerated by the British Parliament. Towards the close of the seventeenth century, Palliot, the historiographer, printer, and bookseller to the King of France, was also highly distinguished as a genealogist. As a proof of his untiring perseverance and industry, it is recorded that he left, at his decease, thirteen volumes of MSS., in addition to the five folios which he had already published, the plates of which were likewise executed by his own hands. Contemporary with him, lived Rothscholtz, the bookseller, of Nuremberg, whose name is distinguished in the world of letters by his great work, in two volumes quarto, entitled, *A Short Essay towards an Ancient and Modern History of Booksellers.*

In early times, bookselling and printing were not only often combined, but, in some instances, it appears, authorship also was united with these several branches of handicraft.

Numerous instances attest that a natural and intimate connection subsists between printing and knowledge, and that printers have themselves contributed by their genius to adorn the annals of their age: rising from the servile labors of the press to eminent distinction, and diffusing the light of science even in the darkest times. Bayle speaks of one who composed and printed a work simultaneously, setting up the types with his hands, as fast as his brain concocted his sentences, without the intervention of manuscript corrections.

Lackington, the well-known bookseller, insists that there is an affinity between the two pursuits. He writes: "among all the schools where a knowledge of mankind may be acquired, I know of none equal to that of a bookseller's shop, where, if any one have any taste for literature, he may be said to feed his mind, as cooks' and butchers' wives get fat by the smell of meat."

It cannot be denied, however, that there are numerous exceptions to this supposed rule; for the instances of eminent printers and booksellers we have presented, are from the many whose commerce with literature seemed to have awakened little or no sympathy with its pleasures, its pains, or its pursuit. The remark is not less applicable to our own times.

Perhaps the most curious instance that ever occurred of an author-publisher, if we may venture so to style him, was that of an individual well known, years since, in the streets of London, who was no less remarkable for the novel method he adopted for displaying his productions before the world, even without the aid of the press, than as presenting the singular anomaly of writer and publisher combined, giving to the public his labors anonymously. How often have we seen him in our boyish peregrinations, and lingered to gaze on his ingenious performances. The "mammoth sheets" of our own day, stupendous as they are, shrink into a paltry insignificance as we trace out in mental vision the broad superficies of the former. Nor was the literary department the only feature that exhibited the skill of this luminous writer; he united within himself the artist also, equally excelling in design, engraving, and chirography. A black's head, with a ring through his nose, and a group of fish, were portrayed upon the pavement with inimitable fidelity. This singular genius, who used to fix his location wherever the pavement was sufficiently smooth, was a cripple, and it was amusing to observe, if among the admiring crowd, any inquisitive little urchin happened to encroach too closely on his prescribed limits, the implement which supplied to him the lack of limbs, was made the summary instrument to visit upon the shins of the offender the penalty of his trespass. His writing was exceedingly well executed, and his poetic lucubrations were generally no less admirably pointed—we regret that our recollection supplies us with no more than the following specimen :

> " Let no rude footsteps on this pavement tread,
> For know, these very flags to me are bread !—
> Oh, spare a penny, or indeed 'tis plain,
> The very stones themselves cry out in vain !"

This hapless votary of the muse has passed away ; and though unchronicled in any " Curiosities of Literature," we trust we have said enough to rescue his memory—*non omnis moriar !*—from utter annihilation.

Craving indulgence for the digression into which the recurrence of an early association has beguiled us, we retrace our steps, while we solicit the reader to accompany us adown the stream of time a few centuries back. In the olden time, prior to the era of printing, the MSS. of authors were obliged to be subjected to the ordeal of critical censorship, previous to their being allowed public perusal ; their works being required to be read over before the Universities, for three successive days, or by appointed judges ; when, if approved, copies were allowed to be executed by the monks, scribes, and illuminators.

Even in the classical days of Greece and Rome, we find a trade carried on in books ; those works most in demand being multiplied by the scribes and copyists. An exclusive traffic in the MSS. of those days seems to have been carried on along the shores of the Mediterranean, and the Greek colonies of the Euxine.

During the middle ages, the booksellers were styled *Stationarii* at the Universities of Paris and Bologna ; they used to sell and loan MSS. This was the commencement of the bookselling business. A species of literary censorship, it appears, was first established at Paris, in 1342, when a license from the

University was requisite previously to engaging in such business. The booksellers were, in fact, regularly matriculated by entry on its roll, and considered as its officers; the prices of all books were also fixed according to the tariff of four sworn booksellers, by the institution; a fine was imposed for selling an imperfect copy of a work, and a catalogue, with the prices annexed, was further required to be always kept in the shops. This censorship was afterwards invested in the person of Berthold, Archbishop of Mentz, in 1486, and again renewed with greater vigor, with respect to books, by the Council of Trent, in 1546, being subsequently enforced by the popes, down to 1563, by whom several *Indices Librorum Prohibitorum*, were issued. In France the censorship was vested in the Chancellor; in England it was exercised by the well-known Star-Chamber; and after the abolition of that court, by Parliament itself; it was abolished in England about 1694, although it still continues in force, we believe, in several of the Continental States.

The *first* bookseller, so called, on record was Faustus. He is said to have carried his books for sale to the monasteries in France and elsewhere; and the first bookseller who purchased MSS. for publication, without possessing a press of his own, was John Otto, of Nuremberg (1516).

Resuming our notices of eminent bibliopoles, the next name we find in the order of date is that of John Dunton (temp. 1659—1733). Of his literary performances, his *Life and Errors* is the best known. His critical acumen, or good fortune, were certainly not much at fault; for it is recorded, that of the 600 works which he published, only seven proved unsuccessful.

Chiswell, styled for pre-eminence the metropolitan bookseller of England, and whose shrewdness and wit stood the test so admirably, that he is reported never to have issued a bad book, was also, at about the same period, an author of some consideration. Contemporary with him, we find the name of the learned linguist and bibliopolist Samuel Smith, the appointed bookseller to the Royal Society; and Thomas Guy, the founder of "Guy's Hospital" (whose munificence and philanthropy have immortalized his name, and often invoked the blessing of suffering humanity), was originally, it will be remembered, a bookseller.

John Bagford, an industrious antiquarian bookseller, who lived to the early part of the eighteenth century, was the author of the *Collectanea*, bearing his name, contained in the Harleian MSS. of the British Museum.

The Tonsons were a race of booksellers who did honor to their profession for integrity, and by their encouragement of authors. Malone published several letters from Dryden to Tonson, and Tonson to Dryden. Tonson displays the tradesman, acknowledging the receipt of the Translations of Ovid, which he had received for the third Miscellany, with which he was pleased, but not with the price, having only one thousand four hundred and forty-six lines for fifty guineas, when he expected to have had one thousand five hundred and eighteen lines for forty guineas; adding that he had a better bargain with Juvenal, which is reckoned not so easy to translate as Ovid. Most of the other letters relate to the translation of Virgil, and contain repeated acknowledgments of Tonson's kind attentions. "I thank you heartily," he says, "for the sherry; it was the best of the kind I ever drank." The current coin was at that period wretchedly debased. In one letter Dryden says, "I expect forty pounds in good silver, not such as I had formerly. I am not obliged to take gold, neither will I, nor stay for it above four and twenty hours after it is due." In 1698, when Dryden published his Fables, Tonson agreed to give him two hundred and sixty-eight pounds for ten thousand verses; and to complete the full number of lines stipulated, he gave the bookseller the Epistle to his Cousin, and the celebrated Ode.

Lintot, Pope's publisher, was also an author: not to

speak of Miller, Evans, Griersson, Motte, and Ruddiman, the last-named, a man of profound attainments as a grammarian and critic ; or Richardson, the author of " Sir Charles Grandison," and other popular works, which have procured for him the title of the English Rousseau ;—and Alexander Cruden, the renowned compiler of the " Concordance to the Sacred Scriptures," whose stupendous labors turned him mad. A curious anecdote is related of him ; one evening having prepared an excellent supper for some friends, whom he had invited to partake of a favorite dish of roast turkey, no sooner had Mr. Cruden arrived and made his appearance in the room, heated with walking, than before the covers could be removed, while his guests were eagerly anticipating their pleasurable repast, up walked the distinguished host, and advancing to the smoking joint in question, *sans cérêmonie* pushed back his wig, and with both hands plunged in the gravy, began to wash his head and face over the bird, to the horror and dismay of the astonished group !

John Buckley, who lived to about 1746, was a learned linguist ; and Paterson, his contemporary, was also author of many works, as well as a book-auctioneer ; he was indeed one of the most prominent bibliopoles of his age.

About the same date, we meet with the name of Harris, the author of *Lexicon Technicum.* *Chambers' Cyclopædia* was the basis of Dr. Rees' voluminous work, which extended to forty volumes, quarto. This celebrated work was styled "the pride of booksellers, and the honor of the English nation." Rees is represented as a man equally indefatigable, perspicacious, and observant. He was a Quaker, a member of Gray's Inn, and at his demise, which occurred at Canonbury House, Islington, a relic of the times of Elizabeth, he was interred within the cloisters of Westminster Abbey.

Hutton, of Birmingham, who has been not inaptly styled the English Franklin, from the very depths of obscurity and poverty, fought his way single-handed to wealth and literary eminence. His "History of Birmingham" was followed by other productions, including his interesting auto-biography. His literary labors were concluded in 1811, by a "Trip to Coatham," a watering-place in Yorkshire, written in his eighty-sixth year, in which he thus takes leave of his readers: "As it is perhaps the last time I shall appear before the world as an author, I may be allowed the liberty of exhibiting my performances in that character. I took up my pen, and that with fear and trembling, at the advanced age of fifty-six, a period when most would lay it down. I drove the quill thirty years, during which time I wrote and published fourteen books."

We might refer to the names of Rushton, of Liverpool, M'Creery, Debrett, Allan Ramsay, the poet, Hansard, Bulmer, Boydell, Griffiths, Harrison, and many others we stay not to enumerate. Worrall, of Bell Yard, who died 1771, was a well-known author-bookseller, as well as the eccentric Andrew Brice, of Exeter, and Sir James Hodges, who lived at the sign of the Looking-Glass, on London Bridge. The names should not be omitted of Faulkner, Gent, Goadby, and also Smellie, the first edition of whose work on philosophy, yielded him one thousand guineas, and a revenue of fame. Thomas Osborne, of Gray's Inn, was also a very eminent bookseller, although, if we are to decide with Dr. Dibdin, not eminent in philological attainments. Boswell relates an amusing circumstance connected with the professional career of this worthy bibliopole, who, it is said, was inclined to assume an authoritative air in his business intercourse. One day Johnson happening to encounter a similar exhibition of temper, the Doctor became so exasperated, that he actually knocked Osborne down in his shop with a folio, and put his foot upon his neck; and when remonstrated with on such summary proceeding, he coolly replied, "Sir, he was impertinent to me, and I beat him."

Paternoster Row, the great literary emporium of the world,

did not assume any importance till the reign of Queen Anne, when the booksellers began to forsake their former principal mart, Little Britain,* which had become the resort of all the bibliopoles about the time of the renowned John Day, terminating with the equally celebrated Ballard. In earlier times Paternoster Row seems to have been more noted for mercers, lacemen, and haberdashers, for a newspaper periodical of 1707, adds to the list, "the *sempstresses* of Paternoster Row." We find, however, the record of a solitary member of the craft, one Denham, who lived then and there, at the sign of the Star, as early as 1564, and whose significant motto ran as follows :

"Os homini sublime dedit."

There also dwelt turners of beads, and they were called Paternoster makers, from which, of course, this noted place originally derived its name. It is also worthy of notice, that the parish of St. Bride has been, from the days of Pynson, in 1500, down to the days of Strahan, the location of the "King's Printer ;" while the number of those carrying on the profession in this vicinity are singularly numerous, and far beyond the average of any other parish in England, or perhaps the world ; the site seems to have become, from its first introduction, the *Alma Mater* of the printers. Alex. Hogg, called the king of Puffers, was moreover reputed a man of considerable learning. He published numerous standard works in the serial form, and was the first to introduce that convenient, and, for the spread of literature, important mode of publication. He seems to have exhausted the vocabularies of superlatives, to express the beauty, elegance, and magnificence of his editions. He also was reputed to possess singular tact in revivifying a dull book by re-christening it, and otherwise metamorphosing

* Anciently Breton street, from the mansion of the Duke of Bretagne on that spot, in more modern times became the "Paternoster Row" of the booksellers ; and a newspaper of 1664 states them to have published here within four years, 464 pamphlets. Here lived Rawlinson ("Tom Folio" of *The Tatler*, No. 158), who stuffed four chambers in Gray's Inn so full, that his bed was removed into the passage.

its contents when its sale, under its original condition, had ceased.

Among our notices of eminent bibliopolists we must not omit the name of Andrew Millar, or the laconic missives that passed between him and Dr. Johnson—although the incident may be already familiar to the reader.

The great lexicographer having wearied the expectation of the trade for his long promised work, and no less the patience of his publisher, who had already advanced him, in various sums, the amount of £1,500, he was induced, on receipt of the concluding sheet of his Dictionary, to send to the doctor the following :—" A. Millar sends his compliments to Mr. Samuel Johnson, with money for the last sheet of copy of Dictionary, and thanks God he has done with him." To which our author replied, " Samuel Johnson returns compliments to Mr. Andrew Millar, and is very glad to find (as he does by his note), that Mr. A. M. has the grace to thank God for anything."

Honorable mention also should be made, of a name which has never, perhaps, been eclipsed in the annals of book-craft. We refer to that of Nicholls, whose "Literary Anecdotes," as well as his numerous other works, will link his memory to many a distant year, and whose otherwise immense industry and labors, as printer, compiler, and publisher, would scarce require the aid of "Sylvanus Urban" to immortalize his name. The mantle of the sire has descended upon the son, who has published several historical works, and among others, an "Account of the Guildhall, London," historical notices of "Fonthill Abbey," &c. Sotheby, the celebrated book-auctioneer of London, whose establishment, originally founded by Baker (his great uncle), in 1744, was one of the earliest that ever existed in London. He was a man of extensive learning and literary acquirements, and had been many years occupied in collecting materials for an elaborate work on the "Early History of Printing." He is favorably known to the literary world by his interesting work, in folio, on the " Hand-writing of Melanchthon and Luther." Davy of Devonshire, once a bookseller of eminence, was afterwards distinguished for his attainments in biblical literature, and will be long remembered by his voluminous "System of Divinity in a series of Sermons," comprising 26 vols. 8vo. John Gough, of Dublin, bookseller, was also author of "A Tour in Ireland," "History of Quakers," and other works of note. William Harrod was a worthy but eccentric bookseller, whose pen produced several topographical works. Samuel Rosseau, who, when an apprentice to Nicholls, used to collect old epitaphs, it is said actually taught himself in the intervals of business, Latin, Greek, Hebrew, Syriac, Persian and Arabic, as well as two or three of the modern languages; besides having edited, in after life, several useful and popular works on elementary education. To name Dodsley, would prove almost his sufficient eulogy; his valuable series of "Annual Registers," and collected edition of "Old Plays," being literary performances sufficient to form a monument to his memory. Nicholson, of Worcester, is another member of the bookselling fraternity, who has added to the stores of literature; and the name of Constable, of Edinburgh, whose literary taste and great bibliographical knowledge, independently of his having been the originator of the Edinburgh Review, sufficiently entitle him to be noticed among the class. Ballantyne, the publisher and confidant of Sir Walter Scott, who was the sprightly author of the "Widow's Lodgings," and other works in the department of elegant literature, in addition to his vast fund of anecdote, is equally entitled to distinction; as well as Blackwood, for seventeen years the editor of the inimitable periodical that still retains his name. James Lackington—the well-known London bookseller—may be said to have established his claim to our notice from the publication of his "Auto-biography." From the shades of obscurity, he was indebted to thriftiness and parsimony, no less than to his untiring zeal and exertions, for his ultimate distinction. Although we may not assign to his character any literary eminence, his career was marked by singular eccentricity; his spacious establishment in Finsbury Square, around which it is said that he actually drove a coach-and-four, contained an immense collection of books. Among his many expedients to excite notoriety, was the publication of an advertisement, stating that his coach-house in Old Street had been robbed of 10,000 volumes, consisting chiefly of Dr. Watts' "Psalms and Hymns," a manœuvre that answered the two-fold purpose of letting the world know that he kept a coach, and that even so large a quantity of books could scarce be missed from his collection. He also had the vanity to hoist a flag at the top of his house as a signal, whenever he arrived from his country-seat at Merton. His vanity was certainly very amusing, and excusable when we consider the disadvantages of his humble origin. At ten years old he commenced crying apple-pies in the streets, so that, as he himself intimates, he soon began to make a noise in the world. His success in this his first essay, induced speedily the exchange of tarts for books; thus he commenced his business as a bookseller, which one year yielded him a profit of £5,000. Here we might mention the name of John Trusler, who was distinguished as a doctor, parson, printer, and author; having fabricated many useful books, and amongst others, an "Essay on the Rights of Literary Property"—a subject, even at the present day, we regret to find, so very imperfectly understood among the mass of those to whose enjoyments it is made to yield so large a contribution. Davies, in 1817, compiled and published several amusing bibliographic works, one entitled, *An Olio of Bibliographical and Literary Anecdote and Memoranda,* and *A Life of Garrick,* which went through several editions. Richard Beatniffe, bookseller, of Norwich, wrote a *Tour through Norfolk,* and other works. Parkhurst (Johnson's friend) was of distinguished repute, and occupied many years in preparing a Talmudic Lexicon! Upham, of Exeter, also translated sacred books of the Buddhists.

Dr. William Russell, who died at the close of the last century, the well-known author of the *History of Modern Europe*, was originally apprenticed to a bookseller ; a few years after which, he was engaged as a corrector of the press, and subsequently was enabled to devote himself to authorship. His historical works were the product of his maturer years. Whiston, the celebrated translator of *Josephus*, was also in his early days a bookseller. The same might be remarked of the renowned naturalist, Smellie, equally celebrated as having produced the best edition of *Terence*. He was, moreover, the antagonist of Hume, the refutation of whose atheistical opinions became the theme of his pen. Walwyn was a bard-bookseller of eminence, "a worthy associate of Dryden." Watton, who kept a shop near St. Dunstan's many years, published and compiled several excellent works—among them the earliest history we possess of Baronets, occupying five octavo volumes. Godwin, whose *Caleb Williams* alone is sufficient to preserve his name from oblivion, was for a considerable time a bookseller, and ushered many books of value into tangible existence. Dr. Olinthus Gregory also was once a bookseller at Cambridge, and a teacher of mathematics at the same time.

John Lander, brother of the African traveller, was originally a bookseller. Devoting his leisure to literary pursuits, and his mind being inspired with a love of enterprise, he not only rendered important services to physical science, by the discovery of a problem which had long baffled the literati of Europe, and which has placed his name among the proudest in the annals of science, but he bequeathed to the world one of the most delightful and interesting narratives of travel in the English language. Sir Richard Phillips, of whose elementary writings, it is enough commendation to remark that they were sufficiently productive to become the adequate support of his declining years, was not only the first publisher to introduce a reduction in the price of books, but the originator of a fund for oppressed debtors—two things that go to his glory. In the same category was Booth, of London, whose knowledge of books, critical, not titulary, rendered him eminently distinguished ; his collection was exceedingly rare and extensive. His literary capabilities were so far respected by Malone, the commentator of Shakespeare, that he consigned to him the onerous task of editing and arranging the annotations and remarks for his edition of the great dramatist. He also edited and compiled several documents for his *Account of the Battle of Waterloo*, two volumes quarto, which passed through the unprecedented number of nine editions in less than two years.

The race of author-booksellers, far from being extinct, is not less flourishing at the present day than it has been at any former period—while it embraces not a few of those who are emulous of the classic honors of their sires, and whose genius and labors will supply a worthy sequel to the past, and add a new lustre to the bibliographic history of the nineteenth century. We will commence with noticing the son of the senior member of one of the most distinguished bookselling houses in the British metropolis—we refer to the Longmans. William Longman has distinguished himself in the science of entomology, a subject that has already successfully engaged his pen. William Wood, the natural history bookseller, is undoubtedly deserving a place among the scientific writers of the day, which his esteemed work, *Zoography, or the Beauties of Nature Displayed*, in three large volumes, sufficiently attests. He is author of some four or five other important works, as well as editor of the beautiful edition of Buffon, in twenty volumes octavo, and contributor of several interesting papers to the *Philosophical Transactions*.*

Moxon, in early life, published *Christmas*, a poem, and a volume of *Sonnets*, which were so favorably noticed by Rogers, the poet, that a friendship ensued, which has since ripened with

* The principal publishers of London are Longman & Co., Rivingtons, Whittaker & Co., Hamilton & Co., Simpkin & Co., Smith, Elder & Co., and at the "West End," Mur-

its growth, and contributed very materially to the success of this enterprising and accomplished publisher. To the classical reader we need only mention the name of A. J. Valpy, whose edition of the *Variorum* Classics, extended to 161 vols., 8vo., to prove his cultivated taste and liberality of enterprise. M'Cray has translated and published some beautiful Lyrics from the German; William Clarke, originally a bookseller, gave to the antiquary an exceedingly curious and interesting account of libraries, under the name of *Repertorium Bibliographicum;* and Rodd was the translator of several volumes from the Spanish. One of the best bibliographers was R. H. Evans, the auctioneer and bookseller of Pall-Mall; his namesake, J. Evans, acted as editor in the instance of Aikin's Essays; Dolby, bookseller, gave to the public a work of ingenuity and labor, *The Shakspearian Dictionary;* and Christie, the auctioneer, has also produced four abstruse works, on the taste and literature of the ancient Greeks, which he compiled during the intervals of his business occupation; Griffith, the bookseller, compiled a catalogue of ancient and modern poetry, entitled *Bibliographia Anglo-Poetica;* and Dr. Koller and Mr. Bach were both translators and German critics, as well as booksellers. Another conspicuous member of the class was Cochrane, who was for some time an eminent bookseller, and the able and discriminating editor of the *Foreign Quarterly Review*, for seven years. He was also selected by the trustees to draw up the catalogue of Sir Walter Scott's choice and valuable library at Abbottsford—a most delightful labor of love; and on the formation of the London Library, was, among a host of competitors, unanimously elected to the offices of librarian and secretary.

We might also mention Stewart, the eminent linguist, and

ray, Bentley, Saunders & Otley, Hatchard, Nisbett, Bohn, Moxon, and although now deceased, we should not omit the well-known publisher of the Aldine edition of the Poets—Pickering. Many others might be named, among them Tegg, Routledge, Bogue, Chapman & Hall, Weale, &c.

known as the skillful compiler of the celebrated catalogue of Miss Currer's library, which he embellished by drawings from his own pencil. If any one is sceptical enough, after what has been adduced to the contrary, to assert that the bookselling and printing business has been wanting in literary distinction, we pity his want of candor, while we further refer him to such names as the following: Arrowsmith, the celebrated map-publisher, and author of *Ancient and Modern Geography*, as well as several elementary works in geography, some of which, with the former, were used as text-books at Oxford, Cambridge, and Eton; J. Wilson, editor of the *Bibliographical and Retrospective Miscellany, Shakspeariana*, &c.; Atkinson, of Glasgow, possessed, perhaps, as great an acquaintance with *Medical Bibliography* as any person of his times, as his curious and unique work on that subject proves. One of the leading medical journals of Europe characterized it as "one of the most remarkable books ever seen—uniting the German research of a Plouquet with the ravings of a Rabelais, the humor of Sterne with the satire of Democritus, the learning of Burton with the wit of Pindar." It is to be regretted the ingenious author did not live to complete the whole design.

Ainsworth, the popular historical novelist, was originally a bookseller with John Ebers, of Bond Street, to whom he afterwards became related by marriage.

Godwin (author of *Caleb Williams, St. Leon*, &c.), was once a bookseller in Skinner Street; Rodd, who kept an extensive establishment for the sale of old books, translated the *Spanish Ballads.* His shop was the resort of confirmed bibliomaniacs.

Nor should the name of John Murray—the friend and publisher of Byron—be omitted in this place. It is not our province to remark on the distinguished eminence of this gentleman as a publisher, although in this respect he may unquestionably be entitled to take the highest rank; but his well-known literary abilities and severe critical taste, equally render him conspicuous, as evinced in the immense collection of valuable works which have issued from his establishment. The excellent series of *Hand-Books*, are in part, productions of his son, the present publisher of that name.

The name of Talboys, of Oxford, will be remembered by his admirable translation of Adelung's *Historical Sketch of Sanscrit Literature*, to which he appended copious bibliographical notices. He was, moreover, the translator of the very erudite volumes of Professor Heeren, of which he is also the publisher ; his *Bibliotheca Classica* and *Theologica*, likewise deserve honorable mention for their completeness and excellent scientific arrangement.

Hansard, the printer, who wrote *Typographia*, and another similar work, and who has been also a contributor to the *Encyclopedia Britannica*, also was of the fraternity ; as well as West, the author of *Fifty Years' Recollections of a Bookseller*. Goodhugh, author of the *Library Manual ;* Haas, who translated Dr. Krummacher's *Elisha*, and Zschökke's *History of Switzerland*.

John Russell Smith has rendered himself distinguished by his industry, as well as literary taste. His work on the Bibliography of Kent, *Bibliotheca Cantiana*, as well as his *Bibliographical List of all Works which have been published towards illustrating the Provincial Dialects of England*, evince both his untiring antiquarian research and literary zeal. We come next to a name that has become almost a synonym with antiquarian anecdote—William Hone, the sale of whose *Every Day Book and Year Book* (who has not read them?), during the first year of their publication, produced £500. He was originally a bookseller—his collected works would probably fill ten or twelve octavos. His political satires had a prodigious sale, upwards of 70,000 copies being disposed of in a short time. His infidel publications he lived to repudiate, and publicly to recant, in a work entitled his *Early Life and Conversion.* Henry G. Bohn deserves to be classed among our list; his catalogue, containing a critical description of 300,000 volumes, in all the languages dear to literature, may be ranked among the most remarkable productions of the press of any nation. It contains 2,106 pages, and cost its compiler two thousand guineas and an almost incredible amount of labor. The Chambers, of Edinburgh, editors of the able and valuable works that bear their name, present another noble instance of genius rising superior to all opposing circumstances. They were originally, as intimated, of humble origin—now they are among the largest publishers of their age. Their essays are among the choicest of our periodical literature. There is still another name we cannot, in justice, omit to notice: we allude to that of Timperley, whose *Encyclopædia of Literary Anecdote* discovers curious labor and research. Here, then, we ought to pause in our enumeration of literary booksellers and printers; although the catalogue might be extended to a much greater length. There are three other names, however, we must not omit, in conclusion.

Charles Knight, the well-known editor of the *Pictorial Shakespeare,* of *London Illustrated,* and other excellent works; Thomas Miller, once the basket-maker, since poet, novelist, and essayist; and William Howitt, whose voluminous writings are too well known to require recital—form a triple coronal in bibliography; and the lustre they shed upon the brotherhood of booksellers to which they originally belonged, may well atone for the obliquities, discrepancies, and obtuseness, with which the tongue of scandal has sought to darken the fair escutcheon of its fame.

The first book ever printed in the New World was in the city of Mexico. It was printed in the Spanish language, in the year 1544, and was entitled *Doctrina Christiana per eo los*

Indos. The first publications made in English, in America, were the *Freeman's Oath*, an Almanac for 1639, nearly a hundred years after the work published in Mexico. In 1640 was published the first book, entitled the *Bay Psalm Book.* It was reprinted in England, where it passed through no less than eighteen editions ; the last being issued in 1754. It was no less popular in Scotland, twenty-two editions of it having been published there. Altogether, it is estimated it reached to seventy editions abroad.

We might mention, with no slight honor, the name of John Foster, a man of great literary attainments, a graduate at Harvard University, and, himself an author. At a later date Matthew Carey, and his son and successor, Henry Carey, both of whom have recorded their names in the literary annals of their country, not to omit the name of an author-bookseller, Peter Parley (Goodrich), whose works are alike appreciated in both hemispheres.

Isaiah Thomas has written and published a *History of Printing,* a work of considerable reputation ; Drake, the antiquarian bookseller of Boston, besides being a member of several learned societies, was author of the *Book of the Indians.*

The first Printing-press set up in America, was "worked" at Cambridge, Massachusetts, in 1639.

The Rev. Jesse Glover procured this press, by "contributions of friends of learning and religion," in Amsterdam and in England, but died on his passage to the New World.

Stephen Day was the first printer. In honor of his pioneer position, Government gave him a grant of three hundred acres of land. Among other of his early publications were the *New Testament,* and *Baxter's Call,* translated into the Indian language, by Elliot, the great Missionary, and printed at great cost. The title might be recommended, on account of its obscurity and high-sounding character, to some of the writers of books now-a-days. It was *Wusku-Wuttesthementum Yul-Lordumun Jesus Christ Nuppoqhwussuaenenmun.**

The whole Bible was printed in this language in 1663. The nation once speaking it is now extinct.

Pennsylvania was the second State to encourage printing. William Bradford went to Pennsylvania with William Penn, in 1682, and in 1686 established a printing-press in Philadelphia ; its first issue was an Almanac for 1687 ; it was but a sheet. The first book printed by Bradford was a collection of essays by Francis Bacon. It appeared in 1688, and was called *The Temple of Wisdom.*

In 1692, Bradford was induced to establish a printing-press in New York. He received £40 per annum, and " the privilege of printing on his own account." Previous to this time, there had been no printing done in the Province of New York. His first issue in New York, was a proclamation, bearing date of 1692.

During the latter part of the seventeenth century, Boston contained about forty printers and publishers. The first fruits of the press were devoted to the rights of religion and liberty—fitting tribute of the pioneer pilgrims of a great nation for the altar of Freedom. The bookselling business of Boston, half a century ago, was conducted on a very limited scale compared with present times. The senior publishers of that city are Crocker & Brewster. They began business in 1811. Gould & Lincoln are next in the order of date. Ticknor, Francis, Greene, Little & Brown, with others, form the succession. It is believed that the amount invested in the book

* One long word suggests another—the title of a pamphlet (in the possession of the writer), published years ago in London. The title reads: " *Chrononhotonthologos*, the most tragical tragedy that ever was tragedized by any company of tragedians." The two first lines of this effusion read—

" Aldeborontiphoscophosnio!
Where left you Chrononhotonthologos ?"

We might name another singular title of a work published in 1661, by Robert Lovell, entitled, " *Panzoologicomineralogia;* a complete history of animals and minerals, containg the summe of all authors, Galenical and Chymicall, with the anatomie of man, &c."

business in Boston alone at the present day, cannot be less than three millions of dollars. Now there are nearly one hundred booksellers, and over fifty distinct publishers in the American "Athens."

In New York there are four hundred and forty-four booksellers and one hundred and thirty-three publishers, and in Pennsylvania, four hundred and two of the first and seventy-two of the last. Most of the publishing, and the largest number of the booksellers, centre in the three great cities of Boston, New York, and Philadelphia, which are the leading publishing cities of the country. New York has the most capital invested in the business.*

In Great Britain, the United States, France, and Germany, the book and publishing business is vast. Great Britain gives to the world more than two thousand five hundred new books, or editions, annually; while France publishes about six thousand. There are thirteen hundred books published in the United States annually.

Among modern bibliopoles and printers of Paris, we must name Didot, Plon, Crapelet, Bossange, and Baillière, chiefly known for his valuable medical publications, who has also a house in New York. The number of booksellers reaches nearly to four hundred; their business is divided into the classical book-trade, the old book-trade, the new publications, and the commission trade. Many journals also enter into the trade: the *Revue des Deux Mondes* publishes the works of several eminent authors.

* Stanford and Swords is the oldest existing publishing-house of New York. Harper & Brothers (numerically the largest publishers, from whose establishment the best editions of the Classics have emanated); Appletons; Putnam (publisher of Washington Irving's works); Barnes & Co.; Scribner; Redfield; Ivison & Phinney; Derby; De Witt & Davenport; Carters; Collins, Woods, Wiley, Sheldon, Lamport & Co., are the publishers of New York. In addition, there are several large establishments connected with religious societies, including the Methodist Book Concern. The booksellers and publishers of Cincinnati, Buffalo, Auburn, and other cities of the West, are rapidly competing with their brothers of the Atlantic cities in the magnitude of their operations. In Philadelphia, the more prominent publishers are, Lindsay & Blakiston, Blanchard & Lea, Lippincott & Co., E. H. Butler, Cowperthwaite & Co.

On the quays, on the Boulevards, near the Louvre, and in a few retired streets, there are more than two hundred second-hand booksellers.

In earlier times, Francis de Bure, a bookseller of Paris, wrote, among others, a work of great research and skill, *A Treatise on Scarce and Curious Books*, in seven large volumes. The originator of the great work, *Encyclopédie Méthodique*, which has extended to above 150 volumes, was M. Panckoucke, a Parisian bookseller. Peter Vander, of Leyden, who died 1730, was another eminent instance of an author-bookseller, as his singular work, *Galerie du Monde*, in 66 folios, sufficiently attests ; and Lascaile, of Holland, was no less celebrated as poet and publisher, having been honored with the poetic crown by the Emperor Leopold ; and even his daughter so largely inherited her father's genius, that she was styled the Dutch Sappho, or tenth muse.

The renowned publisher, Tauchnitz, of Leipsic, achieves a great work for the diffusion of literature over continental Europe. His popular series of *British Classics* alone includes over 300 volumes, of which he annually sells about 150,000 copies. His will doubtless become the greatest publishing establishment in the world, if it progresses as it has since 1840, as it is now the largest on the continent of Europe.

In the sixteenth century, Trithemius died in Germany, after having, from time to time, assembled the literary world to behold the wonder of that age—a library of two thousand volumes. And yet, incredible as it may seem, nearly forty years ago the estimate was made, that since the invention of printing, there had been issued from the press of Germany three billions of volumes.

Next to the desire to know something about the *personnel* of an author, is the interest with which the public regard that intermediate personage between him and themselves, yclept the publisher. In a subordinate sense, he may justly be considered a member of the literary profession, for he enacts the part of agent for the author and his readers ; and if not an indispensable, he is at least a most important auxiliary in these relations. Publishers have, however, not unfrequently been characterized as selfish in their pursuits, and alike injurious to the interest of the author, and the commonwealth of literature. This aspersion upon their fair fame is at length fast passing away, if indeed it has not already disappeared. Their position in society, as the purveyors of its literary aliment, is at length appreciated. In former times, many a poor, unoffending publisher paid the penalty due to the sins and misdemeanors of a seditious or erratic scribe ; having been held responsible for sentiments never avowed, and of which, in some cases they were unconscious, since they were incapable of their comprehension. In the majority of instances the bookselling fraternity are a plain, plodding set of men, whose movements are for the most part regulated by the laws of that universal pecuniary arithmetic—profit and loss. They deal in books very much after the same manner as do the purveyors of meat and bread, estimating their merchandise by the size, if not the weight avoirdupois. The history of "book-craft," which yet remains to be written, would form a book of "Chronicles," if less important, scarcely less interesting than those of Froissart ; it would abound with strange anomalies, and curious portraitures. In early times, the monks—the *custodes* of the learning of their day—combined within themselves both author and publisher ; if indeed the latter term may be allowed in this case. They were styled the *Commercium Librorum*, their office comprehending that of the scribe, as well as the dealer in manuscripts. Between the years 1474 and 1600, it has been estimated about 350 printers flourished in England and Scotland, and that the products of their several presses amounted in the aggregate to 10,000 distinct productions.*

* D'Israeli, in his *Curiosities of Literature*, states, that the four ages of typography have produced no less than 3,641,960 works ! Taking each work at three volumes, and

"The titles of books," writes the author of the *Tin Trumpet*, "are decoys to catch purchasers." There can be no doubt that a happy name to a book is like an agreeable appearance to a man; but if in either case the final do not answer to the first impression, will not our disappointment add to the severity of our judgment? "Let me succeed with my first impression," the bibliopolist will cry, "and I ask no more." The public are welcome to end with condemning, if they will only begin with buying. Most readers, like the tuft-hunters at college, are caught by titles. How inconsistent are our notions of morality! No man of honor would open a letter that was not addressed to him, though he will not scruple to open a book under the same circumstances. Colton's *Lacon* has gone through many editions, and yet it is addressed "To those who think." Had the author substituted for these words, "Those who think they are thinking," it might not have had so extensive a sale, although it would have been directed to a much larger class. He has shown address in his address.

Scott is known to have profited much by Constable's bibliographical knowledge, which was very extensive. The latter christened *Kenilworth*, which Scott named *Cumnor Hall*. John Ballantyne objected to the former title, and told Constable the result would be "something worthy of the kennel;" but the result proved the reverse. Mr. Cadell relates that Constable's vanity boiled over so much at this time, on having his suggestions adopted, that, in his high moods, he used to stalk up and down his room, and exclaim, "By Jove, I am all but the author of the Waverley Novels!"

But for booksellers, intellect would die of famine. London is the great Sanhedrim of the authorcraft of the world. London is the very brain of Britain, the centre of its literature, the seat of its intelligence. There the great emporium of

reckoning each impression to consist of only 300 copies (a very moderate supposition), the actual amount of volumes which have issued from the presses of Europe, down to the year 1816, appears to be 3,277,640,000!

book-craft is time-honored—it is an ancient and worthy order. Paternoster Row is full of the odor and spirit of learning—it has an aroma of paper and print. There is no spot on the globe like it. The London book-trade is divided into the following branches—the general retail bookseller, the dealer in black-letter, or second-hand books, the wholesale merchant, who executes country and foreign orders, and the publishing, or manufacturing bookseller. The second class formerly did chiefly congregate in Little Britain—now they are scattered about Holborn, Covent Garden, and the Strand. These are depositories of those choice relics of the olden time, that often tempt such premiums from the bibliomaniac.

While on this point, we cannot refrain from a recollection or two of the brotherhood. One was named Nunn ; he kept an old-book establishment in Great Queen street, and although a singularly large and corpulent personage, was scarcely less remarkable for his activity in early life, than for his austerity and moroseness in its later stages. By his parsimony and patient application to business, he became ultimately possessed of considerable wealth ; and although this was no secret, yet his two daughters, who were (if one may hazard gallantry for truth) remarkably ugly, lived in single blessedness to the very autumn of life ; but, strange to add, immediately after the demise of their venerable parent at the advanced age of eighty, they each entered into matrimonial alliances. Old Nunn possessed many peculiarities, and although not particularly remarkable for indulging any "sudorous brain-toils" of his own, he yet never appeared so contented as when immersed among the musty tomes of those who have left us in no condition of doubt as to that matter. We well remember, his curious custom of cramming his capacious coat-pockets, which, on one occasion, actually yielded four-and-twenty large octavo volumes before their contents were exhausted. D'Arcy, also a dealer in second-hand and black-letter books, in Holborn, rendered himself conspicuous, among other eccentricities, for the whim of having female attendants in his establishment, some of whom were decidedly pretty ; and what is not less singular, it is said, he regulated their remuneration according to the ratio of their personal attractions. He died wealthy, like his eccentric contemporary before alluded to.

The wholesale trade has always resided in and near Paternoster Row, but the chief house of this class was for many years on London Bridge. Osborne lived under the gateway of Gray's Inn. Tonson, opposite the Strand Bridge. Millar, facing St. Clement's Church, Strand. Dodsley, on the site of the Shakespeare Gallery, in Pall Mall.

Publishers are said to keep the keys of the Temple of Fame. They minister at the altar of learning, and furnish the intellectual wealth of the world. Dr. Johnson considered booksellers the patrons of literature, liberal, generous-minded men. Another quaintly asks, " Can a bookseller live, move, and have his being, in an atmosphere of intellect, and not absorb the very soul and spirit of his books through his pores ?" An experienced bookseller is often better qualified to judge of a book, than all the critics that ever praised or blamed, since the days of Diogenes. Comparatively few, however, of the publishing fraternity pretend to critical censorship ; they usually defer to the critical judgment of some literary friend, in determining the claims of any work for publication.

Booksellers, moreover, evince an affinity of feeling in more instances than one, with the "*genus irritabile*." We remember an incident, among others, to this effect. Goldsmith, who was originally poor and unknown, after the publication of the *Traveller* became of much greater consequence ; and one day, on learning that a scandalous attack had appeared against him in a paper published by Evans, he called at the shop of the offending bibliopolist, and announcing his errand, proceeded to administer summary chastisement. The pugilistic encounter, however, proved ultimately to the overwhelming disadvantage of the worthy *Vicar*, who got well beaten himself and rolled upon the floor, to the amusement of the real offender, the author of the offensive article, who complaisantly stood by as bottle-holder on the occasion.

As somewhat german to our chapter, we shall add a few supplemental words about printing and book-binding.

In the United States the Press is represented by the illustrious Franklin, the Bacon of the New World—a *tria juncta in uno,* printer, author, and one of the great fathers of modern science ; and who has been thus *technically* described by one of the fraternity, " the * of his profession, the type of honesty, the ! of all, and although the ☞ of death has put a . to his existence, every § of his life is without a ‖."

Types have been likened to

> " A thousand lamps at one lone altar lighted,
> Turning the night of error into day."

Type-setting in early times was not remarkable for its exactness and accuracy. In the year 1561, a book was printed, called the *Anatomy of the Mass.* It had only 172 pages in it ; but the author—a pious monk—was obliged to add fifteen pages to correct the blunders. These he attributes to the special instigation of the "devil," to defeat the work ; and hence may have come the use of the title, " Printer's Devil."

A printer's wife in Germany lost her life by feloniously meddling with the types. She went into the office by night, and took out the word "lord," in Genesis iii. 16, where Eve is made subject to her husband, and made the verse read, "he shall be thy fool," instead of "he shall be thy lord." It is said that she was put to death for her wickedness. It is well known that printers of an early edition of the Scriptures were so heavily fined as to be utterly ruined, for leaving out the word "not" from one of the Ten Commandments. There is an edition of the Bible, called the " Vinegar Bible," from the parable of the " Vineyard " being printed " vinegar."

Other equally notorious instances of errata in editions of the Vulgate, which provoked the anathemas of the Vatican, are on record. In one case there were six thousand errors, and after a *revision*, nearly as many more were detected on a subsequent inspection. It is, perhaps, scarcely possible to produce a book faultless, but the art, at the present day at least, approximates very closely to perfection, some of the more costly publications of London being of exquisite typographic beauty. Punctuation is as important to the sense as orthography. This is so self-evident that we need not cite any illustrations in proof.

The oldest printing establishment in Europe, if not in the world, is that of M. Barth of Breslau, still extant, which we believe, has been for 350 years uninterruptedly in existence, in the hands of his ancestors and himself. The first book printed there was a German legend, in 1504.

Bookmaking must be classed among the Fine Arts, for indeed it is an art in itself, whether we consider it in its exterior or interior decoration. The English excel all others in the tasty arrangement that is required in a really exquisite work. They understand it in all its minutiæ. The very title-page is a model of neatness and elegance ; and of such importance is the superintendence of their labors, that artists, "trained men in their vocation," are employed in most of the large establishments to attend to it in all its artistic capabilities. Contrast an English with a French or German work of equal pretensions—how quiet, yet how genial is the one in its superior refinement above all the others. Neither ought it to be forgotten that, while speaking about books, those who administer in such a wonderful degree to their attractiveness, claim some notice at our hands, for it is mainly owing to the engraver that a new dawning in this species of literary luxury has taken place, and those beautifully illustrated works that are ventured upon the broad waters of the Atlantic to gratify the fastidious, giving delight to numbers by their kindly remembrances, and laden affections, are the result of those silent workers. Their names, famous in this phase of decorative art on the other side of the great highway, are familiar as "household words." Yet we, too, have those in our midst who would make their impress in any nation. Danforth, Jones, Seely, Burt, and John Halpin, in historical; Smilie and Beckwirth, in landscape; and Fred. Halpin, in portraiture, are names that could not be lightly passed over anywhere; and among our artists on wood, Bobbett, Childs, Andrews, Lossing, and others, keep up in a corresponding degree the merits of their particular professions.

Bookbinding is an art of great antiquity. It is two thousand years and more since Phillatius, a Greek, divided the rolled volume into sheets, and glued these together in the form which is familiar to us. The rolls had been preserved from dust and injury by being kept in cylindrical cases, and a protection for the book in its new shape was soon found to be more necessary than before. This was supplied by securing the leaves between stiff covers, probably of wood at first, and thus began the modern art of bookbinding.

Soon the board was covered with leather, making in external appearance a still nearer approach to the workmanship of our day; but it was not until the close of the fifteenth century, or the beginning of the sixteenth, that the stout pasteboard, called mill-board, which unites lightness with sufficient strength, was used as the foundation of the book-cover.

When the sheet of paper of which a book is made is folded in two leaves, the book is called a folio; when into four leaves, it is called quarto; when folded into eight leaves, it is called octavo; when into twelve leaves, duodecimo, or 12mo.; when folded into 16 leaves, 16mo.; and when into eighteen leaves, 18mo., &c.

The ancient Romans ornamented the covers of their books very elaborately. Those of wood were carved; and upon some of these, scenes from plays, and events of public interest, were represented. About the commencement of the Christian era, leather of brilliant hues, decorated with gold and silver, had come into use. In the Middle Ages the monks exhausted their ingenuity, and frequently, it would seem, their purses, in adorning the covers of those manuscripts which they spent their lives in writing and illuminating. Single figures and groups, wrought in solid gold, solid silver, and gold gorgeous with enamel, precious stones and pearls, made the outside of the volume correspond to the splendor within. Less expensive works were often bound in oaken boards very richly carved; scenes from the life of Christ, the Virgin, or the Apostles, furnishing the subjects. Many still exist upon which the Nativity, or the Crucifixion, is carved in high relief.

In the latter part of the fifteenth century, and the beginning of the sixteenth, kings, princes, and wealthy nobles, expended much money upon the binding of their libraries, which were, in many cases, very extensive. Carved ivory covers, protected by golden corners, and secured by jewelled clasps, were common, as were also those of velvet, silk brocade, vellum, and morocco, elaborately ornamented after designs made by great artists, and protected with bosses, corners, and clasps of solid gold. The precious stones and metals upon these book-covers, cost us the loss of many a more precious volume, for they frequently formed no inconsiderable part of the plunder of a wealthy mansion in a captured city. Mr. Dibdin tells us of one library of thirty thousand volumes—that of Corvinus, King of Hungary—which was destroyed on this account by the Turkish soldiers, when Buda was taken in 1526.

Quite an era in the history of bookbinding in England was formed by the publication of the Great Bible, by Grafton, in 1539. His first edition was of 200 copies, and within three years there were seven editions. A substantial binding was thus needed for nearly twenty thousand volumes, and from this time there was a noticeable advance in the art in England; chiefly, however, in the mechanical department; for Henry VIII. had many books richly and beautifully bound. In his reign the use of gold tooling was introduced, and the designs for some of the rolls are attributed to Holbein. Queen Elizabeth herself embroidered velvet and silk book-covers, some of which were also tooled in gilt.*

The art has been carried to a high degree of excellence and finish in France. Many have acquired great renown there, in this department of handicraft. They hold themselves far above their brethren of England ; and Duru once said that he should consider himself insulted if he were told that he could bind as well as Hayday. Their prices were enormous—three times as great as those of the best London binders, large as those were. The French books are remarkable for the firmness of their boards, the smoothness of their leather, and the delicacy, the richness of design, and the sharpness of outline of their gold tooling. The designs upon one of Beauzonnet's Capé's, or Lortic's books, seem hardly to be stamped upon the leather, but rather to be inlaid in it. But for pleasure and convenience in use, the work of the French binders is inferior to that of the English. Books bound by the former are very stiff ; that is, they open with great difficulty, and require constant pressure to keep them open.†

The father of the English school of binders was Roger Payne, who lived towards the close of the last century. The great modern English binders are Hayday, Clarke, Bedford, Riviere, and Wright. The Remnants have a very large establishment, and bind richly and substantially. The work of Charles Lewis was highly prized, and merited its reputation.

The fitness of the binding to the character of the volume which it protects, though little regarded by many binders, and

* Illustrated Record of Art.

† It may be well to say here, for the benefitof those not familiar with the bookbinder's vocabulary, that gilt tooling is what is commonly called gilding, the figures in gilt being produced by the impression of a hot tool, sometimes stamped, sometimes rolled, upon gold leaf. Blind tooling is produced by the use of the hot tool without gold leaf. The forwarding of a book is the sewing and putting it into the cover. Finishing is the tooling, gilding, &c.

still less by those for whom they work, is of the first importance. Many a good book is mercilessly sacrificed by an incompetent binder ; persons of fastidious taste will prefer the services of one who is possessed of artistic taste and feeling.

Here, then, we finish with the binder, as he finishes his book, and here also we reluctantly conclude our chapter upon Book-craft—a theme of exhaustless interest to all who have any affinity of taste for books and the intellectual sweets they contain—since our too lavish indulgence in such refined epicurism might challenge our mental digestion too severely. We therefore offer a change by way of dessert.

THE MODERN MOLOCH.

> "God of the world and worldlings,
> Great Mammon! greatest god below the sky."
>
> SPENSER.

> "What is here?
> Gold! gold, yellow, glittering, precious gold,
> Saint-seducing gold?"
>
> SHAKSPEARE.

THE question proposed by little Paul, in *Dombey and Son*, is suggested by the caption of our chapter—"What's money?" The reply of many would doubtless be the same as that returned to the young querist referred to—a mere mercantile one—namely, that it is currency, specie, and bank-notes, or gold, silver, and copper. But this did not suffice for little Paul; he repeated his inquiry—"I mean, what's money after all?" This is the question we propose to discuss in an illustrative way. First as to its *material*. Gold and silver, styled the precious metals—are both pure, ductile, and malleable, and unaffected by most conditions of atmosphere. They are of intrinsic and positive worth, and were therefore adopted as the standards of value, to represent all commercial exchanges.

The *Numismatic Journal* states, in reference to the attempt to establish the true origin of coins, that according to the Parian Chronicle, a record of the third century before Christ, Phiedon, king of Argos, in order to facilitate commerce, stamped silver money in the island of Ægina, in the year before Christ, 895. Now as Homer existed immediately *prior* to this epoch, and makes no mention of coined money, whilst he does mention the system of barter, we may infer that it was unknown in his time; for it is impossible to imagine a writer, by whom no art or science has been overlooked, to have passed over so useful an invention as stamped coin, had it existed. In the time of Lycurgus, which followed that of Homer—certainly not later than a century, though there is some difficulty in ascertaining a more positive data, it is equally certain that gold and silver coin, as money, existed in Greece, as proved by his law prohibiting their use in Sparta, and substituting iron: probably rings, similar to the iron ring money of the early Celtic nations, of which specimens have been discovered in Ireland. This brings the introduction of coins between the epochs of Homer and Lycurgus, in fact to the precise period assigned to the invention of Phiedon; and the coins of Ægina, from the rudeness of their devices, and imperfection of their execution, may fairly be supposed to be of the age in question. This, compared with the assertion of the Parian Chronicle, the silence of Homer, and the law of Lycurgus, seems fairly to authenticate the claim of Phiedon, and to establish the origin of the first *current money as having occurred nearly nine hundred years before the Christian era, in the island of Ægina.*

Numa Pompilius caused money to be made of wood and leather—hence the Latin word, *Pecunia:* afterwards bits of copper, marked according to weight, were stamped with figures or images. Money, as to its name, is derived from *Juno Moneta*, the Roman Temple where it was coined 260, B. C.

The most ancient Jewish coins represented a *pot of manna* on one side, and *Aaron's blossoming rod* on the other; the inscription being in Samaritan.

Jewish *shekels* were 1*s.* 7*d.*; a *talent* was 3,000 shekels, or £342,3*s.* 9*d.* sterling.

The Egyptians did not coin till the accession of the Ptolemies, nor the Jews till the age of the Maccabees; the most ancient known coins are the Macedonian, of the date of about 500 years before Christ.

Athelstan first established a uniform coin in England. The Egbert silver coins were *shillings, thrimsas, pennies, halflings,* and *feorthlings.* Gold coin was introduced by Edward III., in six-shilling pieces, nearly equal in size, but not in weight, to modern sovereigns. *Nobles* followed at 6*s.* 8*d.*, and became the lawyers' fee. Edward IV. coined *angels*, with a figure of Michael and the Dragon.

Money had its equivalent in salt in Abyssinia—a small shell called *cowery*, in Hindostan—dried fish in Iceland—and wampum among the North American Indians.* Nails were

* The first money in use in New York, then New Netherlands, and also in New England, was *Seawant, Wampum,* or *Peague,* for it was known by all those names. *Seawant* was the generic name of this Indian money, of which there were two kinds; *wompam* (commonly called *wampum*), which signifies, *white*, and *suckanhock, sucki* signifying *black.* Wampum, or wampum-peague, or simply peague, was also understood, although improperly, among the Dutch and English, as expressive of generic denomination, and in that light was used by them in their writings and public documents. *Wampum*, or white money, was originally made from the stem or stock of the *metean-hock*, or periwinkle; *suckanhock*, or black money, was manufactured from the inside of the shell of the *quahaug* (Venus Mercenaria), commonly called the hard

formerly in use in Scotland, as we learn from Smith's *Wealth of Nations.*

The three principal mints in the world are those of London, of the United States, and of Paris. Their total coinage during 1853, according to the *London Economist,* was as follows, in pounds sterling: Paris, £14,901,702; London, £12,666,008; United States, £11,101,120. The total amount of this in dollars is $193,644,150.*

To lack money, it has been remarked, is to lack a passport or admission ticket into the pleasant places of God's earth—to much that is glorious and wonderful in nature, and nearly all that is rare, curious, and enchanting in art.

Hood's lines suggest a little moralizing:

"Gold! gold! gold! gold!
Bright and yellow, hard and cold,
Molten, graven, hammered, rolled;
Heavy to get, and light to hold;
Hoarded, bartered, bought and sold;
Stolen, borrowed, squandered, doled;
Spurned by the young, but hugged by the old,
To the very verge of the church-yard mould;
Price of many a crime untold;
Gold! gold! gold! gold!"

What has not man sacrificed upon the altar of Moloch? his time, his health, his friendships, his reputation, his conscience,

clam, a round thick shellfish that buries itself a little way in the sand in salt water. The Indians broke off about half an inch of the purple color of the inside, and converted it into beads. These, before the introduction of awls and thread, were bored with sharp stones, and strung upon the sinews of animals, and when interwoven to the breadth of the hand, more or less, were called a belt of seawant, or wampum.—*Denton's New York.*

* Mr. Jacob has estimated the existing gold of the world, previously to 1848 (four-fifths of it existing in manufactured articles) at £650,000,000. Add our new acquisition of £55,000,000, and we have a present world-wealth of gold of £705,000,000. Taking the cubic yard of gold at £2,000,000, which it is in round numbers, all the goldof the world at this estimate might, if melted into ingots, be contained in a cellar twenty-four feet square, and sixteen feet high. All our boasted wealth already obtained from California and Australia would go into an iron safe, nine feet square, and nine feet high. So small is the cube of yellow metal that has set populations on the march, and roused the world to wonder!

and even life itself, and all its great issues. Rightly used, money is the procurer of the domestic comforts and luxuries, as well as the necessaries of life, but when inordinately cherished and coveted, it becomes the bane of happiness and peace. In the affair of marriage, how much of disaster has it superinduced—how much of infelicity entailed upon the domestic relations. Instead of surrendering to Cupid, how many have been led captive by cupidity, vainly dreaming of *hearts'-ease* when they have shown their preference to *marry gold.* But money cannot purchase love, or virtue, or happiness. A philosopher has said, "though a man without money is poor, a man with nothing but money is still poorer." Fuller wisely insists that it is much better to have your gold in the hand than in the heart. A man's character is often indicated by his mode of using money.

A vain man's motto is, 'win gold and wear it'—a generous man's, 'win gold and share it'—a miser's, 'win gold and spare it'—a profligate's, 'win gold and spend it'—a broker's, 'win gold and lend it'—a fool's, 'win gold and end it'—a gambler's, 'win gold and lose it'—a wise man's, 'win gold and use it.'

Of all the evil propensities to which human nature is subject, there is no one so general, so insinuating, so corruptive, and so obstinate, as the love of money. It begins to operate early, and it continues to the end of life. One of the first lessons which children learn, and one which old men never forget, is the value of money. The covetous seek and guard it for its own sake, and the prodigal himself must first be avaricious, before he can be profuse. This, of all our passions, is best able to fortify itself by reason, and is the last to yield to the force of reason. Philosophy combats, satire exposes, religion condemns it in vain: it yields neither to argument, nor ridicule, nor conscience.*

* Hunter's Biography.

—— "I riches read,
And deeme them roote of all disquietnesse ·
First got with guile, and then preserved with dread;
And after spent with pride and lavishnesse,
Leaving behind them grief and heavinesse.
Infinite mischiefes of them doe arize;
Strife and debate, bloodshed and bitternesse,
Outrageous wrong, and hellish covetize,
That noble hart in great dishonour doth despize." *

This love of money, which Holy Scripture tells us is "the root of all evil," Jeremy Taylor describes as a vertiginous pool, sucking all into its vortex, to destroy it. That this love of gold is the master passion of the age, few will question. It is "the age of gold;" the auriferous sands of the Pacific for the western hemisphere, and those of Australia for the eastern, are incessantly pouring out their treasures to feed the insatiate cravings of avarice. The liturgy "on Change" seems to read—Man's chief end is to make money, and to enjoy it while he can. The votaries of Mammon, however, do not enjoy their possessions—they have no leisure, in their ceaseless, toilsome efforts, to augment their fortunes. A contemporary observes, with great justice:

"Many a man there is, clothed in respectability, and proud of his honor, whose central idea of life is interest and ease—the conception that other men are merely tools to be used as will best serve him; that God has endowed him with sinew and brain merely to scramble and to get; and so, in the midst of this grand universe, which is a perpetual circulation of benefit, he lives like a sponge on a rock, to absorb, and bloat, and die. Thousands in the great city are living so, who never look out of the narrow circle of self-interest; whose decalogue is their arithmetic; whose Bible is their ledger; who have so contracted, and hardened, and stamped their natures, that in

* Spenser.

any spiritual estimate they would only pass as so many bags of dollars."

It is indispensable, in some cases, that men should have money, for without it they would be worth nothing. This, however, offers no apology for the universal scramble after money. Is this money-mania the highest development of our vaunted civilization ?—the *summum bonum* of human existence ? the *Ultima Thule* of human effort ?

> " The plague of gold strikes far and near.
> And deep and strong it enters ;
> The purple cymar which we wear,
> Makes madder than the centaurs ;
> Our thoughts grow blank, our words grow strange,
> We cheer the pale gold-diggers,
> Each soul is worth so much on 'Change,
> And marked, like sheep, with figures."

" Men work for it, fight for it, beg for it, steal for it, starve for it, lie for it, live for it, and die for it. And all the while, from the cradle to the grave, Nature and God are ever thundering in our ears the solemn question—' What shall it profit a man to gain the whole world and lose his own soul ?' This madness for money is the strongest and the lowest of the passions ; it is the insatiate Moloch of the human heart, before whose remorseless altar all the finer attributes of humanity are sacrificed. It makes merchandise of all that is sacred in human affections ; and even traffics in the awful solemnities of the eternal world."

> " Gone, the spirit-quickening leaven,
> Faith, and love, and hope in heaven—
> All that warmed the earth of old.
> Dead and cold,
> Its pulses flutter ;
> Weak and old,
> Its parched lips mutter,

Nothing nobler, nothing higher
Than the unappeased desire,
The quenchless thirst for gold!"

Money is a very good servant, but a bad master. It may be accused of injustice towards mankind, inasmuch as there are only a few who make false money, whereas money makes many false men.

Mammon is the largest slaveholder in the world—it is a composition for taking stains out of character—it is an altar on which self sacrifices to self.

"How many a man, from love of pelf,
To stuff his coffers, starves himself;
Labors, accumulates, and spares,
To lay up ruin for his heirs;
Grudges the poor their scanty dole,
Saves every thing except his soul;
And always anxious, always vexed,
Loses both this world and the next!"

:e defines the sordid passion as—

"Worse poison to men's souls,
Doing more murders in this loathsome wor...
Than any mortal drug."

In the words of Johnson, it is the

"Wide wasting pest! that rages unconfined,
And crowds with crimes the records of mankind:
For gold, his sword the hireling ruffian draws,
For gold, the hireling judge distorts the laws;
Wealth heaped on wealth, nor truth nor safety buys,
The dangers gather as the treasures rise."

"A miser," observes Hazlitt, "is the true alchemist, the magician in his cell, who overlooks a mighty experiment, who sees dazzling visions, and who wields the will of others at his nod, but to whom all other hopes and pleasures are dead, and who is cut off from all connection with his kind. He lives in a splendid hallucination, a waking trance, and so far it is well; but if he thinks he has any other need or use for all this endless store (any more than to swell the ocean) he deceives himself, and is no conjuror after all. He goes on, however, mechanically adding to his stock, and fancying that great riches is great gain—that every particle that swells the heap is something in reserve against the evil day, and a defence against that poverty which he dreads more the further he is removed from it, as the more giddy the height to which we have attained, the more frightful does the gulf yawn below — so easily does habit get the mastery of reason, and so nearly is passion allied to madness." This is the turn the love of money takes in cautious, dry, recluse, and speculative minds. If it were the pure and abstract love of money, it could take no other turn but this.

> "The wretch concentered all in self,
> Living, shall forfeit fair renown,
> And, doubly dying, shall go down
> To the vile dust from whence he sprung,
> Unwept, unhonored and unsung."

"A miser grows rich by seeming poor," says Shenstone, "an extravagant man grows poor by seeming rich."

Wealth usually ministers to the baser passions of our nature —it engenders selfishness, feeds arrogance, and inspires self-security, and deadens and stultifies the nobler feelings and holier aspirations of the heart. Wealth is a source of endless discontent; it creates more wants than it supplies, and keeps its incumbent constantly craving, crafty, and covetous. Lord Bacon says, "I cannot call riches by a better name than the 'baggage' of virtue: the Roman word is better—'impediment.' For as baggage is to an army, so are riches to virtue. It cannot be spared or left behind, and yet it hindereth the march." "Misery assails riches, as lightning does the highest towers: or as a tree that is heavy laden with fruit, breaks its own boughs, so do riches destroy the virtue of their possessor."

Old Burton quaintly but forcibly observes—"Worldly wealth is the devil's bait; and those whose minds feed upon riches, recede in general, from real happiness, in proportion as their stores increase; as the moon, when she is fullest of light, is furthest from the sun."

A miser is, moreover, the most oblivious, as well as the most vindictive of mortals; he is said to be always for-getting, and never for-giving. He lives unloved, and dies unlamented. His self-denial is only surpassed by his denial of the poor and destitute. The miser starves himself in the midst of plenty, that he may feast his imagination on his useless hoards. Avarice, unlike most other passions, becomes more exacting as its victim increases in age. Fielding speaks of a miser, who consoled himself on his death-bed "by making a crafty and advantageous bargain concerning his funeral, with an undertaker who had married his only child." There have been examples of misers who have died in the dark to save the cost of a candle. How debasing the passion which can survive every other feeling, sear the conscience, and deaden the moral sense! "Of all creatures upon earth none is so despicable as the miser. He meets with no sympathy. Even the nurse who is hired to attend him in his latest hours, loathes the ghastly occupation, and longs for the moment of her release, for although the death-damp is already gathering on his brow, the thoughts of the departing sinner are still upon his gold; and, at the mere jingle of a key, he starts from his torpor in a paroxysm of terror, lest a surreptitious attempt is being made upon the sanctity of his strong box. There are no prayers of the orphan or widow for him—not a solitary voice has ever breathed his name to heaven as a benefactor. One poor penny given away in the spirit of true charity would now be worth more to him than all the world contains ; but notwithstanding that he was a church-going man, and from his infancy familiar with those texts in which the worship of Mammon is denounced, and the punishment of Dives told, he has never yet been able to divorce himself from his solitary love of lucre, or to part with one atom of his pelf. And so, from a miserable life—deserted, despised, he passes into a dread eternity ; and those whom he has neglected or misused, make merry with the hoards of the miser !"*

> "The aged man that coffers up his gold,
> Is plagued with cramps, and gouts, and painful fits,
> And scarce has eyes his treasure to behold ;
> But like still pining Tantalus he sits,
> And useless barns the harvest of his wits ;
> Having no other pleasure of his gain
> But torment that it cannot cure his pain."†

The ingenious author of the *Tin Trumpet* remarks—that a miser is one who, though he loves himself better than all the world, uses himself worse : for he lives like a pauper in order that he may enrich his heirs, whom he naturally hates, because he knows they hate him.

Perhaps the severest reproach ever made to a miser, was uttered by Voltaire. At a subscription of the French Academy for some charitable object, each contributor putting in a *louis d'or*, the collector, by mistake, made a second application to a member noted for his penuriousness—"I have already paid," exclaimed the latter with some asperity. "I beg your pardon," said the applicant, "I have no doubt but you paid ; I believe it though I did not see it." "And I saw it, and do not believe it," whispered Voltaire.

Misers have been compared to many strange things ; some

* Blackwood. † Shakspeare.

liken them to oysters with a pearl in the shell ; others style them amateur paupers.

Again, misers have been supposed to resemble the hog ; a resemblance between them, it has been suggested, has long been recognized by popular tradition ; and if we examine the subject closely, we shall find they have more points of likeness than we should at first suppose. The hog is omnivorous and voracious—so the miser grows rich by gathering and converting into money those odds and ends which others throw away. The hog is the scavenger of nature ; the miser is the scavenger of society. Both, also, benefit mankind only after their death—the fat of the hog and the wealth of the miser, which they have spent their lives in accumulating, being of no use during their existence.

The animating principle of both miser and hog is, of course, selfishness. Both are delvers of the grovelling sort, both are ill-tempered and sometimes cruel. It is noticed, by a Swedish writer, that "the hog does not enjoy the society of man, as the dog does. He likes going about by himself, grunting in an undertone, which he prefers to raising his voice to its highest pitch." This is eminently true of the miser. He is thoroughly unsocial in his disposition, burrows by himself, and mutters to himself, not daring to raise his voice in manly tones, lest it should draw attention to his ill-gotten gains.

The wretched victim of avarice is ever striving to amass wealth by every expedient that will not subject him to the criminal laws, and to place it in security, is the great and ultimate object of his pursuit. Mammon is the great idol he worships, and whatever the specious and plausible pretexts he may assume, he pays homage at no other shrine. In his selfish isolation, he surrenders himself up to the domination of his debasing passion—a voluntary exile from the endearing offices of friendship, and the gentle charities of domestic and social life. The benign and blessed influence of heaven-born Peace sheds not her halcyon rays upon his dark and desolate heart.

A victim to the sordid lust of gold, his mercenary spirit is susceptible of no generous impulse or sentiment, worthy of an immortal being—every thought and desire being absorbed in his insatiate cravings after riches. In the words of Dr. Dick, who presents the miser's portrait in all his hideous deformity, "all the avenues to true enjoyment are interrupted, and closely shut up by the cold hand of avarice. He denies himself those sensitive comforts with which Providence has so richly replenished the earth, and has placed within his reach; and even almost starves himself in the midst of plenty. As he approaches the close of his career, and descends to the grave, whither his coveted wealth cannot follow him, his passion for gold acquires an increased intensity, and he clings to his useless but ardently cherished treasures with a fearfully tenacious grasp." The prodigal "spends his substance in riotous living," in the delusive attempt to secure present enjoyment; and the distribution of his money is at least a benefit to society; but the covetous man is alike injurious to himself and all around him. This passion is not only detestable in its nature, and destructive of every virtue, it is also a disease like that of intemperance, that seldom, if ever, admits of cure. "Other passions have their holidays," says an old writer, "but avarice never suffers its votaries to rest."

> O, cursed love of gold! when for thy sake
> The fool throws up his interest in both worlds—

"Joshua," said Ambrose, "could stop the course of the sun, but all his power could not stop the course of avarice. The sun stood still, but avarice went on; Joshua obtained a victory when the sun stood still; but when avarice was at work Joshua was defeated." We have other recorded facts in sacred story illustrative of the crime of cupidity. Achan's covetous humor made him steal that wedge of gold which served "to cleave his soul from God:" it made Judas betray Christ; and Absalom to attempt to pluck the crown from his father's head.

To a reflecting mind it may well cause surprise that the world at large set such paramount value upon the acquisition of wealth To what voluntary inflictions, sufferings and life-toils, will not men submit for its attainment? Vast wealth brings with it increase of cares, and with multiplied resources we find usually ever-growing wants to be supplied. What material difference is it to us, provided we inhale the perfume of the fragrant flowers, whether they belong to our neighbor or ourself: or whether the fair estate be the property of and called after the name of another, so we are refreshed with the vision? We share a community of interest in this respect, in all the fair and beautiful things of earth.

"For nature's care, to all her children just,
With richer treasures and an ampler state
Endows at large whatever happy man will deign to use them.
His the city's pomp, the rural honors his—
Whate'er adorns the princely dome, the column, and the arch,
The breathing marble, and the sculptured gold—
Beyond the proud possessor's narrow claim,
His tuneful breast enjoys."

The beautiful soliloquy of Jeremy Taylor will occur to the reader; he exclaims—

"I am fallen into the hands of publicans and sequestrators and they have taken all from me. What now? Let me look about me. They have left the sun and moon, fire and water, a loving wife and many friends to pity me, and some to relieve me; and I can discourse; and, unless I list, they have not taken away my merry countenance and my cheerful spirits, and a good conscience; they have still left me the providence of God, and all the promises of the gospel, and my religion, and my hope of heaven, and my charity for them too. And still I sleep, and I digest, and eat, and drink; I read and meditate; I can walk in my neighbor's pleasant fields, and see the varieties of natural beauty, and delight in all that in which God delights—that is, in virtue and wisdom, in the whole creation, and in God himself."

> "O, blissful poverty!
> Nature, too partial to thy lot assigns
> Health, freedom, innocence, and downy peace."*

Sand has written a beautiful apostrophe to Poverty—"the good goddess Poverty:" we cite a sentence or two:

"They have chained the good goddess—they have beaten her and persecuted her; but they cannot debase her. She has taken refuge in the souls of poets, of peasants, of artists, of martyrs, and of saints. Many children has she had, and many a divine secret has she taught them. She does all the greatest and most beautiful things that are done in the world; it is she who cultivates the fields, and prunes the trees—who drives the herds to pasture, singing the while all sweet songs—who sees the day break, and catches the sun's first smile. It is she who inspires the poet, and makes eloquent the guitar, the violin and the flute; who instructs the dextrous artisan, and teaches him to hew stone, to carve marble, to fashion gold and silver, copper and iron. It is she who supplies oil for the lamp, who reaps the harvest fields, kneads bread for us, weaves our garments, in summer and winter, and who maintains and feeds the world. It is she who nurses us in infancy, succors us in sorrow and sickness, and attends us to the silent sleeping-place of death. Thou art all gentleness, all patience, all strength and all compassion. It is thou who dost reunite all thy children in a holy love, givest them charity, faith, hope, O, goddess of Poverty!"

Every man is rich or poor, according to the proportion between his desires and enjoyments. Of riches, as of everything else, the hope is more than the enjoyment; while we consider them as the means to be used at some future time for

* Fenton.

the attainment of felicity, ardor after them secures us from weariness of ourselves ; but no sooner do we sit down to enjoy our acquisitions, than we find them insufficient to fill up the vacuities of life. We are poor only when we want necessaries ; it is custom gives the name of poverty to the want of superfluities.

Good old Izaak Walton has something to say on this subject, too good to be omitted. Here it is :—

"I have a rich neighbor that is always so busy that he has no leisure to laugh ; the whole business of his life is to get money, more money that he may still get more. He is still drudging, saying what Solomon says: 'The diligent hand maketh rich.' And it is true, indeed ; but he considers not that it is not in the power of riches to make a man happy; for it was wisely said by a man of great observation, 'that there be as many miseries beyond riches as on this side of them.' And yet heaven deliver us from pinching poverty, and grant that, having a competency, we may be content and thankful. Let us not repine, or so much as think the gifts of God unequally dealt, if we see another abound in riches, when, as God knows, the cares that are the keys that keep those riches, hang often so heavily at the rich man's girdle, that they clog him with weary days and restless nights, even where others sleep quietly. We see but the outside of the rich man's happiness ; few consider him to be like the silk-worm, that, when she seems to play, is at the same time spinning her own bowels, and consuming herself. And this many rich men do, loading themselves with corroding cares to keep what they have already got. Let us, therefore, be thankful for health and competence, and, above all, for a quiet conscience."

La Bruyère wisely remarks, "Let us not envy some men their accumulated riches ; their burden would be too heavy for us ; we could not sacrifice, as they do, health, honor, quiet, and conscience, to obtain them. It is to pay so dear for them that the bargain is a loss."

The classic page furnishes examples of a noble contempt of wealth, and a virtuous preference of poverty over venality and lust of riches. These, however, are rather exceptions to the rule which sustains the converse of the proposition ; and before turning to the bright side, let us briefly refer to one or two instances of the baneful effects of avarice on the human heart.

The inordinate desire of wealth has been the occasion of more mischief and misery in the world than anything else. Some of the direst evils with which the world has ever been afflicted, have emanated from this source. No sooner had Columbus solved the problem of the Western Continent, than the accursed lust of gold began to fire the sordid hearts of his successors. Every species of perfidy, cruelty, and inhumanity, towards the aborigines was practised against them, in order to extort from them their treasures. These mercenary wretches, forcing the natives of Hispaniola so mercilessly to delve and toil for the much coveted ore, that they actually reduced their numbers, within less than half a century, from two millions to about one hundred and fifty. The conquest of Mexico, by Cortez and his followers, impelled by the same insatiable passion, was accompanied with horrors, atrocities, and slaughters, more dreadful and revolting than almost any recorded in the annals of our race. To prepare the way for enjoying the plunder they had in view, the unoffending Indians were butchered by thousands ; while carnage and every species of heartless cruelty marked their progress of spoliation. In the siege of Mexico, no less than a hundred thousand of the natives were sacrificed ; and, as if to add to the effrontery and depravity of the act, it was perpetrated under the standard of the *cross*, and with the invocation of the God of armies to aid the conquests. The like atrocities characterized the expedition of Pizarro for the conquest of Peru. Under perfidious professions of amity, they captured the Inca, butchering some four thousand of his unresisting attendants. The unfortunate emperor, vainly hoping to regain his freedom, offered them as many vessels of gold as would fill an apartment twenty-four feet long, sixteen wide, and eight high; and after having dispatched messengers to collect the promised treasures, he had fulfilled his engagement, when they vilely broke truce, and burnt their wretched victim. What a fearful catalogue of crime might be cited from the history of religion—Pagan, Papal, and even Christian. The baneful effects of avarice, whether displayed in individual conduct, or among communities of men, are the same. We must content ourselves with referring briefly to a few instances of the former, as illustrative of the force of this debasing evil.

In the year 1790, died at Paris, literally of want, the well-known banker—Ostervald. This miserable victim of this disease, a few days prior to his death, resisted the importunities of his attendant to purchase some meat for the purpose of making a little soup for him. "True, I should like the soup," he said, "but I have no appetite for the meat; what is to become of that? it will be a sad waste." This poor wretch died possessed of £125,000 sterling. Another desperate case was that of Elwes, whose diet and dress were alike of the most revolting kind, and whose property was estimated at £800,000 sterling. Among other characteristic incidents related of him, it is said that on the approach of that dread summons which was to divorce him from his cherished gold, he exclaimed, "I will keep my money—nobody shall rob me of my property." We meet with the name of Daniel Dancer, whose miserly propensities were indulged to such a degree, that on one occasion, when, at the urgent solicitation of a friend, he ventured to give a shilling to a Jew for an old hat—"better as new"—to the astonishment of his friend, the next day he actually retailed it for eighteen pence. He was in the habit of carrying a snuff-box about with him, not for the purpose of regaling his olfactory organ, but for what does the reader suppose? to collect pinches of the aromatic dust from his snuff-taking friends; and when the box was filled, he would barter its contents for a farthing rushlight! He performed his ablutions at a neighboring pool, drying himself in the sun, to save the extravagant indulgence of a towel. Other eccentricities are chronicled of this remarkable "case"—such as lying in bed during the cold weather to save the cost of fuel, and eating garbage to save the charges for food: yet this poor mendicant had property to the extent of upwards of £3,000 per annum. There was a Russian merchant—never mind his name, it is too barbarously burdened with consonants to spell or pronounce—who was so prodigiously wealthy, that on one occasion he loaned the empress Catherine the Second a million of rubles, although he lived in the most deplorable state of indigence, privation, and wretchedness. He buried his money in casks in his cellar, and was so great a miser that he seemed almost to thrive upon his very passion. He had his troubles, however, for reposing his trust for the security of his possessions upon the fierceness and fidelity of his favorite dog, his bulwark of safety failed him. The dog very perversely died, and his master was driven to the disagreeable alternative of officiating in the place of the deceased functionary, by imitating the canine service—going his rounds every evening and barking as well as any human dog could be expected to do.

M. Vandille, of Paris, was one of the most remarkable instances on record of immense wealth being combined with extreme penuriousness; he lodged as high up as the roof would admit, as certain poor poets are said to do, and lived on stale bread and diluted milk; notwithstanding he possessed great property in the public funds. Chancellor Hardwicke, when worth £800,000, set the same miserly value on a shilling as when he possessed but £100; and the great Duke of Marlborough, when near the close of life, was in the habit of exhibiting singular meanness to save a sixpence, although his property was over a million and a half sterling. The cases we have adduced are extreme instances of the influence of avarice;

but it should not be forgotten that the principle of covetousness is the same in its tendency wherever it exists, and it is only in consequence of the counteracting force of circumstances that all its victims fail to present the same degree of degradation and wretched moral deformity.

More recently, we read of an instance which occurred at Newby, in Westmoreland. This individual, when a young man, became possessed of a little property ; he worked as a laborer, and added to his store ; through a long series of years he scraped and saved, denying himself every comfort and almost real necessaries. During his latter years he lived in a cottage alone, in the most wretched style. Several estates had been mortgaged to him ; and a box which he kept at the foot of his bed, and upon which his eyes were fixed when dying, contained money and securities of the value of £20,000.

The well-known Nat Bentley (alias Dirty Dick) of London, belongs to this category. This eccentric specimen of humanity was the victim not only to a craving for gold, but also for *old iron.* We have a dim recollection of the dingy old shop in Leadenhall street, piled up with heaps of all kinds of old iron and lumber. The last twenty years of his miserable existence were spent in dirt and destitution. Another deplorable case might be cited—that of Thomas Pitt, of Warwickshire. All his solicitude was about his money ; his pulse rose and fell with the public funds. He lived over thirty years ensconced in a gloomy garret, never enlivened with light of lamp or fire, or the cheering smile of friendship. It is reported, that some weeks prior to the sickness which terminated his despicable career, he went to several undertakers in quest of a cheap coffin. As he lived without the regards, so he died without the regrets, of his neighbors—a miserable illustration of the corrupting influence of cupidity. He left behind him £2,475—in the public funds. Another instance is that of the notorious Thomas Cook. His ruling passion showed itself in all its intensity at the close of his life, for on his physician intimating the possibility of his not existing more than five or six days, with a fierce look of indignation, he protested against the useless expense of sending him medicine, and charged the doctor never to show his face to him again. This wretched man died unlamented in his 86th year—a long lease shamefully abused and dishonored. His property was estimated at about £130,000! How horribly debased a man becomes when he surrenders himself up to the fiendish passion for gain. His influence is moral poison. Audley was another notorious instance. He lived in the days of the Stuarts, and amassed much wealth during the reign of the first Charles, and the Protectorate. He made most of his money by usury and legal chicanery. On one occasion, having obtained for fifty pounds the debt of an insolvent for £200—he induces the party under obligation to sign a contract that he should pay, within twenty years from that time, one penny, progressively doubled on the first day of twenty consecutive months, and in case of failure, to forfeit £500. Not suspecting the cunningly devised cheat, the poor debtor recommences business, succeeds, and at the appointed time is called upon by the miser for the instalments. After making several payments, he began to figure up the amount for which he had made himself liable, in liquidation of his debt of £200. To what sum, do you suppose would his new liabilities amount? To no less than £2,180! and to what the aggregate sum of all these twenty monthly payments? Why, the enormous total of four thousand three hundred and sixty-six pounds, eleven shillings, and three pence!

Misers like to feast their eyes with their treasure, as well as to handle it. We cite an instance from a recent writer,* to this effect. It is an anecdote related of Sir William Smyth, of Bedfordshire. He was immensely rich, but most parsimonious and miserly in his habits. At seventy years of age, he was entirely deprived of his sight, unable to gloat over his hoarded

* Merryweather.

heaps of gold ; this was a terrible affliction. He was persuaded by Taylor, the celebrated oculist, to be couched ; who was, by agreement, to have sixty guineas if he restored his patient to any degree of sight. Taylor succeeded in his operation, and Sir William was enabled to read and write, without the aid of spectacles, during the rest of his life. But no sooner was his sight restored, than the baronet began to regret that his agreement had been for so large a sum ; he felt no joy as others would have felt, but grieved and sighed over the loss of his sixty guineas ? His thoughts were now how to cheat the oculist ; he pretended that he had only a glimmering and could see nothing distinctly ; for which reason, the bandage on his eyes was continued a month longer than the usual time. Taylor was deceived by these misrepresentations, and agreed to compound the bargain, and accepted twenty guineas, instead of sixty. At the time Taylor attended him, he had a large estate, an immense sum of money in the stocks, and six thousand pounds in the house.

Our last citation exhibits an involuntary case of immolation to Moloch.

A miser, of the name of Foscue, who had amassed enormous wealth by the most sordid parsimony and discreditable extortion, was requested by the government to advance a sum of money, as a loan. The miser, to whom a fair interest was not inducement sufficiently strong to enable him to part with his treasured gold, declared his incapacity to meet this demand ; he pleaded severe losses, and the utmost poverty. Fearing, however, that some of his neighbors, among whom he was very unpopular, would report his immense wealth to the government, he applied his ingenuity to discover some effectual way of hiding his gold, should they attempt to institute a search to ascertain the truth or falsehood of his plea. With great care and secrecy, he dug a deep cave in his cellar ; to this receptacle for his treasure he descended by a ladder, and to the trapdoor he attached a spring-lock, so that, on shutting, it would fasten of itself. By-

and-by the miser disappeared : inquiries were made ; the house was searched ; woods were explored, and the ponds were dragged ; but no Foscue could they find ; and gossips began to conclude that the miser had fled, with his gold, to some part where, by living incognito, he would be free from the hands of the government. Some time passed on ; the house in which he had lived was sold, and workmen were busily employed in its repair. In the progress of their work they met with the door of the secret cave, with the key in the lock outside. They threw back the door, and descended with a light. The first object upon which the lamp reflected was the ghastly body of Foscue the miser, and scattered around him were heavy bags of gold, and ponderous chests of untold treasure ; a candlestick lay beside him on the floor. This worshipper of Mammon had gone into his cave, to pay his devoirs to his golden god, and became a sacrifice to his devotion !

Occasionally, these wretched monopolizers of money are really more indulgent to the world than to themselves. Guyot of Marseilles, was a despised tatterdemalion all his life, yet many benefited by his parsimony. His executors, on opening his will, found these remarkable words :—" Having observed, from my infancy, that the poor of Marseilles are ill-supplied with water, which can only be procured at a great price, I have cheerfully labored the whole of my life to procure for them this great blessing, and I direct that the whole of my property shall be expended in building an aqueduct for their use !"

We might here glance at the effects of an opposite disposition, as illustrated in a few examples of distinguished benevolence. Alfred the Great, among other noble traits of character, exhibited, on a certain occasion, an instance of exemplary sympathy for the suffering, under circumstances which tested unequivocally the goodness of his heart. Shortly after the retreat from his enemies, a beggar came to his little castle, soliciting alms. The queen informed him that they had but one small loaf remaining, which was insufficient for themselves and their friends, who were gone in quest of food, though with little hope of success. The king replied, "Give the poor Christian one half of the loaf. He that could feed five thousand with five loaves and two fishes, can certainly make that half loaf suffice for more than our necessity." His fortitude and faith were rewarded, for the messengers and adherents of the monarch soon after returned with a liberal supply of provisions. The late king of Prussia affords another instance of benevolence. On a certain occasion he rang the bell of his cabinet, but, as nobody answered, he opened the door of the ante-chamber, and found his page fast asleep upon a chair. He went up to awake him; but, on coming nearer, he observed a paper in his pocket upon which something was written. This excited his curiosity. He pulled it out, and found that it was a letter from the page's mother, the contents of which were nearly as follows: "She returned her son many thanks for the money he had saved out of his salary, and sent to her, and which had proved a very timely assistance. God would certainly reward him for it, and, if he continued to serve God and his king faithfully and conscientiously, he would not fail of success and prosperity in this world." Upon reading this the king stepped softly into his closet, fetched a rouleau of ducats, and put it, with the letter, into the page's pocket. He then rang the bell again, till the page awoke, and came into his closet. "You have been asleep, I suppose?" said the king. The page could not deny it, stammered out an excuse (in his embarrassment), put his hand into his pocket, and felt the rouleau of ducats. He immediately pulled it out, turned pale, and looked at the king with tears in his eyes. "What is the matter with you?" said the king. "Oh," replied the page, "somebody has contrived my ruin: I know nothing of this money!" "What God bestows," resumed the king, "he bestows in sleep. Send the money to your mother—give my respects to her, and inform her that I will take care both of her and you."

Take a passage from the Life of Washington: "Reuben Rouzy, of Virginia, owed the General about one thousand pounds. While President of the United States, one of his agents brought an action for the money; judgment was obtained, and execution issued against the body of the defendant, who was taken to jail. He had a considerable landed estate, but this kind of property cannot be sold in Virginia for debts, unless at the discretion of the owner. He had a large family, and for the sake of his children, preferred lying in jail to selling his land. A friend hinted to him that probably General Washington did not know anything of the proceeding, and that it might be well to send him a petition, with a statement of the circumstances. He did so, and the very next post from Philadelphia after the arrival of his petition in that city, brought him an order for his immediate release, together with a full discharge, and a severe reprimand to the agent, for having acted in such a manner. Poor Rouzy was, in consequence, restored to his family, who never laid down their heads at night without presenting prayers to Heaven for their 'beloved Washington.' Providence smiled upon the labors of the grateful family, and in a few years Rouzy enjoyed the exquisite pleasure of being able to lay the one thousand pounds, with the interest, at the feet of this truly great man. Washington reminded him that the debt was discharged; Rouzy replied, the debt of his family to the father of their country, and the preserver of their parent could never be discharged: and the general to avoid the pleasing importunity of the grateful Virginian, who would not be denied, accepted the money, only, however, to divide it among Rouzy's children, which he immediately did."

There is an interesting fact related of the hero of Poland, indicative of his customary practice of almsgiving. Wishing to convey a present to a clerical friend, he gave the commission to a young man of the name of Teltner, desiring him to take the horse which he himself usually rode. On his return, the messenger informed Kosciusko that he would never again ride his horse unless he gave him his purse at the same time; and on the latter inquiring what he meant, he replied: "As soon as a poor man on the road takes off his hat and asks charity, the animal immediately stands still, and will not stir till something is bestowed upon the petitioner; and as I had no money about me, I had to feign giving in order to satisfy the horse, and induce him to proceed." This noble creature deserved a pension and exemption from active service for the term of his natural life, on account of his superior education and refined moral sensibility.

Among the bright galaxy of noble names, that of John Howard will ever take prominent rank in the list of benefactors. After inspecting the receptacles of crime and poverty throughout Great Britain and Ireland, he left his native country, relinquishing his own ease, to visit the wretched abodes of those who were in want, and were bound in fetters of iron in other parts of the world. He travelled three times through France, four through Germany, five through Holland, twice through Italy, once through Spain and Portugal, Russia, Sweden, Denmark, and part of Turkey—occupying a period of about twelve years. Without the few bright spots in the world's arid waste of selfishness, that occasionally irradiate the gloomy lot of the oppressed and poor, what a dreary life of deprivation and sorrow would be their portion. Man is necessarily a selfish being to a certain extent, but the social principle is no less an attribute of his nature; and the divine injunction requiring him to love his neighbor as himself, was doubtless imposed for the preservation of the weak and dependent, as well as being the palladium of all the virtues of our social economy. As a class, the poor are, indeed, often prodigal of their gifts, while the affluent are no less penurious; the former may almost be said to rob themselves, while the latter defraud society of the common inheritance of mankind. To choose between the two conditions, indeed, were not difficult; the "golden mean"—neither poverty nor riches—should be the aim of all ; yet, in the words of the prince of poets,

> Poor and content, is rich, and rich enough :
> But riches endless is as poor as winter
> To him that even fears he shall be poor.

The author of "Notes on Life" judiciously sums up the question in the following paragraph.

"The philosophy which affects to teach us a contempt of money, does not run very deep ; for, indeed, it ought to be still more clear to the philosopher than it is to ordinary men, that there are few things in the world of greater importance. And so manifold are the bearings of money upon the lives and characters of mankind, that an insight which should search out the life of a man in his pecuniary relations would penetrate into almost every cranny of his nature. He who knows, like St. Paul, both how to spare and how to abound, has a great knowledge ; for if we take account of all the virtues with which money is mixed up—honesty, justice, generosity, charity, frugality, forethought, self-sacrifice—and of their correlative vices, it is a knowledge which goes near to cover the length and breadth of humanity ; and a right measure and manner in getting, saving, spending, giving, taking, lending, borrowing, and bequeathing, would almost argue a perfect man."

We must not forget that, while some few abuse wealth, there are vastly more who know its appropriate use and worth. With such, money is the procurer of our common blessings. Money is then the universal talisman, the mainspring of our social system, the lever that moves the world. Some moderns, like Socrates (who wrote in praise of poverty on a table of solid gold), cynically speak against wealth. It is, however, the great motive agent in all departments of the social economy ; helping on the civilization of the world, and ministering not merely to the elegances, but also the essentials of life. Money represents labor. An eloquent writer* asks "who can adequately describe the triumphs of labor, urged on by the potent spell of money? It has extorted the secrets of the universe, and trained its powers into myriads of forms of use and beauty. From the bosom of the old creation, it has developed anew the creation of industry and art. It has been its task and its glory to overcome obstacles. Mountains have been levelled, and valleys been exalted before it. It has broken the rocky soil into fertile glades; it has crowned the hill-tops with fruit and verdure, and bound around the very feet of ocean, ridges of golden corn. Up from the sunless and hoary deeps, up from the shapeless quarry, it drags its spotless marbles, and rears its palaces of pomp. It tears the stubborn metals from the bowels of the globe, and makes them ductile to its will. It marches steadily on over the swelling flood, and through the mountain clefts. It fans its way through the winds of ocean, tramples them in its course, surges and mingles them with flakes of fire. Civilization follows in its paths. It achieves grander victories, it weaves more durable trophies, it holds wider sway than the conqueror. His name becomes tainted and his monuments crumble; but labor converts his red battle-fields into gardens, and erects monuments significant of better things. It rides in a chariot driven by the wind. It writes with the lightning. It sits crowned as a queen in a thousand cities, and sends up its roar of triumph from a million wheels. It glistens in the fabric of the loom, it rings and sparkles from the steely hammer, it glories in shapes of beauty, it speaks in words of power, it makes the sinewy arm strong with liberty, the poor man's heart rich with content, crowns the swarthy and sweaty brow with honor, and dignity, and peace."

We have not mentioned a class who have been styled *parvenu*, such as have acquired wealth, and with it the vulgar passion for display. Such characters are to be found in all

* Rev. Mr. Chapin.

communities, but especially in those of recent formation. Unless culture and refinement accompany the possession of great wealth, the deformity is but the more obtrusive.

> "Worth makes the man, the want of it the fellow,
> The rest is naught but leather and prunello."

A gentleman has been defined "a Christian in spirit that will take a polish." The rest are but plated goods, and, whatever their fashion, rub them as you may, the base metal will show itself still.

Whether in ermine or fustian, there is no disguising character : the refined may be seen in the latter, as palpably as the vulgar in the former :

> "You may daub and bedizen the man as you will,
> But the stamp of the vulgar remains on him still."

It is from this class that virtuous poverty has most to suffer. These are they who "grind the faces of the poor," who, notwithstanding the proverb that "poverty is no crime," yet treat a man without money as if he were without principle ; who gauge the wit and worth of a man by his wearing-apparel and his wealth ; who deem it absurd for a poor man to assert his possession of intelligence, learning, or, in fact, any endowment whatever. Goldsmith, referring to this depreciating influence of poverty, says—a poor man resembles a fiddler, whose music, though liked, is not much praised, because he lives by it ; while a gentleman performer, though the most wretched scraper alive, throws the audience into raptures.

The want of money but deprives us of friends not worth the keeping ; it cuts us out of society to which dress and equipage are the only introduction, and deprives us of a number of needless luxuries and gilded fetters.

"I am rich enough," says Pope to Swift, "and can afford to give away a hundred pounds a year. I would not crawl upon the earth without doing a little good. I will enjoy the pleasure of what I give by giving it alive, and seeing another enjoy it. When I die I should be ashamed to leave enough for a monument, if a wanting friend was above ground." That speech of Pope is enough to immortalize him; independently of his philosophic verse.

That which was so diligently sought by the alchemists of old, the contented man has discovered. Contentment is the true philosopher's stone which transmutes all it touches to gold; and the divine maxim that "a man's life consisteth not in the abundance of the things which he possesseth," is itself a golden maxim.

"Why need I strive or sigh for wealth?
It is enough for me
That Heaven hath sent me strength and health,
A spirit glad and free;
Grateful these blessings to receive,
I sing my hymn at morn and eve."

Of all the artificial distinctions which obtain in civilized life, none are more absolute in their nature, or tyrannical in their effects, than those which divide the poor from the rich. Difference of condition tends more to disturb the harmony of the social compact, and to annihilate the common sympathies of mankind, than anything else in the world. It not only often sunders the nearest and dearest ties of relationship, but also perverts the best feelings of our nature, and thus becomes the fruitful source of most of the social evils which afflict humanity. Few comparatively become possessed of great wealth, and fewer still of the affluent are found among the magnanimous almoners who delight to minister to the necessities, and mitigate the sufferings of the children of want. It is proverbial that the poor are the most generous, and that the acquisition of wealth has a direct tendency to make men selfish and parsimonious. As a general rule, the opulent become more and more the victims of a heartless insensibility to the claims of others in proportion as they indulge a lavish prodigality upon self. What outrage and wrong have been perpetrated by some of the minions of fortune, upon those whom it was their duty to befriend! "To be able to soften the calamities of mankind," said Melmoth, "and inspire gladness into a heart oppressed with want, is indeed the noblest privilege of fortune; but to exercise that privilege in all its generous refinements, is an instance of the most uncommon elegance, both of temper and understanding. In the ordinary dispensations of bounty, little address is required; but when it is to be applied to those of a superior rank and more elevated minds, there is as much charity discovered in the *manner* as in the *measure* of our benevolence. It is extremely mortifying to a well-formed spirit to see itself considered an object of compassion; and it is the part of improved humanity to honor this honest pride in our nature, and to relieve the necessities without offending the delicacy of the distressed."

Comparatively few homesteads are found exempt from some "poor relation." Indeed, it has become so proverbial, that the very name seems to inspire a feeling of the comic as well as the pathetic. A poor relation, according to Charles Lamb, is the most irrelevant thing in nature—a piece of impertinent correspondency—an odious approximation—a haunting conscience—a preposterous shadow, lengthening in the noontide of our prosperity—an unwelcome remembrancer—a perpetually-recurring mortification—a drain on your purse, a more intolerable dun than your pride—a drawback upon success—a rebuke to your rising—a stain in your blood—a blot on your escutcheon—a rent in your garment—an apology to your friends—the one thing not needful—the hail in harvest—the ounce of sour in a pound of sweet. He is all this; and, more than all the rest, he is a severe test upon the claims of consanguinity; and often the only link that binds the poor neglected object to his "kith and kin," is the fear of the world's scorn and reprobation, which most men "well to do in the world" have not the hardihood to brave.

Touching "poor relations," we are reminded of the amusing instance of the sister of Sir George Rose, speaker of the House of Commons. Margaret Rose was proof against the meanness and insensibility of her brother, and bravely resented his inhumanity in the following manner. She hired a small cottage on the road-side, leading to the country mansion of Sir George, and placed over the door this intimation, for the especial benefit of the baronet's friends.

MARGARET ROSE,
SISTER OF SIR GEORGE ROSE,
TAKES IN WASHING HERE.

The ingenious expedient had its effect upon the vanity and heartless selfishness of Sir George, who immediately sent word to her that if she would take down her sign he would give her an annuity for life. This offer, it is said, however, the high-minded lady indignantly disdained to accept, preferring rather to punish the titled offender against humanity and decency, although at her own cost. This is but the type of a class still extant.

The French, whose imaginative faculty is in advance even of the gravity of their matter-of-fact neighbors on the opposite side of the channel, thus reduce our theme into the form of an enigma.

There is a being who is a citizen of the world, who travels incessantly. The air is not more subtle; water is not more fluid. He removes everything—replaces everything. He is mute, yet speaks all languages, and is the most eloquent of orators. He appeases all quarrels, all tumults, and he foments and encourages all laws and lawsuits. He excites courage, and instigates cowardice; braves all seas, breaks down all barriers, and will never sojourn anywhere. He diminishes all geographical distances, and increases all moral ones. He makes rougher all social inequalities, or levels them. He has power over all trades. He procures repose, and banishes sleep. He is the strong arm of tyranny, and the guarantee of independence. Virtue despises, and yet cannot do without him. His presence gives birth to pride ; his absence humbles it. He is audacious, imperious, and impudent : he is benevolent, and willing to relieve. He is the best of friends, and the most dangerous of enemies ; the wisest, and most fatal of advisers. At the voice of the prodigal, he transforms his land and house into dust which may be given to the winds ; and he assists the provident man to heap up his savings. Innocent himself, he corrupts innocence. He provokes all crimes, protects all vices, and attacks all virtues. He is no less the idol of universal worship. Nations, individuals contend for his exclusive possession, although he is their mutual and necessary interpreter. He causes pleasure and satiety. He is equally serviceable to caprices and wants, as to taste and passions. He gives nourishment and toys to infancy, and he is nourishment and toys to old age. He conveys bread to the mouth of the paralytic, and daggers to the hand of the assassin. He is deaf to the poor who implore him, and he forces himself upon the rich who prostitute him. He is the maker of all marriages, and the divider of all families. His natural disposition is to travel unceasingly. He is fit for every kind of service, but withal a wanderer. If he comes to you, it is but to leave you. If you retain him, he is good for nothing—he sleeps. Take care that he returns, for he knows how to do everything ; he is successful in all. If you want employment, orders, titles, honors, or even absolutions, address yourself to him ; he knows all the magazines ; he has all the keys. Are you weak, or powerful ? No matter, he will make you either a Crœsus or an Irus. He is in the midst of all good and all evil. He burned

Copenhagen, and built Petersburgh. He is inactive, and yet the universal mover. He is inanimate, yet the soul of the world. In the plenitude of his power, would he bestow health, he sends Hippocrates; would he defy death, he raises pyramids. Lastly, sprung from the dirt, he is regarded as a divinity. But of whom or what are we speaking?—

THE TOILET AND ITS DEVOTEES.

"Smilingly fronting the mirror she stands,
Her white fingers loosening the prisoned brown bands
To wander at will—and they kiss, as they go,
Her brow, and her cheek, and her shoulders of snow.
Her violet eyes, with their soft, changing light,
Growing darker when sad, and when merry more bright,
Look in at the image, till the lips of the twain
Smile at seeing how each gives the smile back again."

Dean Swift proposed to tax female beauty, and to leave every lady to rate her own charms. He said the tax would be cheerfully paid, and very productive.

The intimate relations between woman's beauty, and her toilet-glass render it impossible for the fair possessor to be unconscious of her endowment, and consequently it would be always at a premium. We remember a young surgeon once professed he would any day prefer a good dissection to a good dinner ; we question his taste, and if the dinner challenge were presented to us, in behalf of beauty, we would greatly prefer to accept of it. A good dinner, it is true, makes its appeal to the hungry, but a vision of beauty is a delectation to the eye, if less substantial, far more refining.

Beauty is inflexible : it appears to us a dream, when we contemplate the works of the great artists ; it is a hovering, floating, and glittering shadow, whose outline eludes the grasp of definition. Mendelsshon, the philosopher, grandfather of the composer, and others, tried to catch Beauty as a butterfly, and pin it down for inspection. They have succeeded in the same way as they are likely to succeed with a butterfly. The poor animal trembles and struggles, and its brightest colors are gone ; or, if you catch it without spoiling the colors, you have at best a stiff and awkward corpse. But a corpse is not an *entire* animal, it wants what is essential in all things, namely, life—spirit, which sheds beauty on everything.*

Lord Bacon observed justly, that the best part of beauty is that which a picture cannot express.

Beauty is indescribable and inexplicable ; it fascinates, dazzles, and bewilders us with its mystic power. Woman has been defined something midway between a flower and an angel ; as the sunny half of earth. It has been well said that woman's beauty does not consist merely in what is called a pretty face. An old lyric writer of the seventeenth century thus apostrophizes it.

"There is a garden in her face,
Where roses and and white lilies grow ;
A heavenly Paradise is that place,
Wherein all pleasant fruits do flow.
There cherries grow, that none may buy
Till cherry ripe themselves do cry.

"These cherries fairly do enclose
Of orient pearl a double row,

* Goethe.

Which when her lovely laughter shows,
They look like rosebuds filled with snow:
Yet these no peer, nor prince, may buy,
Till cherry ripe themselves do cry.

" Her eyes, like angels, watch them still;
Her brows, like bended bows, do stand,
Threatening, with piercing frowns to kill
All that approach with eye or hand,
Those sacred cherries to come nigh,
Till cherry ripe themselves do cry."

" Women are the poetry of the world, in the same sense as the stars are the poetry of heaven. Clear, light-giving, harmonious, they are the terrestial planets that rule the destines of mankind."*

" I saw her, upon nearer view,
A spirit, yet a woman too.
Her household motions light and free,
And steps of virgin liberty;
A countenance in which did meet
Sweet records, promises as sweet.
A creature not two bright or good
For human nature's daily food,
For transient sorrows, simple wiles,
Praise, blame, love, kisses, tears, and smiles."

Wordsworth's charming portraiture of womanly sweetness is worthy alike of the subject and the writer: it is doubtless familiar to the reader.

Another pen has dilated upon it in prose, as followeth:

Those who are accustomed to enlightened views of female beauty, well know that there are different kinds of personal beauty, among which that of form and coloring hold a very inferior rank. There is a beauty of expression, for instance, of sweetness, of nobility, of intellectual refinement, of feeling, of animation, of meekness, of resignation, and many other kinds of beauty, which may be allied to the plainest features, and yet

* Hargrave.

may remain to give pleasure long after the blooming cheek has faded, and silver grey has mingled with the hair. And how far more powerful in their influence upon others, are some of those kinds of beauty! For, after all, beauty depends more upon the movement of the face, than upon the form of the features when at rest; and thus, a countenance habitually under the influence of amiable feelings, acquires a beauty of the highest order, from the frequency with which such feelings are the originating causes of the movement or expressions which stamp their character upon it. Who has not waited for the first opening of the lips of a celebrated belle, to see whether her claims would be supported by "the mind, the music breathing from her face;" and who has not occasionally turned away repelled by the utter blank, or worse than blank, which the simple movement of the mouth in speaking or smiling, has revealed? The language of poetry describes the loud laugh as indicative of the vulgar mind; and certainly there are expressions, conveyed through the medium of a smile, which need not Lavater to inform us that refinement of feeling, or elevation of soul, has little to do with the fair countenance on which they are impressed. On the other hand, there are plain women sometimes met in society, every movement of whose features is instinct with intelligence; who, from the genuine heart-warm smiles which play about the mouth, the sweetly modulated voice, and the lighting up of an eye, that looks as if it could "comprehend the universe," becomes perfectly beautiful to those who live with them and love them. Before such pretensions as these, how soon does the pink-and-white of a merely pretty face vanish to nothing!

Among the many tributes to beauty is an old epigram, that may be new to some—it runs as follows,—

"This world's a prison, a sad gloomy den,
Whose walls are the heavens in common:
The jailer is Sin—and the prisoners men,
And the fetters are nothing but women."

Fontenelle thus daintily compliments the sex, when he compares women and clocks—the latter serve to point out the hours, the former to make us forget them.

There is a magic power in beauty that all confess—a strange witchery that fascinates and enchants us with a potency as irresistible as that of the magnet. It is to the moral world what gravitation is to the physical. It is easier to write about beauty in woman and its all-pervading influence, than to define what it is : and, to aid in the dilemma, we cite from an old French writer, its elements in detail :

"Thirty points of perfection each judge understands,
The standard of feminine beauty demands,
Three white :—and, without further prelude, we know,
That the skin, hands, and teeth should be pearly as snow.
Three black :—and our standard departure forbids
From dark eyes, darksome tresses, and darkly fringed lids.
Three red :—and the lover of comeliness seeks
For the hue of the rose in the lips, nails, and cheeks.
Three long : and of this you, no doubt, are aware,
Long the body should be, long the hands, long the hair.
Three short :—and herein nicest beauty appears—
Feet short as a fairy's, short teeth, and short ears.
Three large :—and remember this rule, as to size,
Embraces the shoulders, the forehead, the eyes.
Three narrow :—a maxim to every man's taste—
Circumference small in mouth, ankle, and waist.
Three round :—and in this I see infinite charms—
Rounded fullness apparent in leg, hip, and arms.
Three fine :—and can aught the enchantment eclipse,
Of fine tapering fingers, fine tresses, fine lips ?
Three small :—and my thirty essentials are told—
Small head, nose, and bosom compact in its mould.
Now the dame who comprises attractions like these,
Will need not the cestus of Venus to please :
While he who has met with an union so rare,
Has had better luck than has fall'n to *my* share."

It has been observed that God intended all women to be

beautiful, as much as he did the morning-glories and the roses. Beauty is

"Like the sweet South,
That breathes upon a bank of violets,
Stealing, and giving odor."

Ideal beauty, as well as beautiful objects of art and nature, affect us with a sort of sweet contagion. In the contemplation of a fine picture, we drink in the spirit of beauty through the eye ; and this is probably the reason why lovely women are occasionally addicted to æsthetics—the study of their charms in the mirror.

Milton supposes Eve was fascinated with her own charms as mirrored in the waters of Paradise, and her daughters have faithfully followed her example, for they are seldom disinclined to contemplate ideal beauty in their own symmetrical forms and features. If the "proper study of mankind is man," why may not woman be allowed a like privilege, for thereby a blemish may be removed and many a charm heightened.

The love of ornament creeps slowly, but surely, into the female heart ; the girl who twines the lily in her tresses, and looks at herself in the clear stream, will soon wish that the lily was fadeless, and the stream a mirror.*

Southey, in his *Omniana*, relates the following :—"When I was last in Lisbon, a nun made her escape from the nunnery. The first thing for which she inquired when she reached the house in which she was to be secreted, was a looking-glass. She had entered the convent when only five years old, and from that time had never seen her own face." There was some excuse for her.

A mirror has been thus variously described, as the only truth-teller in general favor—a journal in which Time records his travels—a smooth acquaintance, but no flatterer. We may add, that it is the only tolerated medium of reflection upon

* Mrs. S. C. Hall.

woman's beauty, and the last discarded ; and Queen Elizabeth, we learn, did not desert her looking-glass while there was any vestige left in the way of beauty with which to regale herself.*

The standards of beauty in woman vary with those of taste. Socrates called beauty a short-lived tyranny ; Plato, a privilege of nature ; Theophrastus, a silent cheat ; Theocritus, a delightful prejudice ; Carneades, a solitary kingdom ; and Aristotle affirmed that it was better than all the letters of recommendation in the world.

In truth, it is difficult to form any notions of beauty. Qualities of personal attraction, the most opposite imaginable, are each looked upon as beautiful in different countries, or by different people in the same country. " That which is deformity at Paris, may be beauty at Pekin ?"

> —— " Beauty, thou wild fantastic ape—
> Who dost in every country change thy shape ;
> Here black, there brown, here tawny, and there white !"

The frantic lover sees "Helen's beauty in an Egyptian brow." The black teeth, the painted eyelids, the plucked eyebrows of the Chinese fair, have admirers ; and should their feet be large enough to walk upon, their owners are regarded as monsters of ugliness. The Lilliputian dame is the *beau ideal* of perfection in the eyes of a northern gallant ; while in Patagonia they have a Polyphemus-standard of beauty. Some of the North American nations tie four boards round the heads of their children, and thus squeeze them, while the bones are yet tender, into a *square* form. Some prefer the form of a sugarloaf ; others have a quarrel with the natural shortness

* When Queen Elizabeth was far advanced in life, she ordered all pictures of herself painted by artists who had not flattered her ugliness, to be collected and burned, and in 1593 issued a proclamation forbidding all persons save " special cunning painters" to draw her likeness. She quarrelled at last with her looking-glass, as well as with her painters. During the last years of her life, the maids of honor removed mirrors as they would have removed poison from the apartments of royal pride. It is said that at the time of her death, her wardrobe contained more than two thousand dresses.

of the ears, and therefore from infancy these are drawn down upon the shoulders !

With the modern Greeks, and other nations on the shores of the Mediterranean, *corpulency* is the perfection of form in a woman ; and those very attributes which disgust the western European, form the attractions of an oriental fair. It was from the common and admired shape of *his* countrywomen, that Rubens in his pictures delights so much in a vulgar and odious plumpness :—when this master was desirous to represent the " beautiful," he had no idea of beauty under two hundred-weight. His very Graces are all fat. But it should be remembered that all his models were Dutch women.

The hair is a beautiful ornament of woman, but it has always been a disputed point which color most becomes it. We account red hair an abomination ; but in the time of Elizabeth it found admirers, and was in fashion. Mary of Scotland, though she had exquisite hair of her own, wore red fronts. Cleopatra was red-haired ; and the Venetian ladies to this day counterfeit yellow hair.

Lord Shaftesbury asserts that all beauty is truth. True features make the beauty of a face ; and true proportions the beauty of architecture ; as true measures that of harmony and music. In poetry, which is all fable, truth still is the perfection.

It has been with no less truth observed, that homely women are altogether the best at heart, head and soul. A pretty face often presides over a false heart and a weak head, with the smallest shadow of a soul.

" The bombastic misrepresentations of the encomiasts of Beauty," observed Ayton, " have exposed her just claims to much odium and ill-will. If a perfect face is the only bait that can tempt an angel from the skies, he adds, what is to be the recompense of the unfortunate with a wide mouth and a turn-up nose ? The conduct of men, since the deluge, has proved, however, that love (the true thing) is not mere fealty to a face.

If an ugly woman of wit and worth cannot be loved till she is known—a beautiful fool will cease to please when she is found out."

In the words of a contemporary :—

"Woman has never failed, since the world began, to illustrate, in instances, the glory of her nature—never ceased to manifest the divine in the human. With the regal Esther, yearning to bless her enslaved kindred, and the filial-love inspired daughter, who sustained the life of her grey-haired father through a prison's bars, there have not been parallels wanting in all ages, to prove that the angels of God still wander on earth, to remind man of Eden, and give him a foretaste of heaven."

Of such type of virtue, were Penelope, weaving amid her maidens through weary years the web that shielded her virtue until her royal husband returned from his wanderings, and was to gladden her heart ; or, courteous Rebecca, at the well ; or, timid Ruth, gleaning in the field ; or, nobler still, the Roman Cornelia, who, taunted in Rome's decaying age by rivals with her poverty, held up her virtuous children, exclaiming—"These are my jewels !" Fit woman to have been the "mother of the Gracchi."

Richter observes, "A woman's soul is by nature a beautiful fresco-painting, painted on rooms, clothes, silver waiters, and upon the whole domestic establishment."

Beautiful women may be admired, but who can refrain from loving the impersonation of grace and virtue we every day encounter in the charmed circles of domestic life. Love is a hallowed passion ; it is angel-like—a gleam of the celestial to gladden the dark places of our earthly pilgrimage.

"She was a queen of noble Nature's crowning,
A smile of hers was like an act of grace ;
She had no winsome looks, no pretty frowning,
Like daily beauties of the vulgar race :
But if she smiled, a light was on her face ;

A clear, cool kindliness, a lunar beam
Of peaceful radiance, silvering in the stream,
Of human thought of unabiding glory,
Not quite awaking truth, not quite a dream,
A visitation bright and transitory."

It is not the smiles of a pretty face—the delicate tint of complexion—the enchanting glance of the eye—the beauty and symmetry of person—nor the costly dress or decorations, that compose woman's loveliness. It is her pleasing deportment—her chaste conversation—the sensibility and purity of her thoughts—her affable and open disposition—her sympathy with those in adversity—her comforting and relieving the afflicted and distressed, and, above all, the humbleness of her soul, that constitute true loveliness.

D'Israeli observes, "It is at the foot of woman we lay the laurels that, without her smile, would never have been gained: it is her image that strings the lyre of the poet, that animates the voice in the blaze of eloquent faction, and guides the brain in the august toils of stately councils. Whatever may be the lot of man—however unfortunate, however oppressed—if he only love and be loved, he must strike a balance in favor of existence; for love can illumine the dark roof of poverty, and can lighten the fetters of the slave.'

"Honored be woman, she beams on the sight
Graceful and fair like a being of light,
Scatters around her wherever she strays
Roses of bliss on our thorn-covered ways,
Roses of Paradise fresh from above
To be gathered and twined in a garland of love."*

Comets, doubtless, answer some wise and good purpose in the creation; so do women. Comets are incomprehensible, beautiful, and eccentric; so are women. Comets shine with peculiar splendor, but at night appear most brilliant; so do

* Hood.

women. Comets confound the most learned, when they attempt to ascertain their nature ; so do women. Comets equally excite the admiration of the philosopher and of the clod of the valley ; so do women. Comets and women, therefore, are closely analogous ; but the nature of which being inscrutable, all that remains for us to do is, to view with admiration the one, and, almost to adoration, love the other.*

It was probably under such hallucination that the following confession of returning consciousness was perpetrated :

> " When Eve brought *woe* to all mankind,
> Old Adam called her *wo*-man ;
> And when he found she *wooed* so kind,
> He then pronounced her woo-man.
> But now, with smiles and artful wiles,
> Their husbands' pockets trimmin',
> The women are so full of *whims*,
> That people call them *whim*-men."

An old author quaintly remarks :—Avoid argument with ladies. In spinning *yarns* among *silks* and *satins* a man is sure to be worsted and twisted. And when a man is *worsted* and *twisted*, he may consider himself *wound up*.

After all that may be said or sung about it, beauty is an undeniable fact, and its endowment not to be disparaged. Sidney Smith gives some good advice on the subject.

" Never teach false morality. How exquisitely absurd to teach a girl that beauty is of no value, dress of no use ! Beauty is of value—her whole prospects and happiness in life may often depend upon a new gown or a becoming bonnet ; if she has five grains of common sense, she will find this out. The great thing is to teach her their just value, and that there must be something better under the bonnet, than a pretty face, for real happiness. But never sacrifice truth."

" No persons have a more hyperbolical opinion of the power

* Rymett.

and glory of beauty, than the unelect; and *hinc illæ lachrymæ;* hence undoubtedly their peevishness and spite. If an ugly woman of wit and worth cannot be loved till she is known—a beautiful fool will cease to please when she is found out. Instantaneous and universal admiration—the eye-worship of the world, is unquestionably the reward of the best faces; and the malcontents had much better come into the general opinion with a good grace, than be making themselves at once unhappy and ridiculous, by their hollow and self-betraying recusancy."* Now an ill-conditioned countenance, accompanied, as it always is of course, with shining abilities and all the arts of pleasing, has this signal compensation—that it improves under observation, grows less and less objectionable the more you look into it and the better you know it, till it becomes almost agreeable on its own account—nay, really so—actually pretty; whereas beauty, we have seen, witless beauty, cannot resist the test of long acquaintance, but declines, as you gaze, while in the full pride of its perfection; "fades on the eye and palls upon the sense," with all its bloom about it. Young thus apostrophizes the union of moral and physical graces:—

"When charms of mind,
With elegance of outward form are joined:
When youth makes such bright objects still more bright,
And fortune sets them in the strongest light;
'Tis all of Heaven that we below may view,
And all but adoration is their due."

Another authority affirms: If its possession, as is too often the case, turns the head, while its loss sours the temper; if the long regret of its decay outweighs the fleeting pleasure of its bloom, the plain should rather pity than envy the handsome. Beauty of countenance, which, being the light of the soul shining through the face, is independent of features or complexion, and is the most attractive, as well as the most enduring charm.

* Ayton's Essays.

Nothing but talent and amiability can bestow it, no statue or picture can rival, time itself cannot destroy it.

A good and true woman is said to resemble a Cremona fiddle in one respect—age increases its worth and sweetens its tone. Gay has some well-remembered lines apposite to our point :—

"What is the blooming tincture of the skin,
To peace of mind and harmony within?
What the bright sparkling of the finest eye,
To the soft soothing of a calm reply?
Can comeliness of form, or shape, or air,
With comeliness of words or deeds compare?
No, those at first the unwary heart may gain,
But these, these only, can the heart retain."

Thomas Carew thus apostrophizes female beauty :

"He that loves a rosy cheek,
Or a coral lip admires,
Or from star-like eyes doth seek
Fuel to maintain his fires,
As old Time makes these decay
So his flames must waste away ;
But a smooth and steadfast mind,
Gentle thoughts and calm desires,
Hearts with equal love combined,
Kindle never-dying fires.
Where these are not, I despise
Lovely cheeks or lips or eyes."

Byron also condenses the same sentiment in a single line—

"Heart on her lips, and soul within her eyes."

The last word—eyes, and the eloquent language they express—have been a prolific theme with the poets. Some have dilated on their brilliancy till they have been bewildered and blinded to all things else around them, and some are fastidious as to their color, size and expression. One thus describes the respective claims of black and blue :

Black eyes most dazzle at a ball :
Blue eyes most please at evening fall.
Black a conquest soonest gain ;
The blue a conquest most retain ;
The black bespeak a lively heart,
Whose soft emotions soon depart ;
The blue a steadier flame betray,
That burns and lives beyond a day ;
The black may features best disclose ;
In blue may feelings all repose.
Then let each reign without control,
The black all mind—the blue all soul.

Leigh Hunt says of those who have thin lips, and are not shrews or niggards—I must give here as my firm opinion, founded on what I have observed, that lips become more or less contracted in the course of years, in proportion as they are accustomed to express good humor and generosity, or peevishness and a contracted mind. Remark the effect which a moment of ill-humor and grudgingness has upon the lips, and judge what may be expected from an habitual series of such moments. Remark the reverse, and make a similar judgment. The mouth is the frankest part of the face ; it can the least conceal its sensations. We can hide neither ill-temper with it, nor good ; we may affect what we please, but affectation will not help us. In a wrong cause it will only make our observers resent the endeavor to impose upon them. The mouth is the seat of one class of emotions, as the eyes are of another ; or rather, it expresses the same emotions but in greater detail, and with a more irrepressible tendency to be in motion. It is the region of smiles and dimples, and of trembling tenderness ; of a sharp sorrow, of a full breathing joy, of candor, of reserve, of a carking care, of a liberal sympathy.

There is a charm that brighter grows
'Mid beauty's swift decay,
And o'er the heart a glory throws,
That will not fade away.

When beauty's voice and beauty's glance,
The heart no longer move,
This holy charm will still entrance,
And wake the spirit's love.

Woman may be said almost to enjoy the monopoly of personal beauty. A good-humored writer thus defines her position in this respect as contrasted with the opposite sex :—

If you, ladies, are much handsomer than we, it is but just you should acknowledge that we have helped you, by voluntarily making ourselves ugly. Your superiority in beauty is made up of two things ; first, the care which you take to increase your charms ; secondly, the zeal which we have shown to heighten them by the contrast of our finished ugliness—the shadow which we supply to your sunshine.

Your long, pliant, wavy tresses are all the more beautiful because we cut our hair short ; your hands are all the whiter, smaller and more delicate, because we reserve to ourselves those toils and exercises which make the hands large and hard.

We have devoted entirely to your use flowers, feathers, ribbons, jewelry, silks, gold and silver embroidery. Still more to increase the difference between the sexes, which is your greatest charm, and to give you the handsome share, we have divided with you the hues of nature. To you we have given the colors that are rich and splendid, or soft and harmonious ; for ourselves we have kept those that are dark and dead. We have given you sun and light ; we have kept night and darkness.

We have monopolized the hard, stony roads that enlarge the feet; we have let you walk only on carpets.

Long hair in woman is an essential element of beauty. The Roman ladies generally wore it long, and dressed it in a variety of ways, bedecking it with gold, silver, pearls, and other ornaments. On the contrary, the men amongst the Greeks and Romans, and amongst the Jews at a later period, wore their hair short, as may be collected from books, medals, statues, and other models or remains. Amongst the Greeks we know that both sexes, a few days before marriage, cut off and consecrated their hair as an offering to their favorite deities. It was also customary amongst them to hang the hair of the dead on the doors of their houses previous to interment. The ancients imagined that no one could die till a lock of hair was cut off; and this act they supposed was performed by the invisible hand of death, or some other messenger of the gods.

"How often do we see a really good face made quite ugly by a total inattention to lines. Sometimes the hair is pushed into the cheeks, and squared at the forehead, so as to give a most extraordinary pinched shape to the face. Let the oval, where it exists, be always preserved: where it does not, let the hair be so humored that the deficiency shall not be perceived. Nothing is more common than to see a face which is somewhat too large below, made to look grossly large and coarse, by contracting the hair on the forehead and cheek; but the hair should be made to fall partially over, so as to shade and soften off the lower exuberance. A good treatise, with examples in outline of the defects, would be of some value upon a lady's toilet, who would wish to preserve her great privilege—the supremacy of beauty. Some press the hair down close to the face, which is to lose the very characteristic of hair—ease and freedom. Let her locks, said Anacreon, lie as they like; the Greek gives them life and a will. Some ladies wear the hair like blinkers; you always suspect they will shy if you approach them. A lady's head-dress, whether in a portrait or for her daily wear, should, as in old portraits by Rembrandt and Titian, go off into shade, not to be seen too clearly, and hard or round."*

The custom of decking the hair with pearls and gems, although not a modern invention, is still in vogue with royalty and courtly circles; yet the author of *The Honeymoon*, thus repudiates the fashion:

* Blackwood.

—— "Thus modestly attired,
A half-blown rose stuck in thy braided hair,
With no more diamonds than those eyes are made of,
No deeper rubies than compose thy lips,
Nor pearls more precious than inhabit them;
With the pure red and white, which that same hand
Which blends the rainbow, mingles in thy cheeks;
This well-proportioned form (think not I flatter)
In graceful motion to harmonious sounds,
And thy free tresses dancing in the wind,
Thou'lt fix as much observance, as chaste dames
Can meet, without a blush."

The Roman patrician ladies had from two to three hundred slaves chiefly appointed to attend their persons. Their hair used to be perfumed and powdered with gold dust.

"Of all the articles of luxury and ostentation known to the Romans, pearls seem to have been the most esteemed. They were worn on all parts of the dress, and such was the diversity of their size, purity, and value, that they were found to suit all classes, from those of moderate to those of the most colossal fortune. The famous pearl earrings of Cleopatra are said to have been worth about £160,000, and Julius Cæsar is said to have presented Servilia, the mother of Brutus, with a pearl for which he had paid above £48,000; and though no reasonable doubt can be entertained in regard to the extreme exaggeration of these and similar statements, the fact that the largest and finest pearls brought immense prices is beyond all question. It has been said that the wish to become master of the pearls with which it was supposed to abound, was one of the motives which induced Julius Cæsar to invade Britain. But, though a good many were met with in various parts of the country, they were of little or no value, being small and ill-colored. After pearls and diamonds, the emerald held the highest place in the estimation of the Romans."*

In France, during the reign of Louis XIV. the use of dia-

* M'Culloch.

monds revived. Robes were embroidered with them, and besides necklaces, aigrettes, and bracelets, they were employed to ornament the stomachers, shoulders, waistbands, and skirts of the dress. This costly fashion subsided about the end of the French Revolution.

The favorites of fortune are too frequently the servile votaries of fashion ; and this passion for dress entails many social evils. While it fosters imperious pride in its victim, it destroys all the finer sensibilities of our nature. The gentle hand of charity, that ministers to the children of want, belongs not to the flaunting lady of fashion ; her ambition is rather to dazzle and bewilder the gazing, thoughtless multitude—to become the "cynosure of all eyes." To the reflective mind, such a spectacle is suggestive of emotions far opposite to those of pleasure. To such the luxury of doing good is unknown ; for their benefactions, instead of being diffusive, are directed exclusively to self. Self is the idol they adore and worship ; it is idolatry of the worst type, and the most to be deprecated by noble minds.

"There are certain moralists in the world, who labor under the impression that it is no matter what people wear, or how they put on their apparel. Such people cover themselves up—they do not dress. No one doubts that the mind is more important than the body, the jewel than the setting ; and yet the virtue of the one and the brilliancy of the other is enhanced by the mode in which they are presented to the senses. Let a woman have every virtue under the sun, if she is slatternly, or even inappropriate in her dress, her merits will be more than half obscured. If, being young, she is untidy, or, being old, fantastic, or slovenly, her mental qualifications stand a chance of being passed over with indifference."*

A right loyal scribe thus enacts the champion for beauty : Plain women were formerly so common that they were termed *ordinary*, to signify the frequency of their occurrence ; in these

* Chambers.

happier days the phrase *extra*ordinary would be more applicable. However parsimonious, or even cruel, Nature may have been in other respects, they all cling to admiration by some solitary tenure that redeems them from the unqualified imputation of unattractiveness. One has an eye that, like Charity, covers a multitude of sins ; another is a female Samson, whose strength consists in her hair ; a third holds your affections by her teeth ; a fourth is a Cinderella, who wins hearts by her pretty little foot ; a fifth makes an irresistible appeal from her face to her figure, and so on to the end of the catalogue. An expressive countenance may always be claimed in the absence of any definite charm ; if even this be questionable, the party generally contrives to get a reputation for great cleverness ; and if that too be inhumanly disputed, envy itself must allow that she is "excessively amiable."

Countenance, however, is not within the reach of any of these substances or combinations. It is a species of moral beauty, as superior to mere charm of surface as mind is to matter. It is, in fact, visible spirit, legible intellect, diffusing itself over the features, and enabling minds to commune with each other by some secret sympathy unconnected with the senses. The heart has a silent echo in the face, which frequently carries to us a conviction diametrically opposite to the audible expressions of the mouth ; and we see through the eyes into the understanding, long before it can communicate with us by utterance. This emanation of character is the light of soul irradiating the countenance, as the sun illumines the face of nature before he rises above the earth to commence his celestial career. Of this indefinable charm, all women are alike susceptible : it is to them what gunpowder is to warriors, it levels all distinctions, and gives to the plain and the pretty, to the timid and the brave, an equal chance of making conquests.

Of course, the immediate effect of a well-chosen feminine toilet operates differently in different minds. In some it causes a sense of actual pleasure ; in others, a consciousness of passive enjoyment. In some, it is intensely felt while it is present; in others, only missed when it is gone.

Beauty is the flowering of virtue. [The true art of assisting beauty consists in embellishing the whole person by the proper ornaments of virtuous and commendable qualities. By this help alone it is, that those who are the favorites of Nature become animated, and are in a capacity for exerting their influence ; and those who seem to have been neglected by her, like models wrought in haste, are capable, in a great measure, of finishing what she has left imperfect.]

Chevreul remarks : " Drapery of a lustreless *white*, such as cambric muslin, assorts well with a fresh complexion, of which it relieves the rose color ; but it is unsuitable to complexions which have a disagreeable tint, because white always exalts all colors by raising their tone ; consequently, it is unsuitable to those skins which, without having this disagreeable tint, very nearly approach it. Very light white draperies, such as point lace, have an entirely different aspect. *Black* draperies, lowering the tone of the colors with which they are in juxtaposition, whiten the skin ; but if the vermilion or rosy parts are to a certain point distant from the drapery, it will follow that, although lowered in tone, they appear relatively to the white parts of the skin contiguous to this same drapery, redder than if the contiguity to the black did not exist."

Some ingenious gallant has taxed his skill in stringing together some valuable cosmetics, and, as they may prove serviceable to a lady's toilet, we introduce them :

THE ENCHANTED MIRROR—*Self Knowledge.*

This curious glass will bring your faults to light,
And make your virtues shine both strong and bright.

WASH TO SMOOTH WRINKLES—*Contentment.*

A daily portion of this essence use,
'Twill smooth the brow, tranquillity infuse.

FINE LIP SALVE—*Truth.*

Use daily for your lips this precious dye,
They'll redden and breathe sweeter melody.

MIXTURE GIVING SWEETNESS TO THE VOICE—*Prayer.*

At morning, noon, and night this mixture take,
Your tones improved will richer music make.

BEST EYE-WATER—*Compassion.*

These drops will add great lustre to the eye;
When more you need, the poor will you supply.

SOLUTION TO PREVENT ERUPTIONS—*Wisdom.*

It calms the temper, beautifies the face,
And gives to woman dignity and grace.

MATCHLESS PAIR OF EAR-RINGS—*Attention and Obedience.*

With these clear drops appended to the ear,
Attentive, lessons you will gladly hear.

INDISPENSABLE PAIR OF BRACELETS—*Neatness and Industry.*

Clasp them on carefully each day you live,
To good designs they efficacy give.

AN ELASTIC GIRDLE—*Patience.*

The more you use, the brighter it will grow.
Though its least merit is external show.

RING OF TRIED GOLD—*Principle.*

Yield not this golden bracelet while you live,
'Twill both restrain and peace of conscience give.

NECKLACE OF PUREST PEARL—*Resignation.*

This ornament embellishes the fair,
And teaches all the ills of life to bear.

DIAMOND BREAST-PIN—*Love.*

Adorn your bosom with this precious pin,
It shines without and warms the heart within.

A Graceful Bandeau—*Politeness.*

The forehead neatly circled with this band
Will admiration and respect command.

A Precious Diadem—*Piety.*

Whoe'er this precious diadem shall own,
Secures herself an everlasting crown.

Universal Beautifier—*Good Temper.*

With this choice liquid gently touch the mouth ;
It spreads o'er all the face the charms of youth.

If Nature has given man a strong instinct to dress, says a writer in the *Quarterly Review*, it is because she has given him woman as an object for it ; whatever, therefore, may be the outward practice of the present day, the moral foundation is right. She dresses herself to please him, and he dresses her to please himself ; and this is a distinction between the two animals which will perhaps apply to more subjects than that of *dress.*

Yet by nothing, perhaps, save his boasted reason, is man more signally distinguished from the lower orders of creation, than by the decorations of the toilet—the drapery and various appendages with which he invests his person. So universal is the custom among all civilized communities, that an individual would as soon think of intermitting his necessary food as to attempt to infringe upon the claims of so irreversible a decree. Some there are, it is true, of more pristine habits, whose unsophisticated tastes induce a preference for the purely natural over the artificial in this respect—a state of nature to that of art : but these belong to the untutored and the rude of savage life, and therefore the less said about them the better. There is, moreover, less of the feeling of compulsion in complying with the requisition, from the prevalent passion for adornment and decoration, of which all are, to a greater or less degree, the victims. It seems somewhat strange that Nature, in her lavish distribution of fleece, and fur, and gaudy plumage, should have left the monarch of all mundane creatures in a state of destitution, which it so sorely taxes his purse to supply; but such is the fact, and against it there is no appeal. The world has been long accustomed to do homage to elegance and refinement in costume; it is not surprising, therefore, that it should have become a matter of such universal regard among the various classes of society.

Pride of personal appearance was naturally one result of a passion for dress, alike evinced by the rude trappings of the savage, and the gorgeous appendages of refinement and luxury.

> "Because you flourish in worldly affairs,
> Don't be haughty and put on airs,
> With insolent pride of station;
> Don't be proud and turn up your nose,
> At poorer people, in plainer clothes,
> But learn for the sake of your mind's repose,
> That Wealth's a bubble that comes and goes!
> And that all Proud Flesh, wherever it grows,
> Is subject to irritation."*

It is in fact difficult to determine whether the same may not be affirmed of those who affect the greatest simplicity in their habiliments—for it is not certain that the Quaker, even, is wholly divested of vanity, although he may be of the finery he repudiates. Dr. Gall, in remarking upon the innate love of approbation, states that in the south of France it is customary for drivers to decorate their mules with bouquets when they travel well, and that it is a most painful infliction upon their complacency to be deprived of the distinction. Many a similar proof of this susceptibility of the complimentary in the brute creation might be adduced, especially in domesticated animals; but we will let one case suffice. It is that of a female ape, belonging to the learned doctor just referred to: "Whenever they give her," he says, "a handkerchief, she throws it over

* J. G. Saxe.

her head, and seems to take a wonderful deal of pleasure and pride in seeing it drag behind her, like the train of a court robe."

Fashion, the veriest despot in her decrees, arbitrates through the agency of her devotees—the milliner, the modiste, and the tailor—the style and manner of one's habiliments; and so absolute is her sway in this matter, that it is difficult perhaps, to indicate any class that may boast exemption from her jurisdiction.

Fashion rules the world, and a most tyrannical mistress she is—compelling people to submit to the most inconvenient things imaginable, for her sake.

She pinches our feet with tight shoes—or chokes us with a tight handkerchief, or squeezes the breath out of our bodies by tight lacing; she makes people sit up by night when they ought to be in bed, and keeps them in bed when they ought to be up. She makes it vulgar to wait on one's self, and genteel to live idle and useless. She makes people visit when they would rather be at home; eat when they are not hungry, and drink when they are not thirsty. She invades our pleasure, and interrupts our business. She compels people to dress gaily—whether upon their own property or that of others. She ruins health and produces sickness—destroys life and occasions premature death. She makes foolish parents, invalids of children, and servants of us all. She is a tormentor of conscience, despoiler of morality, an enemy to religion, and no one can be her companion and enjoy either. She is a despot of the highest grade, full of intrigue and cunning—and yet husbands, wives, fathers, mothers, sons, daughters, and servants, all strive to see who shall be most obsequious. Fashion obtains in all countries—there being ever some Beau Brummells at hand to issue her mandates and illustrate her protean shapes and endless metamorphoses.

"Oh, Fashion! it were vain indeed
To try your wondrous flights to follow:

Onward at such a pace you speed,
  Beating the *Belle Assemblée* hollow.
One moment hovering in our coats
  To change the cutting of the skirts:
Then with rude grasp you seize our throats,
  Altering the collars of our shirts.
Now trimming up with ribbons gay,
  And flowers as well, a lady's bonnet;
Then with rash hand tearing away
  Each bit of finery upon it.
Shrouding one day the arm from sight,
  In sleeve so large that six might share it;
And making it next month so tight,
  'Tis scarcely possible to bear it.
Upon a lady's dress again,
  With arbitrary hand it pounces,
Making it one day meanly plain,
  Then idly loading it with flounces."

There are few things that have not been done, and few things that have not been worn, under the sanction of fashion. What could exhibit a more fantastical appearance than an English beau of the fourteenth century? He wore long, pointed shoes, fastened to his knee by gold or silver chains; hose of one color on one leg, and another color on the other; a coat, the one half white, and the other black or blue; a long silk hood, buttoned under his chin, embroidered with grotesque figures of animals, dancing men, &c. This dress was the height of the mode in the reign of Edward III. In view of such facts, shall we upbraid woman for her vanity and love of finery?

Leigh Hunt informs us that fashions have a short life or a long one, according as it suits the makers to startle us with a variety, or save themselves observation of a defect. Hence fashions set by young or handsome people are fugitive, and such are usually those that bring custom to the milliner.

The *Edinburgh Review* observes: "Peculiarities of dress, even amounting to foppery, so common among eminent men, are carried off from ridicule by ease in some, or stateliness in others.

We may smile at Chatham, scrupulously crowned in his best wig, if intending to speak; at Erskine, drawing on his bright yellow gloves, before he rose to plead; at Horace Walpole, in a cravat of Gibbon's carvings; at Raleigh loading his shoes with jewels so heavy that he could scarcely walk; at Petrarch, pinching his feet till he crippled them; at the rings which covered the philosophical fingers of Aristotle; at the bare throat of Byron; the Armenian dress of Rousseau; the scarlet and gold coat of Voltaire; or the prudent carefulness with which Cæsar scratched his head, so as not to disturb the locks arranged over the bald place. But most of these men, we apprehend, found it easy to enforce respect and curb impertinence.

It would be impossible to enter upon the details of a subject so copious in its historic data: nor can we attempt to go into a minute examination of the prodigal magnificence of the wardrobe of distinguished personages, but must confine our remarks to the present fashion, the most prominent feature of which is the number and depth of flounces.

A writer in the *London Quarterly*, likes them when they wave and flow, as in a very light material—muslin, or gauze, or barége—when a lady has no outline and no mass, but looks like a receding angel, or a "dissolving view," but he does not like them in a rich material, where they flop, or in a stiff one where they bristle; and where they break the flowing lines of the petticoat, and throw light and shade where you do not expect them to exist.

The amply-folding robe, cast round the harmonious form; the modest clasp and zone on the bosom; the braided hair, or the veiled head; these were the fashions alike of the wife of a Phocion and the mistress of an Alcibiades. A chastened taste ruled at their toilets; and from that hour to this, the forms and modes of Greece have been those of the poet, the sculptor, and the painter.

The flowing robe, the easy shape, the soft, unfettered hair, gave place to skirts shortened for flight or contest—to the hardened vest, and head buckled in gold or silver.

Thence, by a natural descent, we have the iron bodice, stiff farthingale, and spiral coiffure of the middle ages. The courts of Charlemagne, of Edward, Henry and Elizabeth, all exhibit the figures of women as if in a state of siege. Such lines of circumvallation and outwork ; such impregnable bulwarks of whalebone, wood, and steel ; such impassable mazes of gold, silver, silk, and furbelows, met a man's view, that, before he had time to guess it was a woman that he saw, she had passed from his sight ; and he only formed a vague wish on the subject, by hearing, from an interested father or brother, that the moving castle was one of the softer sex.

These preposterous fashions disappeared in England a short time after the Restoration :

> " What thought, what various numbers can express,
> The inconstant equipage of woman's dress?"

Kar thus designates the epochs of a woman's life :—

Dress is the great business of all women, and the fixed idea of some. Thus, every event in their lives has a change of dress for its result, and often for its cause. In this way, dresses divide a woman's existence into an infinite number of eras and hegiras. Such a thing happened at the time when she had her purple velvet dress ; such another when she bought her pink satin.

Herrick has some sweet lines about a lady's costume, which claim insertion here :—

> " A sweet disorder in the dresse,
> Kindles in cloaths a wantonesse,
> A lawne about the shoulders throwne,
> Into a fine distraction ;
> An erring lace, which here and there,
> Enthral the crimson stomacher ;
> A cuffe neglectful, and thereby
> Ribbands to fly confusedly ;

A winning wave (deserving note)
In the tempestuous petticoat:
A careless shoe-string in whose tye
I see a wilde civility,
Does more bewitche me, than when art
Is too precise in every part."

It is not so much the richness of the material as the way it is made up, and the manner in which it is worn, that give the desired elegance. A neat fit, a graceful bearing, and a proper harmony between the complexion and the colors, have more to do with heightening female attractions than many are willing to believe. "Many a wife looks prettier, if she did but know it, in her neat morning frock of calico, than in the incongruous pile of finery which she dignifies with the title of full dress. Many an unmarried female first wins the heart of her future husband in some simple, unpretending attire, which, if consulted about, she would pronounce too cheap except for ordinary wear, but which, by its accidental suitability to her figure, face, and carriage, idolize her youth wonderfully. If the sex would study taste in dress more, and care less for costliness, they would have no reason to regret it."

Attention to a few general rules would prevent a great many anomalous appearances: for instance, "a woman should never be dressed too little, nor a girl too much—nor should a woman of small stature attempt large patterns, nor a bad walker flounces—nor a short throat carry feathers, nor high shoulders a shawl. From the highest to the lowest, there is not a single style of beauty with which the plain straw hat is not upon the best understanding. It refines the homeliest and composes the wildest—it gives the coquettish young lady a little dash of demureness, and the demure one a slight touch of coquetry—it makes the blooming beauty look more fresh, and the pale one more interesting—it makes the plain woman look, at all events, a lady, and the lady more lady-like still." Bonnets, too, are an index of character. Some wag has furnished the following "Recipe for a Bonnet," free of cost.

"Two scraps of foundation, some fragments of lace,
A shower of French rosebuds to droop o'er the face;
Fine ribbons and feathers, with crape and illusion,
Then mix and *de*-range them in graceful confusion;
Inveigle some fairy, out roaming for pleasure,
And beg the slight favor of taking her measure:
The length and breadth of her dear little pate,
And hasten a miniature frame to create;
Then pour, as above, the bright mixture upon it,
And lo! you possess 'such a love of a bonnet.'"

To instance the broad national characteristics of costume, we find their several peculiarities in the Chinese, the Swiss, French, English, Russian, Turk and Greek; as well as the Laplander, the Tartar and Indian, which last is remarkable, like that of most savage nations, for its paucity. Charles II., Gustavus of Sweden, Napoleon, and other monarchs, issued their edicts for the regulation of court costumes. The love of gay and gaudy attire is a passion not exclusively a weakness incident to the fair sex, notwithstanding an ancient writer has defined woman to be "an animal that delights in finery"—a fact, however, that cannot be questioned if we appeal to the history of the past in all conditions of society. In searching for some of the absurdities of the toilet, we meet with the following. The ladies of Japan are said to gild their teeth, and those of the Indies to paint them red, while in Guzurat the test of beauty is to render them sable. In Greenland, the women used to color their faces with blue and yellow. The Chinese must torture their feet into the smallest possible dimensions—a proof positive of their contracted understandings. The ancient Peruvians, and some of our Indian tribes, used to flatten their heads: and among other nations, the mothers, in a similar way, maltreat the noses of their offspring.

Rings are of remote origin; their use is mentioned by many of the classic writers, and also in the Scriptures: they were worn by the ancient Gauls and Britons on the middle finger, and by the Greeks on the fourth of the left hand, on the supposition that this finger communicated by a small nerve with the heart. The wedding-ring is supposed to be of heathen origin. An old Latin work, which ascribes the invention of a ring to Tubal Cain, contains the following: "The form of the ring being circular, that is, round and without end, importeth thus much: that their mutual love and hearty affection should roundly flow from one to the other as in a circle—and that continually and for ever."

The armlet or bracelet is also of equal antiquity; its adoption is referred to in the 24th chapter of Genesis. Both were in vogue with the Sabine women, and of a very massive kind: they were worn as tokens of valor by warriors, also among the Romans. Ear-rings, or, as they were formerly styled, pendants, are worn by most nations, and, in many instances, by both sexes. In the East Indies they are unusually large, and are generally of gold and jewels. The Sandwich Islanders push the fashion to its utmost extent; they enlarge the incision to such a degree, by the excessive weight of their ear-rings, that the ear is sometimes dragged down to the waist. Of head-dresses, the earliest kind upon record seems to have been the tiara; the caul is also mentioned, in Holy Writ, as having been in vogue in primitive times. It was usually made of net-work, of gold or silk, and enclosed all the hair. Some of the various items of a lady's wardrobe it will not be our venture to dilate upon: we may, however, just refer to the corsets or stays. Tradition insists that corsets were first invented by a brutal butcher of the thirteenth century, as a punishment for his wife. She was very loquacious, and, finding nothing would cure her, he put a pair of stays on her, in order to take away her breath, and so prevent her, as he thought, from talking. This cruel punishment was inflicted by other heartless husbands, till at last there was scarcely a wife in all London who was not condemned to the like infliction. The punishment became so universal at last that the ladies in their defence made a fashion of it, and so it has continued to the present day. The fair sex of our own day seem economic in this respect, for, however prodigal they may be in other matters, they are for the least possible *waist.* Sœmmering enumerates a catalogue of ninety-six diseases resulting from this stringent *habit* among them: many of the most frightful maladies that flesh is heir to, cancer, asthma, and consumption, are among them. Such unnatural compression, moreover, seems to indicate a very limited scope for the play of the affections, for what room is there for any heart at all? As if to atone for brevity of waist, the ladies now indulge in an amplitude of skirt. The merry dames of Elizabeth's court, in a wild spirit of fun, adopted the fashion of hideously-deforming farthingales to ridicule the enormous trunk-hose worn by gentlemen of that period—determined, if not successful in shaming away the absurdity altogether, at least to have a preposterous contrivance of their own. The idea was full of woman's wit. But, alas! they were caught in their own snare. Precious stones were profusely displayed on the bodices and skirts of brocade gowns, and vanity soon discovered that the stiff whalebone framework under the upper skirt formed an excellent show-case for family jewels. The passion thus gratified, the farthingale at once became the darling of court costume, and in its original shape continued in feminine favor till the reign of Queen Anne, when it underwent the modification lately revived for us—the Hoop. In vain did the spectator lash and ridicule by turns the "unnatural disguisement;" in vain did grossest caricatures appear and wits exhaust their invention in lampoons and current epigrams; in vain even the publication of a grave pamphlet, entitled *The Enormous Abomination of the Hoop Petticoat, as the Fashion now is;* the mode, for once immutable, stands on the page of folly an enduring monument of feminine persistency.

Encouraged by the prolonged and undisputed sway of the farthingale, the hoop maintained an absolute supremacy through the three succeeding reigns, though often undergoing changes which only served to make it more and more ridiculous. The most ludicrous of these alterations were the triangular-shaped hoops, which, according to the *Spectator*, gave a lady all the appearance of being in a go-cart; and the "pocket-hoops," which looked like nothing so much as panniers on the side of a donkey—we mean the quadruped. Quite a funny incident is related by Bulwer about the wife of an English ambassador to Constantinople, in the time of James I. The lady, attended by her serving-women, all attired in enormous farthingales, waited upon the sultana, who received them with every show of respect and hospitality. Soon, however, the woman's curiosity got the better of her courtesy, and expressing her great surprise at the monstrous development of their hips, she asked if it were possible that such could be the shape peculiar to the women of England. The English lady in reply hastened to assure her that their forms in nowise differed from those of the women of other countries, and carefully demonstrated to her Highness the construction of their dress, which alone bestowed the appearance so puzzling to her. There could scarcely be a more wholesome satire upon the absurd fashion than is conveyed in the simple recital of this well-authenticated anecdote.

It will be readily understood that at the outset the English ladies had a plausible excuse for adopting this deformity; if they were betrayed into the permanent establishment of it by the very pardonable inducement of a gratified vanity, we may pity their weakness but can scarcely condemn; and in the proud reign of the hoops through a period of unsparing ridicule we are quite forced to admire the unflinching tenacity with which they were adhered to, much as we may deplore the perverted taste which could at any time have consented to their introduction. But what excuse can be offered, what palliating circumstance advanced, to justify a revival of that abomination by the ladies of the nineteenth century—not betrayed into its adoption on the score of novelty, but deliberately dragging it out from the dusty past with all the accumulated ridicule of ages clinging to its skirts ?*

In the early ages of Christianity, gloves were a part of monastic custom, and, in later periods, formed a part of the episcopal habit. The glove was employed by princes as a token of investiture ; and to deprive a person of his gloves was a mark of divesting him of his office. Throwing down a glove constituted a challenge, and the taking it up an acceptance.

Fans have become, in many countries, so necessary an appendage of the toilet with both sexes, that a word respecting them in this place, seems demanded. The use of them was first discovered in the East, where the heat suggested their utility. In the Greek Church, a fan is placed in the hands of the deacons, in the ceremony of their ordination, in allusion to a part of their office in that church, which is to keep the flies off the priests during the celebration of the sacrament. In Japan, where neither men nor women wear hats, except as a protection against rain, a fan is to be seen in the hand or the girdle of every inhabitant. Visitors receive dainties offered them upon their fans : the beggar, imploring charity, holds out his fan for the alms his prayers may obtain. In England, this seemingly indispensable article was almost unknown till the age of Elizabeth. During the reign of Charles II. they became pretty generally used. At the present day, they are in universal requisition. Hats and bonnets are of remote antiquity : it is difficult to say when they took their rise. Of boots, and shoes—those coverings for the extremities—we do not feel in the humor to discourse, since everybody knows sufficient about them, by practical experience, nor are they subject to so many absurd changes and metamorphoses. Of perfumeries, also, little need be said ; they were always, like flowers, artificial and real, favorites with the fair, as they ever should be, notwithstanding we learn that scents and odors are

* New York Tribune.

out of fashion. An old poet thus quaintly chants some good advice suited to all :—

"Ye who would save your features florid,
Lithe limbs, bright eyes, unwrinkled forehead,
From age's devastation horrid,
Adopt this plan—
'Twill make, in climates cold or torrid,
A hale old man:

"Avoid in youth, luxurious diet;
Restrain the passions' lawless riot;
Devoted to domestic quiet,
Be wisely gay;
So shall ye, spite of age's fiat,
Resist decay.

"Seek not, in Mammon's worship, pleasure,
But find your richest, dearest treasure
In books, friends, music, polished leisure;
The mind, not sense,
Make the sole scale by which ye measure
Your opulence.

"This is the solace, this the science,
Life's purest, sweetest, best appliance,
That disappoints not man's reliance,
Whate'er his state;
But challenges, with calm defiance,
Time, fortune, fate."

We endorse the foregoing, and commend it to the ladies. Will they accept it as a little advice gratis? It is invidious to point out defects in beings so near perfection, and we cautiously refrain from such audacity, but that notorious punster, *Punch* affirms, "there are several things which you never can by any account get a lady—be she young or old—to confess to." Here are some of them :—"That she laces tight; that her shoes are too small for her; that she is ever tired at a ball; that she paints; that she is as old as she looks; that she has been more than five minutes dressing ; that she has kept you waiting ; that she blushed when a certain person's name was mentioned ; that she ever says a thing she doesn't mean ; that she is fond of scandal ; that she can't keep a secret ; that she—*she* of all persons in the world—is in love ; that she doesn't want a new bonnet ; that she can do with one single thing less when she is about to travel ; that she hasn't the disposition of an angel, or the temper of a saint—or how else could she go through one-half of what she does ? that she doesn't know better than every one else what is best for her ; that she is a flirt or a coquette; that she is ever in the wrong."

A curious correspondent in *Notes and Queries* observes that, notwithstanding the mutations of fashion in England, some old *habits* are still retained with great tenacity. The Thames watermen rejoice in the dress of the age of Elizabeth, while the royal beef-eaters (buffetiers) wear that of private soldiers of the time of Henry VII., the blue-coat boy, the costume of the reign of Edward VI., and the London charity-school girls the plain mob cap and long gloves of the time of Queen Anne. In the brass badge of the cabman we see a retention of a dress of Elizabethan retainers, while the shoulder-knots that once decked an officer now adorn a footman. The attire of a sailor of William the Third's era is now seen among our fishermen. The university dress is as old as the age of the Smithfield martyrs. The linen bands of the pulpit and the bar are abridgments of the falling collar.

We find some interesting historic anecdotes illustrative of our subject in an English magazine :*

" Shoes with very long points, full two feet in length, were invented by Henry Plantagenet, Duke of Anjou, to conceal an excrescence on one of his feet.

" Others, on the contrary, adopted fashions to set off their peculiar beauties—as Isabella of Bavaria, remarkable for her

* Eliza Cook's Journal.

gallantry and the fairness of her complexion, who introduced the fashion of leaving the shoulders and part of the neck uncovered.

"In the year 1735 the men had no hats, but a little *chapeau de bras;* in 1745, they wore a very small hat; yet in 1725 they wore an enormous one, as may be seen in Jeffrey's *Curious Collection of Habits in all Nations.* Old Puttenham, in his very rare work, *The Art of Poesie,* gives some curious information: 'Henry VIII. caused his own head, and all his courtiers,' to be polled, and his beard to be cut short; before that time, it was thought more decent both for old men and young to be all shaven, and 'weare long haire, either rounded or square. Now again at this time (Elizabeth's reign) the young gentlemen of the court have taken up their long haire trayling on their shoulders, and think this more deacent; for what respect I would be glad to know.'

"It is observed by the lively Vigneul de Marville that there are flagrant follies in fashion which must be endured while they reign; and which never appear ridiculous till they are out of fashion. In the reign of Henry III. of France, they could not exist without an abundant use of comfits. All the world, the grave and the gay, carried in their pockets a *comfit-box,* as we do snuff-boxes. They used them even on the most solemn occasions. When the Duke of Guise was shot at Blois he was found with the comfit-box in his hand.

"A shameful extravagance in dress has been a most venerable folly. In the reign of Richard II., the dress was sumptuous beyond belief. Sir John Arundel had a change of no less than fifty-two new suits of cloth of gold tissue. Brantome records of Elizabeth, Queen of Philip II. of Spain, that she never wore a gown twice."

It cannot be denied that the votaries of fashion too often starve their happiness to feed their vanity and pride.

A passion for dress is nothing new; an old satirist thus lampoons the ladies of his day:

"What is the reason—can you guess,
Why men are poor, and women thinner?
So much do they for dinner dress,
That nothing's left to dress for dinner."

It is not women alone that evince a proclivity in this direction; there are as many coxcombs in the world as coquettes. The folly is more reprehensible in the former instance than the latter, because it has even less show of excuse. If Nature, according to Anacreon, has given to woman the empire of beauty, it is right that she should be allowed all the requisite accessories for its fit illustration.

Old Burton has a quaint tirade, as verbose as it is scurrilous: "Why do women array themselves in such fantastical dresses and quaint devices—with gold, with silver, with coronets, pendants, bracelets, earrings, chains, guales, rings, pins, spangles, embroideries, shadows, rebatoes, versi-color ribands, feathers, fans, masks, furs, laces, tiffanies, ruffs, falls, calls, cuffs, damasks, velvets, tassels, golden-cloth, silver-tissue, precious stones, stars, flowers, birds, beasts, fishes, crisped locks, wigs, painted faces, bodkins, setting-sticks, cork, whalebone, sweet odors, and whatsoever else Africa, Asia, and America can produce; flaying their faces to produce the fresher complexion of a new skin, and using more time in dressing than Cæsar took in marshalling his army; but that, like cunning falconers, they wish to spread false lures to catch unwary larks, and lead, by their gaudy baits and meretricious charms, the minds of inexperienced youths into the traps of love?"

Leigh Hunt says: "Beauty too often sacrifices to fashion. The spirit of fashion is not the beautiful, but the willful; not the graceful, but the fantastic; not the superior in the abstract, but the superior in the worst of all concretes—the vulgar. It is the vulgarity that can afford to shift and vary itself, opposed to the vulgarity that longs to do so, but cannot. The high point of taste and elegance is to be sought for, not in the most fashionable circles, but in the best bred, and such as can dispense with the eternal necessity of never being the same thing."

The mere devotees of Fashion have been defined as a class of would-be-refined people, perpetually struggling in a race to escape from the fancied vulgar. Neatness in our costume is needful to our self-respect; a person thinks better of himself when neatly clad, and others form a similar estimate of him. It has been quaintly said that "A coat is a letter of credit written with a needle upon broadcloth."

Character is indexed by costume. First impressions are thus formed, which are not easily obliterated. Taste and neatness in dress distinguish the refined from the vulgar. Persons of rude feelings are usually roughly attired; they evince none of the grace and delicacy of the cultivated in intellect, morals, and manners.

Vanity, like laudanum, and other poisonous medicines, is beneficial in small, though injurious in large quantities. No man, who is not pleased with himself, even in a personal sense, can please others, for it is the belief of his own grace that makes him graceful and gracious. If it be a recommendation to dress our minds to the best advantage, and to render ourselves as agreeable as possible, why should it be an objection to bestow the same pains upon personal appearance?

Girard, the famous French painter, when very young, was the bearer of a letter of introduction to Lanjuinais, then of the Council of Napoleon. The young painter was shabbily attired, and his reception was extremely cold; but Lanjuinais discovered in him such striking proofs of talent, good sense, and amiability, that on Girard's rising to take leave, he rose too, and accompanied his visitor to the ante-chamber. The change was so striking that Girard could not avoid an expression of surprise. "My young friend," said Lanjuinais, anticipating the inquiry, "we receive an unknown person according to his dress—we take leave of him according to his merit."

Ben Jonson, in one of his plays, expresses the same opinion :

> "Believe it, sir,
> That clothes do much upon the wit, as weather
> Does on the brain ; and thence, sir, comes your proverb,
> The tailor makes the man."

One of our greatest historians says : " Dress is characteristic of manners, and manners are the mirror of ideas."

A writer in a recent periodical also remarks : " Tailors must live ; at least they think so, and we have no objection. Yet they are great tyrants, and have ingenious ways of torturing their victims. One way is this : they invent a fashion which is strikingly peculiar, and get it into vogue by various arts best known to themselves ; for example, very short overcoats, with long waists, which look well on men whose figure is faultless. The next movement, after everybody is overcoated for the winter, is to bring out a garment which differs as much as possible from the one in fashion ; that is, an overcoat with skirts to the heels, and waist under the armpits. They get half a dozen men of high fashion, who look well in anything, to parade this new invention, and make the short-coated majority appear out of date. The manœuvre succeeds ; all the dandies are driven to the extravagance of ordering a superfluous coat ; the tailors smile, and the dandies bleed, or their fathers do.

Old coats are essential to the ease of the body and mind ; and some of the greatest achievements of men have been executed when the owners were in rags. Napoleon wore an old, seedy coat during the whole of the Russian campaign ; and Wellington wore one out at the elbow at Waterloo. Poets are proverbial for a *penchant* for seedy garments.

A hat is the symbol and characteristic of its wearer. It is a sign and token of his avocation, habits, and opinions—the creature of his phantasy. Minerva-like, it bursts forth in full maturity from his brain. Extravagance, pride, cold-heartedness, and vulgarity, with many other of the ruling passions, may be detected by its form and fashion. One may ascertain whether a man is whimsical, grotesque, or venially flexible in his taste, by this test. Much may be deduced from the style in which it is worn.

Beau Brummell's wardrobe cost him £8,000 a-year. In his simple elegance, he eclipsed his successor, Count D'Orsay. His great rival was the Prince of Wales (afterwards George IV.), whose wardrobe cost £100,000 a year.

Beau Nash was another mirror of fashion and foppery. No wonder that men of mind are found disdainful of their personal attire when their sense of propriety is startled by such absurd caricatures of the species being held at a premium solely for their clothes.

The celebrated poet and professor, Buschin, who was very careless in his dress, went out in his dressing-gown, and met in the street a citizen with whom he was acquainted. The gentleman, however, passed him, without even raising his hat. Divining the cause, the poet hastened home, and put on a cloak of velvet and ermine, in which he again went out, and contrived once more to meet the same citizen, who this time raised his hat, and bowed profoundly. This made the poet still more angry, when he saw that his velvet cloak claimed more respect than his professorship and poetical fame. He hastened home, threw his cloak on the floor, and stamped on it, saying—" Art thou Buschin, or am I ?"

A curious instance of the importance of dress occurred at Paris a short time since—we refer to the exclusion of the celebrated Chateaubriand from the *Académie Française*, in consequence of his wearing a frock-coat. In some cases, as in this, the man is of less consequence than his coat.

An American writer describes the fop as "a complete specimen of an outside philosopher. He is one-third collar, one-sixth patent leather, one-fourth walking stick, and the remainder gloves and hair. As to remote ancestry, there is some doubt, but it is now pretty well settled that he is the son of a tailor's goose. He becomes ecstatic at the smell of new cloth. He is somewhat nervous, and to dream of a tailor's bill gives him the nightmare. By his hair, one would judge he was dipped like Achilles, but it is evident that the goddess held him by the head instead of the heels. Nevertheless, such men are useful. If there were no tadpoles there would be no frogs. They are not entirely to blame for being so devoted to externals. Paste diamonds must have a splendid setting to make them sell. Only it does seem a waste of material to put five dollars' worth of beaver on five cents' worth of brains."

Byron designates fops as,

> "Ambiguous things, that ape
> Goats in their visage, women in their shape."

Our modern beaux mimic the Germans in covering their faces as much as possible, as if they felt the necessity of some disguise for the want of expression.

It is a well-known fact that ladies seldom become grey, while the heads of the "lords of creation" are often early in life either bald or grey—sometimes both. Douglas Jerrold tells a piquant joke as follows: "At a private party in London, a lady—who, though in the autumn of life, had not lost all dreams of its spring—said to Jerrold—'I cannot imagine what makes my hair turn grey; I sometimes fancy it must be the "essence of rosemary" with which my maid is in the habit of brushing it.' 'I should rather be afraid, madam,' replied the dramatist, 'that it is the essence of Time' (thyme)."

> "What is life—the flourishing array
> Of the proud summer meadow which to-day
> Wears her green flush, and is to-morrow hay."

Compared with earlier times, with some slight exceptions, our modern costume certainly has the preëminence: it has been said that to this cause is to be attributed the seeming absence, in our day, of any transcendent instances of remarkable beauty in the fair sex : all may be *made up* attractively where even nature has been niggard of her endowments. Dress confers dignity and self-satisfaction, besides possessing the advantage of attractiveness. We are startled to hear a man well attired use vulgar speech, but our amazement is materially lessened if the party be attached to a very menial employment and is enveloped in meaner clothes. Over-fastidiousness at the toilet is, nevertheless, an evil equally to be deprecated : a fop is as much to be despised as a slattern or shrew—both are obnoxious to good breeding and good taste.

The attributes of personal beauty may be reduced to four : color, form, expression, and grace. Colors please by opposition, and it is in the face that they are most diversified and exposed. Thus contrasts are essential, and sallow complexions should be set off by dark cravats and clothing ; whilst fairer features may adopt lighter hues—Beauty of form includes the symmetry of the whole body, even to the turn of the eyebrow or the graceful flow of the hair. Hence the perfect union and harmony of all parts of the body is the source and general cause of beauty ; and whilst the peculiar attraction of the female form should be softness and delicacy, that of manly beauty should be apparent strength and agility. Expression may be considered as the effect of the passions on the muscles of the countenance, and the different gestures. The finest combination is a just mixture of modesty and sensibility. Indeed, all the benign affections—such as love, hope, joy, and pity—add to beauty ; while the predominance of hatred, fear, or envy, in the mind, deforms or injures the countenance. Grace is the noblest part of beauty.

An anonymous writer thus apostrophizes beauty : "There is something in beauty, whether it dwells in the human face, in the pencilled leaves of flowers, the sparkling surface of the fountain, that makes us mourn its ruin. I should not envy that man his feelings who could see a leaf wither, or a flower fall, without a slight tribute of regret."

"Oh, human beauty is a sight
To sadden rather than delight,
Being the prelude of a lay,
Whose burden is decay."

Prompted by their loyalty to woman, we find the poets have ever made her charms the inspiring theme of their muse; not however, in the realm of song merely has she been celebrated; sober writers in prose have been scarcely less enthusiastic in their laudations. Jeremy Taylor styles woman "the precious porcelain of human clay." Not only is she potent in physical endowment—hers is the more enduring excellence of moral beauty, for her heart is the home of the virtues; and while the fascinations of her personal beauty captivate the sense, our grateful love and veneration do willing homage to her moral excellence and worth. While, therefore, with one who felt the mystic power of her bewildering charms, we exclaim—

"Denied the smile from partial beauty won,
Oh, what were man—a world without a sun!"

We yet instinctively yield to the still more potent influence of her enduring love, her patient faith, and the nameless clusters of graces which constitute her moral beauty.

It was a pertinent and forcible saying of the Emperor Napoleon that "a handsome woman pleases the eye, but a good woman pleases the heart. The one is a jewel, and the other a treasure."

A contemporary poet* has epitomized it all in two flowing stanzas:

"What's a fair or noble face,
If the mind ignoble be?
What though Beauty, in each grace,
May her own resemblance see!

* Charles Swain.

Eyes may catch from heaven their spell,
  Lips the ruby's light recall;
In the Home for Love to dwell
  One good feeling's worth them all.

"Give me Virtue's rose to trace,
  Honor's kindling glance and mien,
Howsoever plain the face,
  Beauty is where these are seen!
Raven ringlets o'er the snow
  Of the whitest neck may fall;
In the Home for love we know
  One good feeling's worth them all!"

Beauty being the theme with which our chapter commenced, it should also conclude it. We sum up the case then, as legal gentlemen have it, in the words of an American poetess :—

"Thou wert a worship in the ages olden,
  Thou bright-veiled image of divinity,
Crowned with such gleams, imperial and golden,
  As Phidias gave to immortality!
A type exquisite of the pure Ideal,
  Forth shadowed in perfect loveliness—
Embodied and existent in the Real,
  A perfect shape to kneel before and bless."*

* Mrs. Eames.

THE MYSTERIES OF MEDICINE.

"If physic be a trade, it is a trade of all others the most exactly cut out for a rogue." —*Lacon.*

"Man is a dupable animal. Quacks in medicine, quacks in religion, and quacks in politics know this, and act upon that knowledge. There is scarcely any one who may not, like a trout, be taken by tickling."—*Southey.*

WORTHY Sir Thomas Browne has nobly sought to dignify the medical profession, and it would be undignified in us to attempt to impeach his excellent judgment. There are, however, sundry phases of the Faculty that present points of humor and eccentricity so irresistibly amusing that to indulge a little merriment over them cannot but prove an innocent pastime. There is fun enough in "love, law, and physic," if we seek it out. Any one with an eye for the ludicrous will not need any specifications in point. Much that is farcical in physic is, by the law of electric affinities, transferred to the physician himself.

Judging by the latitudinarianism of some practitioners, and the absurd nostrums of empirics and quacks, in all ages, it has been gravely asked, whether doctors are really not the final cause of disease. It is not, of course, to be disputed, that they have been, to no inconsiderable extent, accessory both to the reduction of disease and—of life itself. But for the inherent tendency of mankind to blind credulity and superstition, it may be doubted whether the profession of medicine would ever have been made the vehicle of such gross absurdities and cunning impostures, as its past, and especially its earlier history reveals. We are not about, however, to cast any imputation upon the science of therapeutics; our purpose being to glance at some of the wild and monstrous follies which have so long disputed its claims to the suffrages of society. Medical practice has been defined to be, for the most part, guessing at Nature's intentions and wishes, and then endeavoring to substitute man's. Medication is *not* the most essential element of cure.

Disease is self-limited. Its tendency, in nineteen out of twenty cases, is toward recovery; and that, uninfluenced as to the ultimate result of death or recovery (more or less complete) by any medical interference; unless, indeed, the latter should be murderously severe.

"Nature," says a French philosophical writer, "is fighting with disease; a blind man armed with a club—that is, the physician—comes to settle the difference. He first tries to make peace; when he cannot accomplish this, he lifts his club and strikes at random. If he strikes the disease, he kills the disease; if he strikes nature, he kills the patient." And to prove, from one who himself turned state's evidence on this point—D'Alembert relates that an individual, after conducting a prominent practice for thirty years, confessed, as his reason for retiring from it, that he was weary of *guessing!* An industrious nosologist has estimated that there are about twenty-four hundred disorders incident to the human frame!

Possibly our great dramatist was not aware to what numerical extent reached "the ills that flesh is heir to," or he would scarcely have so disparagingly suggested that we should "throw physic to the dogs." Or it may be because there is, according to *Punch*, "an evident affinity between physic and the dogs—a fact that shows the master mind of Shakspeare in suggesting the throwing of the former to the latter; for it is clear that every medicine, like every dog, has its day. Pills have had their popularity, and elixirs have had their run. Lozenges have taken their turn on the wheel of fortune, and even pastes have been stuck to for a time by crowds of adherents."

Napoleon once said to one of his physicians (Dr. Antommarchi), "Believe me, we had better leave off all these remedies—life is a fortress that neither you nor I know anything about. Why throw obstacles in the way of its defence? Its own means are superior to all the apparatus of your laboratories. Medicine is a collection of uncertain prescriptions, the results of which, taken collectively, are more fatal than useful to mankind."

The celebrated Zimmerman went from Hanover to attend Frederick the Great, in his last illness. One day the king said to him, "You have, I presume, sir, helped many a man into another world?" This was rather a bitter pill for the doctor; but the dose he gave the king in return was a judicious mixture of truth and flattery: "Not so many as your majesty, nor with so much honor to myself." Colman says, "the medical and military both deal in death;" and if true, that two of a trade never agree, it may be the emperor was jealous of his reputation.

The death of Pope Adrian occasioned such joy at Rome, that the night after his decease *they adorned the door of his chief physician's house with garlands*, adding this inscription—"To the deliverer of his country."

Said an old dramatist—

"These, sir,
Are Death's masters of the ceremonies;
More strangely-clad officials never yet
Ushered the way to Death's cold festival."

A contemporary observes : "The world is peopled by two classes of beings, who seem to be as cognate and necessary to each other as male and female. Charlatans and dupes exist by a mutual dependence. There is a tacit understanding, that whatever the one invents the other must believe. All bills which the former draws, the latter comes forward at once and honors. One is Prospero, the other his poor slave Caliban. The charlatan tricks himself out in a mask, assumes a deep, hollow voice, and struts upon the stage, while the dupe sits gaping in the pit, and takes every word that drops from the rogue's mouth for gospel-truth and genuine philosophy. It would really seem as if the two parties had entered into a solemn compact, that wherever the one exhibited as charlatan, the other, by an absolute necessity, agrees to be present as simpleton. Let the rogue open shop to dispense pills, the simpleton, as soon as he learns the fact, hies to the place of trade, and, pouring down his pence on the counter, takes his box of specifics, and walks complacently away. The knaves seem to consider the world as a rich parish—a large diocese of dunces, into which they have an hereditary and prescriptive right to be installed. They are never at rest until they have some subject on which to hold forth in public ; some novel doctrine running against the grain of the old good sense ; some antiquated sophism dressed in a new suit, to be put forth to surprise and startle the community, and gather around it (as a gay adventurer) an army of disciples. These men constantly assume an attitude of battle."

Addison, who surrounded himself with all the accessories of fortune, seems to have had a depreciating estimate of the Faculty. These are his words : "If we look into the profession of physic, we shall find a most formidable body of men ; the sight of them is enough to make a man serious, for we may lay it down as a maxim that when a nation abounds in physicians, it grows thin of people." This body of men he compares to the British army in Cæsar's time—some of them slay in chariots, and some on foot. If the infantry do less execution than the charioteers, it is because they cannot be carried so soon into all quarters, and dispatch so much business in so short a time. "Besides this body of regular troops," he adds, "there are stragglers, who, without being duly enlisted and enrolled, do infinite mischief to those who are so unlucky as to fall into their hands."

Doctors have by some been called a class of men who live on the misfortunes of their fellow-creatures; by others, the alleviators of life's miseries. Perhaps both are true, depending upon the variety.

Empirics and charlatans are the excrescences of the medical profession; they have obtained in all ages as well as in the present. The "healing art" is not necessarily the occasion for deception, nor the operations of witchcraft, charms, amulets, astrology, necromancy, alchemy, and magic, although it has its mysteries like other branches of occult science. Although the progress of the Materia Medica, in our times, is less impeded by superstition and blind obedience to the axioms of the ancients, still much remains to be achieved before our pharmacopœias will be found to exhibit the certain processes or specifics of ascertained value, by the adoption of those substances only whose effects upon the tissues of the human body are thoroughly understood. Said Dr. Abercrombie, "the uncertainty of medicine—which is thus a theme both for the philosopher and the humorist—is deeply felt by the practical physician in the daily exercise of his art. The uncertainty of medicine resolves itself chiefly into an apparent want of that uniformity of phenomena, which is so remarkable in other branches of physical science. These apparent discrepancies regard the characteristics and progress of disorder, and the action of external agents upon the body—the diagnosis of disease, and its true antidote. It is an admitted fact, that with all the accumulative experience of the past, no certain, infallible data have yet been established for ascertaining the characters or external indications of certain internal diseases, as distinguished from those of others—so many exhibiting appearances in common." It has been asserted, that those persons, generally, are most confident in regard to the character of disease whose knowledge is most limited ; and that more extended observation induces doubt and indecision. If such uncertainty attends the diagnosis of disease, it will not be denied that at least an equal degree of incertitude must interfere in the application of remedial agents. To cite an illustration from the authority already referred to, we may state the various modes by which internal inflammation terminates—as resolution, suppuration, gangrene, adhesion, and effusion ; but, in regard to any particular case of inflammation, how little notion can be formed of what will be its progress, or how it will terminate. An equal, or even a more remarkable uncertainty attends all our researches on the action of external agents upon the body—as causes of disease, and as remedies ; and in both cases their action is fraught with the highest degree of uncertainty. The great difficulty in medicine seems to consist in the tracing effects to their true causes, and *vice versa.*

In justice to the many illustrious benefactors of their age, we must not forget that, although the profession has been disgraced by empirics and quacks, a host of great names have ennobled it by their virtues, their brilliant attainments and services, as well as their self-denial. If Hippocrates be regarded as the father of physic, science was then in its infancy, and it is to the collective wisdom and experience of his successors that it owes all its present glory and renown. Such men have been indeed blessings to their age, and to the world at large ; and the fragrant memory of their benevolence and skill, would, of course, go far to redeem the profession they ennobled from the rebuke of charlatanism. It is to such men as Harvey, Garth, Radcliffe, Meade, Askew, Pitcairn, Baillie, Cullen, Freind, Linacre, Cains, Hunter, Denman, Velpeau, Liston, Mott, and

Brocklesby, the friend of Johnson, with many others of refined literary attainments, that it owes much of its glory.

Pope, a few days prior to his decease, records the following high testimony to the urbanity and courtesy of his medical friends—"There is no end of my kind treatment from the Faculty; they are in general the most amiable companions, and the best friends, as well as the most learned men I know." And Dryden, in the postscript to his translation of Virgil, speaks in a similar way of the profession. "That I have recovered," says he, "in some measure the health which I had lost by too much application to this work, is owing, next to God's mercy, to the skill and care of Dr. Guibbons and Dr. Hobbs, the two ornaments of their profession, whom I can only pay by this acknowledgment."

It will be remembered possibly, and it is a somewhat curious fact to commence with, that we have an instance on record of David in his youth, with his harp, striving by the aid of music to cure the mental derangement of Saul; a method of cure in those early times which seems to have been commonly resorted to. Many of the classic writers allude to the practice; some even proposing it as a certain remedy for a dislocated limb, the gout, or even the bite of a viper. The medicinal properties of music were manifold and marvellous. For example: a fever was removed by a song; deafness, by a trumpet; and the pestilence chased away by the harmonious lyre! That deaf people can hear best in a great noise, is a fact alleged by some moderns in favor of the ancient mode of removing deafness by the trumpet.

The healing art is not without its heroes. Madame de Genlis relates the story of one who, to save his native city from the ravages of the plague, voluntarily surrendered himself a sacrifice. The incident is as follows: "The plague raged violently in Marseilles. Every link of affection was broken; the father turned from the child, the child from the father; ingratitude no longer excited indignation. Misery is at its height when it thus destroys every generous feeling, thus dissolves every tie of humanity! The city became a desert, grass grew in the streets, a funeral met you at every step. The physicians assembled in a body at the *Hotel de Ville*, to hold a consultation on the fearful disease, for which no remedy had yet been discovered. After a long deliberation, they decided unanimously that the malady had a peculiar and mysterious character, which opening a corpse alone might develop—an operation it was impossible to attempt, since the operator must infallibly become a victim in a few hours, beyond the power of human art to save him, as the violence of the attack would preclude their administering the customary remedies. A dead pause succeeded this fatal declaration. Suddenly a surgeon named Guyon, in the prime of life, and of great celebrity in his profession, rose, and said firmly, "Be it so: I devote myself for the safety of my country. Before this numerous assembly I swear, in the name of humanity and religion, that to-morrow, at the break of day, I will dissect a corpse, and write down as I proceed what I observe." He left the assembly instantly. They admire him, lament his fate, and doubt whether he will persist in his design. The intrepid and pious Guyon, animated by all the sublime energy religion can inspire, acted up to his words. He had never married, he was rich, and he immediately made a will, dictated by justice and piety; he confessed, and in the middle of the night received the sacraments. A man had died of the plague in his house within four-and-twenty hours; Guyon, at day-break, shut himself up in the same room; he took with him an inkstand, paper, and a little crucifix. Full of enthusiasm, never had he felt more firm or more collected: kneeling before the corpse, he wrote, 'Mouldering remains of an immortal soul, not only can I gaze on thee without horror, but even with joy and gratitude. Thou wilt open to me the gates of a glorious eternity. In discovering to me the secret cause of the terrible disease which destroys my native city, thou wilt enable me to point out some salutary remedy—

thou wilt render my sacrifice useful. Oh, God! thou wilt bless the action thou hast thyself inspired.' He began—he finished the dreadful operation, and recorded in detail his surgical observations. He then left the room, threw the papers into a vase of vinegar, and afterwards sought the lazaretto, where he died in twelve hours—a death ten thousand times more glorious than the warrior's, who, to save his country, rushes on the enemy's ranks, since he advances, with hope at least, sustained, admired, and seconded, by a whole army." This was an instance of heroic self-devotion perhaps unparalleled. But to resume our subject:

"Dr. Willis tells us," says Burney, in his *History of Music*, "of a lady who could *hear only while a drum was beating;* insomuch that her husband actually hired a drummer, as a servant, in order to enjoy the pleasure of her conversation." A certain Frenchman, Vigneul de Marville, insists that musical sounds contribute to the health of the body and the mind, assist the circulation of the blood, dissipate vapors, and open the vessels, so that the action of perspiration is freer. He tells a story of a person of distinction, who assured him, that once, being suddenly seized by violent illness, instead of a consultation of physicians, he immediately called a band of musicians, and their violins played so well in his inside, "that his bowels became perfectly *in tune*, and in a few hours were completely becalmed." Naturalists assert that animals are sensible to the charms of the divine art; why not the biped, man? The well-known line will occur to the reader,

> "Music hath charms to soothe the savage breast;"

and the great dramatist predicates moral delinquency where the effects of its dulcet influence is not acknowledged—

> "The man that hath no music in himself,
> Nor is not moved with concord of sweet sounds,
> Is fit for treasons, stratagems, and spoils."

A little plaintive, soothing melody after dinner has long

been resorted to as an auxiliary to the digestive process ; the effect is to induce a temporary state of mental quiescence and repose, while it confers all the advantages of sleep with none of its disadvantages. It is putting the soul in tune, as Milton expresses it, for any subsequent exertion.

Medical lore would not probably have been so far behind the other sciences, had its professors but husbanded, in a collective form, the experience of the past, as has been the case, for example, in the art of navigation. To begin with Galen, as a starting point, it will be sufficient to remark, that he reprobated such prescriptions as were composed of any portions of the human body ; and he severely condemned Xenocrates for having introduced them, as being worse than useless, as well as being positively unjustifiable. Yet these abominable ingredients continued in use till what may be styled the reformation of medicine in the seventeenth century. Human bones were administered internally as a cure for ulcers, and the bones were to be those of the part affected. A preparation called *aqua divina* was made by cutting in pieces the body of a healthy man who had died a violent death, and distilling it.

The mummery of early medicine, with all its cabalistic and unintelligible mysticisms, formed a part of the age which sanctioned such buffoonery. The state of medicine may be considered as the criterion or barometer of the state of morals, as well as science in a nation. This is evidenced by the miserable condition of the science in Europe so late as the tenth century, when there was scarcely a physician in Spain.

The Jews are the first people on record who practised the art of healing, which they probably learned from the Egyptians ; but the Greeks, who worshipped Æsculapius as the god of medicine, first reduced that art to a regular system. Hippocrates is justly considered as the father of physic, being the most ancient author whose writings on that subject are preserved. The most celebrated physicians who succeeded him were Asclepiades, Celsus, and Galen.

After the subversion of the Roman Empire the arts and sciences were totally eclipsed by the barbarous manners of the Europeans, and medicine was translocated to the peaceful regions of Arabia. Before the crusades, several Hebrew, Arabian, and Latin professors of physic settled at Salernum, where Charles the Great founded a college for their reception in the year 802.

The first distinguished quack we find mentioned in medical annals, and who may therefore be styled the prototype of his illustrious successors, rejoiced in the classic name of Asclepiades. His eccentricity and affected contempt of everything in the way of medical lore, that existed prior to his advent at Rome, gave him some considerable notoriety. With all his irregularities and whims, however, he certainly inculcated some good plain common sense. He was the originator of the *Balinea pensilis*, or shower-bath, and the free application of cold water, externally and internally—cheap remedies, and very effective in the cure and prevention of disease; for which discovery alone his memory will live.

Paracelsus was the prince of quacks. In order to give himself dignity, he assumed the names of Philippus, Aureolus, Theophrastes, Paracelsus, Bombastes de Hobenheim. He openly discarded all the commonly-received doctrines and modes of practice, and pretended to have sought for truth many years everywhere and from every body, high and low, learned and illiterate. He made a pompous proclamation of his travels and researches, and pretended to have made great acquisitions in medical science. He styled himself the king of physic, and although he professed to have discovered the elixir of life, he yet died at the age of 48 years.

The commencement of the sixteenth century was rendered memorable by the introduction of chemistry into medicine. Paracelsus endeavored to explain the art of healing on chemical principles at once fanciful and illusory.

A high degree of dignity has been ever claimed for the

medical profession, as mediating between life and death ; some even supposing it to have been of divine origin, from the passage in *Ecclesiasticus:* "For the Lord hath created medicines out of the earth, and he that is wise will not abhor them." Some of the Floridian tribes, as we learn from Southey's *Doctor*, had so high an opinion of medical virtue, that they buried all their dead except their doctors ; them they *burnt*, reduced their bones to powder, and drank the same in water—a delicious decoction for a delicate stomach ! Old astrologers, and the like fraternity, with their mathematical marks and zodaical signs, sought to invest their craft with a mysterious sanctity. Boasting its origin and authority to be heaven-derived, with its blazonry of factitious distinction, would it be suspected, after all, the curative art is to be traced even to the instinct of the brutes? For example, the sagacious dog, when indisposed, may be seen to enact himself the doctor, by a resort to the fields to eat a quantity of prickly grass—an expedient which seldom fails of success, by acting as an emetic. The same with the cat, when she finds herself "a little under the weather," forthwith she sneaks off for some *catnip*. There is a story related of an Arabian shepherd, who, having observed the goats of his flock, as often as they browsed upon the coffee-fruit, to skip about and exhibit signs of intoxication, tasting the berry himself, tested the fact. The apes of Abyssinia, in the same way, indicated to their superior masters the laxative qualities of the *cassia fistula*. One might almost suppose, therefore, a necessity for the resorting to sorcery, witchcraft, stichomancy, and other mysterious agencies, in order to disguise the humble sources of some elementary branches of our famed medical lore. Egypt, India, and Palestine, seem to have been blessed with no small supply of the erudite in these matters ; such as pneumatologists, exorcists, magicians, thaumaturgists, and enchanters. These magi combined, with their exercise of the healing art for the body, the power of curing psychological maladies, and with such an extensive variety of practice, these ancient sages must have made a tolerable good thing of it. In Greece and Rome, sorcery and its kindred arts were extensively resorted to; and even till recent times such incantations were practised in some of the most polished countries of Europe.

It is not surprising that men in early ages of civilization should ascribe the curative art to the potency of some unseen and supernatural agency, since the diseases incident to the human family were supposed to be the result of the ire of the heathen deities. Magic, remarks one of the classic writers, was the offspring of medicine, and after having fortified itself with the help of astrology, borrowed all its splendor and authority from religion. It is seldom now that we find the two professions combined—the cure of the body with that of the soul; but in former ages they seem to have been intimately allied: so much so, indeed, that the early fathers of medicine were accounted worthy of deification. Amulets and charms, and consecrated relics, so rife in superstitious times, served to test the credulity and ignorant subjection of the popular mind. Different kinds of materials were used by different people, but all agreed as to their faith in their efficacy, as preventives against infection or disease, as well as their potency for the removal of maladies. The ignorant, however, were not alone liable to become the victims of the pleasing delusion, for we have testimony to prove that several of the learned were of this class, and Lord Bacon among the number.

Speaking of charms, we might mention the case of a silly old woman, who, according to Dr. Sigmond, applied for a remedy for an affection of the breast; a prescription was given her, and a few days after, she returned to offer her grateful thanks for the cure it had effected. Would it be believed, that she merely tied said prescription round her neck! It is stated in Timb's *Popular Errors*, that the fourth book of the *Iliad* has often cured intermittent fevers in this way; the strength of the language no less than the warmth of action that pervades this portion of Homer's magnificent poem being such, that it was, on one occasion, *metaphorically* said to be sufficient to cure a sick man of the ague. Some sapient individuals, not comprehending poetic tropes and figures, actually converted this saying into a grave reality.

Pliny speaks of one Chrysippas, reputed a famous practitioner of his day, who gained his notoriety by advocating *cabbages* as the panacea for all complaints! The practice of physic, it must be apparent, is easily susceptible of being made the occasion of cheat and imposture. Abernethy, on being appealed to by a patient on behalf of her fancied indisposition, had the frankness (after taking his guinea fee) to state that her symptoms merely indicated the absence of health and also of disease, and handing her back a shilling, advised her to get a *skipping-rope*, and use it! It is a singular enigma in human nature—that tendency of yielding one's-self to the pleasing delusions of a cheat, even though the deception may be revealed, or at least fairly suspected. Dr. Parr defined the term *quack*, as being applicable to all who, by pompous pretences, mean insinuations, and indirect promises, endeavor to obtain that confidence to which neither education, merit, nor experience entitle them. As long, therefore, as this innate love of the mysterious obtains among men, charlatanism will, to a greater or less degree, exist; and anomalous as it is, often the most cultivated and enthusiastic minds are the readiest victims of the cheat. Walpole says that acute and sensible people are frequently the most easily deceived by quacks. A recent writer, referring to the success which generally attends any daring and impudent imposture, remarks: "If the cheat required ingenuity to detect it, there might be some hope for mankind; but it actually lies concealed in its *very obviousness*."

Physicians were formerly ecclesiastics. A curious instance of preferring the medical to the clerical profession, from the conceit of supposed destiny, is thus related:

"Andrew Rudiger, a physician of Leipsic, took it into his

head to form an anagram on his name; and in the words *Andreas Rudigerus* he found a vocation, namely, '*Arare rus Dei dignus.*' Thereupon he concluded that he was called to the priesthood, and began to study theology. Soon after, he became tutor to the children of the learned Thomasius. This philosopher one day told him that he had much better apply to medicine. Rudiger admitted his inclination to that profession, but stated that the anagram of his name—which he explained to Thomasius—had seemed to him a divine vocation to the priesthood. 'What a simpleton you are!' said Thomasius; 'why, 'tis the very anagram of your name that calls you to medicine. *Rus Dei*—is not that the *burial-ground*? And who ploughs it better than the doctors?' In effect, Rudiger turned doctor, unable to resist the interpretation of his anagram."*

In Egypt, medicine was fettered by absurd regulations. The chief priests confined themselves to the exercise of magic rites and prophecies, which they considered the higher branches of the art, and left the exhibition of remedies to the *pastophori*, or image-bearers. They were compelled to follow implicitly the medical precepts of the sacred records contained in the "hermetical books," a deviation from which was punishable with death. From a superstitious dread of evil, and a desire to penetrate into futurity, arose the mystic divination of Greece and Rome, as well as that of the Druids. This divination assumed the sanctity of a religious ceremony, and thus priests became invested with a supposed supernatural power for the cure of diseases. Thus, magic and medicine were allied with astrology and religion.

Among other delusions, was that of the royal gift of healing. It has been remarked as singular, that, with the vulgar errors exposed by Sir Thomas Browne, in his *Pseudodoxia Epidemica*, there should be no mention made of this; but, from a case related in the *Adenochoïradelogia*, it would seem that this eccentric but able man had himself faith in the touch, inasmuch as

* Athenæum.

he recommended the child of a nonconformist, in Norfolk, who had been long under his care, without receiving benefit, to be taken to the king (Charles II.), then at Bruges. The father having no faith, however, in the efficacy of such intervention, the child was secretly conveyed to the king, and being submitted to the royal touch, was returned, it is said, perfectly healed. The father, upon hearing the result, exclaimed—"Farewell to all dissenters and nonconformists: if God puts such virtue into the king's hand for the healing of my child, I'll serve that God and that king, as long as I live, and with all thankfulness." Sir Thomas Browne was not the only eminent man susceptible of gross delusion: it is less surprising that the illiterate should be duped.

In the reign of Henry VIII. many of the medical practitioners were mere horse-farriers. A distinguished patient, the great Lord Burghley, secretary of state to Queen Elizabeth, was addressed by one Audelay, on a certain occasion, in this wise, "Be of goode comfort, and plucke up a lustie, merrie hearte, and then shall you overcome all diseases: and because it pleased my good Lord Admiral lately to praise my physicke, I have written to you such medicines as I wrote unto him, which I have in my boke of my wyffe's hand, *proved upon herselfe and mee both;* and if I can get anything that may do you any goode, you may be well assured it shall be a joye unto me to get it for you." "A goode medicine for weakness or consumption:—take a pig of nine days olde, and slaye him, and quarter him, and put him in a skillat, with a handfull of spearment, and a handfull of red fennel, a handfull of liverwort, half a handfull of red neap, a handfull of clarge, and nine dates, cleaned, picked, and pared, and a handfull of great raisins, and picke out the stones, and a quarter of an ounce of mace, and two stickes of goode cinnamon, bruised in a mortar, and distill it with a soft fire, and put it in a glass, and set it in the sun nine days, and drinke nine spoonfulls of it at once when you list!" "A compost:—item—take a porpin, otherwise called an English hedge-hog, and quarter him in pieces, and put the said beast in a still, with these ingredients : item—a quart of redde wyne, a pinte of rose-water, a quarter of a pound of sugar—cinnamon and two great raisins." "If there be any manner of disease that you be aggrieved withal, I praye you send me some knowledge thereof, and I doubt not but to send you an approved remedie. Written in haste at Greenwiche, y[e] 9 of May, 1553, by your trewe heartie friende, JOHN of AUDELAY."

In Percy's *Reliques* we are informed as to what was common regarding medical lore in those days, namely, that the healing art was enacted by young princes ; the practice being regarded "as commendable to real manners, it being derived from the earliest times, among all the Gothick and Celtic nations, for women, even of the highest ranke, to exercise the arte of surgerie." Formerly, medical practitioners obtained their licences from the bishops of the diocese in which they resided. Burton, in his *Anatomie of Melancholie,* notices many curious receipes and "Bookes of Physicke." One work, entitled *The Queen's Closet Opened,* containing "divers things necessary to be knowne, collected out of sundrie olde written bookes, and broughte into one order. The several things herein contayned may be seen in the bookes and tables following, written in the yeare of our Lorde God 1610." The work commences with the "thirty-three evil dayes" of the yeare, and a general calendar ; there is a curious medley of rules about the weather, astronomical calculations and prognostications. The first book has this : "A coppye of all such medicines wherewith y[e] noble Countess of Oxenforde, most charitably, in her owne person, did manye greate and notable cures upon poore neighboures." The second book is entitled, "Here beginneth a true coppye of such medicines wherewith Mrs. Johan Ounsteade, daughter unto the worshipfule Mr. John Olliffe, Alderman of London, hath cured and healed manye forlorne and deadlie diseases," &c. A few extracts from the above will show the then state of medical science, as contrasted with that of the present day : "To take away frekels—take the bloude of an hare, annoynte them with it, and it will doe them away." "For a man or woman that hath lost theire speeche—take wormwood, and stampe it, and temper it with water, and strayne it, and with a spoone doe of it into theire mouthes."

The laborious professional study of the matriculated physician is unsought by the quack—he, Pallas-like, all armed from the brain of Jove, rushes into his reckless practice, "encased all over in native brass, from top to toe," but wholly destitute is he of the requisite skill for his office. He knows not even the alphabet of medicine ; yet, defiant of reason and responsibility, his supposed intuitive wit and arrogance prevail. It has been said, however, with truth, that the followers of quacks are the cause of quackery : they are the cause of the numberless homicides that have been committed with such impunity. These are skeptics of the faculty, but idolators of the empiricism. These deluded patients persevere with a pertinacity that is invincible, till they discover, too late, that they have been advancing, as the Irishman said, backwards. As illustrative of the reckless wickedness of these pseudo-doctors, we present the following instances. The Duke de Rohan, while in Switzerland, had occasion to send for a physician—the most famous of the day came to him, styling himself Monsieur Thibaud. "Your face," said the Duke, "seems familiar to me ; pray, where have I seen you before ?" "At Paris, perhaps, my Lord Duke," he replied, "when I had the honor to be farrier to your grace's stables. I have now a great reputation as a physician ; I treat the Swiss as I used to do your horses, and I find, in general, I succeed as well. I must request your grace not to make me known, for if you do, I shall be ruined !" There was a notorious charlatan at Paris, some years ago, named Mantaccini, who, after having squandered his patrimony, sought to retrieve his fortune by turning quack. He started his carriage, and made tours round the country, pompously professing to effect cures of all diseases with a single touch, or a simple look. Failing in this bold essay, he attempted another yet more daring—that of reviving the dead, at will! To remove all doubt, he declared that, in fifteen days, he would go to the churchyard, and restore to life its inhabitants, though buried fifteen years. This declaration excited a general rumor and murmur against the doctor, who, not in the least disconcerted, applied to the magistrate, and requested that he might be put under a guard to prevent his escape, until he should perform his undertaking. The proposition inspired the greatest confidence, and the whole city came to consult the clever empiric, and purchase his *baume de vie*. His consultations were most numerous; and he received large sums of money. At length, the noted day approached, and the doctor's valet, fearing for his shoulders, began to manifest signs of uneasiness. "You know nothing of mankind," said the quack to his servant; "be quiet." Scarcely had he spoken the words, when the following letter was presented to him from a rich citizen: "Sir, the great operation you are about to perform has broken my rest. I have a wife buried for some time, who was a fury, and I am unhappy enough already, without her resurrection. In the name of heaven, do not make the experiment. I will give you fifty louis to keep your secret to yourself." Soon after, two dashing beaux arrived, who urged him with the most earnest entreaties not to raise their old father, formerly the greatest miser in the city, as, in such an event, they would be reduced to the most deplorable indigence. They offered him a fee of sixty louis; but the doctor shook his head in doubtful compliance. Scarcely had they retired, when a young widow, on the eve of matrimony, threw herself at the feet of the quack, and, with sobs and sighs, implored his mercy. In short, from morn till night, he received letters, visits, presents, and fees, to an excess which absolutely overwhelmed him. The minds of the citizens were differently and violently agitated: some by fear, and others by curiosity, so that the mayor of the city waited upon the doctor, and said : "Sir, I have not the least doubt, from my experience of your rare talents, that you will be able to accomplish the resurrection in our churchyard, the day after to-morrow, according to your promise ; but I pray you to observe that our city is in the utmost uproar and confusion ; and to consider the dreadful revolution your experiment must produce in every family : I entreat you, therefore, not to attempt it, but to go away, and thus restore tranquillity to the city. In justice, however, to your rare and divine talents, I shall give you an attestation, in due form, under our seal, that you *can revive the dead*, and that it was our own fault we were not eye-witnesses of your power." This certificate, our authority continues, was duly signed and delivered. The illustrious Mantaccini left Lyons, for other cities, to work new miracles and manœuvres. In a short time, he returned to Paris, loaded with gold, laughing at the credulity of his victims. One more citation of the kind. Count Cagliostro and his wife made their *dêbut* at St. Petersburg, pretending to a power of conferring perpetual youth—investing old people with rejuvenescence. The countess, who was not more than twenty, spoke of her son, who had long served in the army. This expedient of making old people young again could not fail to affect certain aged ladies, who are expert in diminishing instead of adding to their years. This experiment upon popular credulity did not, however, last long ; but it yielded a golden harvest while it continued.

Among notable and eccentric physicians of former times, was Jerome Cardan of Milan, who flourished, and physicked the valetudinarians of the sixteenth century. In the *Dictionnaire Historique de la Médecine*, we have the following summary of the qualities and accomplishments of our quondam physician :—"His immense knowledge and extraordinary sagacity, his freedom of thought, and his style, in general, manly and spirited, would place him at the head of the celebrated writers of the sixteenth century, *if* he had not united with these qualities a decided love of paradox and of the marvellous, an infantile credulity, a superstition scarcely conceivable, an insupportable vanity, and a boasting that knew no limits. His works, full of puerilities, of lies, of contradictions, of absurd tales, and charlatanry of every description, *nevertheless* offer proofs of a bold, inventive genius, which seeks for new paths of science, and succeeds in finding them." Leibnitz is reported to have said of him, that, with all his puerilities, he was a great man.

The intellectual character of Cardan presents a problem sufficiently intricate to excite the labors of a biographer; and when we add that his life, also, was full of various incidents—that he endured the extreme of misfortune, and rose to the height of professional honor—that he was battling throughout his life both with men and with books, we need not wonder that he became notorious.

His name has been placed in succession to that of Galen, who was the great authority when he made his professional appearance. His first book bore the title *De Malo Medendi Usa*—denouncing seventy-two errors in existing practice! Most of *his* corrections, have been re-corrected by his successors. Astrology by no means satisfied his thirst for divination. He had a system of Cheiromancy, and was very profound on the lines in the human hand, and a science completely his own, which he called *Metoposcopy*. The following extract will show that the character and fortunes of an individual are thus revealed by the lines in his forehead:

"Seven lines, drawn at equal distances, one above another, horizontally across the whole forehead, beginning close over the eyes, indicate respectively the regions of the Moon, Mercury, Venus, the Sun, Mars, Jupiter, and Saturn. The signification of each planet is always the same, and forehead-reading is thus philosophically allied to the science of palmistry."

It is related of a certain quack, in some country town in England, that he resorted to the following expedient, for creating a little notoriety, by way of a *start*. On his arrival, he announced himself by sending the bell-man—an official of great importance in former times—to disturb the quiet of the honest people of the place, by proclaiming the reward of fifty guineas for the recovery of his pet poodle; of course, the physician who could be so lavish with his money for such a trifling purpose, could not but be a man of preëminence in his profession. *Millingen* records the curious fact of two miracle-working doctors having taken London by storm, many years ago, who laid claim to the unpronounceable and most outrageous names of *Tetrachymagogon* and *Fellino Guffino Cardimo Cardimac Frames* (!), which were plastered about the walls of the city, exciting the amazement and curiosity of the gullible multitude. Another announced himself by placards, appealing to the sympathies of the selfish, to the effect that *he had studied thirty years by candle-light for the good of his countrymen;* which issue may possibly have been deemed a debateable point. He claimed to have been the seventh-son of a seventh-son—and to have been exclusively possessed of sundry *certain* cures; among others, that of hernia.

The following poetical version of a quack-doctor's professional scope may be familiar to some readers:

"Advice given gratis, from ten until four,
Teeth also extracted (for nothing, if poor).
Prescriptions prepared with care and ability,
And patients attended with skill and civility.
Tonics, narcotics, and anti-splenetics,
Anti-spasmodics, sarcotics, emetics,
With cures for blue devils, by a clever pathologist,
Dispensed with great care by a young anthropologist."

Among the accidental circumstances to which some of the fraternity have been indebted for their first successful *dêbut*, we may refer to the following case of Dr. Case, which briefly consisted in his having the lines "*Within this place lives Doctor*

Case," written in large characters upon his door: he is said to have acquired a fortune by the quaint expedient. Another disciple of Esculapius tumbled into a good practice through a fit of intoxication. Disappointed on his first arrival in London, he sought to drown his sorrows in muddy ale, at a neighboring tavern; while there, being still under the effect of his "potations deep," he was summoned to attend a certain countess. The high-sounding title of this unexpected patient tended not a little to increase the excitement under which he labored: he followed the liveried servant as steadily as he could, and was ushered in silence into a noble mansion, where her ladyship's female attendant anxiously waited to conduct him most discreetly to her mistress' room. Her agitation preventing her discovering the doctor's tendency to describe imaginary circles and curves in preference to a direct course. He was introduced into a splendid bed-chamber, and staggering up to the aristocratical patient, he commenced the mechanical process of feeling the pulse, etc.; but on proceeding to the table to write a prescription his weakness betrayed him. In vain he strove to trace the salutary characters, until, wearied in his attempts, he at length threw down the pen, exclaiming, "*Drunk, 'pon honor!*" and he made the best of his way out of the house. Two days after, he was not a little surprised at receiving a letter from his illustrious patient, enclosing a check for £100, and promising him the patronage of her family and friends, if he would but observe the strictest secrecy as to the condition in which he found her. The patient and her physician were in the same predicament, but by a strange obliquity in the lady, the doctor's intoxication was of a milder type than his patient's.

The next instance we have to introduce to our friends rejoiced in the not uncommon name of Graham, who, in the year 1782, made a great sensation in London. He was gifted with great fluency of speech, and indulged in towering hyperbole and bombast, with which he sought to gull the wonder-loving multitude. He opened a splendid mansion in Pall-mall, which he styled the "Temple of Health." The front was ornamented with an enormous gilt sun, a statue of Hygeia, and other attractive emblems; the suite of rooms in the interior was superbly furnished, and the walls decorated with mirrors, so as to confer on the place an effect like that of an enchanted palace. Here he delivered lectures on health, at the extravagant price of two guineas per lecture; yet the price, together with the novelty of the subjects, drew together considerable audiences of the wealthy and dissipated. He entertained a female, whom he called the goddess of health; and it was her business to deliver a concluding discourse, after the doctor himself had delivered his lecture.

He hired two men of extraordinary stature, provided with enormous cocked-hats, and with showy liveries, whose business it was to distribute bills, from house to house, through the city. He became, therefore, an object of curiosity. When his two-guinea auditors became exhausted, he dropped his lectures successively to one guinea, half-a-guinea, five shillings, and, as he said, "for the benefit of all," to half-a-crown; and, when he could no longer draw at this price, he exhibited the temple itself for one shilling, to daily crowds, for several months.

Among other whimsicalities, he pretended to have discovered the "*elixir of life*," by the taking of a quantum of which, a person might live as long as he wished. His terms for this invaluable invention, were, it is true, rather extravagant for common people—but, of course, so desirable a boon ought not to be made too cheap. More than one nobleman, it is recorded, actually paid him the enormous fee of *one thousand pounds sterling!* Rather an expensive premium for the purchase of a little common sense. This wonderful discovery, however, did not last long, for the delusion soon exploded, and the quack himself died, after vainly practising various other mummeries, at the age of fifty-two years—neglected, and despised by all.

For the sake of variety, we will glance at some comical

patients, the victims of mental illusion, hypochondria, phantasm, and monomania. It is scarcely necessary to inquire into the physical causes to which usually these maladies are to be ascribed: we cite a case, from the numerous instances recorded by Dr. Rush, of mental derangement, and for the accuracy of which he vouches. It was of an unfortunate individual who was possessed with the strange conceit that he was once a calf; the name of the butcher that killed him being given, who kept a stall in Philadelphia market, at which place was sold, without his leave or license, his *bodily* right and title, previous to his inhabiting his present "fleshly tabernacle." We do not venture into the region of spectral illusions, or ghosts, but we may mention, in passing, the case of a crazy young lady, recorded by Dr. Ferriar, who fancied herself accompanied by her own apparition, and who may, of course, therefore, justly be said to have been, indeed, often—*beside herself*. A Lusitanian physician had a patient who insisted that he was entirely frozen, so that he would sit before a large fire, even during the dog-days, and yet cry of cold. A dress of rough sheep-skins, saturated with aqua vitæ, was made for him, and they set him on fire: he then confessed that he was, for the first time, quite warm—rather too much so; and thus this genial remedy cured him of his frigidity altogether.

The following ludicrous story is told in the London *Lancet:* "While residing at Rome," says the narrator, "I paid a visit to the lunatic asylum there, and among the remarkable patients was one, pointed out to me, who had been saved, with much difficulty, from inflicting death upon himself by voluntary starvation in bed, under an impression that he was defunct, declaring that dead people never eat. It was soon obvious to all that the issue must be fatal, when the humane doctor bethought of the following stratagem: Half-a-dozen of the attendants, dressed in white shrouds, and their faces and hands covered with chalk, were marched in single file, with dead silence, into a room adjoining that of the patient, where he observed them, through a door purposely left open, sit down to a hearty meal. 'Hallo!' said he, that was deceased, presently to an attendant; 'who be they?' 'Dead men,' was the reply. 'What!' rejoined the corpse, 'dead men eat?' 'To be sure they do, as you see,' answered the attendant. 'If that's the case!' exclaimed the defunct, 'I'll join them, for I'm famished;' and thus instantly was the spell broken."

In Poyntz's *World of Wonders*, we find, among other remarkable citations, the following instance recorded of an accomplished somnambulist, the circumstances of which are attested by a beneficed member of the Roman Catholic church: "In the college where he was educated was a young seminarist who habitually walked in his sleep; and while in a state of somnambulism, used to sit down to his desk and compose the most eloquent sermons; scrupulously erasing, effacing, or interlining, whenever an incorrect expression had fallen from his pen. Though his eyes were apparently fixed upon the paper when he wrote, it was clear that they exercised no optical functions; for he wrote just as well when an opaque substance was interposed between them and the sheet of the paper. Sometimes an attempt was made to remove the paper, in the idea that he would write upon the desk beneath. But it was observed that he instantly discerned the change, and sought another sheet of paper as nearly as possible resembling the former one. At other times a blank sheet of paper was substituted by the bystanders for the one on which he had been writing; in which case, on reading over, as it were, his composition, he was sure to place the corrections, suggested by the perusal, at precisely the same intervals they would have occupied in the original sheet of manuscript. This young priest, moreover, was an able musician; and was seen to compose several pieces of music while in a state of somnambulism, drawing the lines of the music-paper for the purpose with a ruler, and pen and ink, and filling the spaces with his notes with the utmost precision, besides a careful adaptation of the words in vocal pieces. On one occasion the somnambulist dreamed that he sprang into the river to save a drowning child ; and, on his bed, he was seen to imitate the movement of swimming. Seizing the pillow, he appeared to snatch it from the waves and lay it on the shore. The night was intensely cold ; and so severely did he appear affected by the imaginary chill of the river as to tremble in every limb ; and his state of cold and exhaustion, when roused, was so alarming, that it was judged necessary to administer wine and other restoratives."

A young man had a strange imagination that he was dead, and earnestly begged his friends to bury him. They consented by the advice of the physician. He was laid upon a bier, and carried upon the shoulders of men to church, when some pleasant fellows, *up to the business*, met the procession, and inquired who it was ; they answered :—" And a very good job it is," said one of them, "for the world is well rid of a very bad and vicious character, which the gallows must have had in due course." The young man, now lying dead, hearing this, popped his head up, and said they ought to be ashamed of themselves in thus traducing his fair fame, and if he was alive, he would thrash them for their insolence. But they proceeded to utter the most disgraceful and reproachful language, dead flesh and blood could no longer bear it ; up he jumps, they run, he after them, until he fell down quite exhausted. He was put to bed; the violent exertion he had gone through promoted perspiration, and he got well.*

It is pertinent to our subject to refer, perhaps, to the analogy and reciprocal influence of the body and soul—mind and matter. That such analogy exists, and exhibits itself in a most indubitable manner, exerting also a most powerful sympathy, none, of course, will question ; were it otherwise a matter in dispute, we might offer many able suggestions proposed by various physicians and metaphysicians ; but we shall content ourselves by simply quoting a passage on the subject, from

* Heywood's *Hierarchy*.

Haslam, in his work on *Sound Mind.* Referring to these curious analogies, he says—" There seems to be a considerable similarity between the morbid state of the instruments of voluntary motion (*i. e.* the body), and certain affections of the mental powers. Thus, paralysis has its counterpart in the defects of recollection, where the utmost endeavor to remember is ineffectually exerted. Tremor may be compared with incapability of fixing the attention ; and this involuntary state of the muscles, ordinarily subjected to the will, also finds a parallel where the mind loses its influence in the train of thought, and becomes subject to spontaneous intrusions : as may be exemplified in reveries, dreaming, and some species of madness." Excessive irritation of the brain is the result of inordinate mental excitement ; the physical economy thus becomes deranged, and this condition of bodily disease again reacts prejudicially on the mental powers. These effects are more or less observable under different conditions, much depending on organic structure, constitutional predisposition, climate, or the peculiar circumstances by which the individual may be surrounded. While the effects, however, of this reciprocal influence of mind and matter are apparent, the cause remains unrevealed ; and to this fact may be referred the many ludicrous blunders and wild imaginings of sundry wiseacres, who have sought to account for a matter so occult. So inscrutable and all-pervading is this union and sympathy between the " fleshly tabernacle " and its noble occupant, that in essaying to address any part of the fabric, the dweller is inevitably found to respond to the appeal. Physiologists tell us that our imagination is freest when the stomach is but slightly replenished with food ; it is also more healthful in spring than in winter ; in solitude than in company ; and in modulated light, rather than in the full blaze of the noonday sun. Climate affects the temper, because it first influences the muscular system and the animal solids ; and who does not know that our happiness and repose are dependent upon the well-balanced condition of the biliary system. In such cases, it is the province of medicine to rectify the moral, as well as the physical derangement at the same moment of time. An eminent physician at Leyden, Dr. Gaubius, who styled himself "Professor of the Passions," recites a curious case of a female patient, upon whom he repeatedly enacted venesection, being of an inflammable temperament, as avouched by her liege-lord; which operation, he says, finally induced the happiest results. This notable practitioner was as *au fait* at metaphysics as medicine; he cured morals and manners, as well as maladies of the body. Is there not, therefore, a more intimate connection between these two elements of our being than has been generally admitted? Dryden confessed his indebtedness to cathartics for the propitiating of his muse; his imaginative faculty being thus dependent, as he thought, upon the elasticity of his viscera. And as we before intimated, there are, unquestionably, constitutional moral disorders—such as temporary or periodical fits of passion, or melancholy, as well as other impulsive emotions; these, for the most part, are involuntary, or easily provoked, under certain exciting circumstances. A moral patient, who suffers himself to become the wretched victim of intemperance, is sure to need only opiates; and nature, in due time, recovers from the outrage, although he may not from the disgrace. And when some pitiable wight is found suffering from the master-passion, love (a perfect tyrant in its way, which usually overturns all a man's common sense, and blinds him into the bargain), the unfortunate one is sure to come "right side up," in his sober senses, too, by administering the process of a cold bath in the river, provided some benevolent by-stander rescue him in time to cheat the fishes. A certain Milanese doctor is said to have resorted to a similar expedient for the cure of madness and other distempers. His practice consisted in placing his patients in a great high-walled enclosure, in the midst of which there was a deep well of water, as cold as ice into which his unfortunate victims were plunged, being secured to a pillar; when they were thoroughly saturated, and their courage cooled, they were liberated. In their bodily fear and shock they generally got rid of their complaints.

The effects of the imagination upon bodily health are already familiar to the reader.

Bouchet, a French author of the sixteenth century, states that the physicians at Montpelier, which was the great school of medicine, had every year two criminals, the one living, the other dead, delivered to them for dissection. He relates that on one occasion they tried what effect the mere expectation of death would produce upon a subject in perfect health, and in order to these experiments, they told the gentleman (for such was his rank), who was placed at their discretion, that, as the easiest mode of taking away his life, they would employ the means which Seneca had chosen for himself, and would therefore open his veins in warm water. Accordingly, they covered his face, pinched his feet without lancing them, and set them in a footbath, and then spoke to each other as if they saw blood flowing freely, and life departing with it. Then the man remained motionless; and when, after a while, they uncovered his face, they found him dead.

Hope and success are finer tonics than any to be found in the apothecaries' shops, and even fear may boast its cures. A German physician, so reads the tale, succeeded in curing an epidemic convulsion, among the children of a poor-house, by the fear of a red-hot poker. The fits had spread by sympathy and imitation; and this great physician, mistrusting the ordinary remedies in so grave a case, heated his instrument, and threatened to burn the first who should fall into a fit. The convulsions did not return.

A celebrated scholar was once attacked with fever at a country inn. He was visited by two physicians; and one of them, supposing from the poverty of his appearance that he would not understand a foreign language, said to the other, in Latin,

"Let's try an experiment on this poor fellow." As soon as they were gone, the patient got out of bed, hurried on his clothes, scampered off as fast as he could, and was cured of his fever by his fright.

In England, quite recently, a girl, being attacked with typhus fever, was sent to the hospital. A week afterwards, her brother was seized with the same disease, and was sent to the same institution. The nurses were helping him up the stairs at the hospital. On the way, he was met by some persons who were descending with a coffin on their shoulders. The sick man inquired whose body they were removing, when one of the bearers inadvertently mentioned the girl's name. *It was his sister.* The brother, horror-struck, sprung from his conductors, dashed down stairs, out of the hospital gate, and never stopped running until he had reached home—a distance of twelve miles! He flung himself on the bed immediately, fell into a sound sleep, and awoke next morning, entirely cured of his illness.

Solomon tells us that "a merry heart doeth good, like a medicine," and experience has proved it to be a panacea for many minor ills. Not a few of the Faculty are aware of the fact, and hence they have achieved marvellous cures by their combination of puns, potions, and pills. A renowned physician of New York, is a felicitous illustration of this.

Among the various ills which flesh is heir to, apparently midway between the mental and physical is the headache—a malady by no means uncommon, but which we welcome none the more from its frequency. Like a cold in the head, it is no joke, yet some wag has had the temerity to do this, in the following:

"A cold in the head!
What need be said
Uglier, stupider, more ill-bred:
Almost any other disease
May be romantic, if you please;

But who can scoff
At a very bad cough?
If you have a fever, you're laid on the shelf,
To be sure—but then you pity yourself,
And your friends' anxiety highly excited,
The curtains are drawn, and the chamber lighted,
Dimly, and softly, pleasanter far,
Than the starving sunshine that seems to jar
Every nerve into a separate knock,
And all at our mortal calamities mock.
* * * * * *
Who *do* you suppose
Ever pitied a man for blowing his nose?
Yet, what minor trial could ever be worse—
Unless it be reading this blundering verse,
Never fit to be written, or read;
No—nor said,
Except by a man—*with a cold in his head!*"

Among the long list of cases in the Materia Medica, here is a new and fatal one: During the prevalence of the cholera in Ireland, a soldier, hurrying into the mess-room, told his commanding officer that his brother had been carried off, two days ago, by a fatal malady, expressing his apprehensions that the whole regiment would be exposed to a similar danger, in the course of the following week. "Good heavens!" ejaculated the officer, "what, then, did he die of?" "Why, your honor, he died of a Tuesday."

An extraordinary case, chronicled by *Punch*, was that of a voracious individual who bolted a door, and threw up a window!

There are other maladies that afflict us, which sometimes provoke the mirth rather than the pity of our friends; for instance, how comical are the capers of a victim of St. Vitus' dance, or the more miserable one of intemperance, when he labors to preserve the perpendicular, or to disguise his condition. But we must not sport with human woe—rather deplore its presence, and seek to aid in its reduction, if not expulsion.

The priest and the physician have enough to do in the mitigation of moral and physical evil. The author of the *Tin Trumpet* justly observes :

"There would be but little comfort for the sick, either in body or in mind, were there any truth in the averment, that philosophy, like medicine, has plenty of drugs and quack-medicines, but few remedies, and hardly any specifics. So far from admitting this discouraging statement, a panacea may be prescribed which, under ordinary circumstances, will generally prevent, and rarely fail to alleviate, most of our evils. The following are the simple ingredients : occupation for the mind, exercise for the body, temperance and virtue for the sake of both. This is the *magnum arcanum* of health and happiness. Half of our illness and misery arises from the perversion of that reason which was given to us as a protection against both."

The celebrated Dumoulin remarked, on his death-bed, that he should leave behind him three distinguished physicians—Water, Exercise, and Diet. Sir Philip Sidney defines health in these words : "Great temperance, open air, easy labor, little care."

Hood thus playfully prescribes : "Take precious care of your precious health; but how, as the housewife says, to make it keep? Why, then, don't smoke-dry it, or pickle it in everlasting acids, like the Germans. Don't bury it in a potato-pit, like the Irish. Don't preserve it in spirits, like the barbarians. Don't salt it down, like the Newfoundlanders. Don't pack it in ice, like Captain Rack. Don't parboil it like gooseberries. Don't pot, and don't hang it. A rope is a bad '*cordon sanitaire.*' Above all, don't despond about it. Let not anxiety have 'thee on the hip.' Consider your health as your greatest and best friend, and think as well of it, in spite of all its foibles, as you can. For instance, never dream, though you may have a 'clever hack,' of galloping consumption, or indulge in the Meltonian belief that you are going the pace. Despondency, in a nice case, is the overweight that you may kick the beam and the bucket, both at once. Besides, the best fence against care is —ha! ha! wherefore, care to have one all around you when ever you can. Let your 'lungs crow like the chanticleer,' and as like the game-cock as possible. It expands the chest, enlarges the heart, quickens the circulation, and, like a trumpet, makes the 'spirit dance.'"

There is a world of good advice in this passage from a letter of Charles Lamb to Bernard Barton: "You are too much apprehensive about your complaint. The best way, in these cases, is to keep yourself as ignorant as you can—as ignorant as the world was before Galen—of the entire inner construction of the animal man: not to be conscious of a midriff; to hold kidneys (save of sheep and swine) to be an agreeable fiction; not to know whereabout the gall grows; to account the circulation of the blood a mere idle whim of Harvey's; to acknowledge no mechanism not visible. For, *once fix the seat of your disorder, and your fancies flux into it like so many bad humors.* Those medical gentry choose each his favorite part; one takes the lungs, another the liver, and refers to that whatever in the animal economy is amiss." He goes on to counsel his friend, "*above all, to use exercise*—keep a good conscience; avoid tamperings with hard terms of art, 'viscosity,' 'scirrhosity,' and those bugbears by which simple patients are scared into their graves. Believe the general sense of the mercantile world, which holds that desks are not deadly. *It is the mind, and not the limbs, that taints by long sitting.* Think of the patience of tailors; think how long the Lord Chancellor sits; think of the brooding hen."

Thus much about the mission of medicine, and its purveyors, as well as some of the disasters it proposes to remedy: now a word or two about the subject of all this—man. Physiologists assert that this "paragon of animals" is physically a machine —a steam-engine—his brain the engine, his lungs the boiler, his viscera the furnace. That he glides along the track of life, often at the fearful speed of sixty or seventy pulsations in a minute, never stopping, so long as the machine is in working order. He has also been compared to a steamship, a chemical laboratory, a distillery, a forcing-pump, a grist-mill, a furnace, an electric telegraph.

Man has the power of imitating almost every motion but that of flight. To effect these he has, in maturity and health, 60 bones in his head, 60 in his thighs and legs, 62 in his arms and hands, and 67 in the trunk. He has also 434 muscles. His heart makes 64 pulsations in a minute. There are also three complete circulations of the blood, in the short space of an hour.

Old Francis Quarles furnishes the moral estimate :

"Why, what is man? a quickened lump of earth,
A feast for worms, a bubble full of breath,
A looking-glass for grief, a flash, a minute,
A painted tomb with putrefaction in it,
A map of death, a burden of a song,
A winter's dust, a worm of five feet long.
Begot in sin, in darkness nourished, born
In sorrow; naked, shiftless, and forlorn.
His first voice heard, is crying for relief,
Alas! he comes into a world of grief;
His age is sinful, and his youth is vain,
His life's a punishment, his death's a pain.
His life's an hour of joy, a world of sorrow,
His death's a winter night that finds no morrow.
Man's life's an hour-glass, which being run,
Concludes that hour of joy, and so is done."

In closing our desultory observations on "the fallacies of the faculty," we refer to the testimony of sundry members of the profession, for determining the amount of good or evil of which they are the occasion.

Dr. Akenside, himself a physician, has said, "Physicians, in despair of making medicine a science, have agreed to convert it into a trade." Sir Anthony Carlisle said, "that medicine was an art founded in conjecture and improved by murder ;

that he never could discover any rational principle in a physician's treatment of a case, and that, therefore, it was all guess-work." The late Professor Gregory used often to declare, in his class-room, "that ninety-nine out of one hundred medical facts were so many medical lies; and that medical doctrines were, for the most part, little better than stark, staring nonsense."

"Assuredly the uncertain and most unsatisfactory art that we call medical science, *is no science at all*, but a jumble of inconsistent opinions, of conclusions hastily and often incorrectly drawn, of facts misunderstood or perverted, of comparisons without analogy, of hypotheses without reason, and of theories not only useless but dangerous."* The late Dr. Hooper remarks in his writings, "Medicine is now defined the art of preventing and treating diseases, but formerly it was called the art of preserving health and curing diseases. The word cure is not used at present, because we possess no remedy capable of effecting an immediate cure. There is a great difference between treatment and cure, as many diseases are incurable, but are still proper subjects for treatment." It has often been objected to the physician or practitioner that he is unable satisfactorily to explain the performance of a single function, the phenomena of a single disease, or the operation of a single remedy. However humiliating the admission of such a truth may be, it cannot wholly be denied. But fully to account for the performance of one function would be nearly paramount to the explanation of all, for all are governed by the same general laws, and subject to the same general causes. Dr. James Johnson, of London, has left upon record the following extraordinary admission: "I declare as my conscientious opinion, founded on long experience and reflection, that if there was not a single physician, surgeon, apothecary, chemist. druggist, nor drug on the face of the earth, there would be less sickness and less mortality than now prevail." We are

* Dublin Medical Journal.

told by the ingenious John Brown that he "wasted more than twenty years in learning, teaching, and diligently scrutinizing every part of medicine." The first five passed away in hearing others, studying what he had heard, implicitly believing it, and entering upon the possession as a rich and valuable inheritance. His mode of employment the next five years was to explain more clearly the several particulars, to refine and give them a nicer polish. During the next equal space of time, because no part of it had succeeded to his mind, he became cold upon the subject, and, with many eminent men, even with the vulgar themselves, began to deplore the healing art as altogether uncertain and incomprehensible. Majendie, whose opinion is considered of much weight in Paris, says, "Consider for a moment the state in which medicine exists in the present day. Visit the different hospitals, and you will not fail to observe how physicians are divided between the most opposite systems, on the nature, on the seat, and even on the treatment of the most simple disease; yet each of those systems is supported by arguments more or less specious: each theory is based upon facts more or less certain."*

In coming to a conclusion, therefore, we ask to what cause shall we attribute the past, and even the present anomalous condition of medical science, if not to the inefficiency of its practitioners. Dr. John W. Francis, of New York, furnishes, in part, the solution of the enigma. We quote from an address, delivered by him not long since. It is a noble tribute to the profession.

"That ignorance of the laws of life, of the rules of health, and of the remedial powers of medicinal substances, prevails to a wonderful degree, even in exalted places, is an incontrovertible position; and hence the innumerable calamities which popular delusion in the curative art entails. Most unfortunate for its victims, like fraud in fiscal concerns, it has a wider influence in its effects than with the immediate objects with

* Penney's Organs of Life.

whom it traffics. Its dire malignity is often extended through a large circle of the unconscious and unsuspecting.

"And, on the other hand, there are instances of noble and touching fortitude, of sublime patience, and of heavenly faith, which every medical man that deserves the name must treasure as among the richest lessons of his life. Who that has kept vigils at the couch of Genius, and marked the wayward flickerings of its sacred fire, made yet more ethereal by disease, or seen beauty grow almost supernatural in the embrace of pain, has not felt his mission to be holy as well as responsible? And when a voice that has thrilled millions is hushed, or a mind upon which rests the cares of a nation is prostrated, who has not realized how intimately the healing art is knit into the vast and complex web of human society? Let not that be thought a light office which summons us to minister, as apostles of science, to the greatest exigencies of life; to cheer the soul under the acute sufferings of maternity, and alleviate the decay of nature; to watch over the glimmering dawn and the fading twilight of existence; to stand beside the mother, whose sobs are hushed that the departure of her first-born may be undisturbed; and be oracles at the bedside of the reverend minister of holy truth, the halo of whose piety softens, on his brow, the lines of mortal agony. What a mastery of self! What requisites, mental and corporeal, are demanded in him who is the observer of scenes like these, whose sympathies are awakened to services such as are befitting the mighty crisis, and whose talents are efficiently enlisted for the triumphant accomplishment of his devout trust! The advent of such an ambassador, when his calling is duly understood, must awaken the heart to its profoundest depths, and cannot be inoperative upon minds of intellectual and moral culture."

It seems to be usually less a matter of ambition with medical students to obtain a thorough induction into the theory and practice of their art, than to secure the distinction of too frequently an undeserved diploma, and the coveted monogram

8*

of M. D. attached to their names, as a passport to practice upon poor old women and children, who pay the forfeiture of life for their inexcusable folly and cupidity.

Prof. Carnochan thus sums up the whole subject: If we examine the life of the practising physician, we find it gilded and shining on the surface; but beneath the spangles, how much pain and hardship! The practising physician is one of the martyrs of modern society: he drinks the cup of bitterness, and empties it to the dregs. He is under the weight of an immense responsibility, and his reward is but too often injustice and ingratitude. His trials begin at the very gates of his career. He spends his youthful years in the exhausting investigation of Anatomy; he breathes the air of putrefaction, and is daily exposed to all the perils of contagion. View him in the practice of his difficult art, which he has acquired at the risk of his life! He saves or cures his patient; it is the result of chance, or else it is alleged that it is nature, and nature alone, that cures disease, and that the physician is only useful for form's sake. Then, consider the mortifications he has to undergo, when he sees unblushing ignorance win the success which is denied to his learning and talents, and you will acknowledge that the trials of the physician are not surpassed in any other business of life. There is another evil the honorable physician has to contend with—a hideous and devouring evil, commenced by the world, sustained by the world, and seemingly for evermore destined to be an infliction upon humanity. This evil is Quackery, which takes advantage of that deplorable instinct which actually seeks falsehood, and prefers it to truth. How often do we see the shameless and ignorant speculator arrest public attention, and attain fortune, while neglect, obscurity, and poverty are the portion of the modest practitioner, who has embraced the profession of medicine with conscientiousness, and cultivated it with dignity and honor.

Great was Diana of the Ephesians, and we follow suit, for

great are we in our credulity, great in our manifold sufferings, great in our multitudinous quacks, great in the princely fortunes we bestow upon those vampires who batten upon disease and sorrow. Take up the first newspaper that comes to hand; look over the advertisements entitled Medical; is there not a panacea for every disability—consumption, dyspepsia, in short everything that has or can make up the total of human wretchedness or human infirmity? Every ailment that has baffled skill, science, and intense devotion, all whittled down into a simple "*veni, vidi, vici.*" How wonderful that death is still the great iconoclast, in spite of potions, ointments, and drops; in spite of pills that are infallible, in spite of philanthropists who profess to eradicate all the "ills that flesh is heir to," and others also that never existed—bitters of such a phœnix-like quality that the sick are turned incontinently into angels of happiness, and a debilitated constitution is so summarily dealt with that it shelters itself in no time under a spiritual healthfulness.

Among the excrescences that infest our Broadway, with its ever varying light and shade, its disguised poverty, reckless extravagance, and obtrusive vanity, may be seen two specimens of the real old-fashioned quack. It is a pleasure to look upon something so broad and full of character; there can be no cheating here—all above board; note his peculiar turned-up hat, unlike any other, specs fixed upon the very tip of his nasal protuberance, his bright blue silk neckerchief, a cloak, embroidered with a superfluity of velvet, does the luxurious for his shoulders—and all this weight of material and immaterial eased off into a pair of Hessians; a foreign title too, and the man is developed. The other Samaritan may be known by a certain air of solemnity that accompanies him—enveloped in a coat and continuations of the last century, black silk stockings, and silver buckles to match. Smaller fry there are innumerable; but we cannot stop to select all the prowling vagabonds we meet, so leave them to pursue their Elysium in their own way; but ought ignorance to be tampered with? must our faith ever be abused by this charlatanism? Where are the conservators of public morality? The unfortunate thimble-rigger is hustled about without any compunction: he violates the law; but why is there not a law to prevent this gambling in human bodies and human hearts? must this traffic be continued unchecked and unrebuked, while thousands upon thousands are sacrificed? The selfish cry of "every one for himself, and God for us all," is heard in all its infidelity and apathy, while helplessness and imbecility are left to self-management. If we are to be cut down before our allotment, let it be done scientifically—in other words, let the regulars do it; with them we may have a chance of existence.

Whittier observes: "It is the special vocation of the doctor to grow familiar with suffering—to look upon humanity disrobed of its pride and glory—robbed of all its fictitious ornaments—weak, hopeless, naked—and undergoing the last fearful metempsychosis, from its erect and god-like image, the living temple of an enshrined divinity, to the loathsome clod and the inanimate dust. Of what ghastly secrets of moral and physical disease is he the depository!" With what a sanctity, therefore, is the character of the true physician invested.

It has been well said, that the theory and practice of medicine is the noblest and most difficult science in the world; and that there is no other art for the practice of which the most thorough education is so essential.

A word or two regarding the modern systems of Homœopathy and Hydropathy, both which are, as might have been anticipated, obnoxious to the advocates of the old system of Allopathy. The Hahnemannian theory, however, now numbers among its supporters many intelligent and philosophic minds, although the infinitesimal reduction of its doses to the millionth, billionth, and trillionth part of a grain, is more than enough to stagger the belief of those who have been accustomed to solutions by the pailful, and powders in any quantity.

The principle of the Homœopathists is founded in truth and reason, but its administrators require to be well skilled in its doctrines, as their remedial agents include many of the most subtle and powerful poisons. We are for Homœopathy on account of its modest inflictions upon the poor, afflicted patient, who, in appealing to the old system, has often as much to abide in his shattered corporeity from the attacks of the curative process, as from the original disease. The logic of the following may be questioned, but it is, of course, intended as a sarcasm :

> "The homœopathic system, sir, just suits me to a tittle,
> It clearly proves of physic you cannot take too little ;
> If it be good in all complaints to take a dose so small,
> It surely must be better still, to take no dose at all."*

There is only one suggestion we have to offer in this connection—it is this : ought not the homœopathic practitioners to regulate their fees in the ratio of their doses ? The cold-water system is rapidly extending its popularity among us. It is true, we have no establishment to compare with that of the learned discoverer of hydropathy, Preisnitz ; but the system is daily gaining favor with the reflective and thoughtful. Of mesmerism, and its application to nervous and neuralgic diseases, we shall not pause to speak. The advantages of *chloroform* have been so fully discussed by everybody, that we shall simply give the reader a taste of one of these expositions in a kind of mock heroic verse, cut from a recent English paper :

* It is very evident, however, that people do not become converts to any particular system of Medicine or doctrine of Theology, from the amount of proof that may be adduced in their support, but rather from the peculiar constitution and tendency of their mental organization. A person who is ultra in one thing will be ultra in all; a believer in Homœopathy will be most likely a believer in Spirit Rappings and Mesmerism. Six-sevenths of the followers of Emanuel Swedenborg, it is ascertained, are enthusiastic disciples of Hahnemann. A mystic in religion will be a mystic in medicine. Evidence has nothing to do in the making of such converts.—*Homœopathicus nascitur, non fit.*—*Dr. C. A. Lee.*

"Take but a snuff at this essence anæsthetical,
Dropp'd upon a handkerchief, or bit of sponge,
And on your eyelids 'twill clap a seal hermetical,
And your senses in a trance that instant plunge.

"Then you may be pinch'd and punctured, bump'd and thump'd, and whack'd about,
Scotch'd, and scored, and lacerated, cauterized, and hacked about ;
And though tender as a chick—a Sybarite for queasiness—
Flay'd alive, unconscious of a feeling of uneasiness.

"Celsus will witness our deft chirurgeons presently,
Manage operations as he said they should ;
Doing them safely, speedily, and *pleasantly*,
Just as if the body were a log of wood.

"Teeth, instead of being drawn with agonies immeasurable,
Now will be extracted with sensations rather pleasurable,
Chloroform will render quite agreeable the parting with
Any useless member the patient has been smarting with."

An instance of the disadvantages of this anæsthetical agent is seen in the following incident, which occurred at Taunton Hospital, when, as a patient was undergoing amputation of a limb, while under the influence of chloroform, the nurse let fall the bottle containing the gas, which quickly spread its somniferous effects over the operators, and some time elapsed before they recovered from their partial insensibility.

Doctors have been ever the theme of the satirist, from the days of Horace to the present. Churchill insinuates that

"Most of the evils we poor mortals know,
From doctors and imagination flow."

Dryden, in his lines on the poet-doctor, Garth, says :

"The apothecary train is wholly blind ;—
From files a random recipe they take,
And many deaths of one prescription make.

Garth, generous as his muse, prescribes and gives,
The shopman sells, and by destruction lives."

Byron adds, also, a stanza—

"This is the way physicians mend—or end us,
Secundum artem—but although we sneer,
In health—we call them to attend us,
Without the least propensity to jeer."

Byron hits it exactly—when in health, we throw physic to the dogs, and laugh at the doctor; but, when we are prostrated by disease, when "sickness sits caverned in the hollow eye," we are glad enough to seek his aid, and remunerate him, as far as we can, for it. Some, after having passed under the recuperative process, are ungrateful enough to forget the doctor's fee. Doctor Francis, of New York, tells a good case of management of such an individual. We give it in his own words: "We hear much of the penny-a-liner, as well as the productive genius of a Moore, a Byron, and a Scott; yet never within the compass of our reading, or of common report, have we known of pecuniary results following the business of versification to surpass the instance we have to narrate. An invalid, whose physical sufferings challenged the best medical skill, was at length restored to his wonted health; yet, the realization of the doctor's fee, not unlike the great cure, seemed to be threatened with great protraction. Some time had elapsed with this indifferent state of things, when, on one bright morning, with a cheerful face, the gratified patient meeting the doctor in his ordinary walks, assured him he was then going to a house of worship, to return thanks for his restoration. 'You do rightly,' said the doctor; 'but take along with you a line or two from me, touching your case.' He was handed a polite note, with this enclosure:

'On a thanksgiving day,
Your debts you should pay;—
If you seek to find Heaven,
Why that is the way.'

Within a half-a-dozen hours after the receipt of the lines, the medical bill was responded to by the admonished patient, and some two hundred dollars added to the physician's income. No sermon would have proved more effective." We know not how costly may have been the doctor's drugs, in the premises ; but the doctor doubtless, never wrote a better prescription, or perhaps received a more easily-earned fee.

Fifty dollars a line—and very short ones, at that—for poetry of the above stamp, excels all we find either among the calamities or delectations of authorship. Surely, neither the *Loves of the Plants,* nor the *Loves of the Angels,* ever brought such results. This incident suggests the fact—too apparent to need illustration—that the present incumbents of the curative art, like many of their predecessors, are not among the least rewarded toilers in the hive of human industry—a better fate than that of the two physicians-royal, who, having the misfortune to lose their patient, were doomed to forfeit their own lives, and to be buried along with her.

The eccentricities of Abernethy are already familiar to most readers : we merely cite two anecdotes of the many that are recorded of this feature of his character.

"Abernethy's mind disqualified him from adopting that affected interest which distinguishes many of the well-bred physicians, and he heartily despised their little arts to acquire popularity. He seemed to feel as if he mentally expressed himself thus : 'Here I am ready to give you my advice, if you want it : but you must take it as you find it ; and if you don't like it, egad (his favorite word), you may go about your business—I don't want to have anything to do with you : hold your tongue, and be off.' In some such mood as this, he received a visit from a lady, one day, who was well acquainted with his invincible repugnance to her sex's predominant disposition, and therefore, forbore speaking but simply in reply to his laconic queries. The consultation was conducted, during three visits, in the following manner :

"*First Day.*—(Lady enters and holds out her finger.) *Abernethy.*—'Cut?' *Lady.*—'Bite.' *A.*—'Dog?' *L.*—'Parrot.' *A.*—'Go home and poultice it.'

Second Day.—(Finger held out again.) *A.*—'Better?' *L.*—'Worse.' *A.*—'Go home and poultice it again.'

Third Day.—(Finger held out as before.) *A.*—'Better?' *L.*—'Well.' *A.*—'You're the most sensible woman I ever met with. Good-by. Get out.'

Another lady, having scalded her arm, called at the usual hour to show it, three successive days, when similar laconic conversations took place:

First Day.—(Patient, exposing the arm, says:)—'Burnt. *A.*—'I see it;' and having prescribed a lotion, she departs.

Second Day.—(Patient shows the arm, and says:)—'Better.' *A.*—'I know it.'

Third Day.—(Again showing the arm.) *P.*—'Well.' *A.*—'Any fool can tell that. What d'ye come again for? Get away."

There are several distinct varieties among the medical profession; such as the following: first, the silent doctor, who is evidently a lover of creature comforts, and whose taciturn, dignified, and mysterious deportment passes current with the unsuspecting for profound wisdom. He ingeniously manages to secure the greatest number of patients with the fewest possible words. "The silent doctor is a great favorite with the fair sex; they regard him as Coleridge did his quondam acquaintance of dumpling celebrity, and think that as stillest streams are ofttimes the deepest, so there must be something intensely fascinating in the said doctor, if it only could be discovered. Everybody knows, too, how each individual woman believes herself endowed by nature with peculiar faculties for discovering the occult, for unravelling the mysterious; and who more mysterious than the silent doctor?

"But, leaving him now in their safe keeping, our next illustration shall be of the sceptical doctor. Though confessedly against his interest, he is very slow to believe that anything is the matter with anybody. If people are resolved to be quacked, he finds a bread-pill, to be taken four times a day—a safe and wholesome remedy. Still, though mortally averse to old women and nervous invalids, when there is real suffering, the sceptical doctor feels keenly, all the more, perhaps, from his efforts to conceal it.

"Of all others, perhaps, the most provoking is the talkative doctor. Well versed in almost every subject, fond of literature, of politics, and of science, it is difficult to keep him to the point, and obtain any definite opinion or practical advice from him. Quite forgetful that you are in actual pain or grievous discomforture, a single hint or remote allusion is sufficient to draw forth a learned discussion on ancient or mediæval art, or the marbles of Nineveh. He will harangue on the authenticity of Rowley, or the author of Junius; there is no subject which he cannot render interesting to every one but the poor patient, who needs more philosophy than he has ever dreamed of to bear patiently with it all!

"The morbid doctor is not a common specimen, but occasionally he may be met with. Take a drive with him some fine morning in his chaise, and, however cheerily you start, depend upon it you will come home moping. The morbid doctor sees disease and death before him at every turning. At each corner a death's-head stares him in the face. A gaunt, grim figure, the embodiment of all diseases, sits at his elbow. It would be hard to say how many functional disorders have become organic through his treatment of them. If the morbid doctor pronounces a complaint fatal, how can the patient doubt?

Some people find great difficulty in choosing their medical attendant. 'How,' say they, 'can we ascertain the real standing a man holds in his profession? A large practice is not a criterion; the courting, canting, quack will sometimes secure it, or mere manners will be against it; the public may be deceived; from his medical brethren we can learn nothing. How, then, is the truth to be ascertained?'

"All we can say in reply is, that in this, as in most other things, people must employ common sense—an invaluable quality at all times, and especially needful in choosing a doctor. If you find a medical man shallow on general subjects, or wanting in clearness of perception, he is not likely to be very logical or very deep with regard to his profession. If you find him boasting, bustling, and pompous—disposed to talk of the variety of his engagements, and the value in which his opinion is held, are you not free to regard him as you would any other man who puts forth the same pretensions? At the same time be not carping or suspicious. Medical men are altogether, perhaps, the most valuable members of society; their sphere of usefulness is exceeded by none. A word spoken in season is doubly valued when falling from the lips of those who have ministered to our bodily necessities, and what influence may they not exert in our families! In sickness and by the bed of death, chords may be touched which will never cease to vibrate; love and domestic union may take the place of coldness and neglect; and the family doctor may prove of immense service as the family adviser." *

Altogether, the medical profession, though arduous in the extreme, is very noble; and few, we believe, who have entered upon it would be willing to change it for any other. The variety of learning it requires, the constant accession of new truths, the full, anxious, but interesting occupation it affords to the mind, renders it absolutely absorbing and exciting.

Add to this the society of all kinds into which the medical man is thrown, the knowledge of human nature he acquires thereby, the many beautiful traits of domestic affection and woman's love which pass daily before him, the gratitude of some hearts, the cordial friendship of others, the respect to be

* Chambers' Journal.

attained from all—and it will scarcely be denied that the practice of medicine is one of the most interesting and delightful, as well as responsible, of all professions.

In fine, since there is a sacredness in the trust confided to the professor of the healing art, a corresponding fidelity to its claims and responsibilities is indispensably requisite; and, consequently, he who is recklessly indifferent to these is guilty of the highest style of crime, in a wanton betrayal of the faith reposed in him.

THE CYCLE OF THE SEASONS.

"The shadow on the dial's face,
  That steals, from day to day,
With slow, unseen, unceasing pace,
  Moments, and months, and years away;
This shadow, which, in every clime,
  Since light and motion first began,
Hath held its course sublime."

THE topic we have chosen for the present chapter is so intangible, that the moment we essay to grasp it, it is gone. Although impalpable it is yet real, for, like the circumambient atmosphere, it is ever present with us, although unseen. If we attempt to symbolize it, we fail fully to portray it, and yet images are its only mode of illustration. It is both the longest and the shortest, the swiftest and the slowest; the most divisible and the most indivisible; the most regretted and the least valued; without which nothing can be done; yet, that which devours everything, and gives existence to everything. It is the most paradoxical, yet the simplest of elements. Strictly speaking, it is never palpable, yet it is ever present; a constant succession, an unfathomable duration; the most momentous benefactor to man, yet seldom estimated according to its worth.

It is the account current with all, in which more are found bankrupt than wealthy, when the balance-sheet is demanded. It marks the rising and the setting sun, spreads over us the black veil of night, and gilds with gladness the face of day; it rolls on the revolving seasons, chronicling the deeds of centuries; watching over the birth of infancy, the ardent aspirations of youth, toiling manhood, and the tottering steps of the infirm and aged—his sorrows, loves, and cares, nor forsakes him so long as life shall last. It is always the friend of the virtuous and the true, a tormenting foe to those who abuse the gift; to the former, it is redolent of fragrant and pleasant memories,—to the latter, of gloomy remorse and despair.

"It rolls away, and bears along
A mingled mass of right and wrong;
The flowers of love that bloomed beside
The margin of life's sunny tide;
The poisoned weeds of passion, torn
From dripping rocks, and headlong borne
Into that unhorizoned sea—
Which mortals call eternity!"

And such is that mysterious myth, named Time, who measures our allotted span, from the cradle to the coffin, mingles our joys and griefs in the chalice of life, and then terminates it with his scythe,—

"A shadow only to the eye,
It levels all beneath the sky."

Time is but a name; it is what is done in time that is the substance. What are twenty-four centuries to the hard rock, more than twenty-four hours to man, or twenty-four minutes to the ephemera? "Are there not periods in our own existence," writes an ingenious thinker, "in which space, computed by its measure of thoughts, feelings, and events, mocks the penury of man's artificial scale and comprises a lifetime in a day."

I asked an aged man, a man of cares,
Wrinkled and curved, and white with hoary hairs:
"Time is the warp of life," he said. "Oh tell
The young, the fair, the gay, to weave it well."
I asked the ancient, venerable dead—
Sages who wrote, and warriors who bled:
From the cold grave a hollow murmur flowed—
"Time sowed the seed we reap in this abode."
I asked a dying sinner, ere the tide
Of life had left his veins: "Time," he replied,
"I've lost it—ah, the treasure!" and he died.
I asked the golden sun and silver spheres,
Those bright chronometers of days and years:
They answered—"Time is but a meteor's glare,"
And bade me for eternity prepare.
I asked the seasons, in their annual round,
Which beautify or desolate the ground;
And they replied (no oracle more wise);
"Tis Folly's blank, and Wisdom's highest prize."*

"Time sadly overcometh all things, and is now dominant, and sitteth upon a sphinx, and looketh unto Memphis and old Thebes; while his sister, Oblivion, reclineth semi-somnous on a pyramid, gloriously triumphing, making puzzles of Titanian erections, and turning old glories into dreams. History sinketh beneath her cloud. The traveller, as he paceth amazedly through those deserts, asketh of her, Who builded them? and she mumbleth something, but what it is he knoweth not."†

Locke is of opinion that a man, in great misery, may so far lose his measure, as to think a minute an hour; or, in joy, make an hour a minute.

Shakspeare expands the same idea, where he says—"Time

* Locke. † Heeren.

travels in divers paces, with divers persons; I'll tell you who Time ambles withal, who Time trots withal, who Time gallops withal, and who he stands still withal. He trots hard with a young maid, between the contract of her marriage, and the day it is solemnized; if the interim be but a sennight, Time's pace is so hard, that it seems the length of seven years. He ambles with a priest that lacks Latin, and a rich man that hath not the gout—for the one sleeps easily, because he cannot study; and the other lives merrily, because he feels no pain; the one lacking the burden of lean and wasteful learning—the other knowing no burden of heavy, tedious penury; then Time ambles withal. He gallops with a thief to the gallows—for, though he go softly as foot can fall, he thinks himself too soon there. He stays still with lawyers in the vacation—for they sleep between term and term, and then they perceive not how Time moves."

Time is portrayed with wings to indicate his rapid flight, and if he strew our pathway with life's spring flowers, he also brings, too swiftly, its wintry frosts and desolation. He is also represented with a scythe, to notify that he mows down all alike—the young, the refined and the vulgar, the good and the bad.

"Even such is Time that takes on trust,
Our youth, our joys, our all we have,
And pays us but with age and dust;
Who, in the dark and silent grave,
When we have wandered all our ways,
Shuts up the story of our days."*

The earliest expedient for reckoning time seems to have been the sun-dial. Allusion to its use is to be found in Holy Writ.† It was called by the ancients *sciathericum*, from being marked by shadow. This instrument was in vogue among the Romans; we have an account of one being placed in the court of the Temple of Quirinus.

* Sir Walter Raleigh.

† Isaiah, chap. xxxviii. 8.

Several of the Grecian astronomers and mathematicians constructed dials. Thales is said to have made one; as also Aristarchus and Anaximenes, of Miletus. Herodotus informs us that the Greeks borrowed the invention from the Babylonians. The first sun-dial used at Rome was in use about three hundred years before Christ. Before the use of these instruments in the "Eternal City," there was no division of the day into hours; nor does that word occur in the Twelve Tables. They only mention sun-rising and sun-setting, *before* and *after* mid-day. According to Pliny, mid-day was not added till some years later, an *accensus* of the consuls being appointed to call out that time when he saw the sun from the Senate-house, between the Rostra and the place called Græcostasis, where the ambassadors from Greece and other foreign countries used to stand.

The *klepsydra*, or water-clock,* was introduced by Scipio Narsica at Rome, 157 B.C. It served its purpose in all weathers, while the dial, of course, depended upon the sun. Sun-dials are occasionally still to be seen in Europe.

"I count only the hours that are serene," is the motto of an old sun-dial near Venice. A capital conceit to dispel dulness and discontent. Life is sure to be much brighter if we look at the sunny side of it.

There is a dial in the Temple, London, upon which is inscribed the admonitory line (a good hint for loiterers), "Begone about your business."

The Chinese have been accustomed, as early as the ninth century, to have watchmen posted on towers, who announced the hours of the day and night by striking upon a suspended board. A similar custom still remains among the Russians.

* In the year 807, the King of Persia sent as a present to Charlemagne a water-clock, furnished with some ingenious mechanism. A slight description of it is to be found in *Annales Francorum*, ascribed to Eginhard. The author says:—"Likewise a timepiece wonderfully constructed of brass with mechanical art, in which the course of the twelve hours was turned towards a clepsydra, with as many brass balls, which fall down at the completion of the hour, and by their fall sounded a bell under them."

Alfred the Great measured his time by the constant burning of wax torches or candles, notched for the hours. In some parts of the East, people measure time by the length of their shadow. Consequently, if you ask a man what time of day it is, he will stand erect in the sun and measure his shadow. We find allusion to this in the seventh chapter of Job. "As a servant earnestly desireth the shadow." Hour-glasses were first invented at Alexandria, 150 years before the Christian era.

The monks of old, finding the time hang heavy on their hands, devised some curious expedients to get rid of it. The Abbot of Hirsham (*temp.* 11th century) constructed a time-measurer somewhat similar to our clocks; the machine being different from the sun-dial and the water-clock. It not only pointed out the hours, and exhibited the motion of the earth and other planets, but emitted also a sound, to give an alarm, for the purpose of awakening the sacristan to matins and vespers. Clocks, moved by wheels and weights, also began to be used in the monasteries in Europe about the eleventh century.

In 1232 a curious clock was sent by the Sultan of Egypt to the Emperor Frederic II. "In the same year," writes an old author, "the Saladin of Egypt sent by his ambassadors, as a gift, a valuable machine, of wonderful construction, worth more than five thousand ducats. It appeared to resemble internally a celestial globe, in which figures of the sun, moon, and planets, formed with great skill, moved, being impelled by weights and wheels, so that, performing their course in certain and fixed intervals, they pointed out the hour, night and day, with infallible certainty; also the twelve signs of the zodiac, with certain appropriate characters, moved with the firmament, contained within themselves the course of the planets."

We learn that, in 1288, an artist furnished the famous clock-house near Westminster Hall with a clock, to be heard by the courts of law. This clock was considered, during the reign of

Henry VI., to be of such consequence, that it was consigned to the keeping of William Warby, dean of St. Stephen's, together with the pay of sixpence *per diem*, to be received at the Exchequer. Four years later, in 1292, a clock was placed in the cathedral at Canterbury ; it was purchased at a price equivalent to four hundred pounds. In 1523, the clock of St. Mary's, Oxford, was furnished out of fines imposed on the students of the university.

One of the oldest clocks in England is in the Palace of Hampton Court. It still works well, and wears well, like father Time, who never seems to get older.

A few years back a clock was invented for dividing the year *decimally*. This curious time-measurer made a hundred thousand beats in the day ; and the hands on the dial were so contrived as to divide the whole day of twenty-four hours into ten, a hundred, a thousand, ten thousand, and one hundred thousand parts.

One of the best clocks now in London is that of the Royal Exchange. It was made by Mr. Dent under the immediate direction of Professor Airy ; and the first stroke of each hour is said to be true to a second of time. That placed in the Clock Tower of the New Houses of Parliament is an eight-day one, and strikes the hour on a bell weighing nearly ten tons ; it chimes the quarter upon eight bells, and shows the time upon four dials, about thirty feet in diameter. The length of the minute-hand of the clock of St Paul's Cathedral is 8 feet, and its weight 75lbs. ; the length of the hour-hand is 5 feet 5 inches, and its weight 44lbs. The diameter of the dial is 18 feet. The diameter of the bell is ten feet, and its weight four tons and a quarter. It is inscribed, "Richard Phelps made me, 1716," and is never used except for the striking of the hour, and for tolling at the deaths and funerals of any of the royal family, the Bishops of London, the Deans of St. Paul's, and the Lord Mayor, should he die during mayoralty.

"The *chimes* which are attached to many of our public clocks seem to give a spur to the lazy, creeping hours, and relieve the lassitude of country places. At noon their desultory, trivial song, is diffused through the hamlet with the odor of rashers of bacon ; at the close of the day they send the toil-worn sleepers to their beds." We have a peal of bells at Trinity Church, New York, but we fear they have lost their tongue, since they maintain a persistent silence.

Watches were first introduced at the close of the fifteenth century. Watchmaking has been carried to great perfection by the Swiss, French, and English. Some minute watches have been constructed of less than half an inch diameter.

A watch has been facetiously designated as the image of modesty, since it always holds its hands before its face, and however good its works may be, it is always running itself down.

The astronomical clock at Strasburg is composed of three parts, respectively dedicated to the measure of time, to the calendar, and to astronomical movements. The first thing to be created was a central moving power, communicating its motion to the whole of its mechanism. The motive power, which is itself a very perfect and exact time-piece, indicates on an outer face the hours and their subdivisions, as well as the days of the week : it strikes the hours and the quarters, and puts in motion divers allegorical figures. One of the most curious of these is the Genius placed on the first balustrade, and who turns, each hour, the sand-glass which he holds in his hand. The cock crows, and a procession of the apostles takes place every day at noon. In the calendar are noted the months, days, and dominical letters, as well as the calendar—properly so called, showing all the saints' days in the year. The plate on which these signs are marked revolves once in 365 days for the common, and 366 for the bissextile, year ; marking, at the same time, the irregularity which takes place three consecutive times out of four in the secular years. The moveable feasts, which seem as though they followed no fixed rule, are, nevertheless, obtained here by a mechanism of marvellous ingenuity, in which all the elements of the ecclesiastical computation—the milesimal, the solar circle, the golden number, the dominical letter, and the epacts—combine and produce, for an unlimited period, the result sought. It is at midnight, the 31st of December, that the other moveable feasts and fasts range themselves on the calendar in the order and place of their succession for the whole of the following year. The third division solves the problems of astronomy. It exhibits an orrery, constructed on the Copernican System, which presents the mean revolutions of each of the planets visible to the naked eye. The earth, in her movement, carries with her her satellite—the moon, which accomplishes her revolution in the space of a lunar month. Besides this, the different phases of the moon are shown on a separate globe. One sphere represents the apparent movement of the heavens, making its revolution in the course of the siderial day. It is subjected to that almost imperceptible influence known as the precession of the equinoxes. Separate mechanisms produce the equations of the sun, its anomaly and right ascension. Others, the principal equations of the moon; as its erection, anomaly, variation, annual equation, reduction, and right ascension. Others, again, relate to the equations of the ascending node of the moon. The rising and setting of the sun, its passage to the meridian, its eclipses, and those of the moon, are also represented on the dial.

A word respecting almanacs. Some suppose the term to be of Arabic origin, but whether it be from *al manach*, to count, or *al* and *men*—months, or *manakos*, the course of the months, is not agreed: some give it a *Teutonic* origin, from the words *al* and *moan*, the moon. Each of these conjectures is plausible. Others again assign it a Saxon derivation. The long almanacs of the Saxons, called "al-mon-aght," were constructed of square pieces of wood, horn, and sometimes metal, about a foot in length, and two inches in diameter, on the four sides of which were graven the golden numbers, dominical letters, and epacts of the different Sundays in each quarter of the year.

Johannes de Monte-Regio, in 1472, composed the earliest European almanac that issued from the press ; and, before the end of that century, they became common on the Continent. In England they were not in general use until the middle of the sixteenth century.

The almanac, in its simple form as a calendar, agrees in many respects to the *fasti* or festival-roll of the Romans. It is of ancient date, and at first was no more than a calendar of Pagan festivals. The word *calendar* comes from the Latin verb *calare*, to call, or *calens*, its participle, on account of the custom of the pontiffs summoning the people to apprise them of the festivals occurring in each respective month : these occasions are designated *dies calendæ*—the calends or first days of the month. Such was the beginning of our almanac. The fasti seems to be an extension of the primitive religious calendar, and to the pagan feast-days, added the days on which the magistrates were elected and held court. This was its first civil form.

The calendar of the almanac now in use is an improvement on that of Romulus. He divided the year into ten months, beginning with March. His year consisted of 304 days. Numa improved on Romulus, and added two months, January to the beginning, and February to the end of the year. In 452 B. C., the Decemvirs placed February after January, and fixed the order of the months. The year at this time consisted of 365¼ days. According to the imperfect mode of reckoning by the Romans, after the addition of the months of January and February, B. C., 452, the twenty-fourth of February was called the sixth before the calends of March, *sexto calendas*. In the intercalary year this day was repeated and styled *bis sexto calendas*—whence we derive the term *bissextile*. The corresponding term *leap year*, is, however, infelicitously applied, inasmuch as it seems to intimate that a day was leapt over, instead of being thrust in, which is the fact. It may be remarked that in the ecclesiastical calendar, the intercalary day is still inserted between the twenty-fourth and twenty-fifth of February. Bissextile, or leap-year, therefore contains three hundred and sixty-six days, and occurs every fourth year. Leap-year is, according to traditionary lore, invested with sundry privileges and immunities to the fair. The Comic Almanac says, 'it takes three *springs* to make one *leap year*.'

Sosigenies, the astronomer, induced Cæsar to abolish the lunar year, and regulate time by the sun. Gregory the Thirteenth, in 1582, corrected the calendar, and placed it on its present basis. The Gregorian calendar was received at once by all the Roman Catholic States of Europe. The Protestant powers refused, for some time, to adopt it. England did not receive it till 1752. In that year, the Julian calendar, or *old style*, was abolished, and the Gregorian, or *new style*, adopted. This was done by dropping eleven days, the excess of the Julian over the true solar time. Russia still adheres to the old.

Of the written calendars, perhaps the most interesting, as well as the most ancient, were the "folding-almanacs," of which there are a number still to be seen, in a fine state of preservation, in the British and Oxford Museums. Some are in Latin; but others again, dating in the middle of the fifteenth century, are in English. Not a few of these compositions were of an astrological nature, and amongst them may be instanced one by the famous Roger Bacon, and another by the notorious Dr. Lee.

In some of the almanacs of the sixteenth century may be found the original of the well-known rhymes on the number of days in each month. They appear slightly different from our modern version:

"April, June, and September,
Thirty daies as November;
Each month also doth never vary,
From thirty-one, save February
Which twenty-eight doth still confine,
Save on Leap-yeare, then twenty-nine."

A prominent feature of the earlier almanacs was the prognostications respecting the weather, calculated from the various phases of the moon. *Moore's* Almanac acquired its great notoriety by this, its sale having at one time reached 480,000 copies. These astrological predictions were even sanctioned by the Archbishop of Canterbury.

Astrology is not yet extinct, not only have we even seen a living professor of that occult and venerable science, but the well known "Raphael's Prophetic Almanac," which has existed about thirty-five years, is still annually issued in London. Now as to the origin of the divisions of time!

Before the death of JACOB, which happened in 1689, B. C., we find that several nations were so well acquainted with the revolutions of the *Moon*, as to measure by them the duration of their year. It had been a universal custom among all nations of antiquity as well as the Jews, to divide time into a portion of a *week* or *seven days;* this undoubtedly arose from the tradition with regard to the origin of the world. It was natural for those nations, who lived a pastoral life, or who lived under a serene sky, to observe, that the various appearances of the moon were completed nearly in four weeks; hence, the division of a *month.* Those people again who lived by agriculture, and were acquainted with the division of a month, would naturally remark that twelve of these brought back the same temperature of air, or the same seasons; hence the origin of what is called the *lunar year,* which has everywhere been recognized in the infancy of science. This, together with the observations of the fixed stars (which we learn from the book of *Job*, who, according to the best writers, was contemporary with *Jacob*) must have been very ancient, and led to the discovery of the *solar year.*

The first division of the day was into morning, noon, and night; and these are the only parts of a day mentioned in the Old Testament. But it is probable that men of science had other more accurate divisions, because we find they had *sun-dials.* Afterwards they divided their days into twelve hours ; and to this division our Saviour refers when he says, "Are there not twelve hours in a day ?" But their hours must have been of different lengths, at different seasons of the year ; for their hour was a twelfth part of the time the sun continued above the horizon. And as this time is longer in summer than in winter, their summer hours must therefore have been longer than their winter hours. This difference, however, would not be so very sensible in that country as here, as Judea is much nearer to the equator than we are, and the days there, in consequence, nearer equal. Their hours were computed from sunrise ; their *third hour* divided the space between sun-rising and noon ; the *ninth* hour divided the space between noon and sunset. But in the New Testament, we find that they sometimes made use of the Roman mode of reckoning.

The Roman reckoning was the same as ours, beginning at midnight, and reckoning to noon, twelve hours ; and again from noon till midnight.

The Hebrews divided their night into four watches of three hours each. The *first* from six to nine in the evening ; the *second* from nine to twelve ; the *third* from midnight to three in the morning ; and the last to *six* or sun-rising.

The Jews began their year in March, and the months were :—NISAN, ZIF, SIVAN, TAMUZ, AB, ELUL, TISRI, BUL, CISLIEU, TEBEETH, SHEBAT, ADAR. Their civil year commenced with the new moon near the autumnal equinox, in the month called TISRI, corresponding with part of our *September* and *October*.

The Jewish months were alternately 29 and 30 days and their year of twelve lunations, 354 days. To recover the lost days, they added a whole month after every two or three years, following their twelfth month of Adar, and they called this extra month Ve-adar.

The MOHAMMEDANS reckon their days from sun-set till sunrise. The CHINESE begin theirs an hour before midnight, and divide the rotation into 12 parts of 2 of our hours, and give a name to each division. The HINDOOS divide their days into four watches, and each watch into *guhrees* of 24 minutes each.

The great and lesser divisions of time into cycles, epochs, and eras, years, months, weeks, and days ; not to mention hours, minutes, and seconds—all respectively subserve the purposes of, and to a great extent exert a controlling influence upon mundane affairs. The most apparent sway of these natural or artificial divisions, is observable in the implicit obedience which nature universally yields to the alternations of day and night, as the allotments assigned to activity and repose. It is true there are some slight infringements upon the rule, by the too servile devotees to fashion and folly, who are accustomed to reverse the order of nature : these, however, but add confirmation to the rule. Again, there seems to exist some difficulty as to the right determining of the precise time at which the day should begin and terminate.

Among the ancient nations the day began at sunrise and continued till its light expired : others supposed their day to commence at sunset : the Arabians, again, make theirs to begin at noon, with all navigators and astronomers : while we, in common with the ancient Egyptians, and most of the modern Europeans, date from midnight, which, allowing of all the waking hours of day to come together, is manifestly the most convenient and rational.

The somewhat arbitrary subdivisions of time into morning forenoon, mid-day, afternoon, evening, and night, are yet not without significance : the same can scarcely be claimed for the more minute distributions of time into hours, minutes, and seconds. Of its sidereal measurements we shall hereafter speak in connection with the zodiacal signs of the months.

The Egyptians and Chaldeans dated their new year from the autumnal equinox ; so did the Jews for all civil purposes, but their ecclesiastical year began with the vernal. The Mohammedans begin their year the minute the sun enters Aries, the day that Dremschid, the Persian monarch, made his public entry into Persêpolis ; in commemoration of which event, he transferred the beginning of the year from its previous date of the autumnal equinox to that of the springtide. The Turks and Arabs are said to date their year from the middle of July ; and the Abyssinians on the 26th of August, as if to increase the variety, and confound the calendar.

The origin of the names of the days is so remote as to be somewhat involved in the mists of antiquity. According to the best authorities, they derived their designation from the planets, or deities worshipped by Pagan nations.

The Romans designated their days after the heavenly bodies, or after some of their gods, as follows :

SUNDAY—*Dies Solis*, the day of the SUN.
MONDAY—*Dies Lunæ*, the day of the MOON.
TUESDAY—*Dies Martis*, the day of MARS.
WEDNESDAY—*Dies Mercurii*, the day of MERCURY.
THURSDAY—*Dies Jovis*, the day of JUPITER.
FRIDAY—*Dies Veneris*, the day of VENUS.
SATURDAY—*Dies Saturni*, the day of SATURN.

The French, perpetuating the custom received from the Romans, still retain these names, *Lundi*, *Mardi*, *Mercredi*, &c. While we have adopted from the Saxons the appellations of their idols, which may be traced as follows :—thus Sunday, from *Sunnan-daeg*, from being dedicated to the worship of the sun ; Monday, *Monan-daeg*, to the moon ; Tuesday, from *Tuisco*, the most ancient of the Teutonic deities ; Wednesday, a contraction of *Wodin's*, or *Odin's* day ; Thursday, from *Thor's-day*, or the thunderer's day, devoted to the worship of Thor ; Friday, from *Friga's-daeg* ; and Saturday, from *Seater-daeg*, equivalent to Saturn's day.

Days, weeks, and months serve as the way-marks of Time, by which we measure our progress in the journey of life ; while the succession of the seasons, like the alternations of day and night, remind us of its ever-varying phases and changes. The early budding and blossoming of human existence, so redolent of sportive fancies and gay flowers, finds its emblem in the vernal beauty and freshness of spring; while the russet tints and golden fruits of autumn, and the blanched face and icy breath of winter, present the no less significant symbols of manhood in its prime and its decadence. The seasons and their change are rife with attractive interest to the contemplative mind; they afford an ever-enduring feast, to regale and gladden the sense, and refine the soul. The youth of the year, like the spring-tide of life, is full of hope, buoyancy, and joyousness. Radiant in freshened beauty, spring diffuses the light of her kindling smiles, and the genial influence of her nectared breath, gladdens the face of all created things. The protracted austerity of winter's desolation but inspires us with a more earnest welcome for the ravishing charms and jubilant voices of the new-born spring. What music is there even in her very name! What new beauties greet us on every side—what pleasant objects delight the eye, and what a glowing pleasure does she diffuse about the heart! We revel in the rich influence of her varied fascinations, till the soul longs to mingle in the sunshine, with the breeze, the buds and blossoms, that send upward their fragrant incense.

The ancients seem to have followed the indications of nature in making the commencement of the year to synchronize with the spring month; but modern usage adopted a different standard. We propose to bring in successive review the months. The ancients were accustomed to group together the various clusters of stars, for their more ready recognition. To some of these groups, which they termed constellations, they gave the names of a few celebrated personages of their day, and others they named after such birds, beasts, or insects as seemed to be portrayed in the space described by these stellar objects. The divisions of the heavens designated, to some extent, the seasons of the year, and hence the origin of the signs of the zodiac. In the days of Hipparchus, the month of January was denoted by *Aquarius, or the water-bearer*, because it was observed that when the sun entered this constellation, it was usually a wintry and wet season of the year. Thus it was represented under the figure of a man pouring out water from an urn.

JANUARY, our first month (so called from Janus, an ancient king of Italy, who was deified after his death), is derived from the Latin word Januarius. Janus, was reputed to preside over the gate of heaven, the name of the month is indicative of its being at the opening of the New Year. Janus was represented with two faces, looking in opposite directions: one old, the other youthful, representing the old and the new era. He held a key in his hand, on which were the numbers 365, the number of days in a year which he unlocked and presided over. The temple in Rome, erected to his memory, was quadrangular, having one door and three windows on each side. It stood upon the Janiculum Hill, and was always kept open in time of war. It was closed only three times during the lapse of seven hundred years. It was closed at the time of the birth of Christ, for then the whole world was at peace. Our Saxon ancestors called January, *Wolf-monat*, or "Wolf-month," on account of the famished wolves which invaded their villages; they also styled it *Aeften Yala*, or after Christmas.

Prince, the peasant-poet, thus apostrophizes the initial month:—

He cometh! the elder born child of the year,
With a turbulent voice, and a visage austere;
But his cold, callous hand, and his boreal breath,
Prepare for new life, the low relics of death;
A changeling in temper, but ever sublime,
Is this moody, mad offspring of stern winter time.

The advent of the New Year has been from time immemorial kept as a day of rejoicing. By the Greeks it was a solemn festival: by the Romans one of feasting and congratulation. Throughout Christendom it is kept as a holiday. Bells are rung at midnight to celebrate the exit of the old, and the advent of the new year.

The commencement of the year, has at different times been assigned to the 25th of December, or Christmas day, the 1st of January, or the day of Circumcision, and the 25th of March, or Easter day, commemorative of the Resurrection.

Despite its icy breath and frigid aspect, rugged winter seems to be prophetic of a joyous new existence, as those who have become frosted with age appear for the time to have acquired a spirit of rejuvenescence. It forms a sort of resting-place in the progress of life's journey, from which we all persuade ourselves, however we may deprecate the past, that the future is gilded with Iris hopes of happiness. If the external aspect of nature appear cheerless and chilly, the scene is but the more heightened by the contrast of the sunny smiles and generous hospitalities of the happy fireside of kindred and friends. There is something picturesque as well as grateful in this time-honored custom of commemorating the nativity of the year, by acts of beneficence and votive offerings to friendship.

Friendly interchange of visits, congratulations and the presentation of gifts, seem to have been in vogue in every age. The ancient Druids were accustomed to cut the sacred misletoe, with a golden knife, in a forest dedicated to the gods, and to distribute its branches with much ceremony, as new year's gifts to the people.

Of the special holidays and festivals of this month, the first in order is that of *Circumcision*—a festival of the Romish church, and adopted also by the Episcopacy since the year 1550. The next festival in the Calendar is that styled *Epiphany, or Twelfth-day*—indicating the manifestation of Christ to the Gentile world, which event is ascribed to this date. This holiday used to be characterized in Saxon times by the *wassail-bowl*—a spiced decoction, deriving its name from *wæs-*

hael (be healthy), the toast the sturdy old Saxons adopted on the occasion of their libations.

The second, and briefest of the family of months—February, derives its name from *Februo*, to purify ; hence *Februarius*, the appellation assigned by the Romans to the expiatory sacrifices they were accustomed to offer at this season. *Pisces*, the constellation over which Neptune was supposed to preside, was regarded by the ancients as the last of the winter signs, and was represented under the figure of two fishes ; but at present it is the first in order of the stellar groups of the zodiac, presiding over the vernal equinox.

The Saxon name for this month was *sprout-kele*, also *sal-monath*, or pancake month, from their custom of offering cakes to the sun, for his increasing power.

Midway in this month comes the festival of St. Valentine. All we know of him is that he was canonized in consequence of his having suffered martyrdom in the third century, under the emperor Claudius.* Some have conjectured that the custom of devoting this day to Cupid is traceable to the ancient Romans, whose festivals, called Lupercalia, were celebrated about this time. On these occasions, amidst a variety of ceremonies, the names of young women were placed in a box, from which they were drawn by a band of devotees, as chance directed.

The practical joking which prevails so universally on the day in question, the love of fun and caricature with Cupid, is of comparatively modern date. Formerly, love-making among our sober progenitors wore a much more grave and demure aspect :

* "St. Valentine was a holy priest of Rome, who, with St. Marius and his family, assisted the martyrs in the persecution under Claudius II. He was apprehended, and sent by the Emperor to the Prefect of Rome, who, on finding all his efforts to make him renounce his faith ineffectual, commanded him to be beaten with clubs, and afterwards beheaded; and this occurred on the 14th. About the year 270, Pope Julius is said to have built a church near Ponte Mole, to his memory, which for a long time gave name to the gate afterwards called Porta del Populo. The greatest part of his relics are preserved in the Church of St. Praxedes.

it was not a matter to be trifled with, that of linking hearts and hands, with the joint fortunes or misfortunes of life.

Oh love! how potent is thy sway;
  Thou'rt terrible, indeed, to most men!
But once a year there comes a day
  When thou tormentest chiefly postmen.
Oh hard indeed the lot must be
  Of him who wears thy galling fetters!
But e'en more miserable he,
  Who must go round with all thy letters.

Without pretending to estimate the obligations of many of the devotees to Hymen to this worthy saint's influence, the festival, occurring half-way in this most inclement and unpopular month, certainly tends to beguile many of its objectionable accompaniments—snow, sleet, and that worst of all kinds of weather—a penetrating thaw, against which even a suit of mail may be said to be scarcely impervious. Shrove-Tuesday and Ash-Wednesday occur in this month, both being initiatory days to the season of Lent; the religious observance of which originated with the Romish Church.

Shrove-Tuesday regulates most of the movable feasts. It is the next after the first new moon in the month of February, and follows the first Sunday in Lent. Formerly, the people were expected to prepare themselves for Lent by confessing themselves, hence the word *shrove.*

Ash-Wednesday is the first day of Lent, supposed to have been so called from a custom in the Church of sprinkling ashes that day on the heads of the penitents.

MARCH is so called from *Mars*, the reputed father of Romulus, and god of war. It was, as already intimated, placed as the first month by some of the ancients, and by others as the third, fourth, or fifth, and even the tenth month of the year.

The SAXONS called it *lenct monath*, or length month, because the days then begin in length to exceed the nights.

Lenct, now called Lent, means spring ; hence March was the spring month. The Saxons also called it *Hlyd-monath*, from hlyd, which means stormy, and in this sense March was the stormy month.

March is a rude, and sometimes boisterous month, possessing many of the characteristics of winter, yet awakening sensations more pleasant than the two following months, for it gives us the first announcement and taste of spring. What can equal the delight of the heart at the very first glimpse of spring —the first peeping of buds and green herbs ? It is like a new life infused into our bosoms. A spirit of tenderness—a burst of freshness and luxury of feeling possesses us ; and though fifty springs have broken upon us, their joy, unlike many joys of time, is not an atom impaired.

True it is that blustering, rude Boreas causes boisterous excitement about this time, as if seeking to awaken nature from her long sleep of winter ; while dusty particles scorn all local habitation, performing fantastic gyrations in the air, to the serious discomfiture of our physical organs, especially the optical and olfactory.

The dry winds of lusty March, however they may be deprecated for their personal incivilities, are nevertheless useful to the purposes of agriculture. Its zodiacal sign, *Aries*, was assigned to this, originally the first month of the year, because the ancients considered the ram as the father of the fleecy flock which afforded them both food and raiment.

St. David's Day is celebrated by the Welsh as commemorative of their patron Saint : it occurs on the first of the month.

We now come to the festival held in honor of the tutelar Saint of *Ould Ireland—Saint Patrick*—who, according to ancient lore, in the year of grace 433 landed near Wicklow, having, it is said, been born at Kilpatrick, Scotland. His glorious memory is mnemonized by the well-known *Shamrock.* The real name of this notable apostle of the Irish was Maenwyn. Pope Celestine gave him his ecclesiastical patronymic of *Patri-*

cus, when he consecrated him as bishop to Ireland in 433, A.D. Originally there was a dispute, according to Lover, as to the true anniversary of this renowned saint, some supposing the eighth and others the ninth to be the correct date: the humorist, however, represents a priest as settling the difficulty as follows:

> Says he, "Boys, don't be fighting for eight or for nine;
> Don't be always dividing—but sometimes combine.
> Combine eight with nine, and seventeen is the mark.
> So let that be his birth-day." "Amen," says the clerk.
> So they all got blind drunk—which completed their bliss,
> And we keep up the practice from that day to this.

St. Agnes' Eve was deemed propitious for young maidens in the affair of securing good husbands; and *St. Paul's Day* was also regarded as one among the numerous days of ominous character by the superstitious of olden time.

Easter Sunday is always the first Sunday after the full moon which happens upon, or next after, the 21st day of March, and if the full moon should occur upon a Sunday, Easter day is the Sunday after. It was so fixed in early times, that the Christians might avoid the celebration of Easter at the time of the Jewish passover, held on the very day of the full moon.

Palm, or *Passion Sunday*, is the first Sunday before Easter, so called in commemoration of Christ's entering into Jerusalem, eight days before the passover. The Passover of the Jews closely agrees with the time when the sun crosses or *passes over* the equator, an event that could hardly fail to be celebrated with rites and ceremonies by a people so devoted to astronomy as the Egyptians who had educated Moses. Pascha was the primitive term, the English name passover being derived from God's *passing* over the houses of the Israelites and sparing their first-born, when those of the Egyptians were put to death.

Lady-day occurs on the 25th. Its title is also derived from the Roman calendar and memorializes the Annunciation of the Virgin. It is the high festival of Catholicism, which, in consequence of the extreme honors it pays to the Virgin Mary, has been sometimes termed the Marian Church.

Ascension Day, called also Holy Thursday, is celebrated by the Church as the day on which our Saviour ascended into heaven, which happened the fortieth day after the resurrection.

April, is derived from *aperio*, to open. The first of April was by the Romans consecrated to Venus, the goddess of beauty, as the earth begins at this time to be covered with beautiful flowers.

The Saxons called it *oster*, or *easter month*, it being the time when the feast of the Saxon goddess, Eastre, Easter or Eòstèr, was celebrated.

The month of April is one of alternating smiles and tears. By some writers it has been designated the sweetest of the series, because it ushers in the "delicate-footed May."

Sighing, storming, singing, smiling,
With her many moods beguiling,
  April walks the wakening earth.
Wheresoe'er she looks and lingers,
Wheresoe'er she lays her fingers,
  Some new charm starts into birth.
Fitful clouds about her sweeping,
Coming, going, frowning, weeping,
  Melt in fertile blessings round.
Frequent rainbows that embrace her,
And with gorgeous girdles grace her,
Dropping flowers upon the ground.*

This month, it will be recollected, is introduced by the equivocal practice of imposing upon our credulity, under the style and title of April-fooling. Antiquarians have puzzled them-

*J. C. Prince.

selves and their readers by their vain attempts to account for a custom, which still obtains even among some of the more sapient and refined. Without, therefore, following in their wake, and thus incur the risk of suspicion with the reader, that we mean to illustrate the practice at his expense—we shall content ourselves by simply citing the emphatic words of an old and respectable authority—Mr. Douce. "After all the conjectures," he says, "which have been formed touching its origin, it is certainly borrowed from the French, and may, I think, be deduced from this simple analogy. The French call their April fish (Poissons d'Avril,)—silly mackerel, or simpletons, which suffer themselves to be caught in this month. But, as with us," he continues, "April is not the season of that fish, we have very properly substituted the word—*fools.*"

Be very circumspect on this day of attending to gratuitous advice, given in the street, respecting your costume or appearance. Do not heed any officious person who may insist upon your picking up anything he may imagine you have dropped.

"Few persons are aware of the real derivation of many of the old customs which have been handed down almost from time immemorial. Thus, decking the house with evergreens at Christmas is the remains of a pagan superstition. In Great Britain the holly is used for this purpose, and the holly in the days of paganism was dedicated to Saturn, as the mistletoe was to Friga, the Scandinavian Venus. The yule log bears reference to the constant fire kept up by the priests of Baal, and the Maypole, with all its adjuncts, offers an imitation of the games formerly held in honor of the goddess Flora."

About the nineteenth day the sun enters *Taurus*—a constellation which includes one hundred and forty-one stars, the principal of which is Aldebaran, of the first magnitude: it also comprises two remarkable representations, viz.: the Pleiades, and the Hyades. Alcyone, the principal star in the Pleiades, is supposed by Prof. Madler to be the grand central sun in the universe.

Good Friday is designed to commemorate the crucifixion. It is religiously regarded by the Episcopacy as a solemn festival of the church: and at St. Peter's at Rome, it is kept up in the service of the *Tenebræ*—a ceremonial representing the entombment of the Saviour. Cross-buns used on this day, are in imitation of the ecclesiastical *eulogia*, or consecrated loaves, formerly bestowed in the church as alms, or given to those, who, from any impediment could not receive the host. It will be remembered (speaking of Friday) that popular superstition has marked this day of the week as "unlucky." This vulgar notion arose doubtless from the fact of the crucifixion having been supposed to occur on that day, with all its solemn and ominous accessories of darkness and earthquake. Leigh Hunt records it against no less a name than Byron's, that he was the victim of this silly superstition; and—alas that it is so—there are many still extant who confess to so ludicrous a weakness, especially among sailors and silly women. The conceit doubtless took its rise in heathen times—the monks endorsing the usage in their designating certain days of their calendar by the names dies atri and dies albi.

In order to put a stop to the superstition which attached to this unlucky day, a company of men once laid the timbers of a ship on Friday, launched her on Friday; after some trouble they found a captain of the name of Friday, and with still more trouble procured men who were willing to sail in her on that day. She started on a Friday for her destination, and was never more heard of. This fact is accredited, being stoutly insisted upon by all sailors.

If Friday was ever ill-omened, its reputation is sufficiently redeemed, for it was on that day that Columbus discovered the American continent, that George Washington was born, and that the Pilgrim fathers reached the Plymouth rock.

Ancient calendars designate two days in each month as unfortunate, namely—of January, the first and seventh; February, the third and fourth; March, the first and fourth; April, the tenth and eleventh ; May, the third and seventh ; June, the tenth and fifteenth ; July, the tenth and thirteenth ; August, the first and second ; September, the third and tenth ; October, the third and tenth ; November, the third and fifth ; December, the seventh and tenth. Each of these days was devoted to some peculiar fatality.

"The flowery May, who from her green lap throws
The yellow cowslip and the pale primrose.
Hail, bounteous May, that dost inspire
Mirth and youth, and warm desire ;
Woods and groves are of thy dressing,
Hill and dale doth boast thy blessing.
Thus we salute thee with an early song,
And welcome thee, and wish thee long."

Thus sung the "blind old bard" of English verse, and a right fruitful theme has this "queen month" of the calendar been to the many worshippers of the muse from the days of old Chaucer down to our own.

May is the most instructive and religious, as well as the most delightful of all festival times. It seems to be the bridal season of heaven and earth, and the whole month the honeymoon.

"Buds are filling, leaves are swelling,
Flowers on field, and bloom on tree :
O'er the earth, and air, and ocean,
Nature holds her jubilee."

Wordsworth thus daintily pictures forth the harbingers of spring :—

"Pansies, lilies, kingcups, daisies,
Let them live upon their praises ;
Long as there's a sun that sets
Primroses will have their glory—
Long as there are violets
They will have a place in story."

The following lines of Tennyson seem to glow with the beauty and bloom of spring :

> "In the spring a fuller crimson comes upon the robin's breast,
> In the spring the wanton lapwing gets himself another crest;
> In the spring a lovelier iris changes on the burnished dove,
> In the spring a young man's fancy lightly turns to thoughts of love."

With many other pastoral customs of the olden time, that of the rural celebration of May-day is well-nigh passed into oblivion. Bourne tells us, that in his time, in the villages in the North of England, the youth of both sexes were wont to rise before dawn, and assemble in some neighboring wood, accompanied with music, and there they gathered branches from the trees, and wove garlands and bouquets of flowers, with which they returned to deck their homes.

The rustic festival of the May-pole, and the ceremony of crowning the pride of the village as May-queen, formed one of the most picturesque of the good old pastimes of our English ancestors: and is also as ancient as any of which we have any record; it being doubtless identical with the festival of the Romans in honor of Flora, which they styled *Floralia*, and which occurred on the fourth of the kalends of May. Sometimes the May-pole was brought to the village-green in great pomp, being drawn by twenty yoke of oxen, each being garlanded with flowers, with which, as well as with branches, flags, and streamers, the pole itself was profusely wreathed and decked.

The rural festivities of the May-queen are no longer seen, but the denizens of New York, for the special benefit of the landlords, have substituted a custom instead, of a most moving and exciting character; we refer to their curious passion for changing their habitations on that day. On this eventful day, the entire community is in a transition state. Like a busy swarm of ants, people are hurrying to and fro, hither and thither, in the most amusing confusion; each eagerly in quest of his new abode. This singular fancy for change of habitation seems peculiar to this locomotive people; and so generally is the custom adopted by them, that all business for the time is suffered to fall into a state of collapse. No wonder that scarce a vestige of antiquity is permitted to remain to point the past history of a city, whose inhabitants cease even to venerate the walls of their own consecrated homes. The festivals of this month, include among others, Whit Sunday, and Trinity Sunday ; the former probably derived from the custom in the Romish church of converts, newly baptised, appearing from Easter to Whitsuntide dressed in white.

Maia, the brightest of the Pleiades, from whom this month derived its name, is fabled to have been the daughter of Atlas.

The Anglo-Saxons called this month *tremelki*, because then they began to milk their kine three times a day.

The zodiacal sign of May is Gemini (the twins), named Castor and Pollux, who are fabled to have appeared to sailors in storms with lambent fires on their heads, as propitious to the mariner.

May is synonymous with sunny weather ; the state of the weather, by the way, is an ever-fruitful theme of discourse with all sorts of people. It seems ever uppermost in our thoughts, or upon the tip of the tongue.

It is worthy of note when two friends meet together
The first topic they start is the state of the weather—
It is always the same, both with young and with old,
'Tis either too hot, or else 'tis too cold,
'Tis either too wet, or else 'tis too dry,
The glass is too low, or else 'tis too high ;
But if all had their wishes once jumbled together,
No mortal on earth could exist in such weather.

We now approach the rosy, summer month of June. It was by the Romans called *Junius*, in honor of the youth who served Regulus in the war ; or it was more probably derived from Juno, the goddess of heaven.

The Saxons gave it the name of *weyd-monath*, from the German *weiden*, to pasture.

This is the season for fresh and fragrant flowers—those gaudy and brilliant gems, nature bedecks herself withal: the very air is perfumed with their rich odors: and in the words of Coleridge,

> "Many a hidden brook, in this leafy month of June,
> To the sleeping woods, all night singeth a quiet tune."

Towards the close of the month, that pleasant rural occupation, hay-making, commences: the country now begins to assume a most beautiful aspect—here the corn is already beginning to peep out, here the meadows are mown and cleared, and here again the grass still waves in all the rich luxuriance of wild flowers, awaiting the reapers.

Of the red-letter-days of June, one of the most notable is the longest of the year, the 21st., on which occurs the summer solstice.

We have now completed just half the circuit of the calendar; and it is high noon of the year; suppose we indulge in a brief homily upon Time—by way of tempering our trifling, and in order to save our sobriety from shipwreck. How important is it that we duly value the passing moment—all we can boast of time in possession—yet are we not ever prone rather to indulge vain regrets for the past, or eager anticipations for the future? "Spare minutes are the gold-dust of time," says a quaint author; "of all portions of our life they are the most to be guarded and watched, for they are the gaps through which idleness tempts us astray." An impartial review of the past is fraught with instruction to the future:

> 'Tis greatly wise to talk with our past hours,
> And ask them what report they bore to heaven.

Midsummer, also, naturally reminds us of the meridian of life—a point in our history, when we may with advantage take a retrospective as well as a prospective survey; when the premonitions of an occasional gray hair, or wrinkle on the brow, are too decisive to be mistaken.

The more we live, more brief appear,
  Our life's succeeding stages:
A day to childhood seems a year,
  And years, like passing ages.

The gladsome current of our youth,
  Ere passion yet disorders,
Steals, lingering, like a river smooth,
  Along its grassy borders.

But as the care-worn cheek grows wan,
  And sorrow's shafts fly thicker,
Ye stars, that measure life to man!
  Why seem your courses quicker?

When joys have lost their bloom and breath,
  And life itself is vapid;
Why, as we reach the falls of Death,
  Feel we the tide more rapid?

It may be strange—yet who would change
  Time's course to slower speeding?
When one by one our friends are gone,
  And left our bosoms bleeding.

Heaven gives our years of fading strength
  Indemnifying fleetness;
And those of youth, a *seeming length*,
  Proportioned to their sweetness.*

We now come to the sultry summer month of JULY—when *Sol* is in the ascendant, and in his glowing ardor to entertain his guests, gives to all creation such an ardent greeting. Punch's humorous apostrophe is too good to be omitted in this place: it runs in this wise:

* Campbell.

"Well done, thou glorious orb! well done, indeed,
Thou sun; for nature now is one great feast,
Roasted, and boiled, and fried, and baked, by thee.
Thy fire hath boiled the fishes in the streams;
Roasted the living mutton on the Downs;
Fried all the parsley on its very bed;
And baking the potatoes under ground,
Hath cooked them growing; so that men may dig
'Taters all hot!'"

This month is distinguished by its introducing the celebrated "*Dog-days.*" *That every dog has his day,* is an admitted axiom, but why the canine fraternity at large should thus monopolize this particular part of the calendar, we cannot divine: and as we prefer not to *dogmatize*, we respectfully refer the reader to an old authority, and a witty *dog* into the bargain—*Dogberry.* Whether it is that they expect to *run mad* with impunity during this term, to the terror of all mayors and municipalities; or whether it is because all the rest of the year they get kicked out of sight, that this brief interval is secured for their jubilee, we are alike unable to determine; and must, therefore, leave the learned in such matters to decide, and shall be content to con-cur in their decision.

Tom Hood has something to add on the subject, which we subjoin:

"Most doggedly I do maintain,
  And hold the dogma true—
That four-legged dogs although we see
  We've some that walk on two,
Among them there are clever dogs—
  A few you'd reckon mad,
While some are very jolly dogs
  And others very sad.
I've heard of physic thrown to dogs,
  And very much incline,
To think it true, for we've a pack
  Who only *bark* and *w(h)ine.*"

The "dog-days," or Dies Caniculares, according to *Bailey's*

Dictionary, "are commonly from the 24th of July to the 28th of August, which are very hot—the dog-star increasing the heat—and vulgarly reckoned unwholesome." The dog-days, says Chambers, precede and follow the heliacal rising of the star Sirius, which, in Pliny's time, was on the 18th of July.

Even in modern as well as ancient times, this "heated term" has been connected with the appearance of this star in the morning; though the extreme heat is palpably the effect of the continued high position of the sun. Now the fact is known, that the dog-star cannot increase the heat, because, by the precession of the equinoxes, its heliacal rising will, in a thousand years, take place in the depth of winter.

At Argos, a festival was expressly instituted for the killing of dogs at this season, and the institution seems to be preserved at the present time in other cities.

The first of the summer Signs was called *Cancer*, or the crab, because, when the sun entered this constellation, it was observed to have attained its greatest northern distance from the equator, and then began to assume a retrograde motion, which the ancients represented under the figure of a crab, on account of its creeping or moving backward.

While Hercules was engaged in destroying the famous Lernæan monster, according to mythologists, Juno sent a sea-crab to bite the hero's feet. This new enemy was soon dispatched, but Juno, to reward its services, placed it among the stars.

Proudly, lovely and serenely,
  Power and passion in her eye,
With an aspect calm and queenly,
  Comes the summer-nymph, July,
Crowned with azure, clothed with splendor,
  Gorgeous as an Eastern bride,
While the glowing hours attend her
  O'er the languid landscape wide.*

July (from the Latin name Julius,) was conferred upon this

* J. C. Prince.

month, in honor of Julius Cæsar. The Saxons named it *hen-monath* (foliage month). The zodiacal sign is Sirius, which is apparently the largest, the most refulgent, and one of the nearest objects in the sidereal heavens, is situated in the constellation Canis Major, 21 deg. 40 min. southeast of the belt of Orion. Its distance is computed at not less than 19 billions of miles from the Earth, and if it occupied the place of our sun, it would appear 37 times larger, and would give nearly 14 times as much light?

On the fifteenth of July we have St. Swithin's day—memorable from the tradition that, if there should be rain on that day, it would continue wet weather for forty days afterwards. This conceit has its origin in one of the fables of the Latin Church, which reads as follows, "St. Swithin, bishop of Winchester, before his demise, which occurred in the year 868, desired that he might be buried in the open church-yard and not in the chancel of the minster, as was usual with other bishops; and his request was complied with; but the monks on his being canonized, considering it disgraceful for the saint to lie in a public cemetery, resolved to remove his body into the choir, which was to have been done with solemn procession on the 15th of July—it rained, however, so violently for forty days together at this season, that the design was abandoned."

The "glorious Fourth" is the national birth-day of Freedom in the United States, when the "sovereign people" indulge in the exercise of the "largest liberty," and by way of *canonizing* the goddess, disturb the quiet with incessant discharges of guns, firing of pistols, and rushing of rockets

The golden AUGUST now bursts upon us—that gorgeous month, most rife with all sorts of delicious fruits, as well as of golden crops of wavy corn, and sheaves of garnered grain.

This month is introduced by Lammas-day—one of the great thanksgiving festivals of former times: and it closes under the saintly patronage of Jerome. Harvest-home, the rustic jubilee of rural life, also belongs to this glorious month.

August was called *Sextilis* by the Romans, from its being the sixth month in their calendar, until the Senate complimented Augustus by naming it after him, because he had then first entered upon his consulship, having subdued Egypt to the Roman dominion!

The Saxons called this month *arn-monath*, more rightly barn-monath, indicating the filling of barns with corn.

The zodiacal sign of the month—that of Virgo—the Virgin, is supposed to be the Asbraea, the Goddess of Justice, who, according to mythological lore, lived upon the earth during the Golden Age; but being offended at the wickedness of mankind during the Brazen and Iron Ages, she returned to heaven among the stars, and has since been known under the name of Virgo.

The sign Virgo was represented with ears of corn in her hands, signifying the harvest. Spenser thus refers to it

——— being rich arrayed,
In garment all of gold down to the ground,
Yet rode he not, but led a lovely mayd,
Forth by the lily hand, the which was crown'd
With eares of corne, and full her hand was found.

The 24th of the month is celebrated as *St. Bartholomew's Day*, a holiday of the Church of England. Bartholomew was an apostle, but there is no scriptural account of his labors or death. The legend of the Romish Church represents him as preaching in the Indies, and concluding his life by being flayed alive by order of a brother of the king of Armenia. In memory of his death, it was customary at the monastic institutions, in the middle ages, to distribute small knives among the people. The day has a horrible celebrity in connection with the massacre of the Protestants at Paris, in 1572, by that wretched woman, Catherine De Medicis.

Crowned with the sickle and the wheaten sheaf,
While Autumn nodding o'er the yellow plain
Comes jovial on.

The radiant splendor of the sunny months, now gives place to the sober tints of russet autumn.

A pastoral writer observes,—Autumn, yet with her hand grasped in the feeble clasp of Summer, as if the latter were loth to depart, still retains much green hanging about the woods, and much blue and sunshine about the sky and earth. But the leaves are rustling in the forest paths, the harvest-fields are silent, and the heavy fruit that bows down the branches, proclaims that the labor of Summer is ended—that her yellow-robed sister has come to gather in and garner the rich treasures she has left behind.

Hope, who looked with a cheerful countenance upon the landscape of Spring, has departed. Instead of watching each green and flowery object, day by day, as it budded and blossomed, we now see only the traces of slow and sure decay, the green fading, bit by bit, until the leaves become like the skeleton wings of an insect, the wind blowing through those places which were before marked with azure, and crimson, and gold. The sun himself seems growing older; he rises later from his bed in the morning, and returns to rest earlier in the evening, and seems not to have that strength which he possessed when he rose in the youthful vigor of Spring, and the bright and cheerful manhood of Summer; for his golden eyes seem clouded, and his breath thick and heavy, as he struggles through the surrounding fog. All these are marks of the seasons, telling us that the year is growing gray, and slowly tottering towards the darkness and grave-like silence of Winter.

"A moral character is attached to autumnal scenes—the leaves falling like our years, the flowers fading like our hours, the clouds fleeting like our illusions, the light diminishing like our intelligence, the sun growing colder like our affections, the rivers becoming frozen like our lives—all bear secret relations to our destinies." *

The name SEPTEMBER being derived from *Septem*, seven, indi-

* Chateaubriand.

cates its order in the Roman Calendar, prior to the Julian reform. The zodiacal sign is the constellation of *Libra, or the Balance;* because when the sun entered this asterism it seemed to hold the days and nights in equilibrio, giving the same proportion of light as darkness to the inhabitants of all parts of the globe. It was called *gerst-monath* by the Saxons ; *gerst* signifying barley, which ripens in this month.

The transition from autumnal richness to the desolation of winter is gradual, almost imperceptible, like our own advancing years. Miller the poet writes about it.

Forest scenery never looks so beautiful as in Autumn. It is then that nature seems to have exhausted all the fantastic colors of her palette, and to have scattered her richest red, brown, yellow, and purple, upon the foliage. Every gust of wind that now blows, brings down thousands of golden-colored acorns, that come pattering like little feet among the fallen leaves, leaving empty their smooth, round, hollow cups, from which the old poets in their fables framed the drinking vessels of the fairies.

Hood's ode to Autumn is a gem—we cite a passage from it :—

> Where are the blossoms of summer ?—In the West,
> Blushing their last to the last sunny hours,
> Where the mild Eve by sudden Night is prest
> Like tearful Proserpine, snatched from her flowers,
> To a most gloomy breast.
> Where is the pride of Summer—the green prime—
> The many, many leaves of all twinkling ?—Three
> On the mossed Elm : three on the naked lime
> Trembling—and one upon the old oak tree !
> Where is the Dryad's immortality ?—
> Gone into mournful cypress and dark yew,
> Or wearing the long gloomy winter through
> In the smooth holly's green eternity.

We add another apostrophe in prose, from an unknown pen :

"Like some richly illuminated manuscript of cloistered art, the wonder book of Nature is spreading out its autumn pages in all their wonted brilliancy of mingled coloring; every mountain is a swelling mound of jewelled lustre, and every vale of woodland a blending of rich rainbow tints, over which a bright sun-warmed haze is spread, just as the old missal painters used to canopy the heads of saints and apostles with a halo of golden light. The hoar-frost covers the meadows in the early morning, and lies in crisp, sparkling wreathes upon the fences and barn-roofs, while overhead, a sky of the deepest blue is beginning to soften under the sunshine. Not a leaf quivers, and the pale cottage smoke curls up in a straight, unwavering column through the frosty air, while cloudlets of mist rest lingeringly on the lake, or creep lazily up the hill-sides.

"There is exhilaration in the air, and a new life in the wind that comes careering from the northwest, bearing frost on its wings, and brightness to the autumn woods. The farmer is early afield, with his cheery call, as he guides his oxen to the late harvesting. The maize fields display their tent-like rows, with garniture of yellow pumpkins scattered between ; and the buckwheat patches, no longer yielding their "honied fragrance," are falling before the quick-swinging cradle, and lie like red spots upon the landscape. The orchards are brimming with rosy fruit, and the chestnut burs are showering down their treasures in the woods. Plenty seems to reign, and the fullness of the year has put its stamp of gladness upon all."

" A mellow richness on the clustered trees ;
And, from a beaker full of richest dyes,
Pouring new glory on the autumn woods,
And dipping in warm light the pillared clouds ;
Morn, on the mountain, like a summer bird,
Lifts up her purple wing ; and in the vales
The gentle wind, a sweet and passionate rover,
Kisses the blushing leaves and stirs up life
Within the solemn woods of ash deep crimsoned,

And silver beech, the maple yellow leaved—
Where Autumn, like a faint old man, sits down
By the wayside aweary. Through the trees
The golden robin moves ; the purple finch,
That on wild cherry and red cedar feeds,
A winter bird, comes with its plaintive whistle
And pecks by the wych-hazel ; while aloft
From cottage roofs the warbling bluebird sings."*

OCTOBER is from the Latin *octo*, eight ; with the Saxon it was styled *winterfyllith*—winter-beginning.

The principal Saints' days of this month are those of St. Dennis—who, according to the legend, walked two miles with his head in his hand, after it had been cut off—and of St.Crispin, the patron of the shoe-making fraternity.

One of the *Comic Almanacs*, attempts the facetious on this month, in the following playful stanzas :—

The sum of Summer is cast at last,
And carried to Wintry season,
And the frightened leaves are leaving us fast,
If they stayed it would be high trees-on.
The sheep exposed to the rain and drift,
Are left to all sorts of *wethers*,
And the ragged young birds *must make a shift*
Until they can get new feathers.

In noting the chronicles of Time, we find—

"The pale, descending year, yet pleasing still,"

for although the sere and yellow leaf now greets us, where, a short time since, all was verdant, and nature has doffed her gay attire, yet is there great beauty even in the blanched and frozen landscape, which dull spirits deem all dreary, desolate, and dead.

* Longfellow.

"Come, bleak NOVEMBER, in thy wildness come:
Thy mornings clothed in rime, thy evenings chill;
E'en these have power to tempt me from my home,
E'en these have beauty to delight me still.

Though Nature lingers in her mourning weeds,
And wails the dying year in gusty blast,
Still added beauty to the last proceeds,
And wildness triumphs when her bloom is past."

Nor is Shelley's Dirge less touchingly beautiful:

The warm sun is failing, the bleak wind is wailing,
The bare boughs are sighing, the pale flowers are dying,
And the year
On the earth, her death-bed, in a shroud of leaves dead,
Is lying.
Come months, come away,
From November to May,
In your saddest array;
Follow the bier
Of the dead, cold year,
And like dim shadows watch by her sepulchre.

The chill rain is falling, the nipt worm is crawling,
The rivers are swelling, the thunder is knelling
For the year;
The blythe swallows are flown, and the lizards each gone
To his dwelling.
Come months, come away.
Put on white, black and grey,
Let your light sisters play—
Ye follow the bier
Of the dead cold year.
And make her grave green with tear on tear.

The following beautiful passage, by Washington Irving, might almost make a doleful day cheerful:

"And here let me say a word in favor of those vicissitudes of our climate which are too often made the subjects of exclusive repining. If they annoy us occasionally by changes from hot to cold, from wet to dry, they give us one of the most beautiful climates in the world. They give us the brilliant sunshine of the south of Europe, with the fresh verdure of the north. They float our summer sky with clouds of gorgeous tints of fleecy whiteness, and send down cooling showers to refresh the panting earth and keep it green. Our seasons are all poetical, the phenomena of our heavens are full of sublimity and beauty. Winter with us has none of its proverbial gloom. It may have its howling winds, and whirling snow-storms; but it has also its long intervals of cloudless sunshine, when the snow-clad earth gives redoubled brightness to the day; when at night the stars beam with intensest lustre, or the moon floods the whole landscape with her most limpid radiance; and then the joyous outbreak of spring, bursting at once into leaf and blossom, redundant with vegetation, and vociferous with life!—and the splendors of our summer—its morning voluptuousness and evening glory—its airy palaces of the sun-gilt clouds piled up in a deep azure sky; and its gusts of tempest of almost tropical grandeur, when the forked lightning and the bellowing thunder volley from the battlements of heaven, and shake the sultry atmosphere—and the sublime melancholy of our autumn, magnificent in its decay, withering down the pomp and pride of a woodland country, yet reflecting back from its yellow forests the golden serenity of the sky, surely we may see in our climate 'the heavens declare the glory of God, and the firmament showeth forth his handiwork; day unto day uttereth speech; and night unto night showeth knowledge.'"

November is the next month we reach: its name being derived from *novem*—nine.

The last of the autumnal signs was *Sagitarius;* because when the sun passed it, the trees were nearly divested of their foliage, which the ancients considered as indicative of the season for hunting, and hence they represented the constellation under the figure of an archer, with bow and arrows. The Saxons named it *wint-monath* (wind month). All-Souls' day, occurs on the second of this month—consecrated to the memory of those saintly personages of yore, to the invocation of whom, the church had not assigned any particular date. The closing day of November is St. Andrew's: St. Cecilia has also conferred a ghostly honor on this month, as well as upon music.

We close our notice of this notable month with a brief but elegant passage from the pen of that sunny and healthful writer, Leigh Hunt. "November," he says, "with its loss of verdure, its frequent rains, the fall of the leaf, and the visible approach of winter, is undoubtedly a gloomy month to the gloomy, but to others it brings but pensiveness—a feeling very far from being destitute of pleasure; and if the healthiest and most imaginative of us may feel their spirits pulled down by reflections connected with earth,—its mortalities and its mistakes, we shall but strengthen ourselves the more to make strong and sweet music with the changeful but harmonious movements of nature."

The Comic Almanac intimates that among the comforts of winter you will find:—

Chilblains sore on all your toes,
Icicles hung from your nose,
Rheumatis' in all your limbs,
Noddle full of aches and whims,
Chaps upon your hands and lips,
And lumbago in your hips,
To your bed you shiv'ring creep,
There to freeze, but not to sleep,
For the sheets that look so nice,
Are to you two sheets of ice.

This is considered an ominious time for suicides in London and Paris—victims to this cowardly vice being generally more numerous in this month than any other. It is the pioneer of winter; it is synonymous with a negation to all the pleasurable aspects of the preceding three months. Hood indicates its characteristics in some ingenious lines—each of which commences with lisping the first syllable, and after a protracted effort spells it outright.

"No Sun—no Moon!
No morn—no noon—
No dawn—no dusk—no proper time of day—
No sky—no earthly view—
No distance looking blue—
No roads—no streets—no 'tother side the way;
No end to any row;
No indication where the crescents go;
No tops to any steeple;
No recognition of familiar people;
No courtesies for shewing 'em;
No knowing 'em;
No travellers at all; no locomotion;
No inkling of the way—no motion;
'No go' by land or ocean;
No mud; no post;
No news from any foreign coast;
No park; no ring; no afternoon gentility;
No company; no nobility;
No warmth; no cheerfulness; no healthful ease;
No comfortable feel in any member;
No shade; no shine; no butterflies; no bees;
No fruits; no flowers; no leaves; no birds;
No-VEMBER!"

We now hail the approach of dark DECEMBER,

Last of the months—severest of them all.

The first of the winter signs was called *Capricornus*, from the goat, which delights in climbing up high, craggy places, and hence is an emblem of the winter solstice. This constellation is sometimes called the "southern gate of the sun," for when he enters this sign, Sol begins to ascend higher in the zodiac. This month being formerly reckoned the tenth, was called December, from *Decem*—ten. The Saxons named it *Winter-monath* (winter-month).

We have watched the progress of the year, from its birth to its decline—the dreary season of its old age—the edge of its grave. We have watched the procession of the sister months, and in their course, the successive seasons—the bright, brilliant, and evanescent glories of the joyous, jubilant spring, the gorgeous sunsets of the sultry summer, the rich exuberance of fruit-bearing autumn; and now we are fairly in companionship with the frigid winter, with its brief days and its prolonged nights. We are reminded here of a very *literal* reason a simple-hearted youth once rendered, in reply to the inquiry as to the cause of the length of days in summer, and their brevity in winter: said he, "It is the nature of heat to expand, and of cold to contract."

Punch thus refers to the frozen desolation of winter:

There is a stoppage in the currency
Of all the streams, which cannot liquidate
Their tribute to the sea. The frozen soil,
Hard up, no more repays the husbandman.
Each object, crusted o'er with rime and snow—
Seems white-washed. Of their furniture the trees
Are stripped; and everywhere distringas reign.
On one vast picture of insolvency
We gaze around; and did we not repose
In mother earth's resources confidence,
Should see no prospect of a dividend
Of sixpence in the pound!

Nov*ember* and Dec*ember* are called the *embers* of the dying year.

The famous festival of St. Nicholas—"the boy-bishop," and the tutelar saint of childhood—is celebrated on the sixth. Dreary, indeed, would this ice-clad month be, were it not for the glowing associations of its merry Christmas, with its holly and mistletoe, and the gladsome gatherings and rejoicings of social life. What bright visions of joyous faces, well-spread tables, and happy firesides, does it kindle up in the memory; and with what glowing and grateful contrast does the dreary desolation without invest the radiant and jubilant scenes of the domestic hearth. The hearty and generous hospitality which characterizes Christmas celebrations—with the old, orthodox accessories of that delicious conglomerate of all good things—plum-pudding, and its accompaniment, the glorious sirloin—are enough to tempt the veriest anchorite to participate in the epicurean delights; for surely the palate that could not appreciate, nay, luxuriate over such dainty and delectable dishes, must have become sadly perverted and depraved.

> This month at last Time's annual circle fills,
> But empties pockets with its Christmas bills:
> The prickly holly every place adorns,
> Showing that Christmas pleasures have their thorns.

The term Christmas is derived from the Latin Church—it is properly *Christi Massa* (the Mass of Christ).

In former times, the celebration of Christmas began in the latter part of the previous day—Christmas Eve. The house was first decked with holly, ivy, and other evergreens. Candles of an uncommon size were then lighted under the name of Christmas candles; an enormous log, called the Yule log, or Christmas block, was laid upon the fire, while the people sat round, regaling themselves with beer. In the course of the night small parties went about from house to house, singing what were called Christmas Carols—simple, popular ditties, full of joyful allusions to the Redeemer. A mass was commenced in the churches at midnight, a custom still kept up in the Catholic countries.

These carols were more generally sung in the morning of Christmas day. A contributor to the "Gentleman's Magazine" in 1811, describing the manner in which Christmas was spent in Yorkshire, says:—"About six o'clock on Christmas day, I was awakened by a sweet singing under my window; surprised at a visit so early and unexpected, I arose, and looking out of the window, I beheld six young women and four men welcoming with sweet music the blessed morn." It may scarcely be imagined how delightfully at such a moment upon the half-slumbering ear such strains as the following would fall:

God rest you, merry gentlemen,
  Let nothing you dismay,
For Jesus Christ our Saviour
  Was born upon this day,
To save us all from Satan's power,
  When we were gone astray.
    Oh, tidings of comfort and joy,
    For Jesus Christ our Saviour
    Was born on Christmas Day.

Christmas carols are among the oldest of English songs. Sir WALTER SCOTT gives us the following picture of an old time Christmas:

And well our Christian sires of old
Loved, when the year its course had roll'd,
And brought blithe Christmas back again,
With all its hospitable train.
Domestic and religious rite
Gave honor to the holy night;
On Christmas Eve the bells were rung,
On Christmas Eve the mass was sung;
That only night, in all the year,
Saw the stoled priest the chalice wear,
The damsel donned her kirtle sheen,
The hall was dress'd with holly green.
Forth to the wood did merry men go,
To gather in the mistletoe.
Then open wide the baron's hall,
To vassal, tenant, serf, and all.

Christmas has long since passed into a synonyme for festivity. In olden times, the boar's head, ornamented with rosemary, was carried to table, upon a silver platter, with great ceremony. Holinshed states that, in the year 1170, on the day of the young prince's coronation King Henry II. "served his son at the table as server, bringing up the *boar's head* with trumpets before it, according to the manner, or general custom of the times." With Christmas commenced the season of mumming, and the reign of the "Lord of Misrule," or "Abbot of Unreason," as he was called in Scotland, and which Scott describes in *The Abbot*. These pleasantries, which were carried frequently to great excess, were the remains of the ancient saturnalia, which existed before the introduction of Christianity. The decoration of churches with evergreens, is a pleasing relic of these old times. These old customs, which seem dying away like distant music, find but a faint echo in our modern matter-of-fact days ; yet it is pleasant to catch a glimpse of our jovial forefathers, as they were accustomed to regale themselves at this merry-making season. A very pleasant book has chronicled their story,* and we commend its perusal to all those who have any fancy for such items as the sirloin, the plum-pudding, and good old sack. Twelfth-day—the anniversary of the adoration of the magi—occurs on the twelfth day after Christmas. Many curious customs are associated with its celebration in Great Britain and on the Continent.

Thus, in parts of Ireland, at night, they used to set a sieve of oats as high as they could, and place around it twelve lighted candles, with a larger one, also lighted, in the centre. This, of course, was to typify Christ and his twelve apostles as lights unto the world ; and in Gloucestershire they do it by building twelve small and one large fire in the fields. In Staffordshire, however, the custom differs, for there, on the

* Hervey's work on Christmas.

evening before, they light a large fire to commemorate the guiding-star which led the three magi to Bethlehem.

In many European countries the rulers did, and in some still do, present the gifts, brought by the wise men, at the altar of their chapel on the 6th of January. Thus we find in the *Gentleman's Magazine* for 1759, in the record for January :—'Being Twelfth-day, his majesty went to the Chapel Royal, with the usual solemnity, and offered gold, myrrh, and frankincense, in three purses, at the altar, according to ancient custom."

In some parts of England there exists a practice among the farmers of going under the apple-trees on Twelfth-eve or night, and singing various couplets. This practice is known as "apple-howling," and it is supposed that without it the apples will not grow well during the year.

"Dread Winter spreads his latest gloom,
And reigns tremendous o'er the conquer'd year;
How dead the vegetable kingdom lies!
How dumb the tuneful! Horror wide extends
His desolate domain. Behold, fond man!
See here thy pictured life! Pass some few years—
Thy flow'ring spring, thy summer's ardent strength,
And sober autumn, fading into age;
The pale, concluding winter comes at last,
And shuts the scene."

Our closing pages shall be homiletic, since Young admonishes us that—

"We take no note of Time,
But from its loss; to give it then a tongue
Is wise in man."

Time is the universal talent, subjecting every man living to a charge and an account. Within its circles all our other talents turn. They are the wheels within this great wheel, whose united movement causes it to revolve, for, as they are duly exercised, Time is successfully employed. It is the entail of humanity, come down to us as our inalienable heritage ; and, as in the law of primogeniture, unencumbered with our father's debts. May we prove such wise occupants and inheritors of this invaluable property, that, whatever may be the passing anxieties of its tenure, we may realize its profits hereafter.

> " 'Tis not for man to trifle! Life is brief,
> And sin is here.
> Our age is but the falling of a leaf,
> A dropping tear.
> We have no time to sport away the hours ;
> All must be earnest in a world like ours.
>
> "Not *many* lives, but only *one* have we ;
> One, only one—
> How sacred should that one life ever be—
> That narrow span!
> Day after day filled up with blessed toil,
> Hour after hour still bringing in new spoil."

As in money, so in time, we are to look chiefly to the smallest portions. Take care of the minutes and the hours, and years will take care of themselves. Gold is not found, for the most part, in great masses, but in little grains. It is sifted out of the sand in minute particles, which, melted together, produce the rich ingots that excite the world's cupidity. So the small moments of time, its odds and ends, put together, may form a great and beautiful work.

> "Catch the *seconds* as they're passing,
> Wait not for the *hours:*
> Prize them as a golden treasure—
> Use them not in trifling pleasure—
> Seconds, minutes—prizing, holding
> As you would sweet buds unfolding
> Into choicest flowers."

Hale wrote his contemplations while on his law circuits. Dr. Mason Good translated "Lucretius" in his carriage, while, as a physician, he rode from door to door. One of the chancellors of France penned a bulky volume in the successive intervals of daily waiting for dinner. Kirk White studied Greek as he was going to and from a lawyer's office. Burney learned French and Italian while riding on horseback. Franklin laid the foundations of his wonderful stock of knowledge in his dinner-hours and evenings, while working as a printer's boy.

A day has perished from our brief calendar of days; and *that* we could endure; but this day is no more than the reiteration of many other days, days counted by thousands, that have perished to the same extent and by the same unhappy means, viz., the evil usages of the world made effectual and ratified by our own *lâcheté*. Bitter is the upbraiding which we seem to hear from a secret monitor—'My friend, you make very free with your days; pray, how many do you expect to have? What is your rental as regards the total harvest of days which this life is likely to yield?' Let us consider.—Threescore years and ten produce a total number of 25,550 days; to say nothing of some seventeen or eighteen more that will be payable to you as a *bonus* on account of leap-years. Now, out of this total, one-third must be deducted at a blow for a single item, viz., sleep. Next, on account of illness, of recreation, and the serious occupations spread over the surface of life, it will be little enough to deduct another third. Recollect also that twenty years will have gone from the earlier end of your life (viz., above seven thousand days) before you can have attained any skill or system, or any definite purpose in the distribution of your time. Lastly, for that single item which, amongst the Roman armies, was indicated by the technical phrase "*corpus curare*," tendance on the animal necessities, viz., eating, drinking, washing, bathing, and exercise, deduct the smallest allowance consistent with propriety, and, upon summing up all these appropriations, you will not find so much as four thousand days left disposable for direct intellectual culture. Four thousand, or forty hundreds, will be a hundred forties—that is, according to the lax Hebrew method of indicating six weeks by the phrase of forty days, you will have a hundred bills or drafts on Father Time, value six weeks each, as the whole period available for intellectual labor. A solid block of about eleven and a half continuous years is all that a long life will furnish for the development of what is most august in man's nature." *

Here are we compelled to stay the pen ; for as we have completed our circuit of the seasons, and briefly recounted the characteristics of the calendar—nothing further remains to us, but to wind up anew the "annual clock of Time."

And while we bespeak for the reader a happy new year, we are constrained to thank old father Time for the many pleasant hours he has given us, and to forgive all the inflictions visited in his illiberal designs against our personal comfort—in blanching the ruddy tints of youth, dimming the lustre of the eye, or reducing the elasticity of the step. And, although he has caused us to taste occasionally the bitterness of sorrow, yet has he mingled many sweets in the chalice of life, which it would be ungrateful to forget.

Moreover, Time has infused into us a little sage and cheerful philosophy, inspiring us with a "faith which looks on the bright side of things.

Time brings a philosophic mind ;
Time takes more than he leaves behind ;
Time is a thief of joys ;
Time turns our golden locks to gray ;
Time draws a bill which all must pay ;
Time makes old men of boys.

* De Quincey.

Time, with his scythe and hour-glass, stands
To reap the harvest of our lands,
        To shorten prosperous days;
Time eats the keenest steel to rust;
Time crumbles monuments to dust;
        Time robs us of our praise.

Much fault is found with Father Time,
In books and speeches, prose and rhyme;
        But *we* will not upbraid.
For he has left our hearts as young
As when, long since, we laughed and sung
        In sunlight and in shade.*

"We know what we are," said poor Ophelia, "but we know not what we may be." Perhaps she would have spoken with a nicer accuracy had she said, "we know what we *have been*." Of our present state we can, strictly speaking, *know* nothing. The act of meditation on ourselves, however quick and subtle, must refer to the past, in which alone we can truly be said to live. Even in the moment of intensest enjoyment, our pleasures are multiplied by the quick-revolving images of thought; we feel the past and future in each fragment of the instant, as the flavor of every drop of some delicious liquid is heightened and prolonged on the lips. It is the past only which we really enjoy as soon as we become sensible of duration. Each by-gone instant of delight becomes rapidly present to us, and "bears a glass which shows us many more." This is the great privilege of a meditative being—never properly to have any sense of the present, but to feel the great realities as they pass away, casting their delicate shadows on the future.

Talfourd has some excellent remarks on this subject: "The ordinary language of moralists respecting time shows that we really know nothing respecting it. They say that life is fleeting and short; why, humanly speaking, may they not as well affirm that it is extended and lasting? The words 'short' and

* Park Benjamin.

'long' have only meaning when used comparatively ; and to what can we compare or liken this our human existence ? The images of fragility—thin vapors, delicate flowers, and shadows cast from the most fleeting things—which we employ as emblems of its transitoriness, really serve to exhibit its durability as great in comparison with their own.

Mere time, unpeopled with diversified emotions or circumstances, is but one idea, and that idea is nothing more than the remembrance of a listless sensation. A night of dull pain and months of lingering weakness are, in the retrospect, nearly the same thing. When our hands or our hearts are busy, we know nothing of time—it does not exist for us ; but as soon as we pause to meditate on that which is gone, we seem to have lived long, because we look back through a long series of events, or feel them at once peering one above the other like ranges of distant hills. Actions or feelings, not hours, mark all the backward course of our being. Our sense of the nearness to us of any circumstance in our life is determined on the same principles—not by the revolutions of the seasons, but by the relation which the event bears in importance to all that has happened to us since. To him who has thought, or done, or suffered much, the level days of his childhood seem at an immeasurable distance, far off as the age of chivalry, or as the line of Sesostris. There are some recollections of such overpowering vastness, that their objects seem ever near ; their size reduces all intermediate events to nothing ; and they peer upon us like "a forked mountain, or blue promontory," which, being far off, is yet nigh. How different from these appears some inconsiderable occurrence of more recent date, which a flash of thought redeems for a moment from long oblivion ;—which is seen amidst the dim confusion of half-forgotten things, like a little rock lighted up by a chance gleam of sunshine afar in the mighty waters !

What immense difference is there, then, in the real duration of men's lives ! He lives longest of all who looks back oftenest, whose life is most populous of thought or action, and on every retrospect makes the vastest picture. The man who does not meditate has no real consciousness of being. Such an one goes to death as to a drunken sleep ; he parts with existence wantonly, because he knows nothing of its value.

Hazlitt observes in his "Table Talk :"

"The length or agreeableness of a journey does not depend on the few last steps of it, nor is the size of a building to be judged of from the last stone that is added to it. It is neither the first nor the last hour of our existence, but the space that parts these two—nor our exit, nor our entrance upon the stage, but what we do, feel, and think while there—that we are to attend to in pronouncing sentence upon it. Indeed, it would be easy to show that it is the very extent of human life, the infinite number of things contained in it, its contradictory and fluctuating interests, the transition from one situation to another, the hours, months, years, spent in one fond pursuit after another ; that it is, in a word, the length of our common journey, and the quantity of events crowded into it, that, baffling the grasp of our actual perception, make it slide from our memory, and dwindle into nothing in its own perspective. It is too mighty for us, and we say it is nothing ! It is a speck in our fancy, and yet what canvass would be big enough to hold its striking groups, its endless objects ! It is light as vanity ; and yet, if all its weary moments, if all its head and heart-aches were compressed into one, what fortitude would not be overwhelmed with the blow ! What a huge heap, a 'huge dumb heap,' of wishes, thoughts, feelings, anxious cares, soothing hopes, loves, joys, friendships, it is composed of !"

With what accelerated speed the years
Seem to flit by us, sowing hopes and fears
As they pursue their never-ceasing march !
But is our wisdom equal to the speed
Which brings us nearer to the shadowy bourn
Whence we must never, never more return ?

Alas! the wish is wiser than the deed!
"We take no note of time but from its loss,"
  Sang one who reasoned solemnly and well.
And so it is; we make that dowry dross
  Which would be treasure, did we learn to quell
Vain dreams and passions. Wisdom's alchemy
  Transmutes to priceless gold the moments as they fly.

THE HUMORS OF LAW.

"These are the spiders of society;
They weave their petty webs of lies and sneers,
And lie themselves in ambush for the spoil,
The web seems fair and glitters in the sun,
And the poor victim winds him in the toil,
Before he dreams of danger, or of death."

L. E. L.

"Laws are like spiders' webs, that will catch flies, but not wasps and hornets."

ANACHARSIS.

LAW is law—and, as in such, and so forth, and hereby, and aforesaid, provided always, nevertheless, notwithstanding. Law is like a blistering plaster—it is a great irritator and only to be used in cases of great extremity. Law, again, is compared to a country-dance; people are led up and down in it 'till they are thoroughly tired. Law is like a book of surgery; there are a great many terrible cases in it. It is also like physic; they that take the least of it are best off. It is like a scolding wife; very bad when it follows us. It is like bad weather; people are glad when they get out of it.

Take, again, the following lucid definition of legal science :

"Law always expresses itself with true grammatical precision, never confounding moods, tenses, cases, or genders, except, indeed, when a *woman* happens accidentally to be slain, then the verdict brought in, is *manslaughter*. The essence of law is altercation, for the law can altercate, fulminate, deprecate, irritate, and go on at any rate. Now the quintessence of the law has, according to its name, five points—the first is the beginning or *incipiendum*, the second its uncertainty, or *dubitandum*, the third delay, or *puzzliendum*, the fourth replication without *endum*, and fifth *monstrum et horrendum*."*

"I hope," says the lawyer in Steele's comedy, "to see the day when the indenture shall be the exact measure of the land that passes by it; for it is a discouragement to the gown that every ignorant rogue of an heir should in a word or two understand his father's meaning, and hold ten acres of land by half an acre of parchment. Let others think of logic, rhetoric, and I know not what impertinence, but mind thou tautology. What's the first excellence in a lawyer? tautology. What's the second? tautology. What's the third? tautology; as an old pleader said of action."†

Another facetious writer‡ fortunately comes to our aid in defining our mysterious subject. "Law," he affirms, "is like fire; since those who meddle with it may chance to burn their fingers. It is like a pocket with a hole in it; and those who risk their money therein are liable to lose it. It is a lancet; dangerous in the hands of the ignorant, doubtful even in the hands of an adept. Law is like a sieve; you may see through it—but you will be considerably reduced before you get through it.

It is to the litigant what the poulterer is to the goose; it plucks and it draws him; but here the simile ends, for the litigant, unlike the goose, never gets *trust*, although he may be *roasted* and *dished*.

* Stevens' lecture on Head. † Southey's *Common-place book*.

‡ The author of the "Tin Trumpet."

It is like an *ignis fatuus;* those who follow the delusive guide too often find themselves inextricably involved in a bog.

It is like an eel-trap; very easy to get *into*, but very difficult to get out of.

It is like a razor; which requires "a strong back," keenness, and an excellent temper.

N. B.—Many of those who get once *shaved* seldom risk a second operation.

It is like a flight of rockets; there is a great expense of powder, the *cases* are usually well "got up," the *reports* are excellent, but after all, the sticks (the clients) are sure to come to the ground."

Ray sets the matter to music in the following stanza:

> Law is like longitude, about,
> Never completely yet found out;
> Though practised notwithstanding.
> 'Tis like the fatalist's strange creed,
> Which justifies a wicked deed,
> While sternly reprimanding!

If a man would, according to law, give to another an orange, instead of saying, "I give you that orange," which one would think would be what is called in legal phraseology, "an absolute conveyance of all right and title therein," the phrase would run thus: "I give you, all and singular, my estate and interest, right, title, and claim, and advantage of and in that orange, with all its rind, skin, juice, pulps, and all right and advantages therein, with full power to bite, cut, suck, or otherwise eat the same orange, or give the same away, with or without all its rind, skin, juice, pulp and pips, anything heretofore or hereinafter, or in any other deed or deeds, instruments, of what nature or kind soever, to the contrary in anywise notwithstanding;" and much more to the same effect. Such is the language of lawyers; and it is gravely held by the most learned men among them, that by the omission of any of those words the right to the same orange would not pass to the person for whose use the same was intended.

Lord Brougham once facetiously defined a lawyer thus: "a learned gentleman, who rescues your estate from your enemies, and keeps it himself."

A wag, being left trustee under a will by which the testator left a small freehold property to be sold for charitable purposes, sold it, and discovered the trust to be illegal. As the sum was too small in amount to bear a suit in equity (being not above sixty pounds), he laughed very heartily at the next of kin, pocketed it himself, spent it, and died.

Human laws are designed mainly to protect absolute rights; the laws, or the lawyers, however, often interfere with what seems absolutely right, till there is nothing absolutely left of the original right—and absolute wrong is of necessity the consequence. Those reputed allies—equity and justice—seem in these boasted days of "progress," not only to have repudiated their avowed relationship, but even to have well-nigh lost all kind of respect for each other.* Cato, it is stated, pleaded four hundred cases, and won them all. Charity would lead us to indulge the hope that a sterner virtue existed in his day, at any rate to warrant the adoption of the insignia of the well-balanced scales of the blind goddess. It is with law as with physic—the less we have to do with it the better: still, so long as diseases and discord disturb the social fabric, pacification and pills seem to be indispensable, and we must, therefore, content ourselves with whatever the collective wisdom of ancient and modern sages has prescribed as antidotes. Let us indulge the hope that the

* The difficulty of ascertaining the precise meaning of *law*, led to the establishment of a distinct branch of jurisprudence, called *equity*. Lord Chancellor Eldon, it will be remembered, presided something like half a century over the highest institution of this kind in England; so frequently, indeed, was his mighty mind poised on questions of gravest import, that the utmost his excessive erudition, caution, and modesty would permit him to arrive at, after months, and often years of patient investigation, was—*to doubt*. No master-mind of modern times, perhaps, was a more thorough *doubter*; and yet who dares question his sagacious wit?

hitherto protracted process of law, will, ere long, be divested of its wilderness waste of words, and reduced down to the simple elements of verity and common sense—something analogous to the homœopathic system of medicine. Justinian has reduced the principles of law to three: first, that we should live honestly; secondly, that we should hurt nobody; and thirdly, that we should give to every one his due. These principles have, however, long ago become obsolete in ordinary legal practice. Natural law and artificial, possess, it would seem, little in common; the former indicates man's true happiness and peace—the latter too often proves the bane of both. It is said that no human laws are of any validity if they are contrary to those of nature; but who will, for instance, venture to deny the reality of the Poor-Laws. In this case, as in most others, the law is more beneficial to its administrator—the lawyer—than the party whose interests it is ostensibly designed to subserve.

Of justice, one of the heathen sages has shown, with great acuteness, that it was impressed upon mankind only by the inconveniences which *injustice* had produced. The passage referred to is the following: "In the first ages, men acted without any rule but the impulse of desire; they practised injustice upon others, and suffered it from others in return; but in time it was discovered that the pain of suffering wrong was greater than the pleasure of doing it, and mankind, by a general compact, submitted to the restraint of laws, and resigned the pleasure to escape the pain." Whether to expediency, the Decalogue, or an intuitive moral sense, we trace its source, it cannot be denied that the abstract principle of justice is essential to the hapiness of society. If *law* were but the synonym of equity and justice, and its administrators, without exception, men of inflexible integrity, would any one be found to complain, as now, of the grievous pecuniary costs and trouble attending its dispensation?

Law has been compared to a new boot—a luxury which we approach with undisguised reluctance, and quit with supreme delight—a thing which transforms the ordinary calm and placable man into a living torment to himself and all around him. In more primitive times, our simple-hearted and trusting grandsires seem to have settled their differences in a much more summary mode than we are accustomed to: possibly because they possessed fewer of those learned expounders of legal lore, whose province, at least in part, appears to be to distort plain common sense and truth into all the tortuous twists and sinuosities of which a lawyer's logic is susceptible. Then, an "action at law" was a mere bagatelle;—it is not so now; it forms an era in a man's history. Besides, men in those days were more placable, and soon forgot their squabbles and animosities; now, they are not allowed to do so; it would be a direct fraud and infringement upon the rights of the *legal* subject.

The scene presented at a court of justice (*i. e.* law) is one of strange interest. It is there human nature may be studied with great effect. The passions of men are not only brought into play—they riot in dire confusion. The cupidity and cunning of counsel, the qualms and querulousness of the clients, the stern immobility of the judge, the officiousness of the crier, and the stolid indifference of those ominous individuals who are to decide the fate of the contending parties, contrast broadly with the vulgar curiosity evinced by the promiscuous crowd. A suit at law is, beyond all controversy, a most uncomfortable one—it unfits a man for everything else; it disturbs his peace, wastes his money, and too often ruins his reputation. The very term—suit at law, is, by the way, a misnomer; for it frequently *strips* a man of all he has, for he seldom gets any *re-dress.* In fact, the infelicities of an action at law are too numerous for detail, but we need not make the attempt, since some wag has furnished the following: "A law-suit," he insists, "is like an ill-managed dispute, in which the first object is lost sight of, and the parties end upon a matter wholly irrelevant to that on which they began. It is an ingeniously contrived web, whose meshes are spread out for the ensnaring of the unwary—a maze of inextricable perplexities designed to deprive the artless of their freedom, whom it decoys by its plausible pretences." Gay is somewhat sportive with the legal profession, in the well-known lines :—

"I know you lawyers can with ease,
Twist words and meanings as you please;
That language, by your skill made pliant,
Will bend to favor every client;
That 'tis the fee directs the sense,
To make out either side's pretence—
When you peruse the clearest case,
You see it with a double face:
For scepticism's your profession,
You hold there's doubt in all expression."

Equity is one of our natural wants, but it is not very easy to be obtained, owing to the moral obliquity so prevalent among men; the institution of law has come to be regarded as its substitute. If it were its true equivalent we should have nothing to complain of. Yet law is regarded by many as a necessary evil; and a certain writer * likens it to "war, pestilence, and famine, or lunatic asylums, poor-houses, and penitentiaries, or apothecaries'-shops, with their adulterous abominations, and every other substitute for, and abridgment of, human liberty, human happiness, and health." If even law were proved to be a positive good, we have so much of it that it has come to be a positive evil. Added to its countless statute-books, its codes, civil, common, and canon, we have such voluminous commentaries as no mortal man can comprehend or even read. This prodigality of law has proved the occasion of an equally prolific race of lawyers, scarcely any two of whom interpret law alike.

In large communities there must necessarily exist a need for

* John Neal.

men who shall be empowered to arbitrate between contending parties; and it is unreasonable to expect, where so many conflicting interests exist, there shall not be found frequent occasion for the exercise of the prerogative. Yet that is no reason why good, well-meaning people, who may occasionally come into collision with each other, and whose conscientious scruples induce them to appeal to an accredited authority for the settlement of their disputations, should become the victims of merciless harpies, who, under pretext of defending the right, seek to serve their own, rather than their clients' interests.

> "So law is wrested from her righteous ends,
> And forced to serve the rogue it should convict;
> Justice her weight to the wrong balance lends,
> And her decrees with her own self conflict!
> But, cheated by the solemn scales and hood,
> The multitude applaud, and call it—Good."

The fault, in some instances, rests more with the client than the counsel: the judicial reports exhibit many such absurdities. In the Chancery Court of England, the case of Narty *vs.* Duncan occurred, in which suit actually *two thousand pounds sterling* were expended in determining which party was liable to paint a board and whitewash a sign!

Law itself, when in accordance with justice and equity, is, of course, unimpeachable. It is of its mal-administration we complain.

The ancients, as proof of their reverence for law and justice, represented their goddess, Themis, as the daughter of Heaven and Earth—of Heaven, as typical of her purity and holiness—of Earth, as representing her abode and sphere of action. To denote her strength, she was of Titanic origin; as an appreciation of her consequence, she was placed by the side of Jupiter, the father of gods and men. This respect was awarded to abstract justice, even when men suffered under the bloody code of Draco—when they did not enjoy the more perfect system of the present day. Well may we shout hosannahs and sing anthems, when we remember that the laws of Draco, the Pandects of Justinian, and the Decretals of Gregory, are now among the things that were, and that now we live in an age when men know and realize what are their rights and what is the spirit and genius of law. "The lawyer," said Burke, "has his forms and his positive institutions, and he adheres to them with a veneration altogether as religious as the divine. The worst cause cannot be so prejudicial to the litigant as his attorney's ignorance of forms. A good parson once said, where mystery begins, there religion ends. May not the same be said of justice—that where the mystery of forms begins there all justice ends?" There is, it must be conceded, but too much *justice* in the sarcasm.

The study of law has a sad tendency to pervert the intellect and destroy the capability of distinguishing between right and wrong. Lawyers do not try a question upon its merits, but by legal precedent.

Bishop Hooker, speaking of Law, says: "no less can be acknowledged than that her seat is the bosom of God, and her voice, the harmony of the universe. All things in heaven and earth do her homage: the humblest feeling her influence, and the greatest not exempted from her power. Angels and creatures of all conditions, with uniform consent, unite in admiring her as the mother of peace and joy."

Man needs nothing more than a knowledge of justice and a due regard for it, to secure happiness. Blackstone holds the sentiment that the laws of eternal justice are so interwoven in the web of individual happiness that the latter cannot be obtained without observing the former; and if the former be punctually obeyed it cannot but induce the latter.

The truthfulness of the sentiment is strikingly in accordance with the experience of the good and just, and is worthy of the learning and integrity of that great authority.

In early times, chancellors and judges combined the dispensation of the *Gospel* with that of the *law*. In Campbell's *Lives of the Judges*, we learn that among those clerical chancellors, there occurs but one who did not ultimately reach the mitre. This was John Maunsel (A.D. 1246), who, while holding the Great Seal, became Provost of Beverley, his highest Church preferment—but not his only one. This personage, according to Matthew Paris, held at once 700 livings. He had, it is presumed, presented himself to all that fell vacant, and were in the gift of the Crown, while he was chancellor.

Many noble names have reflected lustre upon the legal profession, such as More, Bacon, Blackstone, Sir William Jones, Burleigh, Lord Mansfield, Brougham, Chitty, Coke, Philips, Starkie, Sugden, Stephens, Webster, Story, Kent, Wirt, Legare, &c.

A curious writer thus accounts for the history of the tutelar saint of this distinguished profession :

"Evona, a lawyer of Brittany, went to Rome to entreat the Pope to give the lawyers a patron saint. The Pope replied that he knew of no saint not already disposed of to some other profession. His Holiness, however, proposed that he should go round the church of Giovanni di Letirano blindfolded, and, after saying a number of Ave Marias, the first saint he laid hold of should be his patron. This the good old lawyer undertook ; and at the end of his Ave Marias, stopped at the altar of St. Michael, where he laid hold of, not the saint, but, unfortunately, the devil under the saint's feet, crying out, 'This is our saint, let him be our patron.'"

Having established the origin of the genius or guardian spirit of this erudite profession, let us now exhibit some of the protean shapes and various designations under which it is recognized amongst us. *Common law* seems to be the basis of all ; it has more of common sense in its composition than its counterpart, *civil law*, which may be said, on most occasions, to treat all who appeal to its sympathies most *uncivilly*.

The term *common law* is used in two distinct senses :—in its legitimate and legal signification it denotes old, unwritten law sanctioned by custom and precedent; comprising, it has been said, "all recognized doctrines and principles, however introduced, which are neither to be found in the statute book, nor depend on the adjudication of courts of equity:—in its conventional and popular sense, it is used to distinguish it from ecclesiastical polity and equity, and thus it comprises all the systems of adjudication, both criminal and civil, administered in courts having trial by jury. In brief, law is subdivided into the following classifications: common and civil law, municipal, constitutional, parliamentary, ecclesiastical, maritime and military. In England there is the Court of Queen's Bench, and both there and in the United States, there are the Superior Court, Chancery, Common Pleas, Court of Appeals, and the Supreme Court, Courts of Errors and Equity, and the Ecclesiastical Court.

Jeremy Bentham, in answer to the question, What is this boasted English law? thus sarcastically replies: "The *substantive* part of it, whether as written in books or expounded by judges, is a chaos, fathomless and boundless; the huge and monstrous mass being made up of fiction, tautology, technicality, circuity, irregularity, and inconsistency. The *administrative* part of it is a system of exquisitely contrived chicanery; a system made up of abuses; a system which constantly places the interest of the judicial minister in opposition to his duty—so places his interest in opposition to his duty, that, in the very proportion in which it serves his ends, it defeats the end of justice. A system of self-authorized and unpunishable depredation—a system which encourages mendacity, both by reward and punishment—a system which puts fresh arms into the hands of the injurer, to annoy and distress the injured."

Most law-suits are a juggle, whose sole object seems to be the plunder of both plaintiff and defendant by the prolongation of their quarrel. "Strange," says old Fuller, "that reason continuing always the same, law, grounded thereon, should be capable of so great alteration." It is *not* grounded upon reason, but upon the artifices of pettifoggers, and therefore its perversions and metamorphoses are infinite. *In Republicâ corruptissimâ plurimæ leges.* When Justinian compiled his Institutes, the writings on the civil law alone amounted to many camel-loads; *ours* may be reckoned by ship-loads, and the money annually expended upon law and lawyers (not upon justice) may be counted by millions."*

During Lord Eldon's chancellorship, such was his high sense of rectitude, that he is said to have retained counsel, in some instances, five, ten, and even twenty years (according to the capacity of the purse of the parties concerned), rather than venture a rash judgment in some equity cases. The longest suit on record, in England, is that of the heirs of Sir Thomas Talbot and the heirs of Lord Berkeley, respecting some property in the county of Gloucester. It began at the close of the reign of Edward IV., and was depending until the beginning of that of James I., when it was finally *compounded*—being a period of not less than one hundred and twenty years! In the United States there was a case recently determined, which had been pending three years, before the courts in Wyoming county, New York. It was a suit to recover $25, the amount of a note given: the verdict was ultimately rendered for the plaintiff in amount claimed, with the modest item of costs of $800!

Lord Brougham, in his celebrated speech on law reform, when he had not the hope of the chancellorship, or the fear of fickle fortune before his eyes, described the law as intended to be—"the staff of honesty and the shield of innocence;" but he added, that "it actually is a two-edged sword of craft and oppression." Æsop has a fable to the effect that a swallow built her nest under the eaves of a court of justice. Before her young brood could fly, a serpent glided out of his hole and devoured them up.

* Tin Trumpet.

The lawyer has frequent opportunities for indulging eccentricity and humor. We offer a specimen or two :

Counsellor Lamb, an old man when Lord Erskine was at the height of his reputation, was a man of timid manners and nervous temperament ; and usually prefaced his plea with an apology to that effect. On one occasion, when opposed to Erskine, he happened to remark that he felt himself growing more and more timid as he grew older. "No wonder," replied the witty, but relentless barrister, "every one knows that the older a *lamb* grows, the more *sheepish* he becomes."

Sergeant Prime—on a certain occasion, when the weather was intensely hot, and the court densely crowded, the case being one of more than ordinary interest—made a speech of three hours' duration, whose soporific influence, aided by the oppressive atmosphere of the court, caused a boy, who had seated himself on a transverse beam over the heads of the spectators, to fall, not only asleep, but also on the people below. His own injuries were unimportant, but several individuals in court were seriously hurt : and as the blame was laid upon the prosy counsel's long yarn, he was tried at the circuit table, found guilty, and sentenced to pay a fine of three dozen of wine, which he did without wincing or complaining. As an instance of noble independence of character, we might refer to the incident recorded of the celebrated Lord Chancellor Thurlow. As Speaker of the House of Peers, he was distinguished for the dignity with which he enforced the rules of debate. Upon one occasion he called the Duke of Grafton to order, who, incensed at the interruption, insolently reproached the chancellor with his plebeian origin, and recent admission into the peerage. Previous to this time, Thurlow had spoken so frequently that he was listened to by the House with evident impatience. When the duke had concluded his speech, his lordship arose from the woolsack, and advanced slowly to the place from whence the chancellor generally addresses the assembled peers ; then fixing upon the duke the look one may suppose Jove to have assumed as he grasped the thunder—"I am amazed," he said, "at the attack which the noble lord has made upon me; yes, my lords, I repeat, I am amazed at his grace's speech," his voice and manner still increasing in earnestness ; "the duke cannot look before him, behind him, or on either side of him, without seeing some noble peer who owes his seat in this House to his successful exertions in the profession to which I belong. Does he not feel that it is as honorable to owe it to these, as to being the accident of an accident ? To all these noble lords, the language of the noble duke is as applicable and as insulting as it is to myself ; but I do not fear to meet it singly and alone. No one venerates the peerage more than I do ; but, my lords, I must say the peerage solicited me, not I the peerage. Nay more, I can say, and will say, that, as a peer of Parliament, as Speaker of this right honorable House, as keeper of the Great Seal, as guardian of his majesty's conscience, as Lord High Chancellor of England, nay, even in that character alone in which his grace would think it an affront to be considered, but which none can deny *me*—as a *man*—I am at this moment as respectable—I beg leave to add, I am at this moment as much respected—as the proudest peer I now look down upon." The effect of this speech, both within and without the walls of Parliament, was prodigious; it gave Lord Thurlow an ascendency in the House, unsurpassed by any previous incumbent of the woolsack, and has placed him in a no less plausible aspect with the people of all times and all political creeds. Not only was this worthy representative of the high court of equity a most convivial *bon vivant*, he was, also, in the popular acceptation of the term, a wit. As brevity is said to be the soul of the article aforesaid, we present the reader with the following small dose. Once at table, Pitt was expatiating on the superiority of the Latin over the English language, and cited as an instance, the fact that two negatives made a thing more positive than one affirmative could do. "Then your father and mother!" exclaimed Thurlow, in his usual gruff style, "must have been themselves two negatives, to have introduced such a positive fellow as you are." Thurlow, in law, has been regarded something in the same light with Abernethy in physic; very rough, rude, and even insolent—a feature that tarnished his reputation, and which ultimately was the cause of his being deprived of the chancellorship.

The following characteristic notice of his lordship's irreligious tendencies, and we take our leave of him. His brother, the bishop of Durham, possessed but slender influence over him in this respect, for, in seeking to vindicate his character before some company on one occasion, he had to admit that his appeals to the Divine Being were only audible when suffering from acute twinges of that fashionable, but by-no-means-to-be-coveted complaint, the gout!

We have already referred to Chancellor Eldon, no less renowned for his *doubting* propensity. Many were the squibs, in prose and verse, of which this Fabius of Chancellors was the subject. To one, by Sir George Rose, a happy retort was made by his lordship, as seen in the subjoined extract:—

"Sir George Rose, when at the bar, having the note-book of the regular reporter of Lord Eldon's decisions put into his hand, with a request that he would take a note for him of any decision which should be given, entered in it the following lines, as a full record of all that was material which had occurred during the day:

Mr. Leach
Made a speech,
  Angry, neat, but wrong;

Mr. Hart,
On the other part,
  Was heavy, dull, and long:

Mr. Parker
Made the case darker,
  Which was dark enough without:

Mr. Cooke
Cited his book,
  And the Chancellor said—'I DOUBT.'

This *jeu d'esprit*, flying about Westminster Hall, at length reached the Chancellor, who was much amused with it, notwithstanding its personal allusion. Soon after, Rose having to argue before him a very untenable proposition, the chancellor gave his opinion very gravely, thus: 'for these reasons, the judgment must be against your clients; *and here, Mr. Rose, the Chancellor* DOES NOT DOUBT.'"

Mr. Plunkett, while pleading one day, observing the hour to be late, said it was his wish to proceed with the trial, if the jury would *set*. "*Sit*, sir," said the judge, correcting him, "not set; hens set." "I thank you, my lord," was the reply. Shortly after, the judge had occasion to observe, "that if such were the case, he feared the action would not *lay*." "*Lie*, my lord," said the barrister, "not lay; hens *lay*."

Lord Kenyon's classical acquirements are well known to have been but slender. He was nevertheless exceedingly fond of ornamenting his judgments with Latin quotations, which did not always fall exactly into their right places. Upon one occasion, he is said to have concluded his summing up in the following manner: "Having thus discharged your consciences, gentlemen of the jury, you may retire to your homes and your hearths in peace; and, with the delightful consciousness of having well performed your duties as citizens, you may lay down your heads upon your pillows, and say, *aut Cæsar aut nullus!*" Upon another occasion, his Lordship, wishing to illustrate in a strong manner the conclusiveness of some fact, thus addressed the jury: "Why, gentlemen of the jury, it is as plain as the noses upon your faces!—*Latet anguis in herbà!*"

To refrain from multiplying instances of the ludicrous in law is, indeed, no easy matter ; since the recollection of the names, even, of prominent members of the Irish bar are so suggestive of fun. Who can think of Philpott, Shiel, Curran, and Norbury, without recollecting their jokes ?

Curran's versatile and ready wit has long been proverbial ; like Lord Norbury, his name has been classed among those of Voltaire, Swift, and the humorists of their day. One or two instances will suffice.

Mr. Curran was engaged in a legal argument ; behind him stood his colleague, a gentleman whose person was remarkably tall and slender, and who had originally intended to take orders. The judge observing that the case under discussion involved a question of ecclesiastical law—"Then," said Curran, "I can refer your lordship to a *high* authority behind me, who was once intended for the church, though in my opinion he was fitter for the steeple."

"No man," said a wealthy but weak-headed barrister, "should be admitted to the bar, who has not an independent landed property." "May I ask, sir," said Mr. Curran, "how many acres make a *wise*-acre ?" "Could you not have known this boy to be my son, from his resemblance to me ?" asked a gentleman. Mr. Curran answered, "Yes, sir, the maker's name is stamped upon the *blade*." Mr. Curran being asked, "what an Irish gentleman, just arrived in England, could mean by perpetually putting out his tongue ?" answered, "I suppose he's trying to catch the English accent."

One of the eminent British lawyers was engaged, sometime since, to defend an Irishman, who had been charged with theft. Assuming the prerogative of his position, the counsel, in a private interview with his client, said to him, "Now, Patrick, as I am to defend you, I want you to tell me frankly whether you are guilty or not. Did you steal the goods ?" "Faith, then," said Pat, "I s'pose I must tell yez. In troth, I did stale 'em !" "Then you ought to be ashamed of yourself, to come here and disgrace your country by stealing !" said the honest counsel. "In troth, sir, may-be I ought ; but then, if I didn't stale, you wouldn't have the honor and credit of getting me off !"

It will be remembered a curious instance occurred, of a witness confounding a counsel, at Gloucester, England, some years ago. The witness on being asked his name, gave it Ottiwell Woodd. He pronounced it hurriedly several times, as the learned counsel did not seem to catch it. "Spell it, sir, if you please," he said, somewhat angrily ; the witness complied thus : "O, tt, i, w, e, ll, W, oo, dd." The spelling more confounded the counsel than ever, and in his confusion, amid the riotous laughter of the court, he took the witness aside, to help him to spell it after him.

In the *Life of O'Connell*, we find several piquant and amusing anecdotes of that great representative of *Repeal*. We have heard him speak in the British House of Commons, and can readily imagine how much of the *spirit* of his humor is lost in its being *retailed*. He was once examining a witness, whose inebriety, at the time to which the evidence referred, it was essential to his client's case to prove. He quickly discovered the man's character. He was a fellow who may be described as "half-foolish with roguery." "Well, Darby, you told the truth to this gentleman ?" "Yes, your honor, Counsellor O'Connell." "How do you know my name ?" "Ah ! sure every one knows our own *pathriot*." "Well, you are a good-humored, honest fellow ; now tell me, Darby, did you take a drop of anything that day ?" "Why, your honor, I took my *share* of a pint of spirits." "Your share of it ; now, by virtue of your oath, was not your share of it *all but the pewter* ?" "Why, then, dear knows, that's true for you, sir." The court was convulsed at both question and answer.

Here is an instance of his ready tact and infinite resource in the defence of his client. In a trial at Cork for murder, the principal witness swore strongly against the prisoner. He particularly swore that a hat, found near the place of the murder, belonged to the prisoner, whose name was James. "By virtue of your oath, are you sure that this is the same hat?" "Yes." "Did you examine it carefully before you swore, in your information, that it was the prisoner's?" "I did." "Now let me see," said O'Connell, as he took up the hat and began to examine it carefully in the inside. He then spelled aloud the name of James, slowly, and repeated the question as to whether the hat contained the name; when the respondent promptly replied, "It did." "Now, my lord," said O'Connell, holding up the hat to the bench, "there is an end of the case—there is no name whatever inscribed in the hat." The result was an instant acquittal.

The following anecdote of two eminent pleaders, Pinckney and Emmet, we copy from the *Knickerbocker:* it is an admirable rebuke upon those who suppose that irony, sarcasm, and invective constitute the essentials of forensic eloquence.

"We do not know when we have encountered a more forcible exemplification of the truth, 'that a soft answer turneth away wrath,' than is afforded in the ensuing anecdote: On one occasion in the Supreme Court of the United States, the eloquent Irish exile, Emmet, and the distinguished orator, Pinckney, were on opposite sides in an important cause, and one which the latter had much at heart. In the course of the argument, he made some offensive personal observations on Emmet, with a view of irritating him, and weakening his reply. Emmet sat quiet and endured it all. It seemed to have sharpened his intellect, without having irritated his temper. When the argument was finished, he said: 'Perhaps he ought to notice the remarks of the opposite counsel, but this was a species of warfare in which he had the good fortune to have little experience, and one in which he never dealt—he was willing that his learned opponent should have all the advantages he promised himself from the display of his talents in that way. When he came to this country he was a stranger, and was happy to say, that from the bar generally, and the court universally, he had experienced nothing but politeness, and even kindness. He believed the court would do him the justice to say that he had said or done nothing in this cause to merit a different treatment. He had always been accustomed to admire and even reverence the learning and eloquence of Mr. Pinckney, and he was the last man from whom he should have expected personal observations of the sort the court had just witnessed. He had been in early life taught by the highest authority not to return railing for railing. He would only say that he had been informed that the learned gentleman had filled the highest office his country could bestow at the court of St. James. He was very sure that he had not learned his breeding in that school.'

"The court and the bar were delighted; for Mr. Pinckney was apt to be occasionally a little too overbearing. When we take into consideration the merit of resistance against the natural impulse of a warm Irish temperament, we must admire still more the manner adopted by Mr. Emmet. Mr. Pinckney afterwards tendered the most ample apology. 'The manner,' said he, 'in which Mr. Emmet has replied, reproaches me by its forbearance and urbanity, and could not fail to hasten the repentance which reflection alone would have produced, and which I am glad to have so public an occasion of avowing. I offer him a gratuitous and cheerful atonement: cheerful, because it puts me to rights with myself, and because it is tendered, not to ignorance and presumption, but to the highest worth, intellect, and morals, enhanced by such eloquence as few may hope to equal; to an interesting stranger whom adversity has tried, and affliction struck severely to the heart; to an exile whom any country might be proud to receive, and every man of a generous temper would be ashamed to offend.'"

One or two other amusing anecdotes we are tempted here to present. We cite them from a veritable "printed boke," and, therefore, need not vouch for their authenticity. A member of the bar in one of the Eastern States had espoused the cause of a man indicted for passing counterfeit money. After a long and severely contested trial, the "learned" gentleman obtained an acquittal for the prisoner, who affecting an overwhelming sense of gratitude, while pleading poverty, and the claims of a family, as an apology for the smallness of the fee, took his leave of his legal friend. When the unsuspecting counsellor, attorney, or barrister—for these terms are generally used interchangeably in the United States—looked at his fee, he found it to be of the spurious coin! This is a rare instance of a lawyer duped.

Special pleaders, sometimes resort to curious expedients for producing an effect on the sympathies of a jury—a body of men distinguished alike for their acute sensibilities and critical sagacity. In a criminal case, in which the culprit was arraigned upon a charge of manslaughter, which seemed to bear very much against the prisoner, the counsel held up his little child, who was crying aloud, as an eloquent appeal to the jury in his behalf. This might have answered very well, had not one of their number put the pertinent question to the youngster, "What are you crying for?" when the artless reply was, "He pinched me, sir."

As no one denies that the bar has been ever distinguished for eloquence, it is not needful for us to cite a list of luminous names to prove the fact. Rather would we present the following curious case of an attorney, who was possessed of a wonderful facility in "facing both ways." A Scottish advocate, we have forgotten his name, having on a certain occasion drank rather too freely, was called on unexpectedly to plead in a cause in which he had been retained. The lawyer mistook the party for whom he was engaged, and to the great amazement of the agent who had feed him, and to the absolute horror of the poor client, who was in court, he delivered a long and fervent speech, directly opposite to the interests he had been called upon to defend. Such was his zeal, that no whispered remonstrance, no jostling of the elbow, could stop him. But just as he was about to sit down, the trembling client, in a brief note, informed him that he had been pleading for the wrong party. This intimation, which would have disconcerted most men, had a very different effect on the advocate, who, with an air of infinite composure, resumed his oration. "Such, my lords," said he, "is the statement which you will probably hear from my learned brother on the opposite side in this cause. I shall now, therefore, beg leave, in a few words, to show your lordship how utterly untenable are the principles, and how distorted are the facts, upon which this very specious statement has proceeded." The learned gentleman then went over the whole ground, and did not take his seat until he had completely and energetically refuted the whole of his former pleading.

Law is a very grave matter to the client, but it abounds with its humor, irony, sarcasm, invective, and even scurrility, for the counsel, or at least the special pleader; yet we are made to believe that all these minister to the claims of justice, and the majesty of law. Possibly it is from this cause that law has been styled one of the *liberal* professions. It is liberal in more senses than one; none will deny this in respect of its volubility, for when it exhausts the mother-tongue, it then falls back upon the dead languages; let not the simple-hearted, therefore, be deceived by the speciousness of a lawyer's "brief."

We now propose to notice some of the peculiarities of pleading, in connection with *briefs*—those legal documentary papers, usually more remarkable for their extraordinary expansion and *verbosity* than anything else. In early times, pleading was carried on without the aid of *briefs*.

Some one facetiously suggests that a briefless barrister ought never to be blamed, because it is decidedly wrong to abuse a man without a *cause*.

A lawyer has been compared to an odd sort of fruit—first rotten, then green, and then ripe. There is no little significancy in the similitude—as the history of many a briefless barrister would attest. How often, like the medical practitioner, has he to suffer from long disappointed ambition and neglect, while the less meritorious are preferred as the favorites of fortune.

A brief has been thus briefly defined, an instrument—

For pay, to prove the honest man a thief,
For pay, to break the widow's heart with grief,
To stifle truth, for lies to gain belief,
That's a brief!

Deeds* are said to be preferable to words; but legal deeds are composed wholly of words; of—

Ten thousand words, where ten would serve the need,
Ten thousand meanings, discord meant to breed,
Where none can understand, and few can read—
That's a deed.

"Oh, Law! There never were such times as these! A barrister could once with ease, have got as many fees, by merely signing pleas, as would have given him something more than bread and cheese; but destiny's decrees have made it feasible no more to get such fees; and if the lawyers please to live, they can no longer live by pleas."

Exparté statements may, and too often do, so essentially violate truth and honesty, that it is to be regretted the learned members of the bar of the nineteenth century are found still so strenuously to insist upon its adoption in legal process. Any one, uninitiated, hearing for the first time the opening up of a case, the examination of a witness, or the summing up of a cause, would, doubtless, be inclined to conclude that lawyers were professionally as great strangers to *veracity* as the simple Hibernian was to the public stocks: who, on being asked if he ever had any money deposited there, admitted he never had,

*Some faint idea of the bulk of the English records may be obtained by adverting to the fact, that a single statute, the Land Tax Commissioners' Act, passed in the first year of the reign of George IV., measures, when unrolled, upwards of 900 feet, or nearly twice the length of St. Paul's Cathedral, within the doors; and if ever it should become necessary to consult the fearful volume, an able-bodied man must be employed during three hours in coiling and uncoiling its monstrous folds!

but confessed to having had his legs there often enough. We subjoin one specimen of a *brief.*—not of the briefest kind it is true, being long enough and large enough to suit the most garrulous of the profession. It is taken from *Butler's Reminiscences:*

"The length of legal instruments is often owing to the necessity of providing for a multiplicity of contingent events, each of which *may* happen, and must, therefore, be both fully described, and fully provided for. Of the nature and extent of this multiplicity, the party himself is seldom aware; sometimes even his professional adviser does not feel it, until he begins to frame the necessary clauses. A gentleman, upon whose will the reminiscent was consulted, had six estates of unequal value, and wished to settle one on each of his sons, and his male issue, with successive limitation over to the other sons, and their respective male issue, in the ordinary mode of strict settlement; and with a provision, that in the event of the death and failure of issue male of any of the sons, the estate devised to him, should shift from him and his issue male, to the next taker and his issue male, and failing there, to the person claiming under the other limitations. It was considered, at first, that this might be effected by one proviso: then by two, and then by six; but upon a full investigation, it was found that it required as many provisos as there can be combinations of the number six; now—

$$1\times2\times3\times4\times5\times6=720;$$

Consequently, to give complete effect to the intention of the testator, 720 provisos were necessary.

"By a similar calculation, if a deed, which the reminiscent was instructed to prepare, had been executed, the expense of the necessary stamp would have amounted to ninety millions, seven hundred and twenty thousand pounds. Ten persons, each of whom was possessed of landed property, having engaged in a mining adventure, a deed of partnership was to be prepared, which was to contain a stipulation that, if any one or more of the intended partners should advance money to another, or others of them, the money lent should be a charge, in the nature of a mortgage, upon the share or respective shares of the borrower, or respective borrowers, and overreach all subsequent charges—and, therefore, the charges were to be considered as mortgages actually made by the deed. Thus, in the contemplation of equity, the estate was actually to be subjected by the deed, to as many possible mortgages as there can be combinations of the number 10. Each of these possible mortgages, being for an indefinite sum, would require the £25 stamp.

$$25 \times 2 \times 3 \times 4 \times 5 \times 6 \times 7 \times 8 \times 9 \times 10 = 90{,}720{,}000.$$

Sterne insinuates that attorneys are to lawyers what apothecaries are to physicians—only that they do not deal in *scruples!*

One day at the table of the late Dr. Pearse (Dean of Ely), just as the cloth was being removed, the subject of discourse happened to be that of an extraordinary mortality among the lawyers. "We have lost," said a gentleman, "not less than *six* eminent barristers in as many months." The Dean, who was quite deaf, rose as his friend finished his remarks, and gave the company grace: "For *this* and every other *mercy*, the Lord's name be praised!" The effect was irresistible.

Having referred to briefs, we are reminded of the opposite. We have not dilated upon "the law's delay." The topic is, however, too trite to talk about—let an instance suffice.

About a hundred years ago, a Scotch gentleman bequeathed to his "poor relations, of whatever degree," the sum of £20,000. In effect, he left them a Chancery suit, which has remained in the family ever since. In the first place, the next of kin disputed the validity of the bequest, but it was established by Lord Chancellor Camden, and 463 persons made out their relationship. Thereupon, in the year 1766, a bill was filed for the distribution of the money amongst them, which has not been effected to this day.

A yet stranger case was that of the famous "Berkeley suit," which lasted upwards of 190 years! It was commenced shortly after the death of the fourth Lord Berkeley in 1416, and terminated in 1609. It arose out of the marriage of Elizabeth, only daughter and heiress of the above baron, with Richard Beauchamp, Earl of Warwick, their descendants having continually sought to get possession of the Castle and Lordship of Berkeley, which not only occasioned the famous lawsuit in question, but was often attended with the most violent quarrels on both sides, at least during the first fifty years or more.

We have at our hand a case, and as it is a very *striking* one, we may as well introduce it with the view of adding force to our observations:

A lawyer, retained in a case of assault and battery, was cross-examining a witness in relation to the force of a blow struck: "What kind of a blow was given?" "A blow of the common kind." "Describe the blow." "I am not good at description." "Show me what kind of a blow it was." "I cannot." "You must." "I won't." The lawyer appealed to the court. The court told the witness that if the counsel insisted upon his showing what kind of a blow it was, he must do so. "Do you insist upon it?" asked the witness. "I do." "Well, then, since you compel me to show you, it was this kind of a blow!" at the same time suiting the action to the word, and knocking over the astonished disciple of Coke upon Littleton.

In this connection we have yet another case to present, in which the irritating and too irritable counsel was completely nonplussed. It is as follows:

"I call upon you," said the counsellor, "to state distinctly upon what authority you are prepared to swear to the mare's age?" "Upon what authority?" said the ostler, interrogatively. "You are to reply to, and not to repeat the questions put to you." "I doesn't consider a man's bound to answer a question afore he's time to turn it in his mind." "Nothing can be more simple, sir, than the question put. I again repeat it: Upon what authority do you swear to the animal's age?" "The best authority," responded the witness, gruffly. "Then why such evasion? Why not state it at once?" "Well, then, if you must have it."—"Must! I will have it," vociferated the counsellor, interrupting the witness. "Well, then, if you must and will have it," rejoined the ostler, with imperturbable gravity, "why, then, I had it myself from the mare's own mouth." A simultaneous burst of laughter rang through the court. The judge, on the bench, could with difficulty restrain his risible muscles to judicial decorum.

Our readers may remember the story of the two Irish friends, who, from long practice, arrived at great proficiency in the science of unlawfully abstracting their neighbor's property, and were not only true to the old maxim of "honor among thieves," but evinced an ingenuity and skill worthy of a better cause. One, having appropriated a goose, was on the point of being condemned by a jury for theft, when the friend appeared and swore that the bird was his, and had been ever since it was a gosling, and the prisoner on this was acquitted. Afterwards, in the course of his calling, the ingenious witness was himself arraigned for stealing a gun. "Don't be onaisey," whispered the former culprit, "I'll relase ye." Thereupon he stepped into the witness-box, and boldly affirmed that the gun was his, and that it had been in his possession ever since it had been a *pistol*.

An exposé of the tender passion often occurs, which the papers recite with heightening effect, so that we are not called upon to say much on that subject; but as we have a sample of that kind which is short and sweet, we place it before the reader. In the Sheriff's Court, London, recently, a Miss Rogers obtained £64 damages against a certain swain, bearing the suspicious name of Bachelor, for breach of promise of marriage. A number of the defendant's love letters were produced, in which the fluctuations of his love were very amusingly exhibited. His first epistles terminated with, "Yours, J. B.;" then fired up to "My ever dearest Maria;" afterwards they softened into "My Darling;" then cooled into "Dear Maria;" then formalized into "Dear Miss Rogers;" and broke off with the following announcement:—"You wish to know how I intend to settle; all I can say is, that I cannot be more settled than I am."

It is reported of Caligula that he caused the laws of Rome to be written in small characters, and stuck up so high that the citizens could not read them; with the same intent and motive, it might be supposed, that our modern legislators and lawyers are actuated by—namely, the placing their sage edicts above the apprehension of common minds, or at any rate beyond their reach for any available purposes. A facetious writer has given the following analysis of a law, and with it we may as well close our rambling essay: "In the first place it is declaratory; in the second, it is directory; in the third, it is remedial; and in the fourth, it is vindicatory. The declaratory says so and so is wrong, and the directory says immediately it shall not be done; but it sometimes contrives to say so in such very civil and mysterious terms as to leave people in doubt whether they may do a thing or not, until they find all of a sudden they are put in possession of its true meaning, and punished into the bargain for their obtuseness in not having been able to understand it before. It is remedial, for it gives a remedy; thus, if you are deprived of your rights you have the remedy of a law-suit, which is a great luxury, and it must be admitted, an expensive one. It is also vindicatory, for it attaches a penalty—and such is the majesty of law, that, whether right or wrong, he is sure to have to bear a portion of the penalty who presumes in any way to meddle with it." The rules for interpreting law are extremely arbitrary. Words are to be taken in their popular sense, without regard to grammar, which is, of late, becoming a matter of such trivial moment amongst us, that it is hardly worth the noticing. Grotius thought that the penalty on crime was a sort of tax on *sin*, which some seem to think might be defined without regard to syntax.

There are many antiquated absurdities and heresies, which have to be reformed, before our legal institutions can be regarded as adapted to the wants of the age. One of the absurd customs still in vogue in courts of justice, is that of inquiring whether the party arraigned, is guilty or not of the offence alleged against him. This was recently rendered ludicrous by the reply to the question : "Guilty or not guilty ?" by a native of the Emerald Isle—"Just as your honor plazes. It's not for the likes o' me to dictate to your honor's worship."

The following is an amusing anecdote of the well-known Cooke, the actor and musician. At a trial in the Court of King's Bench, in 1833, betwixt certain music-publishers as to an alleged piracy of an arrangement of the song of *The Old English Gentleman*, Cooke was subpœnaed as a witness by one of the parties. On his cross-examination by Sir James Scarlett, afterwards Lord Abinger, for the opposite side, that learned counsel questioned him thus :—"Now, sir, you say that the two melodies are the same, but different ; now what do you mean by that, sir ?" To this Tom promptly answered,—"I said that the notes in the two copies were alike, but with a different accent, the one being in common time, the other in six-eight time ; and consequently, the position of the accented notes was different."—"Now, pray sir, don't beat about the bush, but explain to the jury, who are supposed to know nothing about music, the meaning of what you call accent." *Cooke.*—"Accent in music is a certain stress laid upon a particular note, in the same manner as you would lay a stress upon any given word for the purpose of being better understood. Thus, if I were to say, "you are an *ass*,' it rests on ass ; but if I were to say, '*You* are an ass,' it rests on you, Sir James." Shouts of laughter by the whole court followed this repartee. Silence at length having been obtained, the judge, with much seeming gravity, accosted the counsel thus: "Are you satisfied, Sir James?" Sir James (who had become *scarlet* in more than name), in a great huff, said—"The witness may go down."

We close our desultory chapter, by citing a paragraph from the author of "Companions of my Solitude," because it recapitulates, in brief, the "law points" most vulnerable.

"What a loss is there—of time, of heart, of love, of leisure. The myriad oppressions and vexations of law. There are many things done now in the law, at great expense, by private individuals, which ought to be done for all by officers of the State. It is as if each individual had to make a road for himself whenever he went out, instead of using 'the King's highway.' I do not know a meaner and sadder portion of a man's existence, or one more likely to be full of impatient sorrow, than that which he spends at the offices of lawyers. Many of the adjuncts and circumstances of law are made to retain, for the sake of mystery, its uncouth form and size of deeds, its antiquated words, and unusual character of hand-writing. Physicians' prescriptions may have a better effect for being expressed mysteriously, but legal matters cannot surely be made too clear, even in the merest minutiæ."

After all we have to urge against the law, we beg to acknowledge allegiance to its high authority; and, as to its administrators, let the words of an old epigram speak for us:

When we've nothing to dread from the law's sternest frowns,
We all laugh at the barrister's wigs, bags, and gowns;
But as soon as we want them to sue or defend,
Then their laughter begins, and our mirth's at an end.

THE MUTE CREATION.*

> "Know'st thou not
> Their language and their ways? They also know
> And reason not contemptibly."
>
> MILTON.

THE reasoning faculty in man is supposed to be the proud prerogative which confers his preëminent distinction in the scale of being; to institute a comparison, therefore, between it and the instincts of the inferior creation may well excite surprise, and possibly be deemed incongruous, if not absurd. The inculcation of moral precept in the form of fable, dates as far back as the days of Æsop; and this favorite expedient—so attractive and suggestive—has ever since been regarded as equally poetic, elegant, and impressive. Need we higher authority for its adoption, it may be found among the earliest records of the sacred canon: "Ask now the beasts, and they

* A term originating with Lord Erskine, as a substitute for the phrase "brute creation."

shall teach thee; and the fowls of the air, and they shall tell thee;" while, in other passages, we are instructed to gather lessons from the lilies of the field, and to take example from the industry of the seemingly insignificant insects. But "creation's lord"—the "paragon of animals," blinded by the consciousness of his boasted superiority of intellect, renders himself inaccessible to the gentle teachings, the silent, though eloquent persuasions of Nature's voice. We propose to refer to some facts illustrative of the beauty and worth of the moral virtues, deduced from this source.

Instinct *seems* to be the incipient state of reason, although the instinctive sensations of which animals are the subjects can not be properly classed in the same category with the ideas or the rationative process of the human mind. Here is the dividing line between instinct and reason, and yet it is difficult for the metaphysician to define the boundaries of each, since, as in the several kingdoms of nature—animal, vegetable, mineral—they seem to commingle where they unite.

A German author* thus writes on this subject:

"In taking a review of most, if not all, of the actions of the animal world, it must be obvious that, whether we allow them reason or not, the actions themselves comprehend those elements of reason, so to speak, which we commonly refer to rational beings. So that if the same actions had been done by our fellow-creatures, we should have ascribed them without hesitation to motives and feelings worthy of a rational nature. It is certain that most animals, in their several rational acts, show every outward sign of consciousness or knowledge of the end of their actions, not like the fixed and uninformed operations of instinct, which is wholly employed in their self-preservation, or in providing for their young.

"If we compare our own mental constitution with that of brutes, however we may excel them, as we certainly do, in some noble capacities and principles, exclusively belonging to our

* Schleiden.

moral nature, yet we possess many faculties and powers precisely analogous to theirs; and the motives and combined operations of these, it is often as difficult to understand as it is those of the lower animals."

The reason of animals, it has been urged, is limited to memory enlightened by experience; the intelligence of man, on the contrary, is unrestricted and free. This constitutes his superiority.

The peculiarites and habits of animals constitute a theme rife with interest. In Buck's "Beauties of Nature," we find many curious and important facts recorded, some of which exhibit a striking analogy between the characteristics of man and those of animals. "Thus in the jay we may trace the petulant airs of a coquette; in the magpie, the restlessness, flippancy, and egotistical obtrusiveness of the gallant; while the green macaw is the perfect emblem of a suspicious and jealous spouse; for if its master's caresses are transferred to a dog, a cat, a bird, or even a child, nothing can exceed its anxiety and fury, nor will it be appeased till he forsakes the new favorite and returns to it. Envious men and calumniating women we may compare to the porcupine and the secretary-bird; and the selfish will find their type in the rhinoceros, since it is said to be incapable either of gratitude or attachment; while the inebriate may also be classed with the rougette bat, whose propensity to become intoxicated with the juice of the palm-tree is no less proverbial. Again, obstinate or perverse persons may read their lineaments of character in that of the Lapland mouse, or the Arctic puffin; for if the latter should seize the end of a bough, thrust into its hole, rather than let it go, it will suffer itself to be drawn out by it and killed; and the former will not move out of its course for any thing or any body." Some indolent bipeds there are, also, who resemble a certain bird, the *laurus articus*, which is said never to fish for itself, but to live upon the good fortune of other birds, which it pursues for the sake of their spoil. Others again may be said to exhibit a fatal affinity of disposition with that of the parrot of Guinea, one of the most beautiful of its tribe, but which is really the most ferocious in its disposition, when, to all appearance, it seems to be most inclined to enlist one's sympathies.

Thus writes the author of the *Tin Trumpet:* "The implanted principle that determines the will of brutes is generally limited to the great objects of nature—self-preservation, the procurement of food, and the continuance of the species. An intelligent being, having a motive in view for the performance of any particular operation, will set about it either similarly to others or in a different mode, according to circumstances, his views and powers of action being almost infinitely varied; but irrational beings never deviate from the instincts with which they are born, and which are adapted to their particular economy. Hence, animals are stationary, while man is progressive. Beavers construct their habitations, birds their nests, bees their hives, and the spider its web, with an admirable ingenuity; but the most sagacious of them can not apply their skill to purposes beyond the sphere of their particular wants, nor do any of them improve in the smallest degree on their predecessors. Exactly as they respectively built at the time of the creation, so will they continue to build until the end of time. To illustrate the contrary tendency and progressiveness of man in his habitations, we should compare a Hottentot's Kraal, with St. Peter's or St. Paul's."

Man has the power neither to eat, to walk, nor to speak, until he is taught. Being the most helpless of animals, the utmost of his earliest power is to suck, to move his limbs, and to weep. Nor is he the only animal that has the divine faculty of contemplation. Though the most intimate acquaintance with vegetable anatomy discovers no organ that bears any analogy with the seat of animal sensation, it would nevertheless betray a species of ignorance to deny sensation to plants: and it would be as absurd to deny to animals the possession of some faculty analogous to reason, since the faculty of imagination is proved by their capacity of dreaming.

Aristotle concludes there "are between man and animals faculties in common, near and analogous." He ascribes to the elephant the character of being the most teachable and tamable: but he adds, "one sole animal, man, can reflect and deliberate."

It appears that there are certain kinds of intellectual power —of what, in man, at least, is commonly called reason—common, to a certain extent, to man and to some of the lower orders of creation. And again, that there are certain powers wholly confined to man—especially all those concerned in what is properly called reasoning—all employment of language as an instrument of thought; and it appears that instinct, again, is to a certain extent common to man with brutes, though far less in amount, and less perfect in man; and more and more developed in other animals the lower we descend in the scale.

M. Flourens contends that there is a direct opposition between instinct and intelligence, the former being blind, necessary, and invariable, while the latter is elective, conditional, and changeable. Horses learn to obey man, and understand some of his words; this intelligence, in a qualified sense, is the result of experience and instruction or training. Monkeys and cats are taught to drink tea, elephants to fire pistols, donkeys and pigs to find cards or numbers. If brutes are not invested with reasoning powers—though Plutarch, Montaigne, and others have sought to establish the fact—something very analogous to this they seem to possess; indeed it is difficult to account for the proofs of sagacity and intelligence which in some instances they evince, on any other hypothesis. Thus serpents are said to obey the voice of their masters; the trumpeter-bird follows its owner like a spaniel; and the jacana acts as a guard to poultry, preserving them in the fields from birds of prey, and escorting them home regularly at night. In the

Shetland Isles there is a gull which defends the flock from eagles ; it is therefore regarded as a privileged bird. The chamois bounding among the snowy mountains of the Caucasus, are indebted for their safety, in no small degree, to a peculiar species of pheasant. This bird acts as their sentinel ; for as soon as it gets sight of a man it whistles, upon hearing which, the chamois, knowing the hunter to be not far distant, sets off with the greatest speed, and seeks the highest peaks of the mountains. The artifices which partridges and plovers employ to delude their enemies from the nest of their young, may be referred to as a case in point, as well as the adroit contrivance of the hind for the preservation of her young ; for when she hears the sound of dogs, she puts herself in the way of the hunters, and starts in a direction to draw them away from her fawns. Instances of the effect of grief upon animals are also no less remarkable. The writer already cited says : "I knew a dog that died for the loss of its master, and a bulfinch that abstained from singing ten entire months on account of the absence of its mistress. On her return it immediately resumed its song." Lord Kaimes relates an instance of a canary, which, while singing to its mate hatching her eggs in a cage, fell dead ; the female quitted her nest, and finding him dead, rejected all food, and soon died by his side.

That most quadrupeds have all the bodily senses that man has, and that many of them feel the various passions by which our humanity is distinguished, would seem to be no matter of disputation ; for even insects exhibit the emotions of fear, anger, sorrow, joy, and desire, and many of them express those passions by sounds peculiar to themselves. Dupont de Nemours imagined he understood the language of beasts and birds. He actually published "Translations of the Songs of the Nightingale," and the Crows' Dictionary—"Chansons du Rossignol," and "Le Dictionnaire des Corbeaux." Montaigne will have it that beasts have language, "and if we do not understand it, it is not their fault." Milton imagines Adam master of the language of animals, as indicated by the motto to our chapter.

It has been suggested that the Pyramids were erected in honor of bulls, not for the fame of kings; but not to refer to the folly of the ancients in worshipping reptiles, insects, birds, and quadrupeds, it will at least be fair to remind the reader of the memorable instance mentioned in Holy Writ of that supernaturally endowed animal, of a despised race, which administered a merited rebuke to an unrighteous and disobedient prophet.

For the better illustration of our subject we shall now adduce some illustrative anecdotes; and as the dog is a very general favorite, we propose, first, thus to exemplify, not only his superior sagacity, but his exemplary fidelity, which latter feature of character he seems really to possess in greater perfection than his master, if we allow any significancy to the remarkable, and certainly very disparaging inquiry of Solomon—"A faithful man who can find?" As in the case of the human species, the canine exhibits a great variety of character and disposition —from the vicious to the amiable; nor are these various shades of moral development the less remarkable if we consider the family connections and associations of this animal; the dog being a near relative of the fox, the hyena, the jackal, and the wolf—creatures whose characteristics are of a very questionable kind. In the East and elsewhere, the dog wanders about wild: but in more civilized communities his association with man seems to have imparted to his nature somewhat of the polish and temper of refined life. It is said that the dog in his primitive state is dumb, and that he first acquired his faculty of barking from his attempting to imitate the human voice. Many of the canine fraternity lead a miserably degraded existence, it is true; but the opposite cannot, without exception, be affirmed of the race of his master, as in the instance of the inebriate, who degrades himself lower than the level of the brute. Who does not admire the noble and sagacious creature, for his usefulness, fidelity, and attractive manners? "He has been the pampered minion of royalty, and the half-starved partaker of the beggar's crust: in one form he appears as the high-bred hound of the chase; in another, as the lowly but more useful keeper of his master's flocks; in another, as the true and pertinacious tracker of human felons; in another, as the active destroyer of humbler nuisances; and in another, as the laborious beast of burden."* For an instance of canine sagacity we refer to the following: "A dog belonging to a celebrated chemist, had tried upon it the effect of a certain poison, and upon the next day a counter-poison was administered with the effect of preserving the creature's life. The following day another dose was offered him, but he would not touch it. Different sorts of poisonous drugs were presented to him, but he resolutely refused all. Bread was offered, but he would not touch it; meat, but he turned from it; water, but he would not drink. To reässure him, his master offered him bread and meat, of which he himself ate in the dog's presence; and of that the sagacious animal hesitated not to partake. He was then taken to a fountain, but he would drink nowhere but from the spot where the water gushed free and fresh. This continued for several days, until the master, touched by the extraordinary intelligence of the poor creature, resolved to make no more attempts upon him with his poisons."† Take another case, which is no less significant: "A gentleman who was in the habit of walking out with his dog in the evening, on one occasion happened to be engaged beyond the usual hour for the walk, when 'Brush' made his appearance carrying a hat in his mouth. His master took little or no notice of the circumstance, thinking that the dog was acting according to the orders of some of the family; but in a little while he again walked into the room, carrying his master's boots, significantly wagging his tail, and evidently satisfied that he had given a broad hint enough. It was found that the dog

*Dr. Bell. †Edinb. Register.

had been guided solely by his own instinct. The following incident, said to be well attested, and taken from a French work, entitled, *L'Histoire des Chiens Célèbres*, shows that a well-educated dog, under exciting circumstances, cannot only reason and act with wonderful decision and presence of mind, but can also manifest a feeling of revenge, which is not necessarily his natural character, but which can hardly be surpassed in intensity by a *Christian* warrior. "Mustapha, a strong and active greyhound, belonged to a captain of artillery, raised from its birth in the midst of camps, always accompanied its master, and exhibited no alarm in the midst of battle. In the hottest engagements it remained near the cannon, and carried the match in its mouth. At the memorable battle of Fontenoi, the master of Mustapha received a mortal wound. At the moment when about to fire upon the enemy, he and several of his corps were struck to the earth by a discharge of artillery. Seeing his master extended lifeless and bleeding, the dog became desperate, and howled piteously. Just at that time a body of French soldiers were advancing to gain possession of the piece, which was aimed at them from the top of a small rising-ground. As if with a view to revenge his master's death, *Mustapha seized the lighted match with his paws, and set fire to the cannon, loaded with case-shot!* Seventy men fell on the spot, and the remainder took to flight. After this bold stroke, the dog lay down sadly near the dead body of his master, licked his wounds, and remained there twenty-two hours without sustenance. He was at length with difficulty removed by the comrades of the deceased. This gallant greyhound was carried to London, and presented to George II., who had him taken care of as a brave and faithful public servant. Byron thus apostrophises this animal:

"The poor dog! in life the firmest friend—
The first to welcome, foremost to defend;
Whose honest heart is still his master's own;
Who labors, fights, lives, breathes for him alone."

Hogg, the Ettrick shepherd, acknowledges that he "never felt so grateful to any creature under the sun as he did to his honest 'Sirrah!'" The testimony of Burns is scarcely less remarkable; he affirms "that the master is the soul of the dog; all the powers and faculties of its nature are devoted to its master's service; and these powers and faculties are ennobled by the intercourse." He sarcastically adds that the dog sometimes puts the Christian to shame in this respect.

A few days before the overthrow of Robespierre, a revolutionary tribunal had condemned to death a magistrate, who was a most estimable man. His favorite and faithful dog, a spaniel, was with him when he was apprehended, but was not permitted to accompany his master to prison. Day after day the dog repaired to the door of the prison, vainly seeking admission. At last his fidelity won upon the keeper, and he allowed him to enter. The meeting of the old man and his devoted dog may be better imagined than described. The jailer, however, fearing for himself, shortly afterward carried the animal out, although he admitted him for a short time each successive day, as he regularly presented himself. When the day of sentence arrived, the dog, in spite of the guards, made his way into the hall, where he lay crouched between the legs of his master; and at the fatal place of execution the faithful creature was present: the knife of the guillotine fell, but he would not leave the lifeless body. After two days he was discovered stretched upon his master's grave; and for three months the disconsolate animal repaired each morning and evening to the spot, leaving it only to procure food from his new protector, who took pleasure in thus rewarding his surprising devotion to the memory of his deceased master. At the end of the period named he began to refuse food, his patience became exhausted, and for twenty-four hours he was observed to employ his weakened limbs in digging up the earth that separated him from the being he so loved. His powers now gave way; he shrieked in his struggles; and at length ceased to breathe, his last look being intently fixed upon the grave. If we admit that dogs possess the faculty of thought, here is a decided case of a dog dying of a broken heart. A poor tailor, of the Borough, left a small dog inconsolable for his loss. The little animal would not leave his dead master even for food; and when the corpse was removed for burial, he followed the mournful train to the churchyard, and would have remained at the grave but for the sexton, whose ruder sensibilities prompted his expulsion. He was found the next day, on the grave of his master, and there continued to repeat his visit, as often as he was expelled, till one day the circumstance having become known to the clergyman, he had him supplied daily with food, and even built him a kennel on the spot, in order that he might indulge the bent of his inclination. Two years did this mirror of fidelity pass in this manner, till death put an end to his griefs.* Take another instance of canine devotion, that of a dog whose master desired him to guard a bag, which he had inadvertently placed almost in the middle of a narrow street, in the town of Southampton. While the faithful animal was keeping watch over it, a cart passed by; and such was the immovable determination of the creature to obey his master's orders, that, rather than relinquish his trust, he actually suffered the vehicle to crush him to death. As an instance of generous revenge on the part of this noble creature, there is a story told of a person who, being desirous of getting rid of his dog, took it along with him in a boat, and rowing out into the river Seine, threw it overboard. The poor animal repeatedly struggled to regain the boat, but was as often beaten off; till at length, in the attempts to baffle the efforts of the dog, the man upset the boat, and he fell into the water. No sooner, however, did the generous brute see his master struggle in the stream, than he forsook the boat, and held him above water till assistance arrived, and thus saved his life. Was not this dog morally superior to his owner, in thus returning good for evil? Here is another example of generosity:

*Blaine's Canine Pathology.

A favorite house-dog, left to the care of its master's servants, at Edinburgh, while he was himself in the country, would have been starved by them had it not had recourse to the kitchen of a friend of its master's, which it occasionally visited. Not content with indulging himself simply in this streak of good-fortune, this liberally-minded animal, a few days subsequently, falling in with a poor solitary duck, and possibly deeming it to be in destitute circumstances, caught it up in his teeth, and carried it to the well-stored larder that had so amply supplied his own necessities. He laid the duck at the cook's feet, with many polite movements of his tail—that most expressive of canine features—then scampered off, with much seeming complacency at having given his hostess this substantial proof of his grateful sense of favors received.

We read of a surgeon who found a poor dog, with his leg broken. He took him home, set it, and in due time gave him his liberty. Some months afterward the surgeon was awoke in the night by a dog barking loudly at his door. As the barking continued, and the surgeon thought he recognized the voice, he got up, and went down stairs. When he opened the door, there stood his former patient, wagging his tail, and by his side another dog—a friend whom he had brought—who had also had the misfortune to get a leg broken. There is another dog-story related by Mr. Jenyns, which we think is not without its moral. A poodle, belonging to a gentleman in Cheshire, was in the habit of going to church with his master, and sitting with him in the pew during the whole service. Sometimes his master did not come; but this did not prevent the poodle, who always presented himself in good time, entered the pew, and remained sitting there alone: departing with the rest of the congregation. One Sunday, the dam at the head of a lake in the neighborhood gave way, and the whole road was inundated. The congregation was therefore reduced to a few individuals, who came from cottages close at hand. Nevertheless, by the time the clergyman had commenced, he saw his friend, the poodle, come slowly up the aisle, dripping with water: having been obliged to swim above a quarter of a mile to get to church. He went into his pew, as usual, and remained quietly there to the end of the service. This is told on the authority of the clergyman himself.

Dogs perform an important part in street-begging, in London. They have been known, on receipt of a penny, to run to the baker's shop, and bring their master a piece of bread. We have read of a dog, who, on the death of his blind master, followed up his old calling by begging on his own account. Another instance of canine wit, which seems to have a smack of the facetious in it, is that of one who made a living by shoe-blacking, in Paris. The animal, in his desire to serve his master, would roll in the gutter, for the purpose of throwing mud upon the shoes of pedestrians. A gentleman who was the victim of this trick of trade, extorted the confession from his master, that he had taught the dog this expedient, and that it proved a very profitable one.

Instances of the strong attachment of the beggar's dog may often be witnessed. Not only does he enact the guide to the blind, but he performs other services equally essential: taking up the alms dropped for his mendicant master, or holding a cup to receive the contributions of the charitable; and often is he seen placing himself in an erect attitude, with a most beseeching visage, which tells well upon the pocket. Hogg, the Ettrick Shepherd, relates some surprising things about the exceeding fidelity and utility of the shepherd's dog on the highlands of Scotland. The dog is indeed indispensable in that capacity, for no flock could be kept together without his watch-care; and many instances occur in which several hundred sheep are brought home from the ravines and rocks of that northern clime, solely by this useful animal. While most other quadrupeds fear man, the dog seems, by a law seemingly of intuition, to regard him with feelings of strong attachment. How inhumane are they who fail to appreciate this remarkable trait of his character. The spaniel is the most grateful, affectionate, and patient under ill-treatment. If punished, it receives the chastisment with submission, looking up into the face of its offended master with a most deprecating expression of sorrow; whilst at the slightest returning encouragement, its indications of joy and delight are evinced with seeming ecstasy. Here, again, an important moral lesson may be learned by those who have not acquired the difficult and rare faculty of suffering wrongfully without repining or resentment. The Newfoundland dog is known to be superior to most others in the power of swimming, for which it is peculiarly fitted by having the foot partly webbed. Some years ago a nurse was playing with a child on the parapet of a bridge at Dublin; with a sudden spring, the child fell into the river. The agonized spectators saw the waters close over the child, and imagined that it had sunk to rise no more, when a noble dog, seeing the catastrophe, gazed wistfully at the ripple in the stream made by the child's descent, and rushed in to its rescue. At the same instant the poor little thing reappeared on the surface: the dog seized it, and with a firm but gentle pressure, bore it to the shore without injury. Among the spectators attracted to the spot was a gentleman who appeared strongly impressed with admiration for the sagacity and promptness of the dog. On hastening to get nearer to him, he saw, with terror, joy, and surprise, that the child thus rescued was his own! Such was his sense of gratitude, that it is said he offered five hundred guineas for the noble animal. The well-known dogs of the Convent of Mount St. Bernard deserve more than a passing tribute. If they find a child amid the snows, they stay not for instructions, but hasten with it to the hospitable monks. Of their own accord, they roam about these desolate regions day and night, seeking to relieve the distresses of travellers. One of these dogs has a cask of cordial tied about his neck, to which the sufferer may apply for support; and another has a warm cloak fastened to his back, to cover him. It is related that one of these indispensable animals had saved the lives of twenty-two persons, and was at last buried in an avalanche, in attempting to convey a poor courier to his family, who were toiling up the mountain to meet him: all were lost in one common calamity. In many of the canine species we may also perceive an acuteness of perception and sagacity equalled only by that of the elephant. Our illustrations of canine instinct or intelligence would be incomplete were we to omit the following. A gentleman was missed in London, and was supposed to have met with some foul play. No clue could be obtained to the mystery, till it was gained from observing that his dog continued to crouch down before a certain house. The animal would not be induced to leave the spot, and it was at length inferred that he might be waiting for his master. The house, hitherto above suspicion, was searched, and the result was the discovery of the body of the missing individual, who had been murdered. The guilty parties were arrested, confessed their crime; and thus one of the "dens of London" was broken up by the "police-knowledge" of this faithful dog.

The elephant, unwieldy and uncouth as he seems, presents some remarkable features of character, combining the fidelity of the dog, the endurance of the camel, and the docility of the horse, with singular sagacity, prudence, and courage. It is related of one of the soldiers of Pyrrhus, King of Epirus, that, when fighting in the territory of Argos, he fell wounded from his elephant, which rushed furiously among the combatants till he found his master, raised him gently from the ground with his trunk, and placing him on his tusks, carried him back to the town. A similar anecdote is given of King Porus, who, in an engagement with Alexander the Great, meeting with a similar casualty, his faithful elephant is said to have kept the enemy at bay till he had replaced the monarch on his back by means of his trunk; although the poor animal, in this heroic defence, was severely wounded.

In one of the recent accounts of scenes of Indian warfare, a body of artillery was described as proceeding up a hill, and the great strength of elephants was found highly advantageous in drawing up the guns. On the carriage of one of these guns, a little in front of the wheel, sat an artilleryman, resting himself. An elephant, drawing another gun, was advancing in regular order close behind. Whether from falling asleep, or over-fatigue, the man fell from his seat, and the wheel of the gun-carriage, with its heavy gun was just rolling over him. The elephant, comprehending the danger, and seeing that he could not reach the body of the man with his trunk, seized the wheel by the top, and, lifting it up, passed it carefully over the fallen man, and set it down on the other side. An Oriental traveller furnishes some amusing incidents respecting the docility and sagaciousness of this monstrous creature. In his journeys, he says, if he wished to stop to admire a beautiful prospect, the animal remained immovable until his sketch was finished ; if he wished for mangoes growing out of his reach, this faithful servant selected the most fruitful branch, and, breaking it off with his trunk for him, accepted very thankfully of any part for himself, respectfully and politely acknowledging the compliment by raising his trunk three times above his head, in the manner of Oriental obeisance. Docile as he is, this noble quadruped seems conscious of his superiority over the rest of the brute creation ; a proof of this may be seen in the following circumstance related by another Eastern tourist. Some young camels were travelling with the British army in India, when, having occasion to cross the Jumna in a boat, and the driver being unable to urge them forward, the elephant was appealed to to accomplish the task. The animal immediately assumed a furious appearance, trumpeted with his proboscis, shook his ears, roared, struck the ground right and left, and blew the dust in clouds towards them. The camels, in their fear of the elephant, forgot their dread of the boat, and they rushed into it in the greatest hurry, when the elephant resumed his composure, and deliberately returned to his post.

Locke observes, "It seems as evident that some animals do in certain instances reason, as that they have sense." This certainly derives something like corroboration from the following statement. At the siege of Burtpore, in 1805, the British army, with its countless host of followers and attendants, and thousands of cattle, had been for a long time before the city, when, on the approach of the hot season, the supply of water generally fails. On this occasion, two drivers, each with his elephant—the one large and strong, the other rather small and weak—were at the well together. The smaller animal was provided with a bucket, which he carried at the end of his trunk ; but the other elephant, not being furnished with this needful appendage, seized the bucket, and easily wrested it away from his less powerful fellow. The latter was too sensible of his inferiority openly to resent the insult, though he evidently felt it ; but the keepers began to contend and abuse each other. At length the injured brute, watching the opportunity when the other was standing with his side to the well, retired backwards a few paces very quietly, and rushing forward with all his might, he drove his adversary into the well. It may be supposed great consternation among the company was the result ; and some fourteen hours' assiduous and ingenious labor was required to rescue the ponderous animal from his novel, though not unpleasant, situation. If a helpless living creature, or a wounded person, lie in his way, the elephant will protect and succor him. An incident is recorded in the history of the siege of Seringapatam, to this effect : "I have seen," says the officer referred to, "the wife of a Mahoot give an infant in charge of an elephant, while she went about some business, and have been much amused in observing the sagacity and care of the unwieldy nurse. The child, which, like most children, did not like to lie still in one position, would, as soon as left to itself, begin crawling about ; in which exercise it would probably get among the legs of the animal, or entangled in the branches of the trees on which he was feeding ; when the elephant would, in the most tender manner, disengage his charge, either by lifting it out of the way with his trunk, or by removing the impediments to its free progress. If the little creature should happen to stray away too far, its mammoth guardian would lift it back as gently as possible to the spot whence it had started."

Somnini mentions an elephant, at Naples, which was employed with others in fetching water in a copper vessel, and perceiving that the water escaped from some fracture, he took the vessel of his own accord to a smith's for repair, in imitation of what he had seen done before by his master.

Take yet another example of the shrewd wit of this colossal creature. Some men were teasing an elephant they were conveying across a river. In the boat that was towed alongside they had a dog which began to torment it by pulling its ears. The elephant was resolved to resent the impertinence, and what do you suppose was her expedient ? She filled her proboscis with water, and then deluged the whole party. At first the men laughed at the manœuvre, but she persisted until they were compelled to bale, to keep from sinking ; when, seeing this, she redoubled her efforts, and it is said she certainly would have swamped the boat, had the passage across been prolonged a few minutes further. Thus much—although much more might be presented—in behalf of the noble qualities of the elephant. We see that he is in no respect inferior to the dog in character, and yet—since the most excellent things are said to lie in a small compass—and the dog does not, like his monstrous contemporary, require two hundred pounds of solid meat per diem, or take up so much room—the prevailing preference for the canine will, doubtless, long continue to obtain among civilized communities.

Even pigs may lay claim to a species of moral character. It is true they are not over nice as to their personal habits or deportment ; but, then, they seldom or never perpetrate the high misdemeanors of which some human beings are culpable.

A facetious writer remarks: "Whether food is best eaten off the ground or in a china plate, is, it seems to us, merely a matter of taste and convenience, on which pigs and men honestly differ. They ought, then, to be judged charitably. At any rate, pigs are not filthy enough to chew tobacco, nor to poison their breath by drinking whisky. As to personal appearance, you don't catch a pig playing the dandy, nor picking his way up muddy streets in kid slippers. Pigs have some excellent traits of character. If one chances to wallow a little deeper in some mire-hole than his fellow, and so carriès off and comes into possession of more of the earth than his brethren, he never assumes an extra importance on that account; neither are his brethren stupid enough to worship him for it. The only question seems to be: 'Is he still a hog?' If he is, they treat him as such. And when a hog has no merits of his own, he never puts on any aristocratic airs, nor claims any particular respect on account of his family connections. They understand full well the common-sense maxim, 'Every tub must stand upon its own bottom.'" If there is an absence of humor in the swinish race, the loss is fully compensated by the love of fun inherent with the monkey tribe. Dr. Guthrie relates the following amusing anecdote of a *reasonable* monkey.

"Jack, as he was called, seeing his master and some companions drinking, with those imitative powers for which his species is remarkable, finding half a glass of whisky left, took it up and drank it off. It flew, of course, to his head. Amid their loud roars of laughter, he began to skip, hop, and dance. Jack was drunk. Next day, when they went, with the intention of repeating the fun, to take the poor monkey from his box, he was not to be seen. Looking inside, there he lay, crouching in a corner. 'Come out!' said his master. Afraid to disobey, he came, walking on three legs—the fore-paw that was laid on his forehead saying, as plain as words could do, that he had a headache.

"Having left him some days to get well, and resume his

gayety, they at length carried him off to the old scene of revel, On entering, he eyed the glasses with manifest terror, skulking behind the chair ; and on his master ordering him to drink, he bolted, and he was on the house-top in a twinkling. They called him down. He would not come. His master shook the whip at him. Jack, astride on the ridge-pole, grinned defiance. A gun, of which he was always much afraid, was pointed at this disciple of temperance ; he ducked his head, and slipped over to the back of the house ; upon which, seeing his predicament, and less afraid, apparently, of the fire than the fire-water, the monkey leaped at a bound on the chimney-top, and getting down into a flue, held on by his fore-paws. He would rather be singed than drunk. He triumphed, and, although his master kept him for twelve years after that, he never could persuade the monkey to taste another drop of whisky."

In a family where a common monkey was a pet, on one occasion, the footman had been shaving himself—the monkey watching him during the process—when he carelessly left his apparatus within reach of the creature. As soon as the man was gone out of the room, the monkey got the razor and began to scrape away at his throat as he had seen the footman do, when, alas ! not understanding the nature of the instrument he was using, the animal cut its own throat, and, before it was discovered, bled to death. A friend of ours possessed one of these creatures, whose disposition seemed very affectionate ; if it had done wrong and was scolded, it immediately seated itself on the floor, and clasping its hands together, seemed to beg earnestly to be forgiven. Mrs. Lee also tells us of one belonging to her eldest daughter, which seemed to know he could master the child, "and did not hesitate to bite and scratch her, whenever she pulled him a little harder than he thought proper. I punished him," she adds, "for each offense, yet fed and caressed him when good ; by which means, I possessed an entire ascendancy over him." The same writer also gives an interesting account of a monkey which a man in Paris had trained to a variety of clever tricks. "I met him one day," says she, "suddenly, as he was coming up the drawing-room stairs. He made way for me by standing in an angle, and when I said, 'Good-morning,' took off his cap, and made me a low bow. 'Are you going away?' I asked; 'where is your passport?' Upon which, he took from the same cap a square piece of paper, which he opened and showed to me. His master told him my gown was dusty, and he instantly took a small brush from his master's pocket, raised the hem of my dress, cleaned it, and then did the same for my shoes. He was perfectly docile and obedient; when we gave him something to eat, he did not cram his pouches with it, but delicately and tidily devoured it; and when we bestowed money on him, he immediately put it into his master's hands."

A monkey tied to a stake was robbed by the Johnny Crows (in the West Indies) of his food, and he conceived the following plan of punishing the thieves. He feigned death, and lay perfectly motionless on the ground, near to his stake. The birds approached by degrees, and got near enough to steal his food, which he allowed them to do. This he repeated several times, till they became so bold as to come within the reach of his claws. He calculated his distance, and laid hold of one of them. Death was not his plan of punishment; he was more refined in his cruelty. He plucked every feather out of the bird, and then let him go and show himself to his companions. He made a man of him, according to the ancient definition of a "biped without feathers."*

In the countries of the Eastern Peninsula and Archipelago, where they abound, the matrons are often observed, in the cool of the evening, sitting in a circle round their little ones, which amuse themselves with various gambols. The merriment of the young, as they jump over each other's heads, make mimic fights, and wrestle in sport, is most ludicrously con-

* Illustrations of Instinct.

trasted with the gravity of their seniors, which might be presumed as delighting in the fun, but far too staid and wise to let it appear. There is a regard, however, to discipline; and whenever any foolish juvenile behaves decidedly ill, the mamma will be seen to jump into the throng, seize the offender by the tail, and administer exactly that extreme kind of chastisement which has so long been in vogue among human parents and Yorkshire schoolmasters.

That there is merriment—genuine, human-like merriment—in many of the lower animals, no one can doubt who has ever watched the gambols of the kid, the lamb, the kitten and monkey.

Examples of docility and patience are suggested to us, in a forcible degree, by the beautiful reindeer, the camel, and the horse: the former, it is known, is of indispensable value to the Laplander, as the camel is to the wanderer over the sultry and sandy wastes, where there are no cool shades, nor refreshing water-courses. Caravans, consisting of from 500 to 3000 merchants, are often saved from perishing from thirst, in their weary passage over the arid and trackless desert, by the acute sense of smelling possessed by the camel; they are able to scent water at the distance of two miles. This remarkable faculty they seem to possess in an equal degree with the dog; they also evince a like teachable and tractable spirit with that favorite animal, while the noble and intelligent horse exhibits a no less striking example of these characteristics. To say nothing of the symmetrical beauty and graceful bearing of this universally esteemed creature, which it will be remembered is to be seen in all its pride of beauty in the land of its nativity, the East, its many excellent qualities would, apart from its attractive form, commend it to preference. Like other quadrupeds, it possesses the faculty of memory in a singular degree, and also evinces no less its attachment for its owner. It may, moreover, be trained to many ingenious tricks, such as dancing, as the feats of the circus sufficiently attest. Among others, there is a story told of a horse kept by a gentleman of Leeds, who used to pump water from a well with wonderful dexterity, for his own use, by taking the handle in his mouth, and working it with his head, in imitation of his groom; he also was taught to open and shut the gate for himself. In this connection, we might refer to the mule, the zebra, and the poor, despised ass, as exhibiting examples of patience under suffering and burdens—for, with the exception of the beautiful yet untamed zebra, they have been subjected to severe tests in this respect. The ass, indeed, seems almost behind the age, his movements being too tardy, and his laggard pace being rendered the more marked by the lightning speed of the locomotive. Although almost unknown to us, yet, in early times, and in the East, his fame was in the ascendant; and it will be recollected this was the animal chosen by the Saviour when He made his entry into Jerusalem. This demure-looking and docile creature retains a strong love of home, and is also possessed of no mean share of intelligence, although his name is made synonymous with stupidity. It is true, he is sometimes obstinate, and addicted to kicking; but he is, in this particular, no worse than many a biped under circumstances of like provocation. Another zoological specimen which we propose to introduce to the notice of the reader is the cat—a sort of counterpart to the dog in most domestic establishments. Cats have the reputation of great vital tenacity—the possession of nine lives; and juveniles seem by common consent resolved to test the fact. The cat also has the wretched reputation of always falling upon her feet, from whatever height she may be thrown, and many a cruel experiment has been made to ascertain that fact. We repeat that people having a taste for dogs are seldom catholic enough in their animal fondness to extend it to cats. You never heard of drowning dogs, or pelting dogs, or having dogs worried for mere amusement. The creature's more conspicuous gifts are appreciated by those rougher-judging estimates, which are unable to make out the subtler delicacies of the cat organization. The man with a prime terrier for rats—or a mastiff which can throttle a bull-dog—or a hound which can pull down a red-deer—or even a poodle which can sit upon its hind legs and yelp at the word of command—not one of these amateurs but will discover and admire the points and motions of the creatures while performing these achievements; but it is twenty to one that they never studied, or never thought it worth while studying, one of the most perfectly graceful things beneath the sun—a cat curving herself for a spring; or one of the most dexterous performances which animal nature is capable of—a cat picking her way among a series either of movable or hurtful petty articles, without touching a single one.*

Cats differ as much in character as human beings do; and like human beings, their character is very much to be predicated from their countenances. No two are ever seen alike, and they vary as much in the conformation of their skulls as do the different races of mankind. Southey, in his "Doctor," gives a curious chapter upon the cats of his acquaintance—a chapter in which humor and natural history are agreeably mingled together; he was evidently a close observer of the habits of poor puss, and took much delight in the whims, frolics, and peculiarities of his favorites. Proofs of the domestication and strong attachment of the cat might be adduced *ad nauseam.* The story of M. Somnini and his favorite cat may be recollected as a case in point: "This animal," he writes, "was my principal amusement for several years: how vividly was the expression of her attachment depicted upon her countenance! how many times have her tender caresses made me forget my troubles, and consoled me in my misfortunes! My beautiful and interesting companion at length perished: after several days of suffering, during which I never forsook her, her eyes, constantly fixed on me, were at length extinguished; and her loss has rent my heart with grief." Among the admirers of the

* Angus B. Reach.

sleek and gentle cat may be mentioned Mohammed, Rousseau, Petrarch, Johnson, Cowper, and we know not how many other illustrious names. Madame Helvetius had a favorite cat, which, at the death of her mistress, wandered about her chamber, mewing most piteously, and after the body was consigned to the grave, it was found stretched upon the tomb lifeless, having expired from excess of grief! The Earl of Southampton—companion of Essex in the fatal insurrection—having been confined some time in the Tower, was one day surprised by a visit from his pet cat, which is said to have reached its master by descending the chimney of his apartment. The following anecdote of combined attachment and sagacity, equals anything that has been told of the dog, and places poor pussy in a much more favorable light than current opinion would allow. In the summer of 1800, a physician of Lyons was requested to inquire into a murder that had been committed on a woman of that city. He accordingly went to the residence of the deceased, where he found her extended lifeless on the floor, weltering in her blood. A large white cat was mounted on the cornice of the cupboard, at the further end of the apartment, where he seemed to have taken refuge. He sat motionless, with his eyes fixed on the corpse, and his attitude and looks expressing horror and affright: the following morning the animal was found in precisely the same state, and when the room was filled with officers of justice, he still remained apparently transfixed to the spot. As soon, however, as the suspected persons were brought in, his eyes glared with increased fury, his hair bristled, and he darted precipitately from the room. The countenances of the assassins were disconcerted, and they now, for the first time during the whole course of the horrid transaction, felt their atrocious audacity forsake them. No experiment, says a recent writer, can be more beautiful than that of setting a kitten for the first time before a looking-glass; the little creature appears surprised and pleased with the resemblance, and makes several attempts at touching its new acquaintance: and at length, finding its efforts fruitless, it looks behind the glass, and appears highly astonished at the absence of the figure. This certainly evinces a degree of intelligence. We might instance cases in which the reasoning process appears to be exhibited; but let the following, related by Dr. Smellie, in which ingenuity of performance was combined with sagacity, suffice. "A cat frequented a closet, the door of which was fastened by a common iron latch; a window was situated near the door: when the door was shut, the cat gave herself no uneasiness, for so soon as she was tired of her confinement, she mounted on the sill of the window, and with her paws dexterously lifted the latch and came out. This practice she continued for years." Many instances of the kind are upon record; let one, however, suffice—of a cat, who, having been neglected at the regular dinner hour, which was usually announced by the ringing of the bell, would agitate the bell-wire. The sagacity of the feline race is so clearly evinced in the following anecdote, that we cannot help inserting it. "Mr. Tiedeman, the famous Saxon dentist, had a valuable tortoiseshell cat, that for days did nothing but moan. Guessing the cause, he looked into its mouth, and seeing a decayed tooth, soon relieved it of its pain. The following day there were at least ten cats at his door—the day after, twenty; and they went on increasing at such a rate that he was obliged to keep a bull-dog to drive them away. But nothing would help them. A cat who had the tooth-ache would come any number of miles to him. It would come down the chimney even, and not leave the room till he had taken its tooth out. It grew such a nuisance at last, that he was never free from one of these feline patients. However, being one morning very nervous, he accidentally broke the jaw of an old tabby. The news of this spread like wildfire. Not a single cat ever came to him afterwards. It is extraordinary how the cats, in the above instances, acted like human beings. It is so extraordinary, indeed, that we think we must have reached the culminating point of our illustrations of animal instincts.

We now propose to draw our illustrations from the history of the insect and feathered tribes. Although one of the minutest of living things, yet as the *ant* is placed by the inspired-writer among the "four things which are little upon the earth, but exceeding wise;" and as it is the lessons of wisdom or prudence, which the habits of this interesting little creature so strikingly illustrate, that we wish to present, we shall take a brief survey of its peculiarities. Insignificant and unimportant as it may seem to the unthinking observer, the ant has engaged the scrutiny and curious study of some of the greatest minds. With the single exception of its associate, the "busy bee," it is unrivalled for its activity, industry, and its social economy; and to such an universal extent has it attracted human observation, that its name has long since passed into the synonym for virtue. The sluggard is told to observe the ant, "to consider her ways, and be wise;" the prodigal to imitate her thrift; the young are told that she "provideth her meat in the summer, and gathereth her food in the harvest;" and the unruly and turbulent have a powerful monitor in the harmony of her busy communities. These traits are amongst the cardinal virtues—indeed they form the bases of all human happiness. The value of prudence is so apparent, that without it even the most unremitting industry would prove of no avail. To find their excellence, therefore, so beautifully illustrated in this, one of the tiniest of created beings, may well excite our wonder and warmly enlist our interest. Ants have parental, filial, and social affections and sympathies, and they are supposed by Huber to hold intercourse with each other by signs and the sense of touch. And as to their fruits of industry, in some countries their hills are twenty feet in height, and in Sweden, they erect structures which Dr. Clarke considers far more wonderful in their proportion, than the Pyramids of Egypt. According to the arrangement of entomologists, ants form the seventh family of Hymenopterous insects, those having four membranous wings; this may surprise those who have been accustomed to regard them merely as wingless creatures, that burrow in little hillocks, but the discrepancy will disappear when it is recollected that, like other social insects, ants are of three sexes, and that it is only the perfect sexes that are furnished with wings—those of the neuter gender, called workers, being without. The first class form but a small proportion to the latter; the first-named being devoted to the re-production of their race, and the vast numbers of the wingless insect to the construction of their ingeniously-contrived dwellings, and the social duties of their several communities or colonies. There are numerous species of ants, distinguished by their size and color, but chiefly by their habits. Paramount with the erection of their habitations and the procuring of food, is the assiduous care they bestow upon their young, which usually extends, not only for a few days, but even weeks, and sometimes months. If an ant-hill be molested, the first care of the workers is to protect the young; and they may be seen running about in a state of distraction, each carrying a juvenile, frequently as big as itself. Ants swarm once or twice a summer, when the youngsters build new habitations for themselves, and live together in the same social and orderly manner as their progenitors. The females are the queen-mothers; but whether there is only one queen, as among bees, or several, is not determined by naturalists; the latter is thought most probable. The neuters or workers are true republicans, for they enjoy equal immunities and do all that is to be done of actual toil; and yet, if nature has assigned to them their allotted labor, she has also bequeathed to them a longer lease of existence, for after the winged males and females have left the hive in summer, a few days of "aërial dalliance" limit the term of their natural being. The little conical mounds, familiarly called "ant-hills," evince wonderful architectural ingenuity and skill; with their arched galleries, domes, pillars, and partitions, which rise in pyramidal succession. As these nests are liable to be destroyed by heavy rains, by the accidental tread of colossal man, and also require to be enlarged as the colony increases, the labor of re-constructing or repairing affords an endless round of busy entertainment to these industrious little workers. Their cells have none of the geometrical regularity so much admired in the combs of the honey-bee; and as they do not, therefore, like their *sweet* neighbors, necessarily act in concert, they may often be found working at cross-purposes. Such an occurrence does not seem, however, much to disconcert them; for, more sagacious than human blunderers, no sooner does an ant discover his mistake, than he sets to work to undo what he has erected, and follows instinctively that portion of the plan which was more advanced than his own. In general, however, when ants, according to Huber, commence any important undertaking, they convene a council in their own way, to deliberate upon some concerted plan of action, for the result seems to indicate the existence of design and a preconceived idea. The actual mode of working of these insects has been examined by the ingenious entomologist just referred to. According to his observances, there were two or three small openings on the surface of the nest, but none of the laborers were seen to pass out that way, on account of their being too much exposed to the sun, which these insects dread; for when the freshness of the air, and the dew invited the ants to take a walk, or survey their performances, they made new apertures.

"I remarked," says our naturalist, "that their habitations changed in appearance hourly, and that the diameter of those spacious avenues, where so many ants could freely pass each other during the day, was, as night approached, gradually lessened. The aperture at length totally disappeared, the dome was closed on all sides, and the ants retired to the bottom of their nest.

"In further noticing the apertures of these ant-hills, I fully ascertained the nature of the labor of its inhabitants, of which

I could not before even guess the purport ; for the surface of the nest presented such a constant scene of agitation, and so many insects were occupied in carrying materials in every direction, that the movement offered no other image than that of confusion.

"I saw then clearly that they were engaged in stopping up passages ; and for this purpose they at first brought forward little pieces of wood, which they deposited near the entrance of those avenues they wished to close ; they placed them in the stubble ; and then went to seek other twigs and fragments of wood, which they disposed above the first, but in a different direction, and appeared to choose pieces of less size in proportion as the work advanced. They at length brought in a number of dried leaves, and other materials of an enlarged form, with which they covered the roof—an exact miniature of the art of our builders, when they form the covering of any building! Nature, indeed, seems everywhere to have anticipated the inventions of which we boast, and this is doubtless one of the most simple. Our little insects, now safely in their nest, retire gradually to the interior before the last passages are closed ; one or two only remain without, or concealed behind the doors on guard, while the rest either take their repose, or engage in different occupations in the most perfect security. I was impatient to know what took place in the morning upon these ant-hills, and therefore visited them at an early hour. I found them in the same state in which I had left them the preceding evening. A few ants were wandering about on the surface of the nest, some others issued from time to time from under the margin of their little roofs formed at the entrance of the galleries; others afterward came forth, who began removing the wooden bars that blockaded the entrance, in which they readily succeeded. This labor occupied them several hours. The passages were at length free, and the materials with which they had been closed scattered here and there over the ant-hill. Every day, morning and evening, during the fine weather, I was a witness to similar proceedings. On days of rain, the doors of all the ant-hills remained closed. When the sky was cloudy in the morning, or rain was indicated, the ants, who seemed to be aware of it, opened but in part their several avenues, and immediately closed them when the rain commenced. Could the most enlightened reason, which ascribes such procedure to mere animal instinct, have done more?"

The several species of ants found in warm countries are indeed so numerous that volumes might be devoted to the delineation of their character and habits, which in most instances are marked by the finest displays of instinctive sagacity. We need not, however, attempt even their enumeration; for "every group of plants has particular species, and many trees are the exclusive abode of a kind that does not occur anywhere else;" it may safely be admitted, therefore, that ants are amongst the most numerous forms of life on the globe, teeming as it is with animated existence. That such an insignificant, though ingenious insect, should have been regarded as the standard emblem of foresight, industry, and perseverance—whether the result of unreasoning instinct, or of indubitable sagacity—need not excite our surprise, although it may well elicit our profound admiration.

Many speculations have been recently broached respecting the conditions of insect life. Some appear to regard them as endowed with the attributes of human reason in a modified degree; others admit the perfection of their senses, and ascribe their conduct to instinct; while a third class will allow them neither sense nor feeling, but consider them mere animated machines, as it were, propelled in all their movements by a power they cannot control. With the latter class the writhings of a trampled emmet are not evidences of pain, any more than the movement of its antennæ or feelers is of touch, or the direction of its eyes of sight. In fact, they deny insects the use of these organs altogether—a doctrine which will receive but few adherents; for however much their organs of sense may differ from those of man, it is clear that they were not given without some function to fulfill. It is absurd, of course, to ascribe memory, reflection, and the like, to creatures which have no brain; but it is equally absurd, seeing that these creatures avoid obstacles, evince symptoms of pain, have a choice in food, and so forth, to suppose that their organs are not capable of sight, touch, and taste. Their sensations may be very different from those of other animals, just as their organization is different; but whatever they are, there can be no doubt of their perfect aptitude to direct the animal in its manifold and highly curious operations.

We leave, however, the learned to settle a subject so involved and subtle, and proceed to give an illustrative anecdote, selected from many that might be adduced, of the ingenuity of this curious little creature in removing obstacles.

A gentleman of Cambridge one day observed an ant dragging along what, with respect to the creature's strength, might be denominated a log of timber. Others were severally employed, each in its own way. Presently the ant in question came to an ascent, where the weight of the wood seemed for a while to overpower him: he did not remain long perplexed with it, for three or four others, observing his dilemma, came behind and pushed it up. As soon, however, as he had got it on level ground, they left it to his care, and went to their own work. The piece he was drawing happened to be considerably thicker at one end than the other. This soon threw the poor fellow into a fresh difficulty: he unluckily dragged it between two bits of wood. After several fruitless efforts, finding it would not go through, he adopted the only mode that even a man in similar circumstances would have taken: he came behind it, pulled it back again, and turned it on its edge; when, running again to the other end, it passed through without the least difficulty.

Some Indian species, according to an anecdote related by Col. Sykes, exhibit feats of dexterity which one can scarcely ascribe to mere instinctive sagacity. It is known, perhaps, that ants, like cats, have a repugnance to water; to prevent their approach, therefore, the legs of a well-garnished sideboard of sweets were immersed in water and detached from the wall; notwithstanding this precaution, however, they committed their depredations upon the colonel's good things. He was curious to discover their mode of effecting their purpose, and he accordingly watched the process. He observed a solitary ant climbing quietly up the wall of the room, and when it had mounted to rather more than a foot above the level of the sideboard, it took a spring to the sideboard; soon after, others followed the example of their pioneer, and each, with like success, safely reached their tempting bait, and presently a host of these carnivorous little epicures were regaling themselves upon the luxurious repast. Sagacious and dexterous as this interesting fraternity are seen to be, we meet with an amusing instance of their folly and want of concert.

"A wise and laborious ant was toiling up the bark of a chestnut-tree, and pulling after him an entire snail-shell, the size of a hazel-nut. He halted occasionally as well he might, but he never lost hold of the shell, though the mere weight of it, one should have thought, would have pulled his mandibles out of joint. In a few minutes he had raised it upwards of three feet, and all was going on prosperously, when it so chanced that three or four idlers of the ant kind, and presently as many more, met him on his way. Our laborer had almost done his work; his hind-legs were already within the hole into which it was his plain purpose to introduce the shell, when the new-comers (who, as we have seen, are always ready to help one another) proceeded to do just the reverse! They got upon the shell, they entered it, they persisted in sticking to it: he could not carry it; and then the shell swerved to one side or the other, according to the disposal of his friends within, who had not even the sense to trim the boat; still, by great exertion, he held fast, and might perhaps have accomplished his task, when two more strangers thought proper to contribute their weight, and brought on the catastrophe. The weary but persevering insect was obliged to 'let go,' and the shell, freighted with three 'insides' and half-a-dozen 'outs,' fell to the ground! They left the conveyance in apparent alarm, and scampered off in all directions, while he remained for some time fixed to the spot of his discomfiture. The shell being subsequently examined, was found exactly to fit the hole in the direction in which the ant was dragging it, and in no other."

Ants possess not only an acute faculty of scent, they also have a mode of communicating intelligence by certain motions of their antennæ, or prominent organs attached to their heads. A nest of ants in a nobleman's garden discovered a closet, many yards within the house, in which conserves were kept, which they constantly attended till the nest was destroyed. Some, in their rambles, must have first discovered this depôt of sweets, and informed the rest of it. It is remarkable that they always went to it by the same track, scarcely varying an inch from it, though they had to pass through two apartments; nor could the sweeping and cleaning of the rooms discomfit them, or cause them to pursue a different route. Here the insects perseveringly followed the same track, a fact which leads one to suspect that they leave some scent or trace perceptible to one another. The ingenuity and intelligence discovered in their actions, whether single or combined, are indeed so surprising, that the Mahommedans have even assigned them a place in their heaven. It has been said, no man is hopelessly bad who can laugh: if we extend the application of the proposition, it may not be absurd to humanize their conduct, and to suppose these little specks of being capable of generous emotions and sympathies, if we judge by their evident habits of sportiveness.

"Whether ants," says Mr. Kirby, "with man and some of the larger animals, experience anything like attachment to individuals, is not easily ascertained; but that they feel the full force of the sentiment which we term patriotism, or the love of the community to which they belong, is evident from the whole series of their proceedings, which all tend to promote the general good. Distress or difficulty falling upon any member of their society generally excites their sympathy, and they do their utmost to relieve it. M. Latreille once cut off the antennæ of an ant; and its companions, evidently pitying its sufferings, anointed the wounded part with a drop of transparent fluid from their mouth: and whoever attends to what is going forward in the neighborhood of one of their nests, will be pleased to observe the readiness with which they seem disposed to assist each other in difficulties. When a burden is too heavy for one, another will soon come to ease it of part of the weight; and if one is threatened with an attack, all basten to the spot to join in repelling it."

We now return to the examples of economy and thrift as evinced in the habits of the bee. In all ages, bees have claimed the admiration of mankind as patterns of industry, economy, cheerfulness, and ingenuity. "Wise in their government, diligent and active in their employments, devoted to their young and to their queen, the bees read a lecture to man that exemplifies their Oriental name "*Deburah—she that speaketh.*" In tracing some of the peculiar habits and characteristics of this useful insect, we may possibly acquire fresh incentives to the cultivation of one of the essential virtues. "A bee amongst the flowers of spring," says Paley, "is one of the cheerfulest objects that can be looked upon: its life appears to be all enjoyment—so busy and so pleased." Would that the like sunny smile of cheerful contentedness shed its radiance over the brow of toiling humanity: how many a secret sorrow would it assuage, how many a weary hour would it beguile, and how much would it tend to enhance the aggregate of human happiness. What valuable lessons of thrift and economy are to be learned from the habits of the "busy bee." Bees belong to the same genera with ants: a colony of the former, occupying a hive, consists, besides the young brood, of one female or queen, several hundreds of males or drones, and many thousand workers. This insect is so familiar to all, that it will not be necessary for us to refer to its peculiarity of structure, further than to state that the worker is invested with an extra stomach, which is called the honey-bag, in which it deposits the sweets or saccharine matter it collects from blossoms, fruits, and flowers. "The most profound philosopher, equally with the most incurious mortals," says Kirby, "is struck with astonishment on inspecting the interior of a bee-hive: he beholds a city in miniature. He sees this city divided into regular streets, these streets composed of houses constructed on the most exact geometrical principles, and the most symmetrical plan—some serving for storehouses for food, others for the habitations of the citizens, and a few, much more extensive than the rest, destined for the palaces of the sovereign. He perceives that the substance of which the whole city is built, is one which man, with all his skill, is unable to fabricate; and that the edifices are such as the most expert artist would find himself incompetent to erect: yet the whole is the work of a society of mere insects!"

Shakspeare has thus sketched the subject:—

"So work the honey-bees;
Creatures, that by a rule in nature, teach
The art of order to a peopled kingdom.
They have a king, and officers of sorts:
Where some, like magistrates, correct at home;
Others, like merchants, venture trade abroad;
Others, like soldiers, armed in their stings,
Make boot upon the summer's velvet buds;
Which pillage they with merry march bring home
To the tent-royal of their emperor:
Who, busied in his majesty, surveys
The singing masons building roofs of gold;
The civil citizens kneading up the honey,
The poor mechanic porters crowding in
Their heavy burdens at his narrow gate;

> The sad-eyed justice, with his surly hum,
> Delivering o'er to executor's pale
> The lazy yawning drone."

A number of honey-combs, composed of cells for the most part hexagonal or six-sided, regularly applied to each other's sides, and arranged in two strata or layers, placed end to end, are fixed to the upper part and sides of the interior of the hive. These combs are arranged vertically at a small distance from each other, so that the cells composing them are placed in a horizontal position, and have their openings in different directions. The distance between the combs is about half an inch, sufficient to allow two bees to pass each other easily: besides these vacancies, the combs are here and there pierced with holes, which serve as a means of communication from one comb to another, without losing time by going round. In the construction of these cells, the singular skill of this ingenious insect is displayed in their strength and perfect adaptation, and the economy of the wax, of which they are composed, as well as of the space they occupy. The patient processes by which they construct these cells no less evince their unremitting diligence and skill. As soon as the cells are ready for their reception, the queen-bee proceeds to deposit her eggs, and such is the astonishing fecundity of this insect, that, according to entomologists, it has been known in a single season to produce the surprising number of one hundred thousand. On the expiration of four days, the infant bee makes its appearance, when the nurse-bees immediately tender their services, very assiduously supplying it with food. After five days more, the attendants seal up the cells with wax, when the inclosed nurseling spins in security its cocoon: in all these labors neither the queen nor the drones render any assistance; they are performed exclusively by the workers, as in the case of the ants. In escaping from its cradle, which is generally about the third week, without any previous instruction, full of life, and buoyant with vigor, it takes its first flight; visits, like the rest, the subjects of Flora, absorbs their nectar, covers itself with their ambrosial dust, and returns, when tired of its gay gambols and delightful toils, richly freighted with sweets, to contribute its mite to the general stock of the colony. Many amusing if not extravagant stories are given by naturalists, respecting the exceeding loyalty of bees to their queen; their passion for monarchy indeed brings them into near connection with the ants. The following anecdote will illustrate this: "A young girl of my acquaintance," says the narrator, "was greatly afraid of bees, and she became completely cured of her timidity by the following incident. A swarm having come off, I observed the queen alight by herself at a little distance from the apiary; I immediately called my little friend, that I might show her the queen; she wished to inspect her more closely; so, having caused her to put on her gloves, I gave the queen into her hand. We were in an instant surrounded by the whole bees of the swarm. In this emergency I encouraged the girl to be steady, bidding her to be silent and to fear nothing, and remaining myself close by her; I then made her stretch out her right hand, which held the queen, and covered her head and shoulders with a very thin handkerchief: the swarm soon fixed on her hand, and hung from it as from the branch of a tree. The little girl was delighted beyond measure at the novel sight, and so entirely freed from all fear, that she bade me uncover her face. The spectators were charmed by the interesting spectacle. At length, I brought a hive, and shaking the swarm from the child's hand, it was lodged in safety, and without inflicting a single wound."

As an illustration of what may be accomplished by perseverance, we may next briefly allude to the habits of the spider—a creature we are accustomed to regard with aversion, but whose beautiful silken net-work, dotted with dew and sparkling in the sunshine, affords traces of exquisite skill and patient toil.

The busy hive of human industry, whether in the department of the mechanic arts, or in the more subtle investigations of pure science, has its counterpart, as we have seen, in the several classes of the subordinate creation. An ingenious writer thus attempts their analogy: "Spiders are geometricians, as are also bees, whose cells are so constructed as, with the least quantity of material, to have the largest sized spaces and the least possible loss of interstices; the mole is a meteorologist; the nautilus is a navigator, for he raises and lowers his sails, casts and weighs anchor, and performs other nautical evolutions; while the whole tribe of birds are musicians. The beaver may be called a builder or architect; the marmot is a civil engineer, for he not only constructs houses and aqueducts, but also drains to keep them dry; caterpillars are silk-spinners; wasps are paper manufacturers; the bird *plocens textor* is a weaver; the indefatigable ants are day-laborers; the monkey a rope-dancer; dogs are hunters; pigs, scavengers; and the torpedo and eel are electricians or *shocking* animals. If they were to turn authors, it has been suggested the eagle would excel in epic; the sheep in pastoral poetry; the horse in chivalry; the elephant in philosophy; the cow in agriculture; the dog in drama; the monkey in burlesque and low comedy: the cat in sly sarcasm; the goose in verbosity; the owl in epitaphs and elegies; the bear in waltzing; the hog in philosophic Bacon; the magpie and the parrot in plagiarism; the turkey in vanity.

The delicate fabric of the spider's web is a miracle of skill; although so fine as to be scarcely visible without the aid of a microscope, the spider's thread is nevertheless composed, not of a single line, as is usually supposed, but, as we learn from good authority, of not less than four thousand strands. And this is true with respect to spiders not larger than a grain of sand, as well as the largest specimens. The gauze-like texture of the web of the house-spider, as well as the beautiful net more commonly found among the foliage, composed of a series of concentric circles, united by radii diverging from the centre, are both exquisite specimens of insect skill. Not only in the ingenious construction of its web, the meshes of which are dexterously spread for the capture of its prey, does the spider evince its remarkable habits of industrious perseverance ; it is also endowed with a strong instinctive love of its offspring, and discovers, like most other members of the animal creation, wonderful fertility of invention. Looking abroad into the world, how incessantly are we reminded of the great ruling condition of our being, that of activity and dilligence ; the book of Nature ever teaches us the lesson. Day and night, summer and winter, cold and heat, succeed each other in their untiring course. The tides of ocean and the rivers ebb and flow; the endless variety of the vegetable kingdom is ever changing into new and fresh forms of beauty—flowers, fruits, and foliage, and all animate things are seen disporting in air, earth, and water, joyously obedient to the mandate, and basking in the sunshine of their beneficent Creator.

"Man thinks that he stands unrivalled as an architect, and that his productions far transcend the works of the inferior order of animals. He would be of a different opinion did he attend to the history of insects; he would find that many of them have been architects from time immemorial; that they had their houses divided into various apartments, and containing staircases, elegant arches, domes, colonnades, and the like. No female ornament is more prized and costly than lace, the invention and fabrication of which, seems the exclusive claim of the softer sex. But even here they been anticipated by these little industrious creatures, who often defend their helpless chrysalides by a most singular covering—and as beautiful as singular—of lace. Other arts have been equally forestalled by these creatures. We imagine that nothing short of human intellect can be equal to the construction of a diving bell or air pump—yet a spider is in the daily habit of using the one, and what is more, one exactly similar in principle to ours, but more ingeniously contrived ;

by means of which she resides unwetted in the bosom of the water, and procures the necessary supplies of air by a much more simple process than our alternating buckets—and the caterpillar of a little moth knows how to imitate the other, producing a vacuum, when necessary for its purposes, without any piston besides its own body.

"If we think with wonder of the populous cities which have employed the united labors of man for many ages to bring them to their full extent, what shall we think of the white ants, which require only a few months to build a metropolis capable of containing an infinitely greater number of inhabitants than even the imperial Nineveh, Babylon, or Pekin, in all their glory?

"That insects should thus have forestalled us in our inventions, ought to urge us to pay a closer attention to them and their ways than we have hitherto done; since it is not at all improbable that the result would supply useful hints for the improvement of our arts and manufactures, and perhaps be the clue to some beneficial discoveries.

Although parrots are excessively amusing in their small talk, yet, as they cannot be supposed to be conscious of what they say, we can only refer to them here, *en passant*, on the ground that they bear some seeming analogy, in this respect, to some human talkers. Mrs. Lee, in her "Anecdotes of Birds," mentions the instance of a parrot that had lost one of its legs, and no sooner did any one remark this, or ask how it had been lost, than it replied: "I lost my leg in the merchant service; pray, remember the lame."

The following story has often been recited before, but it will bear repeating:

"A tradesman who had a shop in the Old Bailey, London, opposite the prison, kept two parrots, a green and a grey. The green parrot was taught to speak when there was a knock at the street-door; the gray, whenever the bell rang; but they only knew two short phrases of English. The house in which they lived, had an old-fashioned, projecting front, so that the first floor could not be seen from the pavement on the same side of the way; and, on one occasion, they were left outside the window by themselves, when some one knocked at the street door.

"'Who is there?' said the green parrot.

"'The man with the leather,' was the reply; to which, the bird answered:

"'Oh! oh!'

"The door not being opened, the stranger knocked a second time.

"'Who is there?' said green poll.

"'Who is there?' exclaimed the man. 'Why don't you come down?'

"'Oh! oh!' repeated the parrot.

"This so enraged the stranger, that he rang the bell furiously.

"'Go to the gate,' said a new voice, which belonged to the gray parrot.

"'To the gate?' repeated the man, who saw no such entrance, and who thought that the servants were bantering him. 'What gate?' he asked, stepping back to view the premises.

"'New-gate,' responded the gray, just as the angry applicant discovered who had been answering his summons."

Parrots have been known to mimic the sound of planing a deal board, the mewing of a cat, or the barking of a dog, so accurately as to deceive the closest observers.

The predilection of animals for particular persons was once the means of deciding, very amusingly, a case before a court of justice. It was at a Dublin police-office, and the object of dispute was a pet parrot, which had been stolen from a Mr. Davis, and sold to a Mr. Moore. The plaintiff, taking the bird upon his finger, said, "Come, old boy, give me a kiss," which the parrot instantly did. A youth, in the defendant's interest, remarked that this proved nothing, as the parrot would kiss anybody. "You had better not try," remarked the plaintiff. Nevertheless, the young man asked the parrot to kiss him. Poll, Judas-like, advanced as if to give the required salute, but seized the youth's lip, and made him roar with pain. This fact, and the parrot's obeying the plaintiff in several other requisitions, caused it to be instantly ordered into the possession of its original master.

Wordsworth has devoted some excellent lines to that favorite of the feathered choristers of England—the sky-lark; in which he is apostrophised as the emblem of cheerfulness—a

> "Type of the wise, who soar—but never roam,
> True to the kindred points of heaven and home."

It has been well observed, that while "mirth is like a flash of lightning that breaks through a gloom of clouds, and glitters for a moment, cheerfulness keeps up a kind of daylight in the mind, and fills it with a steady and perpetual serenity." The matin-song of the lark was in ancient Greece the signal for the reaper to commence his toils; these were suspended during the heat of the day, when the bird was silent, and resumed when the sun began to verge towards the west, and this blithe chorister filled the air anew with its warblings. Other birds may sing gaily, but the sky-lark is jubilant almost sublime, as, in his heavenward flight, he pours forth the rich melody of his hymn of joy. The early spring is the best time to hear the lark's cheerful and exhilarating song; the bird rises on quivering wing, almost perpendicularly, describing a sort of curve in the air, singing as he flies; yet so powerful is his voice, that his wild, rapturous notes can be heard distinctly when the pained eye can trace his course no longer. An ear well-tuned to his song, can even then determine by his notes whether the bird is still ascending, or on the descent. When at a considerable height, should a hawk appear in sight, or the well-known voice of his mate reach his ear, the wings are closed, and he drops to the earth with the rapidity of a stone. What a beautiful and touching picture have we here of cheerfulness and conjugal affection ; it is impossible to witness it without feeling its beneficent influence. The presence of a cheerful spirit has been compared to "a sweet sunshine that awakens a secret delight in the mind ;" happy, indeed, are they who, like this joyous bird, can rise with alacrity, amid the cloudy atmosphere of adversity, upon the bright pinions of Hope. True cheerfulness and contentment are a well-spring of happiness—a treasure well worth the best efforts we can make to secure it ; and it is within the reach of all. The love of home, another of the cardinal virtues, is exemplified in the habits and characteristics of the dove. It is an instinctive feeling possessed by many of the lower animals ; the dog, sheep, and cat, evince the ruling influence of this passion ; but the dove, especially the carrier-dove, or pigeon, discovers this wonderful faculty in a preëminent degree, and under circumstances the most remarkable.

From the earliest ages, doves have been regarded as emblems of gentleness and innocence ; poets have celebrated their praises, and frequent mention of them is made in Holy Writ. The dove was the messenger sent forth from the Ark, to ascertain whether the waters had subsided from the earth ; and returning with an olive branch in her mouth, she became, henceforth, the emblem of peace. Even our Saviour took occasion to enjoin it upon his disciples to become in the midst of enemies, "wise as serpents and harmless as doves ;" and the highest honor was conferred upon this gentle creature, when it was made the type of the Holy Spirit, and thus became the symbol of all that was pure, peaceful, and holy. The cooing of doves is a plaintive and expressive sound, which, it has been fitly said, harmonizes well with the subdued murmuring of brooks, and the sighing of the zephyr in the quiet and sequestered spots which these birds frequent.

"Deep in the wood thy voice I list, and love
Thy soft complaining song—thy tender cooing;
Oh! what a winning way thou hast of wooing!
Gentlest of all thy race—sweet turtle dove."

The instinctive love of home, characteristic of this bird, has been turned to good account among mankind from an early period, and their importance as letter-carriers is well known. The plan adopted is as follows: The bird is first transported to the place from which any letter is to be conveyed, and with a perception altogether unaccountable and wonderful, the aërial letter-carrier speeds its way direct to its former home. A regular system of posting was once established in the East by this means; lofty towers having been erected by the Turkish government, at the distance of thirty miles apart, and each of these was provided with a due supply of pigeons, under the management of sentinels, whose business it was to receive the winged messengers, and transmit the intelligence they brought by others. The message or letter was written on a very thin slip of paper, and inclosed in a small gold box, almost as thin as the paper itself, which was fastened to the neck of the bird. This expedient has been adopted, even down to within a late date, for the more speedy transmission of important news, in various parts of Europe, and in our own country; the electric telegraph has, however, since superseded their use. Here we close our remarks about the winged and walking things of earth, whose characteristic developments are so suggestive of moral instruction to "the paragon of animals;" and although the lessons they teach are fraught with deepest interest, and cannot but reflect a beneficial influence, yet it is to be feared but too many are found inaccessible to their power, and inaudible to their teaching.

In fine, after all that has been adduced on the subject, we must leave the reader to determine the respective limits of reason and instinct; having nothing further to offer to his aid, excepting the lines of Prior, who thus sums up the whole case:

"Evil like us they shun, and covet good;
Abhor the poison, and receive the food.
Like us they love or hate; like us they know
To joy the friend, or grapple with the foe.
With seeming thought their action they intend,
And use the means proportioned to the end;
Then vainly the philosopher avers
That reason guides our deeds, and instinct theirs.
How can we justly different causes frame,
When the effects entirely are the same?
Instinct and reason how can we divide?
'Tis the fool's ignorance and the pedant's pride."

If the subordinate animals are happy in their allotted measure of intelligence or instinct, it is almost more than can be affirmed of "imperial man," for, with his increased mental acquisitions, does he not too often add to his infelicities? If this be not true, why did one of our poets suggest:

"If ignorance is bliss, 'tis folly to be wise?"

And if we suppose the poet to be the most liberally endowed with the imaginative faculty, why is he usually so poorly clad, and so poorly domiciled?

PULPIT PECULIARITIES.

THE "odor of sanctity" which attaches to the office of the Christian ministry has ever claimed and received the deference of mankind. The ancient seers, prophets, and patriarchs who were commissioned to make known the will of the Supreme, under the impulse of a direct inspiration, were regarded as supernaturally endowed, and their utterances deemed oracular. Of this illustrious order of priesthood were Noah, Abraham, Moses, and Isaiah of the ancient world; and in riper times, the Divine Redeemer with his Apostles. A commission divinely authorized and invested with such moral grandeur, demands a corresponding elevation of character—intellectual, moral, and religious—in those who assume its functions; and the world naturally looks for these accessories.

"A parson," writes George Herbert, "is the deputy of

Christ for the reducing of man to the obedience of God." He further quaintly adds, "His apparel is plain, but reverend, and clean without spots or dust; the purity of his mind breaking out and dilating itself, even to his body, clothes, and habitation." This remark of Herbert probably originated the saying that "cleanliness is next to godliness."

Some regard the clerical profession with a blind, superstitious reverence—these are the victims of priestcraft. There are others, with equal absurdity, who deem it the asylum of infatuation and indolence—these are the skeptical and profane. A third class are those who appreciate its worth, and who venerate the sacred office, regarding it as Heaven's expedient for securing the moral elevation and happiness of the race—an institution of the highest importance to man's present and eternal well-being. The history of the Pulpit is fertile of interest. It has spoken in tones of melting tenderness to the penitent, thundered its denunciations against the prevalence of vice; to the one it has brought down "airs from heaven," to the other "blasts from hell." All nations and climes it has sought to reclaim, anneal, and bless: and many of the mighty minds of all times have yielded willing obedience to its teachings and its claims. It has triumphed through the long ordeal of persecution—all the mightier for the mastery it has achieved over the malice of its foes.

It is not necessary for us to analyse the various types of the clerical character—the ascetic and monkish, the devout and devoted, or the ludicrous and the hireling. Each has left its impress, and, with the exception of the latter, has achieved much for the good of mankind. We do not however include in our category the Jesuitical monk, any more than the hireling; both are the negation of all that is good. There are further subdivisions however among the pure types, such as the cheerful and the morbid. A recent writer on the subject observes: "The spiritual heroism of Luther, the religious gloom of Cowper, and the cheerful devotion of Watts, are but varied expressions of one feeling, which, according to the frail conditions of humanity, has its healthy and its morbid phase, its authentic and its spurious exposition, and it is no more to be confounded in its original essence with its imperfect development and representatives, than the pure light of heaven with the accidental media which color and distort its rays. The *prestige* of the clerical office is greatly diminished, because many of its prerogatives are no longer exclusive. The clergy, at a former period, were the chief scholars; learning was not its distinctive quality more than sanctity."

This monopoly no longer obtains: the press has annihilated it. "Independent of the priestly rights, a clergyman, in past times, represented social transitions, and ministered to intellectual wants, for which we of this age have adequate provision otherwise; so that the most zealous advocate of reform, doctrine, or ethical philosophy, is no longer obliged to have recourse to the sacerdotal office in order to reach the public mind. This apparent diminution of the privileges of the order, however, does not invalidate, but rather simplifies its claims."

It is reduced to its normal state now. Notwithstanding this, it is to be admitted, that the intellectual and moral power of the modern pulpit suffers by comparison with the past. A recent writer in the London *Times* remarks: "Pulpit eloquence has fallen to a very low ebb. With the finest theme in the world before them—with all the hopes and anxieties which agitate the human breast during the brief interval which separates the cradle from the grave—as their subject, our preachers miss their opportunity. Are there extant, in print, collections of sermons by twelve living divines from the perusal of which any one would rise a more thoughtful or a better man? We think of the Taylors, Barrows, Souths, who have produced works of this kind which are still operative for good, although a couple of centuries may have passed away since their composition, and wonder what it can be in the constitution of modern society which has so completely dulled the capacities of our spiritual teachers. * * * We ask for no polished periods, for no finished compositions, but simply for burning thoughts, couched in simple and homely phrase, such as those which in other days drew men from earth to heaven."

That the embassy with which the Christian minister is charged is one of difficulty is undeniable, for it has to contend against the moral forces constantly in operation in the human heart, which are antagonistic to its claims. Yet the sublimity and celestial grandeur of its character may well fire the zeal of its advocate, and render him superior to all opposition. Panoplied with the armory of Heaven, with the oracles of Divine truth for his exhaustless treasury, and the accompanying power of Him,

"Who touched Isaiah's hallowed lips with fire,"

for his guidance, what may he not be expected to achieve for the moral subjugation of the world?

There is certainly a vast difference between the ancient preachers and the modern; the entire abnegation of self and of the world, their simplicity and earnestness of style, with their wonderful power of reaching the sublime, must, to say the least of it, have been very extraordinary; and, perhaps, in following the type of the old Apostolic preachers, Bishop Latimer seemed to be a worthy descendant; and in him we appear to have the last of the ancients, and the first of the moderns; although it must be admitted that at times old Bishop Latimer, with others, indulged in terms too gross for modern and polite ears, often preached to the common people under a tree, his Testament hanging from his leathern girdle; while the courtly Ridley, in satin and fur, discoursed the same themes in stately cathedrals;* both, however, were fired with a like zeal. Burnett says of Leighton, that he was a most exemplary character; having the greatest elevation of soul, the largest compass of knowledge, the most mortified and heavenly dispo-

* Bingham's Autobiography.

sition, that he ever saw in mortal. Of this class were Andrews, Cranmer, Jeremy Taylor, South, Luther, Bossuet, and Massillon. Matthew Henry once said, that "the Christian ministry is the worst of all trades, but the best of all professions."

Till Cranmer distributed and chained the Bible to every reading desk of the parochial churches of England, a few passages of Scripture inscribed on the walls were the only consolations of humble Christians.

Among the early Christians, the modern style of preaching was reversed; the preacher generally delivered his exhortation in a sitting posture, while the congregation heard him standing. Chrysostom preached in this manner. Men wore their heads covered in the church, in the time of Elizabeth. Laud alludes to the fact. The habit has been traced to the Hebrew Synagogue. Our Lord sat and disputed among the doctors in the Temple. Public expression of approval by the audience was made by tossing up their garments, or waving their plumes, in the times of Chrysostom and Jerome.

It is related even of Constantine the Great, that he did not resume his seat during a long sermon, by Eusebius, and that all the assembly followed his example.

In the thirteenth century, the Anglo-Norman clergy, according to the Abbé de la Rue, used the vehicle of verse for their sermons. In the Library of the Royal Society of London is preserved a sermon of this kind. One of these rhyming sermons was printed in Paris, 1834, entitled *Un Sermon en vers, publié pour la première fois, par Achille Jubenal.*

The title of clergy, given originally by St. Peter to all God's people, was, by Pope Hyginus, appropriated to the prelates and priests; "condemning," as Milton says, "the rest of God's inheritance to an injurious and alienate condition of laity." The title of Pope was also given to all bishops. The same pontiff (A.D., 138), being the first to adopt it.

Boniface III. induced Phocas, Emperor of the East, in 606, to restrict its use to the Bishop of Rome.

The origin of the term minister is thus given in the *Curiosities of Literatare :*

"The Hall of the School of Equity at Poictiers, where the institutes were read, was called *La Ministerie.* On which head, Florimond de Demond, speaking of Albert Babinot, one of the first disciples of Calvin, after having said he was called '*The good man,*' adds, that, because he had been a student of the Institutes of this Ministerie of Poictiers, Calvin and others styled him Mr. Minister; from whence, afterwards, Calvin took occasion to give the name of Ministers to the pastors of his church."

The old English name, Parson, is supposed to be a corruption of person, the person—by eminence. Fuller remarks that the Scriptures give four names to Christians, taken from the four cardinal graces: *saints,* for their holiness; *believers,* for their faith; *brethren,* for their love; *disciples,* for their knowledge.

The clergy were originally styled clerks, from the Norman custom of their judges being chosen from the sacred order. In the first century, they were distinguished by the titles of presbyter and bishops. Church music is supposed to have been first introduced by Gregory the Great, A.D., 602. Church-steeples were originally parochial fortresses.

Sidney Smith thus defines the object of preaching: "It is constantly to remind mankind of what mankind is constantly forgetting; not to supply the defects of human intelligence, but to fortify the feebleness of human resolutions; to recall mankind from the by-paths where they turn, into the path of salvation which all know, but few tread."

The aims and topics of the Pulpit have been eloquently condensed by Talfourd. We transcribe the passage:

"The subjects of the Pulpit have never been varied from

the day the Holy Spirit visibly descended on the first advocates of the Gospel in tongues of fire. They are in no danger of being exhausted by frequency, or changed with the vicissitudes of mortal fortune. They have immediate relation to that eternity, the idea of which is the living soul of all poetry and art. It is the province of the preacher of Christianity to develop the connection between this world and the next ; to watch over the beginning of a course that will endure forever, and to trace the broad shadows cast from imperishable realities on the shifting scenery of earth. This sublunary sphere does not seem to them as trifling or mean, in proportion as they extend their views onward, but assumes a new grandeur and sanctity, as the vestibule of a statelier and an eternal region. The mysteries of our being, life and death, both in their strange essences and in their sublimer relation, are topics of their ministry. There is nothing affecting in the human conditions, nothing majestic in the affections, nothing touching in the instability of human dignities, the fragility of loveliness, or the heroism of self-sacrifice, which is not a theme suited to their high purposes. It is theirs to dwell on the oldest history of the world ; on the beautiful simplicity of the patriarchal age ; on the stern and awful religion, and marvellous story of the Hebrews ; on the glorious visions of the prophets and their fulfillment ; on the character, miracles and death of the Saviour ; on all the wonders and all the beauty of the Scriptures. It is theirs to trace the spirit of the boundless and the eternal, faintly breathing in every part of the mystic circle of superstition, unquenched even amidst the most barbarous rites of savage tribes, and all the cold and beautiful shapes of Grecian mould. The inward soul of every religious system, the philosophical spirit of all history, deep secrets of the human heart, when grandest or most wayward, are theirs to search and to develop. Even those speculations which do not immediately affect a man's conduct and his hopes, are theirs, with all their high casuistry ; for in these, at least, they discern the beatings of the soul against the bars of its earthly tabernacle, which proves the immortality of its essence, and its destiny to move in freedom through the vast ethereal circle to which it thus vainly aspires. In all the intensities of feelings, and all the realities of imagination, they may find fitting materials for their passionate expostulations with their fellow-men to turn their hearts to those objects which will endure forever."

The author of the *Tin Trumpet* makes the following piquant remark: "Some divines are often too deeply read in theology to appreciate the full grandeur and the proper tendencies of religion. Losing the abstract in the concrete, the comprehensive in the technical, the principal in its accessories. Such are in the predicament of the rustic, who could not see London for the houses."

Others, claiming to be religious teachers and superiors, might have done better service in a different department of duty. A dull and illiterate leader will produce his kind in those over whom he presides, since he but administers theological opiates to them, confirming them in their apathy, ignorance, and bigotry. How few divines dare venture to become original; fewer still have we of rational enthusiasts.

"How comes it," demanded a Bishop of Garrick, "that I, in expounding divine doctrines, produce so little effect upon my congregation, while you can so easily rouse the passions of your auditors by the representation of fiction?" The answer was short and pithy. "Because I recite falsehoods as if they were true, while you deliver truths as if they were fiction."

Robert Hall, even, admitted that he was tormented with the desire of preaching better than he did. He was for greater earnestness and zeal. It was said of Rowland Hill's preaching, that his ideas, like Baxter's, came hot from the heart. This is effective preaching. Keble sweetly suggests—

"Love, on the Saviour's dying head,
Her spikenard drops, unblamed, may pour;

May mount his cross, and wrap him dead,
In spices from the golden shore.
Risen, may embalm his sacred name,
With all a painter's art, and all a minstrel's flame."

Steele observes: "When a man has no design but to speak plain truth, he may say a great deal in a very narrow compass." The true pulpit style is that which brings the intellect down through the heart, and melts all its precious metals in that glowing furnace. Prolixity in preaching is an ancient heresy of the priesthood. As if conscious of this weakness, the Greek and Latin fathers used hour-glasses in their pulpits, to admonish them when to wind up. George Herbert says: "The parson exceeds not an hour in preaching, because all ages have thought that a competency." Southey, in his *Commonplace Book*, cites a passage from the church records, in 1564, of St. Catharine's, Aldgate, London, which is as follows: "Paid for an hour-glass that hanged by the pulpit when the preacher doth make a sermon, that he may know how the hour passeth away."

A rector of Bilbury, Gloucestershire, was accustomed to preach two hours, regularly turning the glass; it is said that the squire of the parish usually withdrew after the text was announced, smoked his pipe, and then returned to the blessing.

During the civil wars in England, one Stephen Marshall divided his text into twenty-four parts; one of his hearers, taking the alarm, it is said, started off home for his night-cap and slippers.

There are few things against which a preacher should be more guarded than prolixity. "Nothing," says Lamont, "can justify a long sermon. If it be a good one, it need not be long; and if it be a bad one, it ought not to be long." Luther, in the enumeration of nine qualities of a good preacher, gives as the sixth, "That he should know when to stop." Boyle has an essay on patience under long preaching. "This was never more wanted," said Jay, of Bath, "since the Commonwealth, than now, in our day, especially among our young divines and academics, who think their performances can never be too much attended to. I never err this way myself," he said, "but my conviction always laments it; and for many years after I began preaching, I never offended in this way. I never surpassed three quarters of an hour *at most.* I saw one excellency was within my reach—it was brevity—and I determined to obtain it."

Geoffrey Chaucer portrays very felicitously the good pastor in the following lines:

He was a shepherd, and no mercenary,
And though he holy was and virtuous,
He was to sinful men full piteous;
His words were strong, but not with anger fraught:
A love benignant he discreetly taught.
To draw mankind to heaven by gentleness
And good example, was his business.

Cowper thus indicates what a true parson should be :

"Simple, grave, sincere,
In doctrine uncorrupt, in language plain,
And plain in manner, decent, solemn, chaste—
And natural in gesture, much impressed
Himself, as conscious of his awful charge,
And anxious, mainly, that the flock he feeds
May feel it, too ; affectionate in spirit,
And tender in address, as well becomes
A messenger of grace to guilty man."

"A good preacher," observes an old writer, "is one who makes all his hearers feel—not one who merely gratifies the learned or awakes the idle." He has been compared to the English verb, to be, to do, and to suffer.

Among uneducated pastors, John Bunyan is the most prominent for earnestness, simplicity, and zeal. It is remarkable that he received the first license from the English government to preach in the times of the Non-conformists. It was dated the 9th of

May, 1672. Who would not have wished to have seen him in his rude pulpit, and to have listened to his impassioned harangues? Doubtless, he prized his privilege, and valued his mission the more for the sufferings he endured on their behalf.

> "When such a man, familiar with the skies,
> Has filled his urn where the pure waters rise:
> And once more mingles with us meaner things,
> 'Tis e'en as if an angel shook his wings."

It has been observed that every sermon should have a topic, as well as a text. The topic should be naturally drawn from the text; well chosen, well stated, well arranged, well argued, well illustrated, and well applied. It is important, too, for all these ends, that it should be well expressed.

The selecting of a text seems to have originated with Ezra. Previous to that time, the patriarchs delivered in public assemblies either prophecies or moral instructions for the edification of the people. It was not until after the return of the Jews from Babylonish captivity, during which period they had almost lost the language in which the Pentateuch was written, that it became necessary to explain as well as to read Scripture to them—a practice adopted by Ezra, and since universally followed. In latter times, the book of Moses was thus read in the Synagogue every Sabbath day. To this custom the Saviour conformed, and in a Synagogue, at Nazareth, read passages from the Prophet Isaiah; then closing the book, returned it to the priest, and preached from the text. The custom, which now prevails all over the Christian world, was interrupted in the dark ages, when the ethics of Aristotle were read in many churches, on Sunday, instead of the Holy Scriptures.

The following are among the instances of wit in choosing texts. It is said that Melanchthon on some occasion arose to preach a sermon on the text, "I am the good shepherd." On looking around upon his numerous audience, his natural timidity overcame him, and he could only repeat the text over and over again. Luther, who was in the desk with him, at length exclaimed, "You are a very good sheep!" and telling him to sit down, took the same text, and preached an excellent discourse from it.

Robert Hall, on one occasion, being disgusted by the egotism and conceit of a preacher, who, with a mixture of self-complacency and impudence, challenged his admiration of a sermon, was provoked to say, "Yes, there was one very fine passage in your discourse, sir." "I am rejoiced to hear you say so—which was it?" "Why, sir, it was the *passage from the pulpit to the vestry.*"

What a sermon should be, may be gathered from the following:

"It should be brief; if lengthy, it will steep
Our hearts in apathy, our eyes in sleep;
The dull will yawn, the chapel-lounger doze,
Attention flag, and memory's portals close.

It should be warm, a living altar-coal,
To melt the icy heart and charm the soul;
A sapless, dull harangue, however read,
Will never rouse the soul, or raise the dead.

It should be simple, practical, and clear;
No fine-spun theory to please the ear;
No curious lay to tickle lettered pride,
And leave the poor and plain unedified.

It should be tender and affectionate,
As His warm theme who wept lost Salem's fate;
The fiery laws, with words of love allayed,
Will sweetly warm and awfully persuade.

It should be manly, just, and rational,
Wisely conceived, and well expressed withal;
Not stuffed with silly notions, apt to stain
A sacred desk, and show a muddy brain.

It should be mixed with many an ardent prayer,
To reach the heart, and fix and fasten there;
When God and man are mutually addressed,
God grants a blessing, man is truly blessed.

It should be closely, well applied at last,
To make the moral nail securely fast;
Thou art the man, and thou, alone, wilt make
A Felix tremble, and a David quake!"

Luther said: "Prayer, meditation, and temptation, make a minister." Another vigorous phrase of his is well known,—"*Bene orasse, bene studuisse,*"—to pray well, is to study well. Prayer, is not, however, the solemn duty of the clergy alone, but of all; the common privilege of dependent creatures. An old writer has quaintly, but very truly, said: "God looks not at the oratory of our prayers, how eloquent they are; nor at their geometry, how long they are; nor at their arithmetic, how many they are; nor at their logic, how methodical they are; but he looks at their sincerity, how spiritual they are."

We are as much under law to religion as to morals; as Longfellow very beautifully expresses it: "Morality, without religion, is only a kind of dead reckoning—an endeavor to find our place on a cloudy sea, by measuring the distance we have to run, but without any observation of the heavenly bodies."

"*Oratio est clavis diei, et sera noctis,*"—the key of the day, and the lock of the night, is prayer. This was the beautiful saying of one of olden time, and it is fragrant for all seasons.

In the exercise of the clerical function, it is not surprising that certain idiosyncrasies of character should occasionally be observable. Many prominent names might be cited as illustrative of the fact, such as Dean Swift, Sydney Smith, Lawrence Sterne, and Rowland Hill, with numerous imitators. During the reign of Charles II., it was the fashion to indulge to excess the habit of humorous preaching. Sterne seems to have revived the custom, and South's discourses sparkle perpetually with wit and pun. From the fourteenth to the sixteenth centuries, the pulpit was characterized by its rudeness of address, jocularity, and even indelicacy. These abuses have been perpetuated in later times, and even in our own, some have been found not altogether innocent of the charge. Another questionable feature of the clerical character, in bygone times, was that of gluttony and intoxication; when persons seemed to evince at least as much devotion to the *flesh* as the *spirit*, their own stomachs as the souls of their people.*

This defection in the ministerial order obtained to a comparatively recent period. The "sporting parson" was, also, once the representative of a recognized class in England, for the pampered monk of the Latin Church was scarcely less notorious. Happier days have since dawned upon the Church. These excrescences required lopping off, and it is to be regretted they ever formed upon the noble tree of Protestantism.

The term Protestantism reminds us of the prompt answer which was given by Wilkes, who, being asked by a Romanist, "Where was your church before Luther?" replied, "Where was your face before you washed it, this morning?"

The austerity and asceticism of the monk seem scarcely less consistent. It is not necessary that either extreme should be indulged; a cheerful piety is the true characteristic. "Cheerfulness is the best hymn to the Divinity," according to Addison. When we have passed a day of innocent enjoyment; when "our bosom's lord sits lightly on his throne;" when our gratified feelings, sympathizing with universal nature, make us sensible as John of Salisbury says, that "*Gratior et dies, et soles melius nitent,*" —we may be assured that we have been performing, however unconsciously, an acceptable act of devotion. Pure religion

*In the books of Darlington parish church, the following items appear, showing that, in the olden time, provision was made for comforting the inner man: "Six quarts of sack to the minister who preached when he had no minister to assist, 9*s*. For a quart of sack bestowed on Jillett, when he preached, 2*s*. 6*d*, For a pint of brandy when Mr. George Bill preached here, 1*s*. 4*d*. For a stranger who preached, a dozen of ale. When the Dean of Durham preached here, spent in a treat in the house, 8*s*. 6*d*." This would hardly be considered orthodox at the present day.

may generally be measured by the cheerfulness of its professors, and superstition by its gloom. *Ille placet Deo, cui placet Deus*—he to whom God is pleasant, is pleasant to God. A melancholy and morose Christian is an anomaly.

There is a great difference between occasionally introducing an illustration, which may serve its end, though slightly tinctured with the comic, and that depraved taste which would desecrate the sacred desk by the exhibitions of buffoonery. A minister should never be insensible to the claims of his mission, as it is taught in that

"Book, wherein his Saviour's Testament,
Written with golden letters, rich and brave:
A work of wondrous grace, and able souls to save."

Or, as a later poet, Cowper, expresses it—

He that negotiates between God and man,
As God's ambassador, the grand concerns
Of judgment and of mercy, should beware,
Of lightness in his speech. 'Tis pitiful
To court a grin, when you should woo a soul.
To break a jest, when pity would inspire
Pathetic exhortation; and to address
The skittish fancy with facetious tales,
When sent with God's commission to the heart!
So did not Paul.

Pascal has been censured for his irony and invective, while Barrow vindicates the use of these weapons. When plain declarations will not enlighten the mind to discern the truth and importance of things, and when argument is too blunt to penetrate the dulness of the understanding, it is then reason resigns its place to wit in the work of instruction. Willmott further remarks: "this argument is ingenious, yet we may well tremble to think, that as the brilliant epigrams of Pascal have re-appeared in the sparkling sophisms of Gibbon, so the bantering smile of Jostin may settle into the malevolent sneer of a modern Voltaire. If there be any instance of what is called *humor* in the Bible, it occurs in the meeting of Elijah and the priests of Baal."

Among humorous and eccentric preachers, Father Andre holds distinguished rank. We cite the following anecdotes relating to him, which, if even already familiar to the reader, may bear repeating. Once, while he was preaching in a country church, *a pack of cards flew out of his sleeve,* and fell among the audience. Every one began laughing. The preacher, without being in the least disconcerted, called on the larger children that happened to be there, to collect them together; and as they brought them, inquired *how* the different cards were called. The answers were *promptly given.* He then put some *questions out of the catechism,* which, however, they were unable to reply to. Then addressing the fathers and mothers—"Is it thus," said he, "that you neglect the education of your children? You introduce them into the vanities of life, and by the most criminal carelessness permit them to lose their immortal souls." The impression produced was powerful, and every one perceived that the cards were brought purposely to introduce this pathetic appeal.

Being called upon to announce a subscription in order to raise a sufficient sum to procure the initiation of a young woman into a sisterhood, which was then required of females taking the veil, he commenced his sermon, "Sirs, I am instructed to recommend to your charity a maiden who has not cash enough to take the vows of poverty." The facetious monk once began a sermon with, "The pope is grass, the king is grass, the queen is grass, the cardinal is grass, you are grass, I am grass—*all flesh is grass.*" Preaching in a monastery which had recently been struck by lightning, Father Andre expatiated upon the goodness of God, who took, as he would show, special care of his children. "For," said he, "among other evidences, consider what has happened to this holy house, in which I am preaching. The lightning struck the *library,* and consumed it, but injured not a single monk. If, however, it had, unfortunately, fallen upon the *dining-room or buttery*, how many brethren would have been killed—how many tears shed—what desolation would have ensued!"

A certain bishop, in a sermon to his parishioners, repeated the above text—"All flesh is grass." The season was Lent, and a few days afterwards, he encountered a parishioner who appeared to have something on his mind. "The top of the mornin' to your riverence," said Terence; "did I fairly understand your riverence to say, 'All flesh is grass,' last Sunday?" "To be sure you did," replied the bishop, "and you're a heretic if you doubt it." "Oh, devil a bit do I doubt anything your riverence says," said the wily Terence; "but if your riverence plases, I wish to know whether in this Lent time, I could not be afther having a small piece of *bafe*, by way of a salad?"

Some amusing dilemmas are on record, as the result of using written sermons: we select the following: A clergyman having picked up a homily composed when the plague was raging in London, unconsciously took the choice document with him, one Sunday, to church, and read it to his congregation. Towards the close, after having sharply reproved vice, he added, "for these vices it is that God has visited you and your families with that cruel scourge, the plague, which is now spreading everywhere in this town! Hearing this astounding announcement, the people were all so thunderstruck that the chief magistrate was obliged to go to the pulpit, and to ask him, "For God's sake, sir, where is the plague, that I may instantly take measures to prevent its spreading." "The plague, sir?" replied the preacher, "I know nothing about the plague; but whether it is in the town or not, it is in my homily."

An eccentric domine, Mathew Byles, of Boston, Mass., in 1776, seems to have been as inveterate a joker as Sydney Smith. Upon a Fast Day, Dr. Byles had negotiated an exchange with a country clergyman. Upon the appointed morning, each of them—for vehicles were not common then—

proceeded, on horseback to his respective place of appointment. Dr. Byles no sooner observed his brother clergyman approaching, at a distance, than he applied the whip, put his horse into a gallop, and with his canonicals flying all abroad, passed his friend at full run. "*What is the matter?*" he exclaimed, raising his hand in astonishment—"*Why so fast, Brother Byles?*" to which the Dr., without slackening his speed, replied over his shoulder, "*It is fast Day!*"

As he was once occupied in nailing some list upon his doors, to exclude the cold, a parishioner said to him, "the wind bloweth wheresoever it listeth, Dr. Byles." "Yes, sir," replied the doctor, "and man listeth wheresoever the wind bloweth."

Dr. Byles was arrested as a *tory*, and subsequently tried, convicted, and sentenced to confinement on board a guard-ship, and to be sent to England with his family, in forty days. This sentence was changed, by the board of war, to confinement in his own house. A guard was placed over him. After a time, the sentinel was removed, afterwards replaced, and again removed, when the Doctor exclaimed, that he had been *guarded, regarded, and disregarded.* He called his sentry his *observ-a-tory.*

There are some curious stories respecting Fra Rocco, the celebrated Dominican preacher and the spiritual Joe Miller of Naples. On one occasion, it is related he preached a penitential sermon, and introduced so many illustrations of terror that he soon brought his hearers to their knees. While they were thus showing every sign of contrition, he cried out, "Now, all of you who sincerely repent of your sins, hold up your hands." Every man in the vast multitude immediately stretched out both his hands. "Holy Archangel Michael," exclaimed Rocco, "thou who with thine adamantine sword standest at the right of the judgment seat of God, hew me off every hand which has been raised hypocritically." In an instant every hand dropped, and Rocco, of course, poured forth a fresh torrent of eloquent invective against their sins and their deceit.

The two celebrated divines and scholars, doctors South and Sherlock, were once disputing on some religious subject, when the latter accused his opponent of using *his wit* in the controversy. "Well," said South, "suppose it had pleased God to give you wit, what would you have done?"

Among the eccentricities of the pulpit, we ought not to omit the ingenious temperance lecture ascribed to Mr. Dodd, of Cambridge, England. On one occasion, when challenged to preach against drunkenness, it is related that he delivered the following unpremeditated short sermon, under a tree, by the road-side, from the word *malt*. He commenced by stating that he had chosen a short text, which could not be divided into sentences, there being none; nor into words, there being but one; he therefore divided it into letters, thus:

M, is moral
A, is allegorical,
L, is literal,
T, is theological,

His exposition ran as follows: the moral is to teach you good manners; therefore, M, my masters, A, all of you, L, leave off, T, tippling. The allegorical is, when one thing is spoken of, and another meant. The thing spoken of is malt, the thing meant is the spirit of malt, which you make, M, your meat, A, your apparel, L, your liberty, and T, your trust. The literal is, according to the letters, M, much, A, ale, L, little, T, trust. The theological is, according to the effects it works in some, M, murder, in others, A, adultery, in all, L, looseness of life, and in many, T, treachery.

The following curious string of puns is taken from a scarce work, published in the reign of James the First. A divine, more willing to play with words than to be serious in expounding his text, spoke thus in his sermon: "This *dial* shows that we must *die all*; yet, notwithstanding, *all houses* are turned into *ale-houses*; our *cares* are turned into *cates*; our *Paradise* into a *pair o' dice; matrimony* into a *matter o' money;* and *marriage* into a *merry age.* Our *divines* have become *dry vines;* it was not so in the days of *Noah—ah no!*"

A certain minister had a custom of writing the heads of his discourse on small slips of paper, which he placed on the Bible before him, to be used in succession One day, when he was explaining the second head, he got so excited in his discourse, that he caused the ensuing slip to fall over the edge of the pulpit, though unperceived by himself. On reaching the end of his second head, he looked down for the third slip; but, alas! it was not to be found. "Thirdly," he cried, looking round him with great anxiety. After a little pause, "Thirdly," again he exclaimed; but still no thirdly appeared. "Thirdly, I say, my brethren," pursued the bewildered clergyman; but not another word could he utter. At this point, while the congregation were partly sympathising in his distress, and partly rejoicing in such a decisive instance of the impropriety of using notes in preaching—which has always been an unpopular thing in the Scotch clergy, an old woman rose up, and thus addressed the preacher: "If I'm no mista'en, sir, I saw thirdly flee out at the east window, a quarter of an hour syne."

As a quaint specimen of clerical brevity, we offer the following; it is ascribed to an old English divine. The text upon which it was based is to be found in Titus ii. 9. He thus unfolded his doctrine.

"I. There are three companions with whom you should always keep on good terms. *First,* Your Wife; *Second,* Your Stomach; *Third,* Your Conscience.

"II. If you wish to enjoy peace, long life, and happiness, preserve them by temperance. Intemperance produces: *First,* Domestic misery; *Second,* Premature death; *Third,* Infidelity.

"To make these points clear, I refer you: *First,* To the Newgate Calendar; *Second,* To the hospitals, lunatic asylums, and work-houses; *Third,* To the past experience of what you have seen, read, and suffered, in mind body, and estate.

"Hearer, *decide!* which will you choose? TEMPERANCE, with happiness and long life; or INTEMPERANCE, with misery and premature death?"

Frederick the Great being informed of the death of one of his chaplains, a man of considerable learning and piety, determined that his successor should not be behind him in these qualifications, took the following method of ascertaining the merits of one of the numerous candidates for the appointment:—He told the applicant that he would himself furnish him with a text the following Sunday, when he was to preach at the royal chapel, from which he was to make an extempore sermon. The clergyman accepted the proposition. The whim of such a probationary discourse was spread abroad widely, and at an early hour the royal chapel was crowded to excess. The king arrived at the end of the prayers, and on the candidate's ascending the pulpit, one of his majesty's aides-de-camp presented him with a sealed paper. The preacher opened it, and found nothing therein. He did not, however, lose his presence of mind; but turning the paper on both sides, he said:—"My brethren, here is nothing, and there is nothing; out of nothing God created all things;" and proceeded to deliver a most admirable discourse upon the wonders of Creation.

Louis XIV. said one day to Massillon, after hearing him preach at Versailles: "Father, I have heard many great orators in this chapel; I have been highly pleased with them; but for you, whenever I hear you, I go away displeased with myself, for I see more of my own character." This has been considered the finest encomium ever bestowed upon a preacher.

When Massillon ascended the pulpit, on the death of that prince, he contemplated for a moment the impressive spectacle—the chapel draped in black—the magnificent mausoleum raised over the bier—the dim but vast apartment filled with the trophies of the glory of the monarch, and with the most illustrious persons in the kingdom. He looked down on the gorgeous scene beneath, then raised his arms to heaven and said, in a solemn, subdued tone, "*Mes frères, Dieu seul est grand!*" "God only is great." With one impulse, all the audience rose, turned to the altar, and reverently bowed.

When Dr. Hussey preached at Watford, on the small number of the elect, he asked, "Whether, if the arch of heaven were to open, and the Son of Man should appear to judge his hearers, it were quite certain that one of us," he exclaimed in a voice of thunder, "would be saved?" During the whole of this apostrophe, the audience was agonized. At the ultimate interrogation, we are told, there was a general shriek, and some fell to the ground.

M. Brideine, a French missionary, and the peer of the most renowned orators of that eloquent nation, preached a sermon at Bagnole. At the end of it, he lifted up his arms, and thrice cried in a loud voice, "O, Eternity!" At the third repetition of this awful cry, the whole audience fell upon their knees. During three days, consternation pervaded the town. In the public places, young and old were heard crying aloud, "O Lord, mercy!"

Rather a remarkable incident is related of the preaching of the venerable Dr. Beecher. Many years ago he was engaged to officiate in Ohio; it was in the depth of winter, and the roads were nearly impassable with snow, yet the doctor pursued his journey, and, on reaching the church, found not a single individual there. With his characteristic decision of purpose, he ascended the pulpit, and waited the arrival of his congregation. One solitary person at length entered, and the doctor commenced the service. At the conclusion, he hastened to greet his auditor, but he had vanished. Some score of years subsequently the parties accidentally met, when the pleasing fact was communicated to the doctor, that that sermon had proved the means of his conversion, and that he had since become himself a minister over a large congregation.

The following anecdote illustrates the peculiarities of character of Western pioneer life, as well as of a certain "presiding elder,"—Peter Cartwright. When the State of Illinois was admitted into the Union, it was as a free State. Not long after, the question was largely discussed whether the Constitution of the State should not be so amended as to permit Slavery. Cartwright, who then resided in Tennessee, was a strong opponent of Slavery, and determined to remove to Illinois to take part in the settlement of the question. So he was appointed "Presiding Elder," over a district about as large as England. He kept his appointments, and after preaching on Sunday, was wont to announce that on Monday he would deliver a "stump speech." He soon became regarded as a politician, and no little anger was excited against him. One day coming to a ferry across the river, where he was not personally known, he heard the ferryman holding forth to a crowd in bitter terms against that "old renegade," prefixing sundry emphatic expletives to that flattering term—Pete Cartwright, declaring that he would drown him if he ever came that way. After a while, Peter engaged the ferryman to put him over. They were alone in the boat, and when they had reached the centre of the stream, in full sight of the shore, the preacher, throwing the bridle of his horse over a post, ordered the ferryman to put down his pole. "What is the matter?" asked the ferryman. "You have just been making free with my name, and threatening to drown me in the river. I want to give you a chance to do so." "You are Pete Cartwright, are you?" "My name is Peter Cartwright," replied the preacher. The ferryman, nothing loath, laid down his pole, and the contest began. The preacher proved the better man, and seizing his antagonist by the nape of the neck and the seat of his nether garments, plunged him three times under water. Then holding his head out of the water, he asked, "Did you ever pray?" "No," was the reply. "Then it is time you should. I will teach you. Do you repeat after me, 'Our Father, who art in Heaven.'" The ferryman refused, and down went his head under water, and there it was held long enough, as Peter thought, to conquer his reluctance. He raised him up, and repeated his demand. "Let me breathe," gasped the ferryman. "Give me a few minutes to think about it." "Not a moment," and under went his head again. The inquiry was again put, when the ferryman's head was next raised, "Will you pray now?" "Yes, I'll do anything," and the fellow obediently repeated the Lord's Prayer, after the dictation of Cartwright. "Now let me up," he added. "No, not yet," replied the inexorable Peter. "You must make me three promises before I let you up. First, you must promise to pray every night and morning as long as you live; then you must promise to put every Methodist preacher who comes along over the river for nothing; and lastly, you must promise hereafter to attend every meeting of the Methodists held within four miles of you." The whole transaction took place in full view of the ferryman's comrades on the shore, but the intervening river insured "fair play," and the ferryman felt himself in Cartwright's hands. He promised faithfully to do all that was demanded of him. The transit across the river was finished; the preacher went on his way; the ferryman kept his word, and in course of time was converted, and became a shining light in the church.* Earnest men were these old preachers. Their souls were firmly convinced of the truth of what they had to say. Rugged in their exterior, like those among whom they mingled, they yet seem to have exhibited much of the stern decision of character and deep-seated piety, that signalized the church in the days of the non-conformists. Their self-denial and heroism were none the less noble, because unchronicled; and, although this type of the pioneer missionary is fast fading away, yet the border legends of the West preserve the memory of those who have lived to make the wilderness become a fruitful field, in more senses than one.

* Rev. Mr. Milburn.

Dean Swift was once solicited to preach a sermon for the benefit of the poor. When the time arrived, he arose and selected his text: "He who giveth to the poor lendeth to the Lord." "Now," said he, "my brethren, if you are satisfied with the security, down with the dust." He then took his seat, and there was an enormous collection.

The Rev. Sydney Smith, preaching a charity sermon, frequently repeated the assertion that, of all nations, Englishmen were most distinguished for generosity and the love of their species. The collection happened to be inferior to his expectations, and he said that he had evidently made a great mistake, for that his expression should have been, that they were distinguished for the love of their *specie.*

He once said, in speaking of the prosy nature of some sermons, "they are written, as if sin were to be taken out of man, like Eve out of Adam—by putting him to sleep."

Dr. Barrow once preached so long, that all his congregation dropped off, leaving the sexton and himself alone. The sexton finding the doctor apparently no nearer a conclusion, said to him, "Sir, here are the keys, please to lock up the church, when you get through your discourse."

Whitfield, when preaching at Princeton, New Jersey, detecting one of his auditory fast asleep, came to a pause, and deliberately spoke as follows: "If I had come to speak to you in my own name, you might question my right to interrupt your indolent repose; but I have come in the name of the Lord of Hosts" (and accompanying these words with a heavy blow upon the pulpit), he roared out, "and I must and will be heard." This had the effect of awakening the sleeper; and on his perceiving it, his reverence eyed him significantly, saying, "Aye, Aye, I have waked you up, have I? I meant to do it." This suggests another similar incident; we forget the name of the party or the place; however, the circumstances were as follows. A clergyman was once preaching, in the sultry summer-time, when many of his hearers yielded to the soporific influence of the weather (or the sermon—perhaps both). The domine seeing this drowsy condition of his audience, paused for some time, when the sleepers returning to consciousness, he thus addressed them, "My good friends, this sermon cost me a good deal of labor, and I do not think you have paid to it the attention it deserves, I shall, therefore, go over it again:" and he was as good as his word. An equally successful expedient was adopted by a minister, in New York, not long since, while holding forth to his congregation in a style that ought to have kept them awake; suddenly he stopped in his discourse, and said, "Brethren, I have preached about half of my sermon, and I perceive that twenty-five or thirty of my congregation are fast asleep. I shall postpone the delivery of the balance of it until they wake up!" There was a dead pause for about five minutes, during which time the sleepers awoke, when the preacher resumed. Another instance might be cited, which proved no less effective. A worthy divine, in a church at Norwich, Connecticut, observing many sleeping, paused awhile, then said, "I come now to the third head of my discourse, to which I ask the serious and candid attention of all who are not *asleep*," giving a marked and peculiar emphasis to the last word.

A preacher in the time of James I. being appointed to hold forth before the Vice-Chancellor and heads of Colleges at Oxford, chose for his text, "What, cannot ye watch for one hour?" which carried a personal allusion, as the Vice-Chancellor happened to be asleep. The preacher repeated his text in an emphatic manner at the end of every division of his discourse, the unfortunate Vice-Chancellor as often awoke, and this happened so often that at last all present could very well see the joke. The Vice-Chancellor was so nettled at the disturbance he had met with, and the talk it occasioned, that he complained to the Archbishop of Canterbury, who immediately sent for the young clergyman, to reprove him for what he had done. In the course of the conference which ensued between the archbishop and the preacher, the latter gave so many proofs of his wit and good sense, that his grace procured him the honor of preaching before the king. Here also he had his joke. He gave out his text in these words, "James the First and Sixth, 'Waver not;'" which, of course, everybody present saw to be a stroke at the indecisive character of the monarch. James, equally quicksighted, exclaimed, "He is at me already." But he was, upon the whole, so well pleased with this clerical wag as to make him one of his chaplains in ordinary. He afterwards went to Oxford, and preached a farewell sermon on the text, "Sleep on now, and take your rest."

The sin of sleeping during service time is of no modern date. In Henry Seventh's chapel, Westminster Abbey, there are ingeniously contrived chairs, for preventing the drowsy monks indulging a nap. These chairs are pleasant enough if you preserve your balance, but if you should become oblivious, you suddenly find yourself on the middle of the floor.

A minister of the "*Kirk*" of Scotland, once discovered his wife asleep in the midst of his homily on the Sabbath. So, pausing in the steady, and possibly somewhat monotonous flow of his oratory, he broke forth with this personal address, sharp and clear, but very deliberate:

"Susan!"

Susan opened her eyes and ears in a twinkling, as did all other dreamers in the house, whether asleep or awake.

"Susan, I didna marry ye for your wealth, sin' ye hae'd none! And I didna marry ye for your beauty, that the hail congregation can see. And if ye have no grace, I have made but a sair bargain!"

Susan's slumbers were effectually broken up for that day.

A clergyman of Cambridge, Mass., was once in a singular dilemma, according to his own showing: he told his people that if he spoke softly, those at the end of the church would not be able to hear him, and if loud, those near the pulpit would awake! We have heard of a worse disaster which befell a certain deacon. He fell asleep, and, as is usual in such cases, made repeated inclinations of his head; when suddenly it rebounded back with such force as to throw his wig into the pew behind him. In his consternation, vainly seeking for his vagrant wig, where it could not be found—in his own pew—he covered his bald pate with his red silk handkerchief, to the great scandal of the congregation and his own greater dismay.

A celebrated clergyman once told his parishioners he should reserve the best efforts of his mind for rainy days—the worse the weather, the better should be his sermons—and he kept his word. The consequence naturally was, that his church was never so well filled as in wet weather, and the harder the rain poured down, the more the people flocked in, until it finally became his practice to include in his prayers, rainy Sundays!

The Rev. Mr. Adams of Leominster, was an eccentric character. A neighboring minister—a mild, inoffensive man—with whom he was about to exchange, said to him, knowing the peculiar bluntness of his character—"You will find some panes of glass broken in the pulpit window, and possibly you may suffer from the cold. The cushion, too, is in a bad condition; but I beg of you not to say anything to my people on the subject; they are poor," &c. "Oh no!—oh no!" said Mr. Adams. But ere he left home, he filled a bag with rags, and took it with him. When he had been in the pulpit a short time, feeling somewhat incommoded by the too free circulation of air, he deliberately took from the bag a handful or two of rags, and stuffed them into the window. Towards the close of his discourse, which was more or less upon the duties of a people toward their clergyman, he became very animated, and purposely brought down both fists with a tremendous force upon the pulpit cushion. The feathers flew in all directions, and the cushion was pretty much used up. He instantly checked the current of his thought, and simply exclaiming,

"Why, how these feathers fly!" proceeded with his sermon. He had fulfilled his promise of not addressing the society on the subject, but had taught them a lesson not to be misunderstood. On the next Sabbath the window and cushion were found in excellent repair.

Dean Swift has the following pointed remarks about absentees from church. "There is no excuse so trivial that will not pass upon some men's consciences, to excuse their attendance at the public worship of God. Some are so unfortunate as to be always indisposed on the Lord's day, and think nothing so unwholesome as the air of a church. Others have their affairs so oddly contrived as to be always unluckily prevented by business. With some it is a great mark of wit and deep understanding to stay at home on Sabbath. Others again discover strange fits of laziness, which seize them particularly on that day, and confine them to their beds. Others are absent out of mere contempt for religion. And, lastly, there are not a few who look upon it as a day of rest; therefore claim the privilege of their cattle, to keep the Sabbath by eating, drinking, and sleeping, after the toil and labor of the week.

The celebrated Robert Hall once visited London, for the purpose of hearing Dr. John W. Mason, of New York, deliver a discourse before the London Missionary Society. The extraordinary effect which the masterly address of Mason had produced, was the theme, for the time, of general observation, and Mr. Hall was among the most enthusiastic of its admirers. Shortly after his return to Leicester, a certain reverend gentleman made him an accidental visit, when Mr. Hall requested him to officiate in his pulpit that evening, assigning, as a reason, that he had just returned from London, oppressed with a sense of the wonderful eloquence of Dr. Mason of New York. The visitor affected great desire to be excused preaching before so distinguished a scholar as Mr. Hall. The latter, however, would take no denial, insisting that if he would not preach, his people would have no sermon that evening. Our clerical friend, who is described as "a little pompous personage, as round as a sugar-barrel—a man of great verbosity, and paucity of thought," at length overcame his scruples, and ascended the pulpit. At the close of the services, Mr. Hall, with great warmth of feeling, thanked him heartily for his discourse; which, he said, had given him more comfort than any sermon he had ever heard in his life. This assertion inflamed the vanity of the one, and superinduced the sarcasm of the other. The former, with ill-concealed eagerness, urged Mr. Hall to state what there was in the effort that afforded him so much pleasure. He replied, "Sir, I have just returned from hearing that great man, Dr. Mason, of New York. Why, Sir, he is my very beau ideal of a minister; he reminds me more strongly than any other of our day, of what one might suppose the Apostle Paul to have been. Such profound thought, such majesty of diction, and such brilliancy of illustration, I have never heard equalled; and it left me with such an overpowering conviction of my own insignificancy, that I had resolved never to enter the pulpit again," and rising up, he energetically exclaimed, "But thank God, I have heard *you*, Sir, and I feel myself a man again!"

A certain noviciate once called upon Mr. Hall, to solicit his advice upon what he considered a very important matter; to wit, his supposed call to the ministry. This gentleman stated that he was impressed with the idea that it was his duty to obey that call, but that as yet he could see "no door open." "No matter for that, Sir," said Mr. Hall, "if the Lord has called you, he will open a door." "But, Sir, there is one passage of Scripture which causes me much trouble." "Well, Sir, what is it?" was the reply. "It refers to the hiding of a talent in a napkin." "Oh! my good fellow," said Mr. Hall, "don't let that give you any concern, this little handkerchief of mine (pulling out his own), would cover a *score* of such talents as yours."

It must not, from the foregoing, be inferred that Mr. Hall was accustomed to indulge in such severe sarcasms, excepting when he saw the weakness of the man usurping the place of his sacred vocation.

Most sermons are short-lived enough, but we have heard of one of extraordinary longevity, and it is said it was eminently productive of good. We refer to a discourse by Dr. Griffin, of New York, which he repeated ninety times. He devoted great pains to it, and revised, and re-revised, it with diligent care.

Some ministers are more forcible with their hands than their heads. It is reported of a clergyman in a county town, that he was a most powerful preacher, since he is known to have knocked to pieces four pulpit Bibles in less than two years.

The Rev. Hamilton Paul, a Scottish clergyman, is said to be a reviver of Dean Swift's walk of wit in the choice of texts. For example, when he left the town of Ayr, where he was understood to have been a great favorite with the fair sex, he preached his valedictory sermon from this passage, "and they all fell upon Paul's neck and kissed him." Another time when he was called on to preach before a military company, in green uniforms, he preached from the words, "and I beheld men like trees, walking." He once made serious proposals to a young lady whose Christian name was Lydia. On this occasion, the clerical wit took for his text, "And a certain woman, named Lydia, heard us; whose heart the Lord opened, that she attended unto the things which were spoken of Paul." He published a volume of *facetiæ* under the title of "Paul's Epistle to the Ladies."

We have heard of a case no less extraordinary, which occurred some fifty years ago, in Virginia. An itinerant preacher being invited to hold forth in one of the early settlements there, took for his text the words "Though after my skin, worms destroy this body, yet in my flesh shall I see God." He divided his text into three parts, thus—"first, the skin-worms; secondly, what they done; and thirdly, what the man seen after he was eaten up."

Some dreary expositors of the Gospel, possibly sent to challenge our patience, seem to be endowed with at least one faculty, that of dulling all its bright and beautiful truths; they see things "through a glass, darkly." Good George Herbert suggests thus charitably our forbearance with such; he says:

> "Do not grudge
> To pick out treasures from an earthen pot;
> The worst speak something good. If all want sense,
> God takes a text and preacheth patience."

This apology, even, can scarcely be admissible in cases like that last cited; they are, however, happily of rare occurrence.

The clerk of a retired parish in Northwest Devon, who had to read the first lesson, always used to make a hash of Shadrach, Meshach, and Abednego; and as the names are twelve times repeated in the third chapter of Daniel, after getting through with them the first time, he afterwards styled them the "aforesaid gentlemen."

The Rev. Daniel Isaac was both a great wag and a great smoker. "Ah, there you are," cried a lady who surprised him one day, enjoying his pipe, "at your idol again." "Yes, my dear madam," he replied, "I hope you do not find fault with me, for I ought to be commended, as you see *I'm burning it.*"

Although this world is "a thorny waste," it seems some good men are not in any hurry to leave it. The Rev. John Skinner, of Linshart, Longside, while passing along a street in the village, was met by an old woman, who was in the habit of begging. As was her practice, she made a great solicitation for a half-penny. On feeling his pocket, Mr. Skinner discovered that he had not a half-penny, but was possessed of a penny-piece, which he handed to the woman. The sum being double what she expected, so excited her gratitude, that she exclaimed: "Lord bless you, sir, and may a' that's gude attend your bonny family; and for yoursel', God sen' that ye may win to the kingdom o' heaven this very night !" "Mony thanks to you, Janet, for your good wishes," said Mr. Skinner ; "but you needna have been so very particular about the *time!*"

An itinerant minister was preaching on a very sultry day, in a small room, and was much annoyed by those who casually dropped in after the service had commenced, invariably closing the door after them. His patience being at length exhausted by the extreme oppressiveness of the heat, he vociferated to an offender, "Friend, I believe if I was preaching in a bottle, you would put the cork in!"

A specimen of an absent-minded parson may be seen in the following extract from the life of Coleridge, by James Gillman: "The father of the bard and metaphysician was a poor country parson, of a very absent mind. It is said of him, that on one occasion, having to breakfast with his bishop, he went, as was the practice of that day, into a barber's shop to have his head shaved, wigs being then in common use. Just as the operation was completed, the clock struck nine, the hour at which the bishop punctually breakfasted. Roused, as from a reverie, he instantly left the barber's shop, and, in his haste forgetting his wig, appeared at the breakfast table, where the bishop and his party had assembled. The bishop, well acquainted with his absent manners, courteously and playfully requested him to walk into an adjoining room, and give his opinion of a mirror which had arrived from London a few days previously, and which disclosed to his astonished guest the consequences of his haste and forgetfulness."

We close our Eccentrities of the Pulpit with a few amusing and characteristic anecdotes of Rowland Hill, the well-known, excellent, though eccentric clergyman of London.

A dissenting minister once complaining of the *dealing* he met with from an ecclesiastical *board*, to Rowland Hill, observed that "for his part he did not see the difference between a board and a bench," meaning, that the rule of his board was as stringent as that of the bishops. "Pardon me, my friend," replied Hill, "I will show you a most essential difference between the two: A board is a bench *that has no legs to stand upon.*"

With many strong points of character, he combined notions prodigiously odd. One of those commonly called Antinomians, one day called on Rowland Hill, to call him to account for his too severe and legal gospel. "Do you, sir," asked Rowland, "hold the ten commandments to be a rule of life to Christians?" "Certainly not," replied the visitor. The Minister rang the bell, and on the servant making his appearance, he quietly added, "John, show that man the door, and keep your eye on him until he is beyond the reach of every article of wearing apparel, or other property in the hall!"

He once said, on observing some persons enter his chapel to avoid the rain that was falling, "Many persons are to be blamed for making their religion a cloak; but I do not think those are much better, who make it an umbrella!" Again, on receiving anonymous letters from some of his congregation, he remarked, "If you wish me to read your anonymous letters, you must enclose a five-pound note in them for some good charity." On another occasion, he said "I do not want the walls of separation between different orders of Christians to be destroyed, but only lowered, that we may shake hands a little easier over them."

He was a great observer of the different modes of preaching, and once drew up in his peculiar style, a string of characteristics of the various kind of pulpit orators. He thus describes them: *Bold Manner.*—The man who preaches what he feels without fear or diffidence. *Self-Confident.*—A man who goes by nobody's judgment but his own. *Rash.*—A preacher who says what comes uppermost, without any consideration. *Rambling.*—A man who says all that pops in his mind without any connection. *Stiff.*—One who pins himself down to think and speak without any deviation. *Powerful.*—The man who preaches from the bottom of his heart the truth of the Gospel with energy, to the consciences of his people. *Finical.*—He who minces out fine words with nothing in them. *Sober.*—The man who lulls you fast asleep. *Elegant.*—The man who employs all his brains upon dressing words, without ever aiming at the heart. *Conceited.*—He who vainly aims at everything, and says nothing. *Welsh Manner.*—A man that bawls out very good things till he can bawl no longer. * * * *Dogmatic.*—A man who goes by his own brains, right or wrong. *Peevish.*—One who picks into everybody's thoughts, and thinks no one right but himself. *Fanciful.*—One who, instead of being led by wisdom, runs after a thousand visionary whimsies and conceits. *Self-Important.*—Thinks nobody like himself. *Noisy.*—A loud roar and nothing in it. He once said of a man who knew the truth, and seemed afraid to preach it in its fullness, "He preaches the Gospel as the donkey mumbles the thistle, very cautiously."

Thus much for the illustration of our subject, which is susceptible of much greater extension. If eccentricity be occasionally a concomitant of genius, it is quite worth while to tolerate it if even allied to the clerical profession ; provided it is restricted within proper limits, and is rendered subservient to the interests of truth. If, however, we could have the genius without the eccentricity, it would be more desirable ; because of all places in the wide world, the sanctuary is the most sacred, and those who minister at the altar, should be the most solemn and sincere.

Yet as Pascal observes, it should not be imagined that the life of a good Christian must necessarily be a life of melancholy and gloominess, for he only resigns some pleasures to enjoy others infinitely greater.

An old writer asks—"Who are the most godlike of men ?" The question might be a puzzling one, unless our language answered it for us—the godliest.

"Religion," said Webster, "is the tie that connects man with his Maker, and holds him to his throne. A man with no sense of religious duty is he whom the Scriptures describe in such terse but terrific language, as living 'without God in the world.'"

The words of Milton may be applied to the possession of that "peace which passeth all understanding," the consciousness of a coming blissful immortality—

> "One sip of this
> Will bathe the drooping spirits in delight
> Beyond the bliss of dreams. Be wise, and taste."

The reader is already familiar with the names of those theological magnates, Luther, Melanchthon, Calvin, Bullinger, Bucer, Latimer, and Ridley, and a score of others, including Jeremy Taylor, Bates, Isaac Barrow, &c., but he may not be so well acquainted with that of Edward Irving; we therefore annex the following high tribute to his genius and worth from a critic no less distinguished than Coleridge. He thus speaks of him. "I hold that Edward Irving possesses more of the spirit and purposes of the first Reformers; that he has more of the head and heart, the life, the unction, and the genial power of Martin Luther, than any man of this and the last century. I see in Edward Irving a minister of Christ, after the order of Paul."

Coleridge, referring to the theological literature of the seventeenth century, asserts it as his conviction "that in any half dozen sermons of Donne or Taylor, there are more thoughts, more facts and images, more incitements to inquiry and intellectual effort, than are presented to the congregations of the present day in as many churches or meetings, during twice as many months. The very length of the discourses, with which these rich souls of wit and knowledge fixed the eyes, ears, and hearts of their crowded congregations, are a source of wonder now-a-days, and we may add, of self-congratulation, to many a sober Christian, who forgets with what delight he himself has listened to a two-hours' harangue on a loan, or tax-bill, or a trial of some remarkable cause or culprit: the transfer of the interest makes and explains the whole difference. For although much may be fairly charged on the revolution in the mode of preaching, as well as in the matter, since the fresh morning and fervent noon of the Reformation, when there was no need to visit the conventicles of fanaticism, in order to,

> " See God's ambassador in pulpit stand,
> Where they could take notes from his look and hand;
> And from his speaking action bear away
> More sermon, than our preachers used to say."

The pulpit may be styled the palladium of the world's virtue—the conservator of its liberties, the panacea for its woes, and the prophecy of its future restoration and glory. Its prerogative is to exert a paramount power over the common heart. Its themes are sublime and momentous—the arcana of science are rendered tributary to its teachings, because the works illustrate the Will of the Supreme. This mission of the Gospel, it was that fired the zeal of that worthy of old, whose eloquent appeals "shook Areopagus, and reverberated through the Forum."

"The Christian priesthood, although the temptation incident to conventional elevation may have served to develope among them many of the subtler forms of evil latent in the undisciplined heart, is yet lustrous with many virtues. What sweetness has baptized the clerical function in the past! What fortitude, what self-denial, what patience, what labor in season and out of season, have been the heritage of the great mass of these men! What stores of learning have they accumulated; what splendid additions have they made to the best literature of every land: how they have enriched the sciences by their observation and studious inquiries; how they have kept the flame of patriotism aglow; how they have encouraged the generous ambition of youth, and directed it to worthy and useful ends; how they have dignified the family altar, and cherished the purity of woman, and diffused through society the charm of honest and gentle manners; all these things must be cordially acknowledged by every one competent to speak on the question."*

* Chapin.

THE LARCENIES OF LITERATURE.

Originality has been defined "unconscious or undetected imitation." "As for originality," wrote Byron, in his journal, "all pretensions to it are ridiculous; 'there is nothing new under the sun.'" Moore, once observing Byron with a book full of paper-marks, asked him what it was. "Only a book," he answered, "from which I am trying to *crib;* as I do whenever I can, and that's the way I get the character of an original poet." "Though, in imputing to himself premeditated plagiarism," observes his biographer, "he was, of course, but jesting; it was, I am inclined to think, his practice, when engaged in the composition of any work, to excite thus his vein, by the perusal of others on the same subject or plan, from which the slightest hint, caught by his imagination as he read, was sufficient to kindle there such a train of thought as, but for that spark, had never been awakened, and of which he himself soon forgot the source."

Emerson says an author is original in proportion to the amount he steals from Plato; and to those who are not much acquainted with Plato, he thus divulges the secret of much of his claim to originality.

Even Seneca complains that the ancients had compelled him to borrow from them, what they would have taken from him, had he been lucky enough to have preceded them. "Every one of my writings," says Goethe, in the same candid spirit, "has been furnished to me by a thousand different persons, a thousand different things; the learned and the ignorant, the wise and the foolish, infancy and age, have come in turn, generally, without having the least suspicion of it, to bring me the offering of their thoughts, their faculties, their experience: often have they sowed the harvest I have reaped. My work is that of an aggregation of human beings, taken from the whole of nature; it bears the name of Goethe."

"It is in the power of any writer to be original, by deserting nature, and seeking the quaint and fantastical; but literary monsters, like all others, are generally short-lived. 'When I was a young man,' says Goldsmith, 'being anxious to distinguish myself, I was perpetually starting new propositions; but I soon gave this over, for I found that generally, what was new was false.' Strictly speaking, we may be original without being new; our thoughts may be our own, and yet commonplace."*

On the other hand, it must be admitted with Pollock, that while "the siccaneous critic or the meagre scribbler may hang his head in despair, and murmur out that what can be done is done already; yet he who has drank of Castalia's fount, and listened to the mighty voice of the Parnassian sisters, and who casts his bold eye on Creation, inexhaustible as its Maker, and catches inspiration while he gazes; will take the lyre in his hand, delight with new melody the ear of mortals, and write his name among the immortal in song. A cotemporary,† writing on this subject, insists that, "what is often termed originality, is more a manufactured article than a natural product. Moore, in dwelling upon the elaborate care with which all the

* Tin Trumpet. † Knickerbocker.

performances of Sheridan were prepared, was led to exclaim, 'genius is patience.' An original thinker may be considered as one who has grown mentally fat upon the food great minds in all ages of the world have afforded him. Montaigne and Emerson, as we have seen, have confessed, with careless frankness, some of the sources of their originality.

"Of course it is necessary that nature should have furnished a tolerably broad and capacious foundation for mental fatness to be laid upon. It is impossible to make a very fat hog of a Guinea pig. All men have not a disposition, and could not cultivate one, to grapple with the deep and subtle thoughts of profound minds. 'Books, books,' says Bulwer; 'magnets to which all iron minds insensibly move.' Minds of a softer metal, of a less investigating character, do not move in that direction. The mind grows by what it feeds upon, and no man can be an original thinker without a good deal of knowledge. All that was wanting, perhaps, to develop the powers of 'the village Hampden,' 'the mute, inglorious Milton,' and 'the guiltless Cromwell,' that the country churchyard contained, was knowledge. But knowledge is of no value unless it is well digested; and in this respect nature is an infallible guide. Minds, like stomachs, have little relish for food they cannot digest; and there is every variety of strength in the digestive powers of the mind as of the body."

The same idea is enforced by another writer, in a more facetious strain. He says; "We prey upon the literary productions of the past, as we do upon the brains of Italian and French cooks of the present, and while our palates will carry a teeth-watering reminiscence of some favorite dish, concocted by the one, while the tongue which discussed it articulates, is it remarkable that our pates should should retain some of the attic flavor of the former? Our constitutions are made or unmade by the food we eat. Our brains, by the books we read. Men of great natural genius, and who have not had opportunities for much book 'culture,' even as the most bodily healthy people, are evidences of the truth that strong, simple food is far superior to the *diablerie* of modern wizard-cooks, in either case."

Emerson assumes, that it is the duty and the province of great minds to adopt the thoughts of others—to embalm them for futurity—to take the roughly hewn blocks from the thought-mines of others and fashion them into mosques, feudal towers, or pyramids, as the loving, chivalrous, or sublime spirit of the builder may suggest.

This communistic appropriation of ideas—this building from another's quarry is a species of *free*-masonry which is qualified entirely by the name of him who is caught in the fact.

It has been gravely asked who are original thinkers; even those who rank as philosophical writers adopt the opinions of their predecessors—some favorite theory of a former age; and having espoused it, they endorse the *new* creed with an enthusiasm as zealous as if it were one of their own creation. There are a few noble exceptions to the rule, however, for the honor of learning; the daring Florentine, for instance: a large proportion of our modern literature might be, with advantage to all parties, suppressed, since it possesses in the main but the questionable merit of a metamorphoses.

The remark ascribed to Pope Ganganelli, that all books in the known world might be comprised in six thousand folio volumes, if filled with original matter—was, we think, an extremely liberal estimate.

One age battens upon its predecessor with gnome-like rapacity, and thus a host of pseudo-authors acquire an undeserved reputation. The quaint lines of Chaucer still apply with full force—

"Out of the olde fieldes, as men sayeth,
Cometh all this new corne fro yeare to yeare,
So out of olde bookes, in good faith,
Cometh all this newe science that men lere."

Homer,* Dante, Rabelais, and Shakspeare, Chateaubriand

* Homer's Gardens of Alcinous in the Odyssey, and the Elysium of the Æneiad, were perhaps taken from the Mosaic account of Eden.

styles the great *universal individualities* and great parent geniuses, who appear to have nourished all others. The first fertilized antiquity; Æschylus, Euripides, Sophocles, Horace, Aristophanes, and Virgil were his sons. Dante in like manner was the father of modern Italy, from Petrarch to Tasso. Rabelais created the literature of France; Montaigne, La Fontaine, Molière, descended from him; while England owes all to Shakspeare. People often deny the authority of these supreme masters—they rebel against them, proclaim their defects, but with as much propriety as one might the spots on the sun's disc; they even accuse them of tediousness, and sometimes absurdity, while in the very act of robbing them and decking themselves in their spoils.

The student in his literary progress will derive no small interest in discovering, as he inevitably will, if he goes deep enough, the hidden germs of many of the happiest expressions which adorn the pages of our distinguished writers.

Almost every author of any standing in the ranks of literature may be regarded as a borrower, in a greater or less degree, from the commonwealth of letters. Even Shakspeare, Milton, Gray, are frequently indebted to their predecessors in "bokecraft."

"Shakspeare is more purely original; but it should not be forgotten, that in his time, there was much less to borrow, and that he too has drawn freely and largely from the sources that were open to him, at least, for his fable and graver sentiment: for his wit and humor, as well as his poetry, are always his own. In our times, all the higher walks of literature have been so long and so often trodden, that it is scarcely possible to keep out of the footsteps of some of our precursors; and the ancients, it is well known, have stolen most of our bright thoughts, and not only visibly beset all the patent approaches to glory, but swarm in such ambushed multitudes behind, that when we think we have gone fairly beyond their plagiarisms, and honestly worked out an original excellence of our own, up starts some deep-read antiquary, and makes it out, much to his own satisfaction, that heaven knows how many of these busy-bodies have been beforehand with us, both in the *genus* and the *species* of our invention!"*

While, however, it is allowed that they have freely used the "shadowed thoughts of more obscure authors, it must also be remembered that they have made a noble restitution in presenting to their readers, not a depreciated capital, but a thought refined, embellished, and stamped with the impress of a brighter genius.

Some are guilty of grand literary larceny, as many know by experience, and as Hood has so humorously described in the following lines:

How hard, when those who do not wish
To lend—that's lose—their books,
Are snared by anglers—folks that fish
With literary hooks.

Who call and take some favorite tome,
But never read it through;
They thus complete their set at home,
By making one of you.

I, of my Spenser quite bereft,
Last winter sore was shaken;
Of Lamb I've but a quarter left,
Nor could I save my Bacon.

They picked my Locke, to me far more,
Than Bramah's patent worth;
And now my losses I deplore,
Without a Home on earth.

Even Glover's Works I cannot put
My frozen hands upon,
Though ever since I lost my Foote,
My Bunyan has been gone.

* Jeffrey.

My life is wasting fast away—
  I suffer from these shocks;
And though I've fixed a lock on Gray,
  There's gray upon my locks.

They still have made me slight return;
  And thus my grief divide;
For oh! they've cured me of my Burns,
  And eased my Akenside.

But all I think I shall not say,
  Nor let my anger burn;
For as they have not found me Gay,
  They have not left me Sterne.

Hudibrastic Butler compares a literary plagiarist to an Italian thief, that never robs but he murders, to prevent discovery. Another definition, somewhat akin, describes the plagiarist as a "purloiner, who filches the fruit that others have gathered, and then throws away the basket."*

"Plagiary had not its nativity with printing, but began when the paucity of books scarce wanted that invention."† After all that may be urged on the score of accidental coincidences of thought and expression, it cannot be questioned that there has been perpetrated a vast amount of literary fraud.

Could we invoke the spirits of the departed, what pitiless plaints would be preferred against the spoliations of many a modern scribe, who, to avoid the trouble of thinking for himself, has chosen the more summary mode of allowing others to do so for him. Yet, after all, who should complain, when such a vast economy of time and trouble may be achieved by the labor-saving process. A poem, indeed, that formerly occupied in its construction twenty long years, can thus be produced, with scarcely inferior success, in as many minutes; and the Herculean task that wasted the midnight oil of a devoted life, is now achieved in a few brief hours.

* Tin Trumpet. † Brown.

To suppose that fewer instances of moral delinquency have been perpetrated in the particular department of letters than in any other, would be, to say the least of it, very unphilosophical, since the risk of purloining the fruits of other men's brains with impunity, is unquestionably less than in that of most other depredations. If the pilferers of the purse are not more amenable to justice than are those who commit like infringements upon the productions of genius, the latter merit a no less rigid requital of rebuke. True, it may be urged in extenuation, that great scope should be allowed in determining the exact limits of literary property—since there must necessarily exist what is termed the "commonwealth of literature,"—yet we venture to premise that the most strenuous advocates of the plea, will, in the main, be found to be actuated by motives, no less equivocal in kind, than they are specious in pretence.

These literary pilferers are too often adroit and shrewd enough to elude detection.

A strong resemblance may occur between two writers, if not indeed a strict identity both of ideas and language, which may be purely accidental; but this must be an occurrence exceedingly rare. A bold or beautiful thought is sometimes likely so to impress the imagination, as to exist in the memory long after its paternity is forgotten, and thus become ingrafted into the mind so as to seem part of itself; such a case would certainly admit of great extenuation in the criminal code of literary jurisprudence.

A writer, it is observed, *may* steal after the manner of bees, without wronging anybody; but the theft of the ant, which takes away the whole grain of corn, is not to be imitated. A French writer* observes, "to take from the ancients, and make one's advantage of what they have written, is like pirating beyond the line; but to steal from one's contemporaries, by surreptitiously appropriating to one's self their thoughts and

* Vayer.

productions, is like picking people's pockets in the open street." And another extract we had marked, insists that, "It is a greater crime to steal dead men's writings, than their clothes." Instances of petty larceny are undoubtedly more numerous than such as may be styled cases of grand literary larceny; and we have even heard it advocated as a meritorious virtue in a writer, when he shall abstract from a previous author some acknowledged beauty, either of rhetoric or thought, and afresh incorporate it as his own, on the plea that a gem may often lie long obscured, and acquire redoubled lustre by the skill of the artist in the resetting."

The doctrines of expediency do not always run parallel with those of equity and even-handed justice; and since we are compelled to adjudicate the question by the moral standard, we must allow no meaner motives to govern our decisions in this matter. It is no easy task, amidst the prolific outpourings of the press of our day, to attempt an *exposé* of the many "dread counterfeits of dead men's thoughts" which living plagiarism is continually recasting and sending forth: for,

> "This trade of knowledge is replete,
> As others are, with fraud and cheat—
> Such cheats as scholars put upon
> Other men's reason, and their own—
> A sort of drapery, to ensconce
> Absurdity and ignorance."

The term *plagiarist* is derived from the word *plagium*, used among the Romans to designate a person who abducted a freeman for the purpose of selling him as a slave, for which offence the culprit was condemned by the Flavian law, *ad plagio*, to be whipped. In a metaphorical sense, the word implies theft, and has been since applied to such as appropriate, without due acknowledgment, the thoughts and expressions of an author.

Plagiarism, like homicide, may be divided into degrees. If the purloiner benefits the estate of literature by his spoliation, one is inclined to regard his offence as venial, but when this is not the case, he deserves the full penalty of his misdemeanor.

"Not every striking coincidence in thought and illustration, however, is to be denounced as plagiarism. Some of the most admired productions of ancient and modern times are only splendid imitations. Much of the poetry of the last and preceding century was moulded after the ancient classics, and abounded in imitations of thought and expression. All this is considered lawful. It has been said that "we are come into the world too late to produce any thing new, that nature and life are pre-occupied, and that description and sentiment have been long exhausted." The same authority allows that "an inferior genius may, without any imputation of servility, pursue the path of the ancients, provided he declines to tread in their footsteps." The extent to which it is warrantable to make use of the intellectual labor of others, how much of their thoughts and illustrations may be employed without endangering moral character and reputation, is not very clearly settled. But with one consent, to steal another's thoughts and language and pass them off as one's own, is an act of which no honorable man would be guilty, and whoever perpetrates it justly forfeits his claim to confidence and respect."

If direct literary plagiarism has been more rife in modern than in ancient times, yet we are not to suppose that this species of fraud did not exist even with the classic writers. Vida, in his "Art of Poetry," indeed, conducts us to such a conclusion in justifying an occasional resemblance between two several authors on the same subject:

> "Aspice ut exuvias veterumque insignia nobis
> Aptemus: verum accipimus nunc clara repertum.
> Nunc seriem atque animum verborum quoque ipsa
> *Nec pudet interdum alterius nos ore locutos.*"

Terence, who has been accused of many depredations, says, "nihil est dictum quod non sit dictum prius."

One substantial reason why this species of legerdemain was not so much in vogue with the early penmen, is to be ascribed to the fact that detection would almost inevitably follow, from the limited number of manuscripts then in existence compared with the almost countless issues since the era of the press.

The following exquisite thought, contained in one of the sonnets of Petrarch,

> "Trefiro torna; e 'l bel tempo ramena :
> E i fiori, e 'l herbe sua dolce familigia,"

has been more frequently incorporated, or rather imitated, than any gem in the whole wealth of poetry. Milton, who, so to speak, ransacked the three worlds for the *materiel* of his sublime effusions, so closely resembles the Italian muse, that it is difficult to reconcile the coincidence upon any other supposition than that even he borrowed. The couplet referred to in allusion to his loss of sight, occurs, it will be remembered, in his great epic,

> "Seasons return, but not to me return
> Day, or the sweet approach of eve or morn."

He also closely copies Ariosto, in his Vision of Paradise, and Astolpho's Description of the Moon, when he mounts the clouds on the winged horse. Lord Littleton, Waller, Gray, Savage, and Kirke White, discover traces of the same thought, and some invest it in language remarkably analogous. Spenser has also been charged as a close copyist of both Tasso and Ariosto. A similar illustration might also be given, showing the double plagiarism upon a fine passage from Dante, which was first rendered into our vernacular without acknowledgment by Merivale, and afterwards closely copied by Byron. But we must narrow our limits, or we shall have to invoke among the culprits a host of such other names, as Ford, Decker, Marlow, and Shirley, with our several specifications against them. We may fairly place in our category of plagiarists, the notorious literary impostors, since they were no less fraudulent.

Scaliger, was an impostor, since he had never been at any war, nor at any court of the Emperor Maximilian, as he pretended. He passed the first thirty years of his life in one continued study. Afterwards, he threw off his monk's frock, and palmed on all Europe the singular imposition of his being a descendant of the Princes of Verona, who bore the name of Scaliger.

One of the boldest and most uncompromising of a very mischievous class of literary impostors was Annius of Viterbo. Annius published a pretended collection of historians of the remotest antiquity, some of whose names had descended to us in the works of ancient writers, while their works themselves had been lost. Afterwards, he subjoined commentaries to confirm their authority, by passages from well-known authors. These, at first, were eagerly accepted by the learned; the blunders of the presumed editor—one of which was his mistaking the right name of the historian he forged—were gradually detected, and at length the imposture was apparent. The pretended originals were more remarkable for their number than their volume, for the whole collection does not exceed one hundred and seventy-one pages, which lessened the difficulty of the forgery; while the commentaries, which were afterwards published, must have been manufactured at the same time as the text. In favor of Annius, the high rank he occupied at the Roman court, his irreproachable conduct, the declaration that he had recovered some of these fragments at Mantua, and that others had come from Armenia, induced many to credit these pseudo-historians. A literary war was soon kindled. One historian died of grief for having raised his elaborate speculations on these fabulous originals; and their credit was at length so much reduced, that Pignoria and Maffei both announced to their readers that they had not referred in their works to the pretended writers of Annius. Yet, to the present hour, these presumed forgeries are not always given up. The problem remains unsolved; and the silence of Annius in regard to the forgery, as well as what he affirmed when alive, leave us in doubt as to whether he really intended to laugh at the world by these fairy tales of the giants of antiquity. Sanchoniathon, as preserved by Eusebius, may be classed among these ancient writings as a forgery, and has been equally rejected and defended.

It should not be forgotten that the statements of Annius received a supposed confirmation in some pretended remains of antiquity which were dug up in the grounds of the Inghirami family. These remains—which were Etruscan—consisted of inscriptions, and some fragments of an ancient chronicle. Curtius Inghirami had no doubt of their authenticity and published a quarto volume of more than 1000 pages in their support.

The imposture of Joseph Vella will be long remembered. Being at Palermo in 1782, he accompanied the ambassador from Morocco in a visit which that diplomatist made to the Abbey of St. Martin, and where he was admitted to see a very ancient Arabic manuscript. Being aware of the desire which existed to find in the Arabic writings materials for the completion of the history of Sicily, in which there was a gap of two centuries, Vella took the hint, and, after the departure of the ambassador, asserted that he had found in the library of the Abbey a precious manuscript containing the correspondence between the Arabian governors of Sicily and the sovereigns of Africa.

To confirm the authenticity of this pretended discovery, and to give it additional importance in the eyes of his protector, Airoldi, archbishop of Heraclea, who paid all the expenses of his researches, Vella manufactured a correspondence between himself and the ambassador, who had returned to Morocco, in which he made the latter give an assurance that there existed in the library of Fez a second and more complete copy of the manuscript found in the library of St. Martin; that another work in continuation of the manuscript had been discovered;

and also a series of medals, confirmatory of the history and chronology of the document in question.

The imposture had such success, that the King of Naples, to whom Vella presented his translation of the supposed manuscript, wished to send him on a mission to Morocco to make further inquiries. This was as unfortunate a turn as the royal favor could take; but, luckily for Vella, circumstances occurred to avert the disaster.

The translation of the Arabic manuscript had been announced in all the journals of Europe. The first volume was published in 1789, under the sanction of Airoldi. The sixth volume appeared in 1792, and was to be followed by two others. Vella was everywhere courted, and loaded with pensions and honors. Airoldi, however, having caused a fac-simile of the original manuscript —which Vella had taken great pains to alter and make nearly illegible—doubts rose as to its authenticity; and finally, after the "translation" had been everywhere read, everywhere celebrated, and everywhere extracted from, the whole was found to be a deception. The original manuscript was nothing but a history of Mahomet and his family, and had no relation to Sicily whatever. Vella was induced to confess his imposture, but not until he had been threatened with torture.

Varillas, the French historian, enjoyed for a long period a good reputation as a veracious chronicler of events, till at length the critics of other countries exploded the secret of his undeserved honors. His professions of sincerity went for little, when it was once discovered that his historic anecdotes derived their existence solely from the wonder-loving and inventive brain of the writer; his affected citations of titles, letters, memoirs, and relations, being all imaginary! Having perused most of the historical books of his day, he discovered a ready facility in imparting fictions as facts, while he quoted his authorities with random recklessness. Another odd genius amused himself, while confined to his room by protracted indisposition, with inflicting on the reading community of his day his "*Voyage*

Round the World," when his physical disability scarcely permitted him to describe the circuit of his own dormitory. His name may be recollected by some—Gemelli Carreri, a Neapolitan.

The next case we shall refer to is that of Psalmanazar, a man of considerable learning and singular ingenuity, who, in his time, acquired much notoriety. He was one of the writers employed in compiling a work on Universal History. Originally a wandering adventurer, and while under the pressure of poverty, having enlisted in the army, he first attracted the notice of Col. Lauder, in the garrison of Sluys, where he artfully circulated a report that he was a native of the island of Formosa, from which place he was expelled by the hostility of the Japanese on account of his religious faith, having been previously proselytised to Christianity from Paganism, by the Jesuits. The plausibility of his story induced the colonel to espouse his cause, and he subsequently was conveyed to England, where he was introduced to the Bishop of London, who listened to his account with pity and implicit faith, became his patron, and generously contributed towards his support. His artful contrivance of producing and speaking a language with alphabet and grammar purely of his own invention, no less than his singular propensity for eating raw meat, roots and herbs, soon rendered him an object of curious speculation and public notoriety. The keen-eyed skepticism of some of the more discerning, however, viewed his pretensions with suspicion: and yet, could he have silenced the secret accusations of his own conscience, the most sanguine wishes of the impostor might possibly yet have been successful. He wrote, in Latin, an interesting description of the island from which he professed to have been expatriated on account of his newly-espoused religion, which was received by the public with favor; a translation was speedily effected, and read with avidity, which was referred to as authority by Buffon, and others, while his characteristic self-complacency and adroitness in warding off every avenue to detection, seemed to have completely established his claim to public confidence. His powers of memory were so tenaciously correct, from the exercise of habit in verbal arrangement, that on being desired to translate a long list of English words into the Formosan language, which were marked down without his knowledge, his credit was considerably corroborated by his correctly affixing the same terms to the same words, on the question being repeated three, six, and even twelve months afterwards. He at length found a warm advocate in the Bishop of Oxford, who procured for him apartments in one of the Universities, for the further prosecution of his studies. To impress his new neighbors at this place with the idea of his intense and indefatigable application, it was his custom to keep lighted candles in his room during the night, and to sleep in an easy-chair, to prevent the impression that so extraordinary a genius indulged in so unphilosophical a relaxation as that of reposing on a bed. His next step was to return to London, and publish a version of the Church Catechism in his pretended vernacular, which, having passed under the close scrutiny and supervision of the learned, was pronounced a real language, and no counterfeit. He had now attained the acmé of his fame: but no sooner had he reached it, than the tide of his popularity began to ebb; for suspicion had already begun to be excited by sundry contradictions which were betrayed in his narrative, and other seeming absurdities, which presently caused his patrons to abate their ardor, and ultimately to withdraw altogether their support. At length the reaction in the public mind became so strong, that it speedily grew into the most violent expressions of malignity and irritated resentment against him; and as his means of subsistence became consequently precarious, he would have become again the victim of abject distress, had it not been for the admitted abilities he possessed, which induced the booksellers to engage his services upon the work already referred to—the laborious task of compiling a Universal History. His real name and place of birth were never revealed—these he studiously concealed on account of his disgrace. He was supposed to have been from the south of France; and although he never publicly avowed his fraud, yet he is said to have confessed it to confidential friends, with tears and repentance; and, but for such acknowledgment on his part, his ingeniously fabricated illusions of an unknown people and their language, might have, to this day, been classed with the mysteries of mesmerism, and other subtle sophisms, which perplex the sagacious and amuse the vulgar. This extraordinary individual died in 1763.

D'Israeli relates, among others, the following curious instance of literary forgery, practised on Capt. Wilford, by a learned Hindoo, who, to ingratiate himself and his studies with the too zealous and pious European, contrived, among other attempts, to give the history of Noah and his three sons, in his "*Purana*," under the designation of *Satyavrata*. The captain having *read* the passage, transcribed it for Sir William Jones, who translated it as a curious extract; the whole was an interpolation, by the dexterous introduction of a forged sheet, discolored and prepared for the purpose of deception; and which, having served his design for the moment, was afterwards withdrawn. As books in India are not bound, it is not difficult to introduce loose leaves. To confirm his various impositions, this ingenious forger had the patience to write two voluminous sections, in which he connected all the legends together, in the style of the *Puranas*, consisting of 1,200 lines.

During the reign of Charles I., numerous political forgeries were perpetrated. The famous *Eikon Basiliké* has been ranked among the number, from the ambiguous claim of Gauden; and, as it appears from the note-book of Sir Nicholas Hyde, chief justice during the reign of that unfortunate prince, Sir Robert Cotton must not be denied his claim altogether to the *honors* of a literary filcher, since there is mention made of a *pardon* he had obtained from King James, for *embezzling the public records;*

and we read even of authors at the solemn hour of dissolution having been the prey of those whose moral obliquity did not prevent the lawless indulgence of the passion.

Sir William Dugdale possessed the minutes of King James's Life, written by Camden, till within a fortnight of his demise; as also, Camden's own Memoirs, which he had from Hacket, the author of the "Life of Bishop Williams;" "who," adds the chronicler Aubrey, "did *filch* it from Mr. Camden as he lay a dying!" It is stated that the renowned Pinelli Collection was the product of skill in an art which lies more in the hand than the head; and Sir Robert Saville, writing to the founder of the Bodleian Library, appointing an interview for Sir Robert Cotton, cautions him that, "if he held any book so dear that he would be loath to lose it, he should not let Sir Thomas out of his sight, but set the book aside beforehand."—a precaution adopted by a friend of Bishop Moore. One calling on him found him busy in *hiding his best books*, and locking up as many as he could; on inquiring the reason of his odd occupation, the bibliopolist replied, "The Bishop of Ely dines with me to-day!"

We will now subjoin a few instances of poetical imitations, or similarities, which we find collated by D'Israeli. We have already alluded to the great Grecian Epic Poet, as being of pre-eminent *original* genius; but it has been justly remarked by Scott, in his Introduction to the Minstrelsy of the Scottish Border, that it is fairly matter of speculation whether Homer is entitled to be considered so altogether beyond the reach of suspicion as an imitative poet, since it is unreasonable to suppose that the rich maturity of the divine art in which he became so eminently distinguished, could have sprung into full-grown existence all at once—it being far more probable that even he possessed a certain standard of design in the ruder attempts of preceding writers.

In his beautiful "Ode to Adversity," Gray thus apostrophises,—

"Thou tamer of the human breast,
Whose iron scourge and torturing hour
The bad affright, afflict the best—"

The expressions employed in the foregoing have been deemed amenable to poetical criticism by Wakefield, but probably he has after all been permitted to enjoy his opinion undisturbed, as we find Milton adopts very similar language:

"When the scourge
Inexorably, and the torturing hour
Calls us to penance."

Perhaps Shakspeare's prolific muse has been more laid under contribution by literary filchers than any other writer of modern times; for instance it is apparent that Pope's oft-quoted lines,

"Honor and shame from no condition rise,
Act well your part, there all the honor lies,"

were but another rendering of the same thought, expressed not less forcibly, by the great dramatic bard—

"From lowest place when virtuous things proceed,
The place is dignified by the doer's deed."

Pope wrote—"The proper study of mankind is man;" but Charron, said it before him. Byron, in *Childe Harold*, has the image of a broken mirror to show how a broken heart multiplies images of sorrow. But the same simile is in Burton. Giordano Bruns said that the first people of the world should rather be called the *youngsters* than the *ancients*. Lord Bacon (a great plagiarist) makes use of the very same idea. Gray sings beautifully about "full many a gem of purest ray serene," and many a flower, concealed in the mine and in the sea. But Bishop Hall first wrote the whole sentiment in prose. Addison speaks of the stars "forever singing as they shine." Sir Thomas Browne talks of "the singing constellations;" though both have followed the idea expressed in the Scripture. Shelly speaks of Death and his brother Sleep. The expression was Sir Thomas Browne's.

Rogers has doubtless availed himself of Gray's beautiful stanza, in his *Elegy:*

> "The breezy call of incense-breathing morn,
> The swallow twittering from the straw-built shed—
> The cock's shrill clarion, or the echoing horn,
> No more shall rouse them from their lowly bed;"

for in his pleasing little poem, "*The Wish,*" he presents us with the following:

> "The swallow oft beneath my thatch
> Shall twitter from her clay-built nest;
> Oft shall the pilgrim lift the latch,
> And share my meal, a welcome guest."

Goldsmith's well-known lines:

> "Man wants but little here below,
> Nor wants that little long,"—

were evidently stolen from Dr. Young, who, in his "*Night Thoughts,*" says,

> "Man wants but little, nor that little long."

That hackneyed line in Campbell's "*Pleasures of Hope,*"—

> "Like angel visits, few and far between;"

is borrowed almost literally from Blair's "*Grave,*" where we have—

> ———————"its visits,
> Like those of angels, short and far between;"*

* Wilmott contends that this beautiful conceit originated with Norris of Benton, in his poem, entitled, "*The Parting.*" The stanza reads:

> "How fading are the joys we dote upon;
> Like apparitions seen and gone;

Moore has been charged with liberal plagiarisms upon Beranger, as well as being a close copyist of some of his other cotemporaries in vernacular verse, a detailed account of which was given in Blackwood, some years ago, exhibiting a series of specifications amounting to *sixty-five!* Even Tennyson has, in his "*Miller's Daughter*," proved himself but a paraphrastic translator of Anacreon, while he also has but marred the expressive lines of Byron,

"Who hath not proved how feebly words essay
To fix one spark of Beauty's heavenly ray?
Who doth not feel—until his failing sight
Faints into dimness with his own delight—
His changing cheek, his sinking heart confess
The might—the majesty of loveliness?"

Tennyson's love song runs thus,—

"How many full-sailed verse express,
How many measured words adore
The full flowing harmony
Of thy swan-like stateliness,
Eleanore?
The luxuriant symmetry
Of thy floating gracefulness,
Eleanore?"

Sir Walter Scott was always esteemed an original writer, but Lord Jeffrey, in reviewing his works, said: "Even in him, the traces of imitation are obvious and abundant."

But to return again a moment to Pope and some of his contemporaries; we ought to mention that his editors charge him with "a palpable plagiarism from Flatman, an obscure

---

But those who soonest take their flight,
Are the most exquisite and strong,
Like angels' visits short and bright;
Mortality's too weak to bear them long."

rhymer of Charles II.'s time, in his sublime ode, 'The Dying Christian to his Soul.'" Many of his expressions, as well as ideas, in his "Essay on Man," were abstracted from Milton; and against his celebrated "Essay on Criticism," Lady Wortley Montague has preferred a far more serious accusation: she writes, "I admired Mr. Pope's 'Essay on Criticism,' at first very much, because I had not then read any of the ancient critics, and did not know *that it was all stolen.*" The fine moral poem of the "Hermit," by Parnell, is taken from Martin Luther's tale of a hermit, who murmured against the decrees of Divine Providence. What Sterne has *not* plagiarized, we shall not stay to notice, notwithstanding he counterfeited most excellent coin. He has been charged with pilfering from Burton, Rabelais, Montaigne, Bayle, and others; his seventh *posthumous sermon* is in a great part cribbed, word for word, from a previous divine, yclept Leightenhouse, 1697.

Another instance of close resemblance occurs in Gray's celebrated "*Elegy*;" so remarkable is the analogy, that one is constrained to suspect it to be a *free* rendering from Lucretius.

> "For him no more the blazing hearth shall burn,
> Or busy house-wife ply her evening care,
> No children run to lisp their sire's return,
> Or climb his knees the envious kiss to share."

There is a slight parallel between the foregoing and the beautiful bursts of pathos in Thomson, which we subjoin; but even these lines are said to be an imitation of a passage in the "*Iliad*:"

> "In vain for him th' officious wife prepares
> The fire fair blazing, and the vestment warm:
> In vain his little children, peeping out
> Into the mingling storm, demand their sire,
> With tears of artless innocence—alas!
> Nor wife, nor children more shall he behold,
> Nor friends, nor sacred home."

The plagiarism of Campbell from an elder poet, Vaughan, is worthy of being cited :

"When o'er the green, undeluged earth,
Heaven's covenant thou didst shine;
How came the *world's gray fathers* forth,
To watch thy sacred sign." *

"Still young and fine! but what is still in view
We slight as old and soiled, though fresh and new:
How bright wert thou, when Shem's admiring eye
Thy burning, flaming arch did first descry;
When Zerah, Nahor, Haram, Abram, Lot,
The youthful *world's gray fathers*, in one knot,
Did, with intentive looks watch every hour
For thy new light, and trembled at each shower!" †

The occasional conceits in this black-letter bard, coupled with his earnest straight-forwardness and sincerity, compensate us for the absence of the rich embellishment of Campbell.

We cannot forbear quoting from the "*English Bards and Scotch Reviewers*," Byron's well-known lines on the death of Kirke White; because the most beautiful figure in them seems evidently copied from Waller. We commence with Byron:

"Unhappy White! while life was in its spring,
And thy young muse just waved her joyous wing,
The spoiler came, and all thy promise fair,
Has sought the grave to sleep for ever there.
Oh, what a noble heart was here undone,
When science' self destroyed her favorite son!
Yes, she too much indulged thy fond pursuit:
She sowed the seeds, but Death has reaped the fruit.
'T was thine own genius gave the fatal blow,
And helped to plant the wound that laid thee low!
So the struck eagle, stretched upon the plain,
No more through rolling clouds to soar again,
Viewed his own feather on the fatal dart,
And winged the shaft that quivered in his heart:

* Campbell. † Vaughan.

Keen were his pangs, but keener far to feel,
He nursed the pinion which impelled the steel,
While the same plumage that had warmed his nest,
Drank the last life-drop of his bleeding breast!"

Waller's stanza which expresses a similar sentiment, is as follows:

That eagle's fate and mine are one,
  Which on the shaft that made him die
Espied a feather of his own
  Wherewith he'd wont to soar so high.

In Thomas Moore's poetic epistle, "*Corruption*," the same figure also occurs:

"Like a young eagle, who has lent his plume
To fledge the shaft by which he meets his doom,
See their own feathers plucked, to wing the dart,
Which rank corruption destines for their heart.

Speaking of Lord Byron, we might here quote a paragraph from Göethe, which may be new to some:

"The tragedy of *Manfred*, is a most singular performance, and one which concerns me nearly. This wonderful and ingenious poet has taken possession of my *Faust*, and hypochondriacally drawn from it the most singular nutriment. He has employed the means in it which suits his object, in a particular manner, so that no one thing remains the same; and on this account, I cannot sufficiently admire his ability. The re-cast is so peculiar, that a highly interesting lecture might be given on its resemblance, and want of resemblance, to its model—though I cannot deny, that the gloomy fervor of a rich and endless despair becomes at last wearisome to us. However, the displeasure we feel is always connected with admiration and esteem. The very quintessence of the sentiments and passions, which assist in constituting the most singular talents for self-commentary ever known, is contained in this tragedy."

Touching poetic coincidences, it may not be amiss to notice the somewhat remarkable fact, and one, perhaps, not very generally known, that there have been three poets of the respective names of Walter Scott, Samuel Rogers and James Grahame, before the excellent authors of "*Marmion*," "*The Pleasures of Memory*," and "*The Sabbath*." Specimens of their published works may be found in Mr. Southey's "*Later English Poets*;" they all three existed in the latter part of the seventeenth century.

The beautiful stanzas entitled, *The Soul's Errand*, "Go, soul, the body's guest," etc., often attributed to Sir Walter Raleigh, were really written by Sylvester. Barnfield is now generally believed to be the author of the following song, sometimes ascribed to Shakespeare.

> "As it fell upon a day,
> In the merry month of May,
> Sitting in a pleasant shade,
> Which a grove of myrtles made."

It may be seen in the collected poems of Richard Barnfield, 1598. The same idea we find repeated by different writers, touching the hopelessness of overruling a "strong-minded woman." An old dramatist, Sir Samuel Tuke (1673) says—

> "He is a fool who thinks by force or skill,
> To turn the current of a woman's will."

And in Aaron Hill's "Epilogue to Zara," bearing date about 1750, we find the following:

> "First, then, a woman will, or won't, depend on't;
> If she will do't, she will; and there's an end on't;
> But, if she won't, since safe and sound your trust is,
> Fear is affront; and jealousy injustice." *

* On a pillar erected on the Mount in the Dane John Field, Canterbury, are engraved the following lines:—

> "Where is the man who has the power and skill
> To stem the torrent of a woman's will?
> For if she will, she will, you may depend on't;
> And if she won't, she won't; so there's an end on't."

Young, in his "*Night Thoughts*' has the well-known line—

"Be wise to-day; 'tis madness to defer."

And Congreve, in his *Letter to Cobham*, introduces a similar thought:

"Defer not till to-morrow to be wise,
To-morrow's sun to thee may never rise."

Dryden says—

"For truth has such a face and such a mien,
As to be loved needs only to be seen."

And we have from Pope—

"Vice is a monster, of so frightful mien,
As to be hated, needs but to be seen," &c.

In *Measure for Measure*, occurs the song, which may be also found verbatim in Beamont and Fletcher, commencing,—

"Take, O! take those lips away,
That so sweetly were forsworn;
And those eyes, the break of day,
Lights that do mislead the morn.
But my kisses bring again,
Seals of love, but sealed in vain."

The well-known lines,

"My mind to me a kingdom is,
Such perfect joy therein I find,
As far exceeds all earthly bliss,
That God and nature hath assigned,"

seem to have had their origin in the couplet of Southwell,

"My mind to me an empire is,
While grace affordeth health."

Cowper's line,

> "God made the country, and man made the town,"

has its parallel (it originated with Varro) in that of Cowley,

> "God the first garden made, and the first city, Cain."

Good old Fuller thus beautifully depicts the last moments of a dying saint:

"Drawing near her death, she sent most pious thoughts as harbingers to heaven; and her soul saw a glimpse of happiness through the chinks of her sickness-broken body;" and Waller versifies the same idea:

> "The soul's dark cottage, battered and decayed,
> Lets in new light through chinks that time has made.
> Stronger by weakness, wiser men become,
> As they draw near to their eternal home."

Addison and Pope may be said to "divide the honors," as to the authorship of the line—

> "Rides on the whirlwind, and directs the storm,"

since it appears in the writings of both.

A similar instance is also observable with respect to the lines of Pope and Milton:

> "Laugh where we must, be candid where we can,
> But vindicate the ways of God to man."

for in *Paradise Lost*, we have the same idea in almost the identical phraseology:

> "And justify the ways of God to man."

Even Wordsworth seems to have copied; he says,

> "The child is father of the man,"

and Milton wrote,

> "The childhood shows the man,
> As morning shows the day."

"Dryden," says Warburton, "borrowed for want of leisure; Pope for want of genius; Milton from pride, and Addison through modesty. The same critic has collated some half-dozen remarkable parallels in Addison's "*Cato*" with *Tully* and *Lucan.*

Lauder, the author of two ambitious but unsuccessful tomes, entitled "*Poetarum Scotorum Musæ Sacræ,*" has assailed the literary reputation of the "blind old master of English song," in a volume which was afterwards roughly handled by Drs. Johnson and Bentley; being conscious it was no slight act of temerity in him to attempt impugning the integrity of such a name, he commences his work in the following apologetic strain, assuring the reader that "he had no intention to derogate from the merits of the author of 'Paradise Lost,' to whom great praise is due for so beautiful a structure; *even if it should be proved that a good part of his materials were borrowed from his neighbors;* but it cannot be denied that he is considerably indebted to the following productions: 'Sarcotidos,' a Latin Drama, written by Grotius; and, lastly, to a volume of poems published in the same language by Andrew Ramsay." A strong resemblance, it is affirmed, is discernible, both in structure and thought, in the parallels he has adduced; and yet we are reluctant to endorse the opinion of this literary censor, preferring rather to adopt the rejoinder of one of the poet's defenders, "admitting that Milton *took* many hints from these writers, yet the great whole of a magnificent epic, the connection of reference of part to part, are undeniably his own."

One of the most deeply interesting biographies we ever read was that of the poet, Chatterton. His brief and hapless career was crowded with touching incidents.

Unquestionably, the most brilliant, successful, and innocent literary forgeries ever committed were those produced in England about seventy years ago, by Thomas Chatterton. Chatterton was the posthumous son of the sexton of St. Mary Redcliffe church at Bristol, and was himself a charity-school boy. He was a singular youth—shy, abstracted, and, as some thought, stupid. When about sixteen years of age, he professed to have found in some old chests belonging to the church, a quantity of poems written by one Rowley, a priest in the fifteenth century. Portions of these manuscripts he exhibited, which bore all the marks of age, and by those to whom they were first shown were considered to be genuine. The poetry of the supposed work was of the highest order, and among the literati of England the utmost excitement prevailed. Chatterton's mother being poor, the boy on leaving school became clerk in a lawyer's office. This fellow, Lambert, shamefully ill-used Chatterton, and at last turned him out doors because he had found on his desk a paper entitled his "will," in which the boy expressed his intention to destroy himself.

The literary forgeries of Chatterton were induced by the cold neglect with which he found his own original effusions were received; and yet Byron, Shelley, Coleridge, Southey, Wordsworth, and other great poets have lauded Chatterton as a precocious and remarkable genius. Keats dedicated his "Endymion" to his memory; and Wordsworth styled him

> "The marvellous boy,
> The sleepless soul that perished in its pride."

The next instance of grand literary larceny that occurs to us is that of Samuel Ireland, of Shakspearian notoriety. It is doubtful if such devout consternation and enthusiastic admiration were ever enkindled among the cognoscenti and dilettanti of the civilized world, as were caused by his fabrications.

This notorious literary impostor was early distinguished for his enthusiastic devotion to Shakspeare; the slightest scrap of ancient writing referring to that great name, was, to Samuel

Ireland, a treasure of priceless worth. What effect upon his nerves the possession of an autograph of the immortal bard produced, may be easily imagined by the reader—he became intoxicated with delight. The precious relic which purported to be a mortgage-deed betwixt Shakspeare and one Michael Frazer, was viewed with such rapturous veneration by all the antiquaries of the day, "that it took several days," continues the narrator, "before any one became sufficiently composed and calm to inquire whence the document emanated." Young Ireland (the son of the afore-named), the discoverer, accounted for its appearance by alleging that he found it among some ancient records in the possession of a gentleman of fortune, but whose name he had been charged to preserve an inviolable secret. Byng, and other literary amateurs conjectured that a rich mine of Shakspearian wealth had been struck, and they became ravenously impatient for its further exploration. With such powerful stimulus these sanguine expectations soon became realized, and presently the following documents greeted the delighted vision of the learned :—Shakspeare's "Profession of Faith," a "Letter to Lord Southampton," a "Letter to Anne Hatharway," some "Poetic Epistles to the same," and a "Letter to Queen Elizabeth," and some "Original plays." Even that sage veteran, Dr. Parr, proved a ready victim to the delusion; also the Earl of Lauderdale, Valpy, Boswell, and Pinkerton, the historian, were among the credulous; and yet these papers, instead of being two centuries old, ultimately proved to be but the fabrication of a lad of eighteen, a few hours before. In his "Confessions," young Ireland admitted, in extenuation of his fraud, that he was incited to the act from the pleasure it afforded his father. The penalty of his imposture was, however, anything but enviable, for the name of Ireland soon became synonymous with obloquy, and a life of voluntary exile paid the forfeit of his folly. We ought to add, that the merit of detection belonged to John Kemble, whose critical acumen respecting the writings and genius of the great dramatic poet, proved in this instance more than a match against the sagacious credulity of the greatest men of letters of his time.

There was a curious work published in 1688, entitled "*Momus Triumphans*," devoted to the exposure of the plagiaries of the English stage: but with such cases of *petit larceny* we shall not meddle, having already discovered more instances of fraud, on a grander scale, than the reader will care to scrutinize.

It is related of the French poet, Despartes, on being accused of having availed himself very liberally of some passages of the Italian poets; so far from denying the charge, when a book appeared upon the subject, entitled "*Rencontre des Muses de France et d'Italie*," He frankly replied, "had I known the author's design, I could have furnished him with a great many more instances than he has collected!"

Here we have a literary sinner who affects no disguise of freebooting. He seems to suffer as little compunction for his detected crime, as if a certain canon of the Decalogue never had existence. Psalmanazar's ingenious fraud, or the daring artifice of Ireland, scarcely exceed in impudent audacity the case of one, Pinkerton, a voluminous writer, who published, in 1786, two volumes, "*Ancient Scottish Poems, never before in print, but now published from the MS. collection of Sir R. Maitland*, &c. Pinkerton maintained that he had found the manuscripts in the Pepysian Library at Cambridge, and among his correspondence, it is stated, he alludes to the circumstance with admirable coolness. We may mention one other variety, however, that of authors selling their names to be prefixed to works which they never even read; take the following case: Sir John Hill, as we learn by a recent writer, "once contracted to translate Swammerdam's work on insects, for fifty guineas;" after the agreement with the bookseller he recollected that he did not understand a single word of the Dutch language, and as no French edition then existed, he sought another to assume his task, and succeeded in effecting an agreement, with a translator, for just one-half the sum he was himself to receive; strange to add, however, the second translator was found to be in precisely the same situation as his employer. The consequence was, that a third was finally engaged to accomplish the work, and, to the disgrace of literature, at the meagre remuneration of twelve guineas; so that while the *actual* translator, the modest drudge, whose name never appeared to the world, broke, in patience, his daily bread, our pseudo-author was allowed to feast upon the spoils, as a reward for his imposture.

Mark Akenside first published his "*Pleasures of Imagination*" anonymously; and very soon after, a pretender of the name of Rolt, actually had the impudence to go over to *Dublin* and publish an edition of that fine poem with his own name attached *to it as the author*. Poor Akenside at length heard of the cheat, and published a genuine edition, exposing the fraud. Dr. Campbell, of St. Andrews, Scotland, wrote "An Inquiry into the Original of Moral Virtue," the manuscript of which he consigned to his friend Mr. Innes, who not only exceeded his commission by publishing the work under *his own name* as the author, but before the imposition was detected, acquired considerable fame and even promotion for his (supposed) great merit! Dr. Blair's early poem, "The Resurrection," while in manuscript, having been copied at college for the use of his private friends, in a short time after appeared in a pompous folio, to the utter amazement of its despoiled author, with the name of Dr. Douglas appended to its title, and arrogantly dedicated to the Princess Dowager of Wales! The "Man of Feeling," by Mackenzie, was also originally published under the assumed name of Eccles, who borrowed the manuscript on pretence of perusing it. This rogue succeeded to such an extent in his imposture, that the real author found at first great trouble in establishing his just claim to its authorship before the world. The true authorship of "*Gil Blas*" has not only been made the matter of speculative inquiry, but a recent writer in Blackwood has even ventured to dispute the claim of Le Sage to its paternity, asserting strong grounds for the belief of its having been the production of a Spanish scribe, Don Antonio de Solis!

Dr. Johnson says, "It is not difficult to conceive of such kind of fraud to be practised with successful effrontery; the filiation of a literary performance being difficult of proof, there being seldom any witness at the birth." The writer from whom we quote did not himself incur any great risk in this matter, however, as his progeny evince a strongly-marked identity; and

> "Shakspeare's magic could not copied be,
> Within that charmed circle none durst walk but he."

A somewhat similar theft, although on a grander scale, was perpetrated by the notorious Sir Everard Home, who, it will be remembered, under pretext of making a catalogue of them, procured from the Royal College of Surgeons the loan of the life-labor manuscripts of Doctor Hunter, forming ten large folio volumes. After much patient waiting and many bootless inquiries for said catalogue, it was at length confessed by this literary corsair, that *he had burnt a large portion of them*, alleging that he did so in accordance with the expressed wish of Dr. Hunter. The grief and consternation that ensued upon such an unpardonable proceeding, was in no degree lessened by the discovery, and subsequent *confession* on the part of Sir Everard, that he previously *stole* the valuable materials of Hunter, from which he compiled his boasted Essays delivered before the Royal Society. These lectures being produced with such astonishing rapidity and frequency, very naturally excited suspicion, and ultimately led to the betrayal of the fraud. The name of John Hunter reminds us of another case of plagiarism: about four years ago there was a paper in the British and Foreign Medical Review purporting to be a review of the character and writings of John

Hunter, ascribed to the pen of Dr. W. B. Carpenter, a distinguished member of the English faculty, but which in reality was a transfer of "A Review of the Genius and Writings of Milton," by William Ellery Channing, each being substantially the same throughout—and for the most part *verbatim et literatim*—the principal change consisting in that of the proper name. What shall we say of the case of the metaphysician, Coleridge, delivering in London a course of lectures on the Greek drama, who resorted to the easy expedient of *translating* the published lectures of Schlegel on the same subject, which had been delivered some few years preceding.

In 1823 a visit to England was made by a singular individual named Hunter, an American, the author of a production—a pure fabrication—entitled "Memoirs of a Captivity among the Indians of North America, from childhood to the age of nineteen, with anecdotes descriptive of their manners and customs," &c. The work contains a highly romantic and interesting narrative of his alleged wanderings among various tribes of the Red-men, which at first not only was regarded as a faithful picture of Indian life, but procured for him an introduction into the best literary society, and enlisted for him the sympathies of the philanthropic, who eagerly sought to aid him in his professed object of aiming to bring about their civilization.

The case of Madame de Genlis is singular. In her latter years, this lady, not content with wholesale plagiarisms from Rousseau and Voltaire, took to filching from herself, and, under a different title, would publish the same work twice, or thrice. She engaged to compile for a bookseller a *Manuel Encyclopédique de l'Enfance.* The manuscript was put into his hands; the stipulated price of four hundred francs was paid; and the work was about to be sent to the press, when the publisher discovered that it was nothing but an exact copy of a book on the same subject which Madame de Genlis had published ten years ago. It has been observed that whenever any age has been distinguished by a great number of excellent authors, they have cultivated different departments of literature, prose or verse, or have adopted different styles of expression. This was the case in the Augustan age, as appears from the works of Virgil, Horace, Ovid, etc. This is also evident in later times; for in the writings of Shakespeare, Swift, Pope, Gray, Bolingbroke, Addison, Scott, Moore, Milton, and others, there are striking idiosyncrasies, and peculiarities of style.

These men were not, like most of their literary contemporaries, servile imitators, but original thinkers, and consequently, original writers.

Coleridge said, that plagiarists are always suspicious of being stolen from: if this is so, the case of Madame de Genlis is rather anomalous. We will close our chapter with a few more instances of analogy in sentiment and verse. For example: Spenser compares the falling of Autumn foliage with the death of man.

> "As withered leaves drop from their dried stocks,
> When the wroth western wind doth reave their locks."

The same idea is employed by Shelley,

> "Thou wild west wind! thou breath of autumn's being,
> Before whose unseen presence the leaves dead
> Are driven, like ghosts from an enchanter fleeing."

Milton embodies the same figure; and Byron also, in the well-remembered stanza:

> "Like the leaves of the forest, when summer is green,
> That host with its banners at sunset was seen;
> Like the leaves of the forest, when autumn hath blown,
> That host on the morrow lay withered and strewn."

Again, in Pope:

> "Like leaves on the trees, the race of man is found:
> They fall successive, and successive rise."

The following is a coincidence between Tennyson and Shakspeare :

——"A dream
Dreamed by a happy man, while the dark east
Is slowly brightening to his bridal morn."
Tennyson.

——"Then music is
As those dulcet sounds in break of day,
That creep into the dreaming bridegroom's ear,
And summon him to marriage."
Merchant of Venice.

In the very fine stanza on a skull—(*Childe Harold*) Byron apostrophizes it as,

"The dome of thought and palace of the soul."

Waller in a short poem on tea, the effect of which he describes, calls the head the

"Palace of the soul."

Can we not trace Mason's "Gadding Ivy" to Milton's "Gadding Vine?" In the dramatic poem of "Elfrida," by the former, there is

"The *ivy, gadding* from th' untwisted stem,
Curtains each verdant side,"

And in Milton's "Lycidas" we read

"desert caves,
With wild thyme, and the *gadding vine o'ergrown.*"

A coincidence of imagery is apparent in the following :

"But let my due feet never fail,
To *walk the studious cloister's pale,*
There let the *pealing organ blow,*
To the full voic'd choir below,
In service high, and anthems clear,

As may with sweetness through mine ear
Dissolve me into ecstacics."

Il Penseroso.

The other passage in "St. Agnes' Eve," where the beadsman returneth :

"*Along the chapel aisle by slow degrees,*
* * * * * * *
Northward he turneth through a little door,
And scarce three steps, ere *Music's golden tongue*
Flattered to tears this aged man—"

In a madrigal by Morley (1600) we have the following :

"April is my mistris face,
And July in her eyes hath place,
Within her bosom is September,
But in her heart a cold December."

and in Robert Greene's "*Perimedes, the Blacksmith,*" 1588—we find another rendering of the same idea :

"Fair is my love, for April in her face,
Her lovely breasts September claims his part,
And lordly July in her eies takes place,
But cold December dwelleth in her heart."

The following speak for themselves :

[*Longfellow.*]

"And like a lily on a river floating,
She floats upon the river of his thoughts."

Spanish Student, Act 2, *Sc.* 3.

[*Tennyson.*]

"Now folds the lily all her sweetness up,
And slips into the bosom of the lake."

Princess, pt. 7.

There is a resemblance in the following lines from Wordsworth and Keble.

"A book, upon whose leaves some chosen plants
By his own hand disposed with nicest care,
In undecaying beauty were preserved."
Excursion, bk. 6.

"Like flower-leaves in a precious volume stored
To solace and relieve
Some heart too weary of the restless world."
Christian Year.

Herrick, seems to have had the finest perception of the delicate and charming, in the following—

"Her pretty feet,
Like smiles, did creep
A little out, and then,
As if they started at bo-peep,
Did soon draw in again."

It is the exquisite intimation of the lively character of the inward spirit, shown in the active movements of the feet, which Sir John Suckling has imitated in his ballad of the Wedding:

"Her feet beneath her petticoat
Like little mice stole in and out,
As if they feared the light;
But, oh, she dances such a way,
No sun upon an Easter day
Is half so fine a sight!"

The literary *faux-pas* of a once celebrated chemist, by his work on "*Chemical Tests,*" is known to the scientific in both hemispheres. He published a work on Poisons, entitled, "*Death in the Pot,*" which at first bid fair to yield its author a moderately good revenue of fame and fortune, but for the discovery which was soon made, that it consisted of a series of pilfered pages, torn out of old books in the British Museum; he was tried upon a criminal suit for felony, and although formally acquitted, yet so strong was the circumstantial evidence of his guilt, that he was compelled to decamp. Among the liberal professions respectively—law, physic, and theology—many curious facts might also be cited; but about theology we must have little to say—of physic, less—and law, the least. Before speaking of the mysterious parallels which may be found to exist with the Biblical Commentaries of such divines as Dr. Adam Clarke, and his approved pioneer, Dr. John Gill, we subjoin the following extract from the Preface to Cobbin's Condensed Commentary:

"All the commentators have drawn largely from the Fathers, especially from St. Augustine; and most of them have made common property of Patrick, South and Whitby. Henry has made very free use with Bishop Hall and others, and Scott has again enriched himself abundantly from Henry; Poole exhausted the continental writers, while Gill, unlike the others, acknowledges his obligations."

The number of commentators is great; yet if the *uncopied* portions were to be collected, they would, perhaps, occupy a single duodecimo.

It was a curious mistake that a celebrated English clergyman recently made; in printing his Philippic against Theatres, he actually copied it wholly from another writer, without the slightest acknowledgment. Bunn detected this, and printing the article from *both in parallels*—simply asked what faith could be reposed in the reverend pilferer.

A few years ago, a work was published in London, under the title of "Anecdotes of Napoleon," and, would it be credited, that this wonderful production was neither more nor less than a compilation literally rendered from the German, of a Life of Frederic the Great, the name of the emperor being substituted for that of the latter. Another instance of fraud occurred in Captain Marryatt's "Narrative of M. Violet," in which some wholesale plagiarisms were perpetrated upon two American authors, Kendall and Gregg.

Punch profanely jokes about some "sprigs of divinity," who are accustomed to "*bone*" their sermons, having recourse to *skeletons*, which they keep in their closets, and with which they are in the habit of terrifying the consciences of their hearers. This fact accounts for their sermons being as dry as a bone! The same humorous authority affirms, there are many thoughts like diamonds, that take much less time to find, than to polish when found. Old thoughts being frequently like old clothes, you put them away for a time, and they become apparently new by "brushing up."

A few years ago a very impressive sermon was delivered by a young man fresh from the seminary. After service a gentle man observed "Not every young man can think like that young man." *It was one of Melville's masterly discourses, word for word!*

A preacher of no remarkable powers undertook, not long since, to astound the congregation of a brother minister by a great sermon. *It was Massilon's on the small number of the saved.* Alas, he could not wield the power of Massilon, and the effort proved a failure.

Another instance of clerical delinquency was that of a printed discourse. It has been heralded to the world with no ordinary parade and display. But in glancing at it, evidences of other authorship were immediately detected—and on comparison it was found that every passage of any beauty or power was stolen. About one half of it, in *language as well as idea,* was found to be from Gilfillan's *Bards of the Bible,* and from Hamilton of London.

Even the Press sometimes makes unacknowledged appropriations of the productions of others. Not many months since, we accidentally noticed in a newspaper emanating from the 'far West,' a poem, entitled "*The World;*" the first stanza of which reads—

"Talk who will of the world as a desert of thrall,
Yet there is a bloom on the waste;
Though the chalice of life hath its acid and gall,
There are honey-drops, too, for the taste."

The authorship of the production, consisting of thirteen

verses, would it be believed—was ascribed to a certain N. H Parker, to whose literary claims the discriminating editor thought proper to devote his rhetorical skill. The poem is to be found verbatim in Eliza Cook's poetical works.

An edition of *Cicero de Senectute*, with annotations, appeared in London about the time of Franklin's mission to that capital, as *translated by himself*, with his portrait annexed, when it is well-known he was incompetent to such a task. The translation was really made by Logan, who founded the Philadelphia Library. Another literary peccadillo should be recorded: we refer to his plagiarism upon Jeremy Taylor's beautiful parable against "Intolerance," which Franklin has incorporated verbatim into his works without the slightest acknowledgment; while even Lord Kaimes, in quoting the extract, gives credit for it to Franklin. It is as follows:

"And it came to pass after these things, that Abraham sat in the door of his tent, about the going down of the sun. And behold a man bent with age, coming from the way of the wilderness leaning on a staff: and Abraham rose, and met him, and said unto him, 'Turn in, I pray thee, and wash thy feet, and tarry all night: and thou shalt rise early in the morning and go on thy way.' And the man said, 'Nay, for I will abide under this tree.' But Abraham pressed him greatly; so he turned and went into the tent, and Abraham baked unleavened bread, and they did eat. And when Abraham saw that the man blesssed not God, he said unto him, 'Wherefore dost thou not worship the most high God, creator of heaven and earth?' And the man answered and said, 'I do not worship thy God, neither do I call upon his name; for I have made to myself a god, which abideth always in mine house, and provideth me with all things.' And Abraham's zeal was kindled against the man, and he arose, and fell upon the man, and drove him forth with blows into the wilderness. And God called unto Abraham, saying, 'Abraham, where is the stranger?' And Abraham answered and said, 'Lord, he would not worship thee, neither would he call upon thy name, therefore have I driven him out from before my face into the wilderness;' and God said, 'Have I borne with him these hundred and ninety and eight years, and nourished him, and clothed him, notwithstanding his rebellion against me; and couldst not thou, who art thyself a sinner, bear with him one night?'"

Having thus taken a brief glance at prominent cases of literary fraud, we are tempted to inquire whether there is such a thing in existence as absolute moral honesty. The earliest indications of childhood afford us no very conclusive evidence in its behalf, however guileless the incipient knavery, while among the unsophisticated rangers of the forest, similar developments of a natural law of *secretiveness* are no less observable. The governing impulse of the robber seems but the exuberant outgrowth of the very principle, otherwise known by the less objectionable epithet—covetousness; and we cannot but conclude that he must be an ingenious sophist who can adduce any substantial reasons against their positive identity. If, then, they are convertible terms, it is solely to our conventional usage we must ascribe the fact, that both are not alike visited by penal enactment. How far such a course may conflict with our notions of abstract justice, we leave the reader to decide, since to both we admit an eager, if not an equal, proclivity.

"In the crowd,
May it please your excellency, your thief looks
Exactly like the rest, or rather better;
'Tis only at the bar, and in the dungeon,
That wise men know your felon by his features."

"L'Envoy is an epilogue, or discourse, to make plain
Some obscure precedence that hath before been sain;
I will example it."

Love's Labor Lost.

VERY few wills are executed without a codicil, so that it may not be inadmissible to offer a little dish of trifles after our *Salad*. If it be true that good wine needs no bush, 'tis true, as Shakspeare has it, that a good play needs no epilogue; yet to good wine they do use good bushes; and good plays do prove the better by the help of good epilogues. Not unfrequently the after-thought which suggests the postscript contains the most important item of the whole epistle: and although this may not be the case in the present instance, yet our pen seems reluctant to resign its office without a few words supplementary—a brief tête-à-tête with our excellent friends who have shared our literary repast. Patroclus is said to have been famous for his "*Olla Podrida*"—in our emulation of the classic hero, we stake our reputation upon *Salad*. Our preference has been confirmed, moreover, by the brilliant success of a more recent *artiste* in the same department of culinary skill—the chevalier D'Aubigné, the story of whose career is too curious to be passed over. "Latour D'Aubigné contrived to live, as many French gentleman did at the time of the French Revolution, in bitter poverty, without a sacrifice of dignity. He had one day been invited by an English friend to dine with the latter at a tavern. In the course of the repast, he took upon himself to mix the salad ; and the way in which he did this attracted the notice of all the guests. Previous to this period, lettuces were commonly eaten, by tavern frequenters at least, *au naturel*, with no more dressing than Nebuchadnezzar had to his grass when he dieted daily among the beasts. Consequently, when D'Aubigné handled the preparation for which he had asked, like a chemist concocting elixir in his laboratory, the guests were lost in admiration, for the refreshing aroma of a *Mayonnaise* was warrant to their senses that the French knight had discovered for them a new pleasure. One of them approached the foreign magician, and said, 'Sir, it is universally known that your nation excels all others in the making a salad. Would it be too great a liberty to ask you to do us the favor to mix one for the party at my table ?' The courteous Frenchman smiled, was flattered, performed the office asked, and put four gentlemen in a state of uncontrollable ecstacy. He had talked cheerfully, as he mixed gracefully and scientifically, and, in the few minutes required by him to complete his work of enchantment, he contrived to explain his position as emigrant, and his dependance on the pecuniary aid afforded by the English Government. The guests did not let the poor Chevalier depart without slipping into his hand a golden fee, which he received with as little embarrassment, and as much dignity as though he had been the Physician De Portal, taking an *honorarium* from the hands of the Cardinal de Rohan.

He had communicated his address, and he, perhaps, was not very much surprised when, a few days after, he received a letter in which he was politely requested to repair to a house in Grosvenor square, for the purpose of mixing a salad for a dinner-party there to be given. D'Aubigné obeyed the summons; and, after performing his mission, returned home richer by a five-pound note than when he went out.

Henceforth he became the 'fashionable salad-maker;' and ladies 'died' for his salads, as they do now for Constantine's simulative bouquets. He was soon enabled to proceed to his responsible duties in a carriage ; and a servant attended him, carrying a mahogany case, containing the necessary ingredients for concocting various salads, according to the respective tastes of his employers. At a later period he sold, by hundreds, similar mahogany cases, which he had caused to be made, and which were furnished with all matters necessary for the making an irreproachable salad, and with directions how to administer them. The Chevalier, too, was, like old Carré—whose will was so cleverly made by the very disinterested friends who had never before spoken to him—a prudent and a saving man; and by the period which re-opened France to the émigrés, he had realized some eighty thousand francs, upon which he enjoyed a dignified retirement in a provincial town."*

This little incident seemed so apposite to our closing pages, that we have been tempted to append it: the moral of which, if it have any, shall be to suggest the hope that our *Salad* may prove as acceptable as that of the French artist.

* Dr. Doran's Table Traits.

THE END.

www.ingramcontent.com/pod-product-compliance
Lightning Source LLC
LaVergne TN
LVHW020109110826
845151LV00001B/112
9781425544027